Cambridge studies in medieval life and thought

Edited by WALTER ULLMANN, LITT.D, F.B.A.
*Formerly Professor of Medieval History in the
University of Cambridge*

Third series, vol. 21

PAPAL GOVERNMENT AND ENGLAND DURING THE PONTIFICATE OF HONORIUS III (1216–1227)

CAMBRIDGE STUDIES IN
MEDIEVAL LIFE AND THOUGHT

THIRD SERIES

PAPAL GOVERNMENT AND ENGLAND DURING THE PONTIFICATE OF HONORIUS III (1216–1227)

JANE E. SAYERS

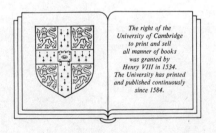

The right of the
University of Cambridge
to print and sell
all manner of books
was granted by
Henry VIII in 1534.
The University has printed
and published continuously
since 1584.

CAMBRIDGE UNIVERSITY PRESS

CAMBRIDGE

LONDON   NEW YORK   NEW ROCHELLE
MELBOURNE   SYDNEY

Published by the Press Syndicate of the University of Cambridge
The Pitt Building, Trumpington Street, Cambridge CB2 IRP
32 East 57th Street, New York, NY 10022, USA
296 Beaconsfield Parade, Middle Park, Melbourne 3206, Australia

First published 1984

Printed in Great Britain by the University Press, Cambridge

Library of Congress catalogue card number: 84–1853

British Library Cataloguing in Publication Data
Sayers, Jane E.
Papal government and England during the pontificate of Honorius III
(1216–1227).——
(Cambridge studies in medieval life and thought. Third series; v. 21)
1. Church government – Papal administration
– England 1216–1227   2. Papal
administration – England 1216–1227 –
Church government   3. England 1216–1227
– Church government – Papal
administration
I. Title
262'.136   DG797.3

ISBN 0 521 25911 8

BR
747
.S29
1984

UP

CONTENTS

Contents

TABLES

FIGURE

PREFACE

I have tried in the present study to appraise the administrative achievement of Honorius III's pontificate by looking in general at the pope's correspondence and in particular at the originals and the copies relating to the English Crown, realm and Church. In the first part of the book I have set out from a detailed analysis of the letters to discover what can be learned about the structure and significance of the papal Chancery and its staff. An assessment of how many letters were issued under Honorius, what proportion of the correspondence was registered, the techniques of registration, the ordering of the business by the use of 'house style' and the development of set forms is essential to an understanding of the institution. Such an influential Chancery not only produced models for other chanceries but also created the richest archive source for studying the development of western Europe. That is not too big a claim.

In the second part I have sought to put the letters in their legal and historical context. There was one official law compilation made at the end of Honorius's pontificate, the *Compilatio Quinta*. I have attempted to show how and from what sources this collection was made and have considered the interpretation and application of the canon law, as it was then known, in England and in English conditions. The law was formed from the numerous decretal letters despatched to the provinces but only a small number of these decisions entered the official law-books for widespread application. Historically the letters are the major source for investigating curial relations with England. The remarkable action of King John in surrendering his kingdom to the papacy to be held by him as a papal fief, and the consequent despatch of powerful papal legates to restore and then oversee secular and ecclesiastical government, are heavily documented from the Roman end. Direct rule from Rome lasted for five years of Honorius's pontificate and arguably dominated the remaining six. The popes had made large claims to government in Europe. Whether Honorius's administrators were capable of realizing them is discussed in the last chapter.

Preface

It is pleasant to thank many persons who have contributed to this book in certain ways. Firstly I wish to express my gratitude to the British Academy for a generous grant that allowed me to explore archive sources throughout England and Wales and in Rome. I have enjoyed the help of archivists and librarians in the following places and institutions: the cathedral and chapter archives at Canterbury (Miss A. Oakley and the late Dr W. G. Urry), Durham (Mr Martin Snape and Mr Alan Piper), Exeter (Mrs Audrey Erskine), Hereford (Miss Penelope Morgan and the late Mr F. C. Morgan), Lincoln (in the Lincoln Archives Office: Miss M. E. Finch), Norwich (now in the County Record Office: Miss Jean Kennedy), Peterborough (Canon Arthur Gribble), Salisbury (Miss Pamela Stewart), St Paul's, London (the late Mr A. E. B. Fuller, and more recently the archivists of the Guildhall Library, Messrs C. H. Cooper and G. Yeo), Wells (Mr L. S. Colchester), Westminster (Mr N. H. MacMichael), Windsor, St George's (Mrs G. Holmes), and York (Miss K. M. Longley and Mr B. Barr). In London I have used the sources in the British Library Manuscripts Room, the Public Record Office, the Lambeth Palace Library (Miss Melanie Barber and E. G. W. Bill), the Lincoln's Inn Library (Mr R. Walker) and St Bartholomew's Hospital (Miss Janet Foster). So many people have aided me in the Long Room of the PRO and in the Students' Room of the British Library that I cannot possibly thank them all by name but my thanks are none the less warm. The librarians of the Institute of Historical Research here in London have been ungrudging in their help. The acquisition by the Institute of a microfilm of Honorius III's registers cut down much of the labour to be carried out in Rome. In particular I wish to thank Mr C. W. Kellaway, Miss Rosemary Taylor and Mr R. Lyons of the Institute and Miss Joan Gibbs of the Palaeography Room in the University of London Library. Archivists in the National Library of Wales at Aberystwyth (Dr Daniel Huws), in the Borthwick Institute at York (Dr David Smith, who also loaned me microfilms from the Borthwick's collection of cartularies), in the university libraries at Nottingham (Mrs M. E. Welch), Cambridge (Mr and Mrs A. E. B. Owen, in particular for access to and help with the King's College and Ely archives) and in Oxford at the Bodleian (Dr D. M. Barratt, and Miss Ruth Vyse of the University Archives) deserve my gratitude; as do the archivists of various colleges at Cambridge, Christ's (Mr E. Carson), Jesus (Mrs Freda Jones), St John's (Mr M. G. Underwood) and Trinity (the librarian, Dr Philip Gaskell, and Miss Rosemary Graham) and at Oxford, Magdalen (Dr G. L. Harriss and Mrs Brenda Parry-Jones), New College (the Rev. G. V. Bennett)

Preface

and St John's (Mr H. M. Colvin). The county archivists of Devon (Mrs M. M. Rowe), Hereford and Worcester (Mr A. Wherry), Norfolk (Miss J. Kennedy), Northamptonshire (Mr P. I. King) and Somerset (Mr D. M. Shorrocks) and the former county archivists of Bedfordshire (Miss Joyce Godber), Essex (Mr F. G. Emmison), Hampshire (Miss M. E. Cash) and Kent (Dr Felix Hull) have kindly assisted me, as have the archivists of Eton College (Mr Patrick Strong) and of Winchester College (Mr Roger Custance). Thanks are also due to the Dukes of Devonshire and Rutland for allowing access to material at Chatsworth and at Belvoir, to Mr B. Benedikz of the Birmingham University Library for advice on Worcester Cathedral material, to the East Sussex Record Office and to Mrs B. Cluer for loaning me a microfilm of the Battle abbey cartulary which is now at the Huntington Library in California, and to Dr Antonia Gransden of Nottingham University for arranging a photocopy and commenting on a reading. In Rome I enjoyed the aid of Monsignor Charles Burns and of the Prefect of the Vatican Archives, Monsignor Martino Giusti. In London the palaeography seminar listened to a talk on Honorius's scribes and looked at their handiwork and Professor T. J. Brown and Dr A. G. Watson gave their opinions on certain papal hands. Others amongst my colleagues, family and friends have been both forbearing and encouraging, in particular my mother, always generous and undemanding, and Dr D. E. Greenway, who has given many hours to read, shape, discuss and improve much of the text.

My debt (and, indeed, the debt of all those who work on the thirteenth century) to the work of the late Professor F. M. Powicke and his pupils, Professor C. R. Cheney, Professor Kathleen Major and Miss Marion Gibbs and Miss Jane Lang, is obvious, but should not go unrecorded. Similarly my debt is great to all those whose speciality is the medieval papal Chancery and the medieval canon law: especially Professors Peter Herde (who loaned me a microfilm of the Durrieu MS), Othmar Hageneder, Agostino Paravicini Bagliani, Leonard Boyle and Stephan Kuttner, whose kindnesses have been many and various since the early 1960s. Finally my greatest debt is to Professor Walter Ullmann, whose learning, matchless inspiration and friendship I enjoyed over nearly thirty years. I dedicate this book to his memory as a small token of gratitude.

University College, London   J.E.S.
December 1982

ABBREVIATIONS

AD	*Archiv für Diplomatik*
AHP	*Archivum Historiae Pontificiae*
ASAR	*Annali della scuola speciale per archivisti e bibliotecarii dell'Università di Roma*
Aug.	Augustinian
BAPP	B. Barbiche, *Les Actes Pontificaux Originaux des Archives Nationales de Paris*
BEC	*Bibliothèque de l'École des Chartes*
Ben., Ben. al.	Benedictine, Benedictine alien
BIHR	*Bulletin of the Institute of Historical Research*
BL	British Library
BMCL	*Bulletin of Medieval Canon Law*
cal.	calendared
Cist.	Cistercian
Clun.	Cluniac
CPL	*Calendar of Entries in the Papal Registers* (*Calendar of Papal Letters*), ed. W. H. Bliss and others (all references are to vol. i unless otherwise stated)
CQ	*Compilatio Quinta* in *Quinque Compilationes*, ed. E. Friedberg
CS	*Councils and Synods* ii 1, ed. F. M. Powicke and C. R. Cheney
CUL	Cambridge University Library
DBI	*Dizionario Biografico degli Italiani*
DDC	*Dictionnaire de Droit Canonique*
DNB	*Dictionary of National Biography*
ed.	edited by, editor(s)
edn	edition
EHR	*English Historical Review*
Gilb.	Gilbertine
HMC JP	Historical MSS Commission Joint Publications
HMSO	His/Her Majesty's Stationery Office
JL	*Regesta Pontificum Romanorum*, ed. P. Jaffé, revsd

	S. Loewenfeld (numbered references are to the letters unless preceded by a volume number)
MGH *Epp.*	Monumenta Germaniae Historiae, Epistolae
MGH *SS*	Monumenta Germaniae Historiae, Scriptores
MIOG	*Mitteilungen des Instituts für Österreichisches Geschichte*
Mon. *Angl.*	Sir William Dugdale, *Monasticon Anglicanum*, ed. J. Caley, H. Ellis and B. Bandinel
n.s.	new series
P	*Regesta Pontificum Romanorum ab 1198 ad 1304*, ed. A. Potthast (numbered references are to the letters unless preceded by a volume number) (where a source reference is given without a Potthast number, the letter is not included in P, see below App. 2 p. 209, n. 2)
pd	printed
PL	*Patrologia Latina*
Prem.	Premonstratensian
PRO	Public Record Office
PRS	Pipe Roll Society
pt	part
PUS	*Die Papsturkunden der Schweiz von Innocenz III bis Martin V ohne Zürich*, ed. A. Largiadèr, 2 vols.
PUZ	*Die Papsturkunden des Staatsarchivs Zürich von Innocenz III bis Martin V*, ed. A. Largiadèr
QFIAB	*Quellen und Forschungen aus Italienischen Archiven und Bibliotheken*
Rec. Soc.	Record Society
Reg. Hon. III	*Regesta Honorii Papae III*, cal. P. Pressutti
repd	reprinted
revsd	revised
RS	Rolls Series
Rymer	Rymer, *Foedera, Conventiones, Litterae...*, ed. A. Clarke and F. Holbrooke
SB	*Schedario Baumgarten*, ed. G. Battelli
Shirley	*Royal and other Historical Letters...of the reign of Henry III*, ed. W. W. Shirley, 2 vols.
trans.	translated
TRHS	*Transactions of the Royal Historical Society*
VCH	*Victoria County Histories*
X	'Decretales', *Corpus Iuris Canonici* ii, ed. E. Friedberg
ZRG	*Zeitschrift der Savigny-Stiftung für Rechtsgeschichte*

PROLOGUE: HONORIUS III (CENCIO SAVELLI)

Honorius III brought the Savelli family to power rather than they him. Like the Conti and the Orsini, the Savelli were one of the new noble families of the twelfth century, but without the acquisition of the papal tiara they would probably have remained of small influence except within the city of Rome.[1] Of Roman birth, 'genere Romanus', as many of the chroniclers note,[2] Cencio Savelli is thought to have been the son of Haimericus. It has been argued that his father's name (and the use of the name Pandulf within the family) suggests a Germanic origin, but by the 1160s the family already possessed moderate-sized estates in the Campagna – in the Sabina and at Castel Gandolfo, Castel Savello (near Albano), Albano and Arricia in the Alban hills.[3] Cencio probably spent his childhood in Rome. The year of his birth is unknown and also the name of his mother. If, however, he was about thirty when he became cardinal deacon of S. Lucia in Orthea in 1193, he was born close to 1163 at the beginning of the long pontificate of Alexander III. Many of the chroniclers describe him as of mature age ('senior venerandus' and 'jam aevo grandior') at the time of his election as pope in 1216.[4] The date of 1163 for his birth would make him fifty-three; he could have been at least ten years older. As a child, he may have been an oblate in the school of St John Lateran, as asserted by both

[1] There is no good modern biography of Honorius III. Clausen, *Papst Honorius III* (1895) is not only outdated but also inaccurate. Potthast (P i 468) gives a brief account and so does Horoy, ed., 'Opera omnia', i. Between 1888 and 1895 Pressutti calendared the registers (*Reg. Hon. III*) but provided no social, historical or diplomatic background to the pope's activities. The upsurge of genealogical interest in the nineteenth century produced Litta's large and elaborate enterprise *Famiglie celebri Italiane*, including Passerini's 'Savelli di Roma' in vol. x, which indicates no sources but is apparently based on Panvinius and Ciaconius, thus incorporating much hearsay and supposition. I have not been able to investigate the short account of Carlo Cecchelli, *I Crescenzi, i Savelli, i Cenci* (Rome 1942) who on pp. 11–12 apparently argues descent from the Crescenzi family.

[2] e.g. Rainer, 'Annales', 675.

[3] Gregorovius, *Rome in the middle ages* v pt 1 118–19; Waley, *Papal state*, 209.

[4] e.g. 'Notae Sancti Emmerammi' in MGH SS xvii (1861) 574, and *Memoriale fratris Walteri de Coventria*, ed. Stubbs, ii 230–1.

I

Prologue

Potthast and Panvinius, but that is far from certain.[5] From this time onwards we are on surer ground. Cencio Savelli entered the household of the Roman cardinal Giacinto Bobone, who held the diaconate church of S. Maria in Cosmedin, serving perhaps at first as *cubicularius*. Under the influence of the Roman pope, Paolo Scolari, Clement III (1187–91), he was made a papal subdeacon and served in the papal chamber.[6] In 1188 he is described as Clement's proctor, although clearly acting in the capacity of chamberlain when he received the oaths of six senators who renounced all actions and claims against the pope and his successors in return for certain payments.[7] This was part of Clement's concordat with the Romans.[8] Probably at about this time he acquired a canonry in the great Roman basilica of S. Maria Maggiore.[9] Scolari's influence was strong over S. Maria Maggiore, where as cardinal bishop of Palestrina he had built a palace.[10] During Honorius's own pontificate one of his chamberlains, Sinibaldus, held a canonry there.[11] With the election to the papacy in 1191 of his old patron, Cardinal Giacinto, who became Celestine III, Cencio Savelli's rise as an administrator continued and he held together the two most powerful household offices of chamberlain and chancellor.[12]

Tangible monuments remain of Cencio's activities as Celestine's chamberlain: the magnificent bronze doors in the south-east corner of the twelfth-century cloister of the Roman episcopal cathedral of St John Lateran and the book of customs, rents and payments due to the Roman Church, the *Liber Censuum*. The doors, studded with raised stars, incorporate the inscription '✠ Incarnacionis dominice anno mcxcvi pontificatus domini Celestini Pape iii anno vi Cencio Camerario ministrante hoc opus factum est. ✠ Ubertus magister et Petrus eius frater Placentini fecerunt hoc opus'. The compilation of the *Liber Censuum*, completed in 1192, illustrated the chamberlain's place within

---

5 P i 468, and O. Panvinius, *Epitome pontificum Romanorum* (Venice 1657). Horoy suggests that he was a canon of St John Lateran: this is not substantiated.
6 On Clement III, see Pfaff, 'Clemens III' 261–316.
7 T. Hirschfeld, 'Zur Chronologie der Stadtpraefekten in der Zeit der Erneurung des Senates', *QFIAB* xvi (1914) 93–107, esp. 103; pd at 106–7.
8 Pd in *Liber Censuum*, ed. Fabre and Duchesne, i no. 84 373 and 374. See also Partner, *Lands of St Peter*, 219–21.
9 Noted in *Liber Censuum*, ed. Fabre and Duchesne, i 1 (of text), trans. and pd in Lunt, *Revenues* ii 34.
10 Pfaff, 'Clemens III', 262.
11 *Reg. Hon. III* no. 3769 and see below pp. 174, 187.
12 On Celestine III, see *DBI*; Pfaff, 'Papst Coelestin III'; id., 'Der Vorgänger: das Wirken Coelestins III. aus der Sicht von Innocenz III', *ZRG* xci Kan. Abt. lx (1974) 121–67, and id., 'Die Kardinäle unter Coelestin III (I)' and '(II)'. The Bobone family, from which Celestine came, was related to the Orsini.

the administration and his control of the household. It probably
accounted for the fame of his activities in the Chamber. Many of the
chroniclers, commenting on his election as pope, remembered that he
had been chamberlain: Burchard of Worms speaking of him, curiously,
as 'chamberlain of the cardinals who faithfully distributed the income
amongst them'.[13] It is easy to be critical of the rather formless shape
of the *Liber Censuum*. It includes a mass of material that was not
carefully organized and prepared – and indeed the volume was
apparently arranged with sufficient space for additions[14] – the result
resembling more a commonplace book than a detailed financial report.
There were forerunners of this type of collection, now no longer
surviving, so that comparison is not possible, but Honorius's own
comments suggest that they were now outdated and useless. Although
Pfaff may have underestimated the curia's income at this time,[15] there
is no doubt that there was a severe financial crisis in the late-
twelfth-century curia and shortage of funds, partly perhaps due to papal
policy and partly to ineffective collection. It was this defect that the
Liber Censuum was intended to rectify. Cencio prepared the *Book of
Taxes*, seeing the inadequacy of the records (on which both Eugenius
III and Adrian IV had commented) and the consequent loss to the
Roman Church 'and seeing myself to be able easily to provide remedy
for this damage, and recognizing that my person was reared, advanced
in all things and made from earliest childhood by the Holy Roman
church'.[16] The 'building up' of the curia in the late twelfth century,
which Pfaff has so clearly shown, cost money and with an increased
number of curial cardinals, resident and active in the Church's
administration, a careful apportioning of the funds was needed – this
is perhaps what Burchard of Worms meant when he referred to Cencio
as distributing the income among the cardinals. Clement III increased
the college to thirty-one internal members and four external: at his
election there had been nineteen, three of whom were on legation.[17]
Celestine III inherited twenty-nine resident cardinals and four non-
resident.[18] Cencio's position as chancellor under Celestine III, which

[13] 'Burchardi et Cuonradi Urspergensium chronicon' (MGH *SS* xxiii) 738.
[14] See Lunt, *Revenues* ii 35.
[15] Pfaff, 'Clemens III', 266; id., 'Aufgaben und Probleme der päpstlichen Finanzver-waltung am Ende des 12. Jahrhunderts', *MIOG* lxiv (1956) 1–24; and cf. Partner, *Lands of St Peter*, 221 n. 3. See also V. Pfaff, 'Der Liber Censum von 1192 (Die im Jahre 1192/3 der Kurie Zinspflichtigen)', *Vierteljahrsschrift für Sozial-und Wirtschaftsgeschichte* xliv (1957) 78–96, 105–20, 220–42 and 325–51.
[16] Lunt, *Revenues* ii 34.
[17] Pfaff, 'Clemens III', 262, 269.
[18] Pfaff, 'Die Kardinäle unter Coelestin III (I)', 62.

will be examined in detail later, points again to his key role in the two most influential household offices. He had by now a firm reputation as an administrator, and on the death of Pope Celestine III in 1198 at the age of eighty-five there must have been many surprised that he was not elected to succeed his old master.

The power base of the Savelli family, at least by 1279 when the properties are described in the will of Cardinal Giacomo Savelli (later Pope Honorius IV),[19] was the area covering the Aventine and extending along the river bank northwards at its foot, including the Marmorata, the quays for unloading marble, and the jetty at the top of which stood the church of S. Maria ad Gradellis (or *Egiziaca*), which had been built within the temple of Fortuna Virilis. There were also certain properties towards the Ripa and in the Rione Ripa, including the theatre of Marcellus.[20] As was common with Roman noble families, the towers and ruins within the quarter they dominated were used and fortified. Certainly by the time of the papacy of Honorius IV (1285–7), the Aventine and Santa Sabina was the *caput* of their territory. Letters of Honorius IV as pope were dated from S. Sabina's,[21] at least one Savelli, Perna, wife of Luca, was buried there in 1315/1316,[22] and Honorius IV built a residence within the precinct behind the basilica.[23] The other, and probably earlier, nucleus of the Savelli estate was the theatre of the emperor Marcellus, in the quarter still called Monte Savelli. The family acquired this property in the thirteenth century and doubtless fortified it. It may have been the centre of their influence when Luca who died in 1266 (possibly Honorius III's nephew) became senator of the city. He was buried in S. Maria in Ara Coeli – as was his son, the senator Pandulf – where the Savelli later at least had a private chapel. Honorius IV's tomb was also there until removed to the Vatican.[24] Probably after the Savelli had withdrawn to the Aventine, the ground floor of the theatre was leased to butchers and craftsmen, and later the property passed to the Orsini, who also had

[19] Pd *Les registres d'Honorius IV*, ed. Prou, no. 823 cols. 577–84.

[20] Krautheimer, *Rome*, 157 and 319–20.

[21] Ibid. 319 and 370. Krautheimer is incorrect in saying that any documents of Honorius III were dated from S. Sabina. Those he cites (*Reg. Hon. III* nos. 89, 153, 196, 553 and 878) are either documents of Honorius IV or the place has been wrongly read, Rome S. Sabina being confused with Rome St Peter; see P 5402–3.

[22] The incised floor slab remains *in situ*; see Passerini in Litta, *Famiglie* x, disp. 168 unnumbered tav. at end. Honorius IV's nephew, Pietro, treasurer of Tours and canon of Rheims (d. 1288) was buried in the church of S. Alessio on the Aventine.

[23] Krautheimer, *Rome*, 312 and 319; Ptolemy of Lucca, 'Historia ecclesiastica', ed. L. A. Muratori, *Rerum Italicarum scriptores* xi (Milan 1727) 1191.

[24] Krautheimer, *Rome*, 213 and pl. 168; Waley, *Papal state*, 180 and 207; and Passerini (in Litta, *Famiglie* x) disp. 167 unnumbered tav. at end.

Prologue

estates in the Sabina,[25] and who shared the senatorship with the Savelli at the time of Benedict XI (1303–4).[26]

Very close to the Savelli properties, perhaps even within their estate, was S. Maria in Cosmedin, which had been the cardinalate church of Celestine III. It is tempting to think that this diaconate church had a close connection with the Savelli. Raniero Capocci, who held the title under Honorius III, and who signs from 13 April 1216 – he died in 1244 × 1250 – was a relative of the family and this was the title given to Giacomo Savelli in 1261/2.[27] Whether the Savelli married into the Capocci family early in the reign of Honorius III or before is not apparent.[28] Pietro Capocci was provided in 1222 to an English benefice which might suggest that a connection between the two families had already been forged. Pietro was the son of Giovanni who in 1203 had fortified a tower against the chief senator – the Capocci dominated the roads to S. Maria Maggiore on the Esquiline. He was an influential administrator, being appointed legate and rector 'in spiritualibus et temporalibus' throughout Italy in 1249.[29] Even more interesting is the suggestion that Thomas of Capua, cardinal priest of S. Sabina and papal penitentiary, was related to the Savelli,[30] being a son of Honorius's brother, Luca, and younger brother of Luca the senator.[31] He held the church of S. Sabina from 1216 until his death in Gregory IX's pontificate in 1239. However, no medieval source, let alone thirteenth-century source, which is known to me confirms this. Passerini suggests that Pandulf, papal chaplain, subdeacon and notary, was one of Honorius's nephews.[32] Pandulf was certainly, at least later, a family name and Gregorovius comments on its Germanic origin,[33] but the relationship seems unlikely as no source at all – and there are numerous letters to Pandulf in the papal registers – indicates such a blood tie.

As cardinal, Honorius's building activities were on no large scale. If the family were rising in property ownership in the city it is certainly

[25] Krautheimer, *Rome*, 283 and 305; Waley, *Papal state*, 83. Passerini, giving no authority, suggests that the Savelli moved back to the theatre of Marcellus in the fifteenth century.
[26] Waley, *Papal state*, 250. [27] P i 679 and ii 1795.
[28] For the Capocci, who also married into the Colonna family, see Carlo Cecchelli, *I Margani, i Capocci, i Sanguigni, i Mellini* (Rome 1946) 20–8; Krautheimer, *Rome*, 147; and Paravicini Bagliani, *Cardinali*, 301.
[29] 'Gesta' (*PL* ccxiv) col. 185 chap. 137f.; Krautheimer, *Rome*, 319. On Pietro see *DBI* 604–8; Waley, *Papal state*, 147.
[30] See P ii 1795, and below pp. 24, 25. A fictitious figure, Thomas cardinal priest of S. Balbina enters the list of the pope's relatives (Clausen, *Papst Honorius III*, 398). The mistake may originate with Ciaconius.
[31] Passerini (in Litta, *Famiglie* x) disp. 167 tav. 1.
[32] Ibid.
[33] Gregorovius, *Rome in the middle ages* v pt 1 119.

5

not apparent in artistic patronage or in munificence lavished on churches. The apse-mosaic of S. Paolo, the work of Venetian craftsmen, which may have been begun by Innocent III, was largely executed under Honorius and included his own small figure in the design, now heavily restored.[34] Honorius's title of cardinal priest of SS. Giovanni e Paolo (to which saints he had a special devotion)[35] may account for his interest and certainly he must have contributed to the costs. Possibly the costliest work undertaken by him in the city was the planning and laying out of the large basilica of S. Lorenzo fuori le mura which was completed in the first quarter of the thirteenth century.[36] Of his association with the basilica of S. Maria Maggiore, nothing remains, although it was in that church that he chose to be buried, in a tomb of red porphyry, which no longer survives.[37] He had died at the Lateran.

Depicted in various paintings and mosaics in the basilicas and churches of the city, of which the best surviving and perhaps the least restored contemporary representation is the mosaic at S. Paolo, Honorius is shown as a white-haired, bearded figure with a long aquiline nose and slightly hooded eyes. He is dressed in dalmatic, chasuble and pallium and wears sandals on his feet. The only characteristic feature, however, of this particular figure which is not shared by the others in the same series of mosaics is the white hair, perhaps a comment on his rank or position rather than his age. As the figure wears the pallium, it must represent him as pope.[38]

The election of Honorius III took place at Perugia, using the method of compromise according to an undated letter of the new pope found in the formulary of Buoncompagno of Florence, the power of election being given to the two senior cardinals, the cardinal bishop of Ostia, Ugolino Conti, himself *papabile* but too young, and the cardinal bishop of Praeneste, Guido Pierleone.[39] The gathering has been described as the first conclave.[40] Innocent III had died on 16 July 1216 at Perugia,

---

[34] Ladner, *Papstbildnisse* ii 80–91.

[35] Raynaldus (in Theiner, ed., *Annales ecclesiastici* xx) ad a. 1216 no. 17.

[36] For his building works and mosaics at S. Lorenzo, S. Bibiana, S. Sebastiano, the basilica of the Holy of Holies and the church of St John Lateran, see Krautheimer, *Rome*, 174–5, 204, 206 and 220; Ladner, *Papstbildnisse* ii 91–6.

[37] 'Chronica...Erphordiensi' (MGH SS xxiv) 196–7. 'Catalogus pontificum Romanorum Viterbiensis' (MGH SS xxii) 352, lists his (smallish) gifts to S. Maria Maggiore, St Peter's and St John Lateran. The omission of S. Paolo may suggest more substantial gifts for it. [38] Ladner, *Papstbildnisse* ii 80–91, esp. figs. 32–4.

[39] Pd Winkelmann, 'Zwölf Papstbriefe', no. 2 376–7.

[40] See P. Herde, 'Die Entwicklung der Papstwahl im dreizehnten Jahrhundert. Praxis und kanonistische Grundlagen', *Österreichisches Archiv für Kirchenrecht Vierteljahresschrift* 32nd year 1/2 (1981) 15, who reviews the evidence.

where the curia had been since the middle of May, and was buried on the following day. Seventeen cardinals attended the funeral and so were presumably present at Honorius's election.[41] Honorius later speaks of 'universi cardinales' being present but this is unlikely to be correct: at least one cardinal, Guala, was on legation. On the third day after Innocent's death (18th), Cencio Savelli was elected to an office which he said 'we would have freely chosen to avoid',[42] given the name of Honorius by the senior deacon ('eidem electo nomen imponit') and invested with the red mantle or cape.[43]

His consecration by the bishop of Ostia – he was not yet in episcopal orders – and investiture with the pallium took place on the following Sunday 24th, the seventh after Trinity and the vigil of St James. In the initial stages the making of the pope followed the procedure of *Ordo Romanus XII*. It is this *Ordo*, indeed, which has been accredited to Cencio during his chamberlainship.[44] It pays scant attention to coronation. In essence it was election and consecration that mattered, for coronation was not constitutive, merely symbolic and confirmatory of the pope's temporal power. If the pope was elected and consecrated outside Rome, could he also have been crowned outside the city and away from St Peter's? Enthronement, of course, could only take place in St Peter's and the curious ceremony in which the new pope was raised from the 'sedes stercorata' could only be performed at St John Lateran. Although the papal crown might have been with Innocent's court at Perugia for the customary crown-wearings,[45] the sources are singularly silent on the matter of coronation. No contemporary source actually mentions crowning: 'elevated', 'elevated and instituted', 'consecrated' are used.[46] Clausen states that the coronation took place at St Peter's on 31 August, citing Potthast, but Potthast speaks only of consecration (on 24 July at Perugia) and quotes chronicles that refer simply to Honorius's 'elevation' and return to Rome, to St Peter's, on 31 August.[47] Four days later on Sunday 4 September, according to the chroniclers, the new pope was received at the Lateran with unparalleled

[41] Cheney, *Innocent III and England*, 10 n. 40.
[42] Winkelmann, 'Zwölf Papstbriefe', no. 2.
[43] *Liber censuum*, ed. Fabre and Duchesne, i no. 58 311.
[44] Pd ibid. 311–13 and in *PL* lxxviii cols. 1063–1106, esp. 1097–1100.
[45] See H.-W. Klewitz, 'Die Krönung des Papstes', *ZRG* lxi (3) Kan. Abt. xxx (1941) 99–100, and Ullmann, *Growth of papal government*, 316 n. 2.
[46] See e.g. 'Annales Placentini Guelfi' in MGH *SS* xviii (1863) 433; Rainer, 'Annales' ad a. 1216 (MGH *SS* xvi) 675; and Raynaldus (in Theiner, ed., *Annales ecclesiastici* xx) ad a. 1216 no. 21.
[47] Clausen, *Papst Honorius III*, 9, and see above n. 46.

scenes of joy.[48] The silence and the difficulties argue against coronation at Perugia and underline the secondary importance of coronation. The pope already exercised full powers from his election and consecration. If the conclusion that Honorius was not crowned in Perugia is correct, the papal registers, clearly running from 24 July, commence the papal year in this case at least from consecration, as Bresslau argued, not from coronation.[49]

What do the chronicles convey about the pontificate and the man who succeeded Innocent III? The majority of them, obviously written at the end of the pontificate, repeat a theme that was perhaps officially issued, rarely deviating from a factual and chronological narrative that mentioned the coronation of Frederick II in St Peter's (of much more interest than the papal coronation) and his promise to take the cross.[50] Most comment also on the papal crowning of Peter Altisodoreus as emperor of Constantinople in the basilica of S. Lorenzo fuori le mura and some mention the French invasion of England and the death of King John.[51] Some, again with an English interest, note the restoration of Langton and the translation of St Thomas of Canterbury.[52] The capture of Damietta by the Christians, and then its loss, figure in most. Many mention Honorius's approval of the rules of the Dominicans and of the Franciscans[53] and a few his confirmation of the Carmelites and the brothers of Val-des-Écoliers.[54] None that I have discovered mentions the pope's canonizations. These appear to have been of interest only to regional commentators and later historians.

The deviations from the common line are often explained, as is to be expected, by the institutional affiliation or by the local associations of the author. Naturally Franciscan and Dominican chroniclers mention the approval of their Orders. Benedictine chroniclers are, for the most part, absorbed by the acquisition of privileges and confirmations,

---

[48] e.g. Richard of San Germano, 'Chronica' in MGH SS xix (1866) 338, and 'Annales Ceccanenses' (MGH SS xix) 300.

[49] Cf. Cheney, *Handbook of dates*, 33, citing Leo X, consecrated on 17 March and crowned on 19 March 1513, when apparently the latter date was used.

[50] e.g. 'Annales Cavenses' (MGH SS iii) 193.

[51] Ibid. and e.g. 'Annales Mosomagenses' in MGH SS iii (1839) 163, and 'Annales S. Benigni Divioniensis' in MGH SS vi (1844) 48.

[52] 'Annales Sancti Rudberti Salisburgenses' (MGH SS ix) 782; 'Auctarium Mortui Maris' in MGH SS vi (1844) 468.

[53] 'Catalogus pontificum et imperatorum Romanorum Casinensis' in MGH SS xxii (1872) 363 and 'Gesta abbatum Trudonensium continuatio' tertia pars II in MGH SS x (1852) 393.

[54] e.g. 'Vincentii Bellovacensis memoriale omnium temporum' in MGH SS xxiv (1879) 160.

stating that they had obtained a given privilege from him, and sometimes quoting the prized documents in full.[55] The Ceccano–Fossanova chronicle (Cistercian) speaks of Honorius's generosity towards their Order, on which of course the Cistercians dwelt at some length, and a few non-Cistercian chronicles take up the story of the pope's liberality to the Order. One chronicler wrote of his 'favouring' the Cistercians, who accordingly kept the anniversary of his death, apparently having in mind the pope's spectacular dedication of the great church of Casamari on 15 September 1217, when all the cardinals, notaries and his whole court, plus two Spanish archbishops and eleven bishops, attended him.[56] The pope himself, at the dedication, spoke of his own gifts towards the building which he had made when 'in minori officio'.[57] Honorius's promotion of the abbot of Cîteaux, Conrad of Urach, to the cardinal bishopric of Porto in 1219 was also perhaps seen as a mark of his esteem for the Order.[58]

Apart from these comments on matters of obvious interest to the specific Orders, the basic account remains much the same, with the one exception of the Chronicle of the Minorites of Erfurt which, having mentioned the compilation of a new collection of decretals (clearly the *Compilatio Quinta*),[59] goes on to comment on four specific legal rulings: concerning the proper handling of the sacrament, the forbidding of the ordeal, the use of lots in elections, and the decision that those teaching or studying in theological faculties were to receive the fruits of their prebends for five years.[60] Local associations are illustrated by a chronicle from Viterbo which is obsessed with the position of its bishopric and the pope's selection of his chaplain, Filippo, as bishop of the see.[61] For the English chronicles, only one or two of which are first-rate for this period, we will defer judgement for the moment, but he is never portrayed as clearly as his predecessor who, from the vivid accounts of Gerald of Wales and of Thomas of Marlborough, we are allowed to see walking and conversing in his gardens and sitting in his

[55] e.g. 'Chronica monasterii S. Bertini' in MGH SS xxv (1880) 833.
[56] 'Chronica pontificum et imperatorum Amiatinum continuationes' in MGH SS xxiv (1879) 836 and 'Annales Ceccanenses' (MGH SS xix) 302, and P note *post* 5602.
[57] P 5594.
[58] 'Ex gestis sanctorum Villariensium' in MGH SS xxv (1880) 223.
[59] A fair number of the chronicles mention this, e.g. 'Cat. pont. et imp. Rom. Casinensis' (MGH SS xxii) 363.
[60] MGH SS xxiv 196–7: c. 1 CQ III 24 = c. 10 X III 41 (P 6166), echoed in 'Flores temporum' in MGH SS xxiv (1879) 248; un. CQ V 14 = c. 3 X V 35 (P 6910); un. CQ V 9 = c. 3 X V 21 (P 7843); and un. CQ V 2 = c. 5 X V 5 (P 6165).
[61] 'Cat. pont. Rom. Viterbiensis' (MGH SS xxii) 352.

consistory, a witty man with a keen sense of humour, a plain speaker verging on the sarcastic.[62]

Honorius's reputation as a preacher and composer of sermons[63] leads in one chronicle to an account of Honorius preaching in Rome to further the fifth crusade. He told how when he was raising money in the city for the legation of Cardinal Giacinto to Spain, a certain old, revered and honourable man predicted that they would not go to Spain because, as he said, the pope (Clement III) would die and his (Honorius's) master, Cardinal Giacinto, would become pope. The speaker then went on the say 'today Jerusalem is taken by the Saracens and it will not be re-taken until the time of your pontificate.' Many people, Honorius continued, thought that this unidentified person was St Peter for, indeed, the first two things had come to pass. As Honorius was now pope, and ill, he firmly believed that the third prediction, the fall of Jerusalem to the Christians, would shortly follow. Hearing this, many Romans, greatly excited, took the cross and when this rumour spread to Germany many more followed suit.[64]

Another story concerned the death of Philip Augustus. The events related are supposed to have taken place shortly after Honorius's election in Perugia. The pope had gone to visit a sick knight. Giving the knight up for as good as dead, Honorius had given him absolution and had performed the last rites, but during the night the sick man had a dream that St Denis appeared to him and ordered him to go to the pope and tell him that King Philip of France had died and was now in purgatory, asking the pope to absolve him from the sentence of excommunication. The knight rose, fully recovered, from his bed, and to the horror of his nurses and companions, who thought he was an apparition, made his way to the papal lodging, where with the following words to the gatekeeper he insisted that the pope be roused: 'I am the knight, known to the pope, who was near death; behold the Lord has revived me. Open the gate because I have wonderful things to tell him.' The keeper, trembling, ran to the pope's bedroom and narrated this story. The pope, amazed yet hesitant, ordered the knight to be admitted. When the pope heard of the knight's vision of St Denis and saw how the knight had been restored to health, he offered prayers of thanksgiving to God, blessed the knight and dismissed him. The next

---

[62] Gerald of Wales, *Opera*, ed. Brewer *et al.*, iii 255–6; *Chronicon abbatiae de Evesham*, ed. W. D. Macray (RS xxix 1863) 189; and see Kuttner and García y García, 'New eyewitness account', 121.

[63] See e.g. 'Cat. pont. et imp. Rom. Casinensis' (MGH SS xxii) 363, and Horoy, ed. 'Opera omnia' i cols. 609–976.

[64] 'Burchardi et Cuonradi Urspergensium chronicon' (MGH SS xxiii) 378–9.

morning, the pope, as he had been instructed, celebrated mass and absolved the king, faithfully fulfilling all.[65] As Philip Augustus did not die until 1223, nearly seven years after Honorius's election, and as the papal court was at Perugia only during the first month after the election, no credence can be given to the chronology of the story.

The two stories break into the monastic and institutional framework of the chronicle, into the usual catalogue of acts and gifts, pestilences, sickness of animals and bad harvests.[66] They represent no 'official' view but may have been stories that were circulated throughout Europe by the troubadours and others. Indeed Honorius's own story in the sermon concludes with a remark on its diffusion. The audience did not desire an account of Honorius III's administrative acts but some token of his spiritual power. Actions and instructions are revealed through visions and dreams, as depicted in the medieval but much restored fresco in the Upper Church at Assisi showing Innocent III's dream of St Francis 'shoring up' the falling Church.[67] The pope is in touch with another world. In the first story he is to be the instrument of the prediction; through him it will be revealed to others and through him it will be effected. The encounter with the unknown person, unless literally understood, is a vision and the unknown man is identified as St Peter. The achievement of the first two predictions – that they would not go to Spain and that Celestine III would soon succeed Clement – throws considerable emphasis on the third, namely that Jerusalem would not be recaptured until Honorius became pope. Did the story really emanate from a sermon by the pope? We shall never know, but what we do know is that the story reflects a contemporary interest in the person of the pope and a contemporary desire, or perhaps anxiety, for proof that the pope was close to the supernatural world. The second story illustrates the importance of the dream as a vehicle of communication between the divine and the mortal. While the knight may act as the agent – subsequent to Honorius's priestly attentions – it is the pope who is the target for the message and who is to aid St Peter in easing the soul through purgatory. The pope as the successor to St Peter has the power to bind and to loose. He has the power to excommunicate and to absolve. Such stories satisfied curiosity and fitted popular preconceptions.

The sad lack of a biography, written by someone close to the pope

[65] 'Gesta Richeri Senoniensis ecclesia' in MGH *SS* xxv (1880) 297.
[66] e.g. 'Annales Sancti Rudberti Salisburgenses' (MGH *SS* ix) 783.
[67] The same series includes a representation of Honorius III listening intently to a sermon by Francis.

and within the papal *entourage*, means that the chronicles are as close as we can get to a delineation of the personality of the man at the centre of papal government between 1216 and 1227. The mighty ambitions and visions of his predecessor, Innocent III, had left a difficult legacy. Lateran IV was only some eighteen months past. The implementation of its decrees – a major task throughout Christian Europe – had hardly begun. There was the problem of England, 'the papal fief'. England represented a threat to the preservation of order in northern Europe. Its church torn apart by the effects of the interdict, its senior churchman suspended and others excommunicate, the country in turmoil from the Great Charter, England was now rent by the effects of the French invasion. A quick settlement was imperative. The re-establishment of monarchic control was to be one of the new pope's first tasks. Nor had Innocent's dealings with the Empire been satisfactorily concluded: the young Frederick II was still in papal tutelage. The crusade and the problem of the East remained to be settled. Even the confirmation of the two new religious orders of friars had not been completed.

How can Honorius's achievements be measured? Medieval chroniclers tended only to assess kings and popes by their munificence, gifts and building works. To have viewed them as administrators would not have been possible. The modern historian, however, has the advantage of being able to explore the archive sources of the pontificate: the products of the curia, and more especially the Chancery, the letters. From a study of the letters, originals and registered copies, it is feasible to make some assessment of the administrative machine, to examine the changes and estimate the strengths and the weaknesses in relation to the pretensions of papal government. Honorius's influence on the administration, his changes and reforms within the curia, and his management of the curial officers and the legates are the real tests. On the basis of the official records, where they survive, some judgement may be made of the actions of a pope who, coming after a dynamic predecessor, has been represented as elderly and cautious.[68]

[68] Clausen, *Papst Honorius III*, 9, citing Burchard: 'bonum, senem et religiosum, simplicem et benignum'; and Erfurt chronicle (MGH *SS* xxiv) 'full of sanctity and virtues'. The 'caution' is somewhat sharpened by Berlière ('Honorius III et les monastères bénédictins', 237), who sees it as conciliatory tact. Elsewhere (p. 245) he speaks of Honorius III as 'in the wake of Innocent III'.

PART I

THE DIPLOMATIC OF THE LETTERS

Chapter 1

THE PAPAL CHANCERY

THE CHANCERY IN THE LATE TWELFTH AND EARLY THIRTEENTH CENTURIES

On his accession to the papacy in July 1216 Honorius inherited an administrative machine which in the previous quarter century had undergone an unparalleled expansion and a radical reformation and rationalization. In this development he had played a personal rôle as papal chamberlain from 1188 to 1198, concerned with the collection of rents, tributes and taxes. The organization of the Chamber is not of direct concern here, but Honorius's *Liber Censuum*[1] exhibits an author who was deeply versed in the administration of the papal curia and one whose administrative efficiency was to influence his activities as pope. Furthermore from 1194, as cardinal deacon of S. Lucia in Orthea,[2] he combined the office of papal chamberlain with that of acting chancellor, in succession to Egidio cardinal deacon of S. Niccolò in Carcere, dating papal letters between 6 November 1194 and 10 September 1197.[3] He controlled both Chancery and Chamber until 1198. The close connection between the two offices is witnessed by the scribe of the *Liber Censuum*, Willelmus Rofio of Saint-Jean-d'Angély in Saintonge, who was described by Cencio as 'clericus camere et cancellarie domini pape scriptor'.[4] When the young Cardinal Lothario dei Conti, consecrated Pope Innocent III, came into power, the cardinal deacon Cencio was not retained under the new régime in either the office of chamberlain or that of chancellor.[5] Cencio's disappearance

---

[1] Besides Fabre and Duchesne's edition, see Fabre, *Étude sur le Liber Censuum*, and Elze, 'Liber Censuum'.

[2] Pfaff in *ZRG* lxii (Kan. Abt. xli, 1955) 94.

[3] Bresslau, *Handbuch* i 242–3. P i 468. Egidio subscribes without the title of chancellor from 1191–4; see von Heckel's useful survey of the subscriptions, 'Studien', 279–86, esp. 284.   [4] See Elze, 'Liber Censuum', 254, 256 and 257–8.

[5] Tillman's assertion (*Pope Innocent III*, 221 n. 84) that Cencio was papal chamberlain under Innocent III has, so far as I know, no factual basis. The sources which she cites (P 7349–50 and Gerald of Wales, *Opera*, ed. Brewer *et al.*, iv 304–5) say nothing about Cencio being chamberlain to Innocent, nor does the secondary work, Gottlob, *Servitientaxe*, 55–9, which she also cites.

from prominence after 1198 can only be explained by Innocent's hostility towards him.[6] Although he subscribes, and was promoted a cardinal priest in 1201, he was not entrusted with any legation or important business: there is only one mention of him in Innocent's register for the first year (when his clerk, the same William Rofio, was provided to a benefice) and none at all in the second year.[7] His unrivalled knowledge, however, of both areas of the curia's administration was to be of importance some twenty years later when he was elected pope.

The dismissal of Cencio by Innocent has been seen as a move to separate the joint administration of Chancery and Chamber.[8] But to think of Chancery and Chamber as very clear-cut and distinct departments, at any stage in the early thirteenth century, is to put a misleadingly modern construction on curial organization.[9] If Innocent did bring about any real administrative changes in this way, which seems doubtful, Cencio, when he became pope, made no attempt to reunite the offices. This might be seen as a measure of his good sense and realism, for in fact the increasing business of both departments would have made this difficult if not impossible. Certainly the two 'departments' were never again administered under one hand. A more realistic interpretation of the administration at this time would seem to be that as the curia's governmental and judicial rôles developed, so there was a corresponding specialization which in time became departmentalized. Some of these tendencies were there before Innocent III's accession; some he hastened or developed; and some took many years to come to maturity.

In the organization of the Chancery, Innocent has been credited with the establishment of the scribes' college or guild.[10] The papal scribes had originally been drawn from the chapel, as were the royal and episcopal scribes. The first major step towards scribal organization came when the scribes were no longer responsible for the duties of the chapel but were involved exclusively in writing documents. Elze has shown the closeness between the papal chapel and the Chancery in the early thirteenth century. The scribes were also often papal chaplains as well,

[6] J. Haller, *Das Papsttum* 2 edn iv (Stuttgart 1952) 1f.
[7] *Reg. Inn. III*, ed. Hageneder *et al.*, i, no. 477. Clausen (*Papst Honorius III*) 'makes' a life for him as the tutor of the young Frederick II but the reference in the letter of Frederick (5 n. 5) to the pope's *tutela* is no more than a general allusion to the papal protection of minors. Some of the difficulties over Cencio's activities under Innocent have arisen from confusion with Cinthius, cardinal priest of S. Lorenzo in Lucina.
[8] Herde, *Beiträge*, 239.
[9] Elze, 'Liber Censuum', 258, makes this point on the situation under Celestine.
[10] von Heckel, 'Studien', 279–86, and Schwarz, *Schreiberkollegien*, esp. 7–22.

The Papal Chancery

and all of Innocent's three cardinal chancellors and five vice-chancellors came from the chapel.[11] It is not clear what precisely were their chapel duties but it is clear that this attachment had not been completely severed by Innocent's pontificate. The *Gesta* is the source for Innocent's building new offices and a second *capellania* at St Peter's in addition to the older *capellania* in the Lateran.[12] This definition may have furthered the distinction between the chapel organization and that of the writing office and encouraged the growth of the scribes' college.

The strongest argument for the development of scribal organization at this time concerns the payment of the scribes. The practice whereby the scribe wrote his name on the *plica* of the engrossment does not appear to pre-date Innocent's papacy. This is connected, at least in part, with the payment of the scribes. Furthermore, the *Gesta* records that Innocent, in attempting to reform the curia's reputation for arbitrary and extortionate financial demands by its officers, decreed that only the scribes and the bullators were to exact approved fees, which were to be strictly controlled.[13] The elaborate taxation system for documents, for which evidence is found on the engrossments from 1255,[14] is undoubtedly foreshadowed here.

The emergence of the scribes' signatures also indicates a growing number of scribes in the Chancery. The superiors of the Chancery could no longer keep in mind all the scribes and follow every document through the stages of its issue. For the purposes of the control of the letters and in case correction was needed, it was necessary to have the scribe's name recorded on the document. So far as is known, there was no corrector of papal documents before Innocent III.[15] The corrector's appearance suggests both the issue of more documents and an increasing desire to supervise Chancery's products.

The increase in the number of scribes in the writing office clearly encouraged the growth of professional conduct and led to restrictive practices. Obviously by this time only members of this office wrote papal letters. A guild system, however, required not only the protection of the group against others (outsiders) but also regulation of the business within. In support of the argument for the establishment of a scribes' college under Innocent, attention has been drawn to the scribe's oath and to the clauses (two only) in the so-called chancery ordinance, which mention the scribes.[16] While the scribe's oath undoubtedly shows

[11] Elze, 'Päpstliche Kapelle', esp. 157, 171–5.   [12] Ibid. 173.
[13] 'Gesta' in *PL* ccxiv col. 80 cap. 41.   [14] *BAPP* i pp. xcv–xcvi.
[15] See Schwarz, 'Corrector', 144, and below pp. 46–7.
[16] Schwarz, *Schreiberkollegien*, 7–9; Tangl, *Kanzleiordnungen*, 37 (no. 5) and 54–5 nos. 2, 10.

growing professional organization, it is by no means certain that it comes from Innocent's reign. It could be earlier; and the existence of an oath does not prove a college structure. The clauses in the chancery ordinance, to which we must turn in detail in a moment, simply comment on the scribes' activities in petitioning in conjunction with other curial officers: they say nothing important about rules for the conduct of the scribes or their organization. There is no mention as yet of the rescribendary who served as the head of the scribes' guild or college, and who was appointed from among the scribes to serve for a period of six months. The rescribendary in no way took the place of the head of the Chancery, the vice-chancellor, to whom he himself was responsible. He was concerned with controlling the activities of the scribes, with their common consent, within the guild. He arranged the 'equal distribution' of the work of engrossment among the scribes and supervised their professional conduct.[17] Until the emergence of the rescribendary in the later thirteenth century, a full 'college' or guild structure cannot be observed.

Innocent's reputation as an administrative reformer in Chancery also rests on the appearance, apparently during his pontificate, of the process of contradicting letters which were read in the *audientia publica*, so that their contents might be modified or altered before issue. The arrangement for these possible alterations was the work of the *audientia litterarum contradictarum*.[18] The first identified description of the operation of this procedure occurs in an English source, the chronicle of Evesham abbey. In 1205–6, in the course of promoting the abbey of Evesham's case of exemption from the bishop of Worcester's jurisdiction, the abbey's proctor, Thomas of Marlborough, describes how he protested in the *audientia publica* against the letters which were to be issued to his opponent, and that he then put his arguments against the issue of the letters in their present form to the *auditor litterarum contradictarum* in the *audientia contradictarum*. There is no mention of the *audientia publica* before this date, and as the *audientia publica* and the *audientia litterarum contradictarum* were dependent structures it looks as though they both came into being at this time. It is probable that Marlborough's excited and racy account describes a relatively new process. Once the mandate in a particular case had been drawn up, not needing the personal approval of the pope, it could be read out in an

---

[17] Herde, *Beiträge*, 154, 158, 181, 184–7. The officer who distributed the petitions to the abbreviators also did not emerge until Innocent IV's pontificate. See below pp. 29, 32–3, 46 for the abbreviators.

[18] Herde, *Beiträge*, esp. 213–39, and id., *Audientia*, esp. i 20–2.

open forum or public audience of the Chancery which was presided over by the vice-chancellor. To this open forum came the proctors with the purpose of objecting if the letters they heard might be claimed to prejudice their clients. If there was no objection (or if the *auditor litterarum contradictarum* found the objection unfounded) the document was sent immediately for bulling. Such in brief were the arrangements for speeding up the issue of relatively unimportant documents, the judicial mandates, which would otherwise have clogged the adminis-trative machine, and it can hardly be doubted that the appearance of the two audiences marked a major administrative advance. Herde has argued powerfully for Innocent's foundation of the *audientia litterarum contradictarum*, whereas Barraclough had suggested that its emergence may be connected with the extension of the judge-delegate system under Alexander III.[19] Without the discovery of further sources the problem cannot be entirely resolved. If the seeds of the reading and the contradiction existed earlier than Innocent's reign it was he who furthered the usefulness of the method by crystallizing the two processes in the sections of Chancery, the *audientia publica* and *audientia litterarum contradictarum*.

THE SOURCES FOR THE ORGANIZATIONAL CHANGES

The official sources for these changes are virtually non-existent. There are no surviving chancery constitutions establishing the college of scribes or the *audientia litterarum contradictarum*. It may be that there were never any such official declarations. The nearest to official ordinances of any kind for Innocent III's reign are the pope's pronouncements concerning the products of his Chancery which were selected for the law-books.[20] These are not particularly expansive, include nothing on the chancery personnel and mainly concern forgery. Also attributed to Innocent has been the short 'Institutio Cancellarie super petitionibus dandis et recipiendis' (the title cannot be other than a later addition). First printed by Tangl in 1894, and dated by him 1192–1236, its seventeen clauses are a composite and ill-fitting collection.[21] It is clear that the argument for assigning the earliest part of it to the time of the original compilation of the *Liber Censuum* (in which it is found) under Celestine III is no longer tenable. At least this cannot be

[19] Barraclough in *DDC* i cols. 1387–99.
[20] e.g. P 365 and 1184 (cc. 5, 6 *X* V 20); *Reg. Inn. III*, ed. Hageneder *et al.*, i 520 no. 349, and c. 28 *X* I 3.
[21] Tangl, *Kanzleiordnungen*, 53–5. Only the first eleven clauses are found in the *Liber Censuum* (i no. 209 461–2).

maintained on the basis of an identification of *capellanus* and *camerarius*, used in clause 1 in a general sense, with two of Celestine's officers, namely with Moyses the chaplain and Cencio the chamberlain.[22] It is also clear that the 'collection' is a false concoction: it is not one document but has several different groups of clauses, some of which may not even fit into groups. Von Heckel, who had from the first attributed it to Innocent III,[23] realized that the last seven clauses were obviously later additions. On the grounds of his later discovery that the first ten clauses were known to the decretal compiler, Alanus Anglicus, whose collection was completed in 1206, von Heckel narrowed the date to between 1198 and 1206.[24] But the first ten clauses have no particular unity and, as Stelzer has argued, the earliest amongst them (arguably 1, 2 and 7) could go back to Celestine III, as Tangl and Bresslau thought.[25] That they were known to Alanus only makes them *earlier* than 1206, and any argument concerning the lack of a permanent chancellor could put the date back as far as 1187.

Such an amorphous collection is fraught with problems. The heading, which is found in the *Liber Censuum*, looks like the attempt of the compiler to give some unity to the scraps on petitions which he had discovered scattered throughout the office. The arguments are convincing that the first ten clauses were in existence before Honorius III's pontificate, but they were certainly not one document. Within the first ten clauses, at least three groups can be detected. 1, 2 and 7 may belong together (the 'item nullus' and the 'item nemo' of 2 and 7 referring to the subject of clause 1, the notary); 3 to 6 might be connected (they all concern petitions as the subject). 8 to 10 do not even have a superficial unity. 11 concerns fraud, as does 10. The final six clauses concern proctors and advocates: the last two (16 and 17) on the advocates have a certain similarity in form, 'prohibemus...' and 'precipimus...' which suggests a connection;[26] the four on the proctors (12 to 15) belong together but not in the order in which Tangl printed them.[27] The order may be 14, 15, 12 and 13. Herde has associated 12 with Honorius's pontificate; this may be likely, but it

22 von Heckel, 'Studien', 274 and 283–4.
23 'Das Aufkommen', esp. 313–14.
24 'Studien', 258–89, esp. 259.
25 W. Stelzer, 'Die Anfänge der Petentenvertretung an der päpstlichen Kurie unter Innocenz III', *ASAR* anno xii (Turin 1973) 130–9, esp. 133. Bresslau, *Handbuch* ii 3 n. 2. Tangl and Bresslau also included nos. 8–10: the numbers are Tangl's.
26 The earnings of the advocates were not to be more than 20 'librarum denariorum senatus' in any one case, and not more than two advocates were to be employed by any one party in a case.
27 On the content, see below pp. 34–5.

cannot be proved.[28] There are no grounds for thinking of these clauses, as they stand, as official chancery regulations. It is not at present possible to know whether any of them were drawn up by the vice-chancellor or by the pope and officially issued for the use of the Chancery. As already mentioned, the first clauses were included in the *Liber Censuum* at some point, but the *Liber Censuum* includes a mass of such material – lists, notes and comments relative to curial rights and customs – which comes from a variety of sources, not all of them official. Nor can anything be said on the circulation. Undoubtedly the origin of this curious amalgam is inside the Chancery, but the texts are so fragmentary and muddled in form and content as to suggest a variety of pronouncements by senior officials (not necessarily the pope or the vice-chancellor) over a period of twenty to thirty years and at least two, probably three, pontificates.

For Honorius's pontificate there is no sudden and dramatic expansion of official evidence, but there is the important treatise or *libellus* 'on the forms of petitions according to the procedure of the Roman curia', completed presumably close to 1226 – the date is mentioned in the text – and surviving in two manuscripts from the second half of the thirteenth century.[29] Although it was not an official collection put out by the curia, it was officially approved by the pope for the use of petitioners at his court, and it had been compiled by the much respected Cardinal Guala. The work consists of thirty-two forms of petition. While a discussion of the historical setting of the documents belongs elsewhere, some appraisal of what the *libellus* tells us about the administrative machine is appropriate here. The treatise begins by distinguishing between the petitions for letters of 'simple' justice, which are easily impetrated because they are not read before the pope, and those for letters of grace – the privileges, protections, confirmations and indulgences – which have to come before the pope for his approval. Ten of the petitions request letters of simple justice for judges delegate to be appointed ('unde petit iudices'), in cases concerning presentation, violence, usury, injuries, undue exactions, despoliation, an inadequate vicarial pension, and a broken agreement or composition (nos. 1–7, 10, 16, 29).[30] Ten are for letters of grace and therefore must be sought from the pope in person, to be granted from his 'beneficence' or 'active kindness'. Two of these are for privileges (nos. 23, 26), four

---

[28] *Beiträge*, 128.
[29] Ed. (with numbered entries) by von Heckel in *Archiv für Urkundenforschung* i 502–10. For a brief résumé of the contents, see Herde, *Audientia* i 33–5.
[30] The application for judges is inferred in no. 4, which is a gloss on no. 3.

for indulgences and indults (nos. 21–2, 25, and 27), and four for confirmations (nos. 11–13 and 19). The remaining petitory forms concern appeals (nos. 8, 9), complaints against negligent judges and executors, and proctorial appointments (nos. 30–2). This fundamental distinction, between the 'easy' mandates and the letters of grace and more difficult questions, which is clearly emphasized in Guala's work, shows how the Chancery was now distinguishing between the relative importance of the business. This was reflected in the different treatment of the petitions and the different modes of issue for the letters. From Guala's 'approved' treatise can be inferred the new methods which the Chancery was in the process of introducing.

Handy collections of forms, or formularies, were clearly needed in a working Chancery to assist the officials – notaries, abbreviators and scribes – in drawing up and issuing the appropriate documents. The existence of at least one such formulary in the pontificate of Honorius III is strongly suggested by Guala's treatise on petitions.[31] It is inherently unlikely, given the existence of Guala's book for petitioners, that no such manuals would have been compiled by or for the chancery officials, whose daily task it was to write the required letters. Herde has pointed out, moreover, that the arrangement of Guala's *libellus* on petitions is in an order which is very similar to that of many of the later clerks' formularies. The form and shape of the *libellus* may, indeed, suggest that it was itself based on an earlier, lost formulary which was used by the chancery officials.[32] The earliest formulary to have survived is one collected under Gregory IX, now in Durrieu MS 5 on fols. 46 to 59.[33] It mentions popes H. and I., presumably Gregory's immediate predecessors, Honorius and Innocent, and it may incorporate material from the formulary of Honorius which was apparently known to Guala or from another early one.[34] Two further formularies of Gregory IX are extant, one also in the Durrieu manuscript[35] and the other in Berlin Staatsbibliothek Cod. lat. fol. 231, which cites 'our predecessor of happy memory', Honorius III, and Otto, cardinal deacon of S. Niccolò in Carcere Tulliano (Otto da Tonengo).[36] Finally MS Lea m. 16 of the University of Pennsylvania in Philadelphia includes a formulary on fols. 8–79, 'Forme Romane curie super beneficiis et questionibus',

[31] Herde, 'Formularies', 327 n. 23.
[32] Ibid., and Herde, *Audientia* i 33–5.
[33] This manuscript is in private hands; see Herde, *Audientia* i 35–7, and Tessier, 'Note sur un manuel', 375f.
[34] Fol. 46–v. [35] Fols. 60–102.
[36] Fols. 122–7v. Otto is mentioned on fols. 126 and 134v. For these two formularies, see Herde, *Audientia* i 37–42, and for Otto, below pp. 38–40, 45.

which comes from the mid-thirteenth century and the pontificate of Innocent IV and includes one document of Honorius III.[37] Such collections were usually of a composite nature, drawing upon suitable material which was added to and changed, often over a fairly long period of time. Changes in decisions were made, too, as to what could be issued without reading and what needed to be read before the pope. Many of the simple confirmations were downgraded to common form in the course of the thirteenth century. One example, the 'littere "cum secundum apostolum"' shows a letter which was downgraded perhaps by the mid-thirteenth century and certainly before 1278, when it was upgraded again, only to become *littere dande* once more under John XXII.[38] This form appears to have been read before the pope in Guala's time, according to the passage in his treatise.

Directives as to what had to be read before the pope and what did not have to be were clearly authoritative and were publicly proclaimed by the pope and published in ordinances, as is known from later examples.[39] It may be assumed that the same would have been true for earlier pronouncements on these important matters. Formularies used by the chancery clerks, on the other hand, were only semi-official.[40] At any one time there might be several formularies in circulation and use. It is quite possible, even likely, that clerks possessing copies of formularies would have added new forms which they considered particularly useful. It is not until Boniface VIII's pontificate that there is anything like a uniform recension. In most, if not in all, instances, their origin must have been in the Chancery. For a later period, Herde has suggested that they were connected with the auditors of the *audientia litterarum contradictarum*.[41]

Much of what contributes to our knowledge of the early-thirteenth-century Chancery comes from similar examples of a later date. In some cases the picture thus drawn may be reasonably faithful, but there is obviously a danger of reading back into the early thirteenth century the well-documented process of the issue of papal letters of later centuries. In a desire, too, to clarify what appears to be a complicated

---

[37] See Herde, *Audientia* i 44, and Haskins, 'Two Roman formularies', who prints (p. 281) the otherwise unknown document of Honorius of May 1224, commending the elect of Cashel to Henry III. Cf. below App. 2 no. 44.

[38] Herde, 'Formularies', 325 & n. 17, 342–4, esp. 344; id., *Audientia* i, see index *sub* 'cum secundum apostolum'; and Guala, *Libellus*, no. 14 in the von Heckel edition.

[39] See G. Barraclough, 'The Chancery ordinance of Nicholas III', *QFIAB* xxv (1933/4) 192–250.

[40] Herde, *Audientia* i 20f., and 'Formularies', 326, 332.

[41] *Audientia* i 169–73, and 'Formularies', 336–8.

procedure, we may be guilty also of making distinctions and deductions that would have much puzzled contemporaries, and of suggesting order and system where there was very little. We have looked briefly at the sources relating to the Chancery that were in existence by Honorius's accession or that date from his pontificate. The next step is to examine the structure and the personnel of the Chancery after 1216. It will then be possible to detect what changes and elaborations were made by Honorius to the developments of the previous quarter century, which Innocent had gone some way towards encapsulating in an 'office' framework.[42] To all intents and purposes, Innocent had laid some of the foundations of an administrative machine which in time might become divorced from the household. Honorius did not revert to the late-twelfth-century system but he used his past administrative experience to implement and to develop it.

THE VICE-CHANCELLOR

Honorius did not prolong the appointment of his predecessor's chancellor, Thomas of Capua, cardinal priest of S. Sabina, who had acted from March to July 1216.[43] Thomas had been a papal notary, and was the author of a well-known treatise on letter writing.[44] If Honorius and Thomas were related it may have been easier for Honorius to remove him. Honorius himself, it will be remembered, had not been retained in office by Innocent III. Apart from these two instances, it was customary in papal administration in both the twelfth and thirteenth centuries to keep one's predecessor's chancellor, at least while considering a suitable permanent appointment. Honorius's acting vice-chancellor at the time of the pope's death in March 1227, Master Sinibaldus Fieschi, became Gregory IX's first vice-chancellor from 8 June 1227 until raised to the cardinalate, and Gregory's last vice-chancellor, the Dominican Giacomo Buoncambio, continued in office for just short of a year under Innocent IV.[45] Confirming or extending

---

[42] Innocent is also credited with the creation of the cardinal penitentiary (Cheney, *Innocent III and England*, 70–1 and 403), whose requirements were soon to be office ones, and with developing the use of auditors. On the papal penitentiaries, see Göller, *Die päpstlichen Pönitentiarie* i. On the auditors, see Sayers, *Papal judges delegate*, 14f: it is questionable whether Innocent contributed as much towards their formation into a court as the mid-thirteenth-century popes, Gregory IX and Innocent IV.

[43] See *Letters*, ed. Cheney, pp. xvii–xviii, esp. n. 5.

[44] Herde (*Audientia* i 18–19) indicates that Thomas of Capua's *Summa dictaminis* (ed. Heller) was 'old-fashioned'.

[45] Sayers, *Papal judges delegate*, 21 and 274; below pp. 26, 38, 41; Herde, *Beiträge*, 1–3.

an appointment of the head of the Chancery after a papal vacancy made for continuity in the administration, although this might be over-emphasized if the majority of Chancery's senior personnel remained the same. There is no obvious reason why either Cencio or Thomas of Capua should not have been retained in office – both survived and were later, if not immediately, in active employment. In the case of Cencio, it can only be deduced that there were personal difficulties in his working with the new pontiff. Thomas, on the other hand, became papal penitentiary,[46] which could certainly not be seen as a demotion, but arguably suited Honorius's decision to appoint no more cardinal chancellors – to demote not the man but the office.

Honorius never appointed a chancellor as Innocent had done. He used acting vice-chancellors, some of whom were given the title, but not all. This experiment had been tried by both Celestine III and Innocent III (and, indeed, by other earlier popes, such as Urban III, Gregory VIII and the anti-pope, Calixtus III). But it was not adhered to by Innocent when he appointed Giovanni, cardinal deacon of S. Maria in Via Lata, chancellor in 1205, to be followed by Giovanni, cardinal deacon of S. Maria in Cosmedin, and after a gap of nearly three years, between May 1213 and March 1216, by Thomas of Capua.[47] Honorius's vice-chancellor from at least 11 October 1216 (and possibly as early as mid-August)[48] to 14 September 1219, who signed again as acting vice-chancellor on 13 December 1219, was Ranerius.[49] There is nothing to suggest that he had administrative experience, but he must have been much trusted by the pope and would appear to have come from outside the chapel. Ranerius was prior of the Augustinian house of S. Fridianus at Lucca and combined the office with that of vice-chancellor until mid-February 1217, when he dropped the title of prior, according to the documents which were registered in the papal registers, presumably as soon as a new prior had been elected.[50] Appointed patriarch of Antioch and consecrated at Viterbo on 19 November 1219, when he was described as 'sprung' from the *comitatus* of Todi from the castle called the Old Castle,[51] he signed as acting

---

[46] Rusch, *Die Behörden und Hofbeamten*, 39–40. For Thomas of Capua's formulary of the office, see Haskins, 'Two Roman formularies', 277, and Lea, *Formulary of the papal penitentiary*.

[47] *Letters*, ed. Cheney, p. xvii n. 5; and see Delisle, *Mémoire*, 44–6.

[48] Reg. Yr. 4, entry between nos. 549 and 550, states that on his resignation in mid-November 1219 he had been vice-chancellor for 3 years and 3 months.

[49] Bresslau, *Handbuch* i 249–50 and P i 679.

[50] Reg. Yr. 1 nos. 247 and 319.

[51] Reg. Yr. 4 entry between nos. 549 and 550; *Reg. Hon. III post* no. 2262.

vice-chancellor ('cancellarii vicem agens') as late as 13 December,[52] very likely while arrangements were being made to replace him. His appointment as patriarch of Antioch suggests that he may have had some knowledge of Greek that would have been useful to the papal Chancery. He appears to have been succeeded immediately by Willelmus the notary, who had acted very temporarily in the capacity of vice-chancellor on one occasion before, dating a document *per manum* on 12 August 1216, a bare three weeks after Honorius's election, when the papal court was still at Perugia. For immediate purposes a notary was used: this may have been the first solemn privilege (for Monte Cassino) of the new reign and it needed the cardinals' subscriptions and the *datum per manum*.[53] On the resignation of Ranerius, Willelmus was given the title of vice-chancellor, signing from 24 February 1220 to 3 April 1222.[54] His successor was Master Guido, papal chaplain and notary, who signed from 24 May 1222 to 9 May 1226,[55] and who was never promoted to the title of vice-chancellor. Master Sinibaldus Fieschi, described as *auditor litterarum contradictarum*, dated *per manum* on 14 November 1226.[56] He was Gregory IX's vice-chancellor by 8 June 1227.[57] None of Honorius's four vice-chancellors or acting vice-chancellors were to be created cardinals while in office. Two out of the four had been notaries, and one, Master Sinibaldus, was versed in chancery business as *auditor litterarum contradictarum*.

The significance of Honorius's action in suppressing the chancellorship lies apparently in the removal of a powerful officer who was usually a cardinal with other commitments. Cardinals were increasingly being used as legates and might be absent from the curia for long periods of time. The chancellor was now replaced by a chancery official who was immersed in chancery practice (though this cannot be proved of Ranerius) and who was available when required. From 1216 onwards the Chancery was headed by what may be termed full-time working superiors. While it is true that Innocent had tried this experiment, he

[52] *Reg. Hon. III* no. 2261. P has this incorrectly as 20 Dec. (6185 = Ughelli, *Italia Sacra*, ed. N. Coleti i (Venice 1717) 231). P 6591 which Potthast thought showed Ranerius signing (i 679) on 15 March 1221 belongs to 1219. The year of grace, said to be 1219, and the indictional year, the seventh, accord; the pontifical year, said to be the fifth (i.e. 1221) has clearly been wrongly copied.

[53] P 5327. There is no absolute comparison with the arrangements of Innocent III when at first he used the notaries, Raynaldus, sometimes described as 'vicem agentis cancellarii', and Blasius, because these arrangements lasted for five years until the end of February 1203 (P i 467).

[54] *Reg. Hon. III* no. 2339. P i 679 has him with the style of chancellor in instances of 1221 (June 11) and 1222 (Feb. 27). These are not originals and the evidence is weak.

[55] P i 679.   [56] P 7610.   [57] P i 938, 939; see Bresslau, *Handbuch* i 250.

did not, probably for reasons beyond his control, carry it through to its logical conclusion. Tout saw the suppression of the office of papal chancellor as an important condition of the enormous development of the Chancery as a department of government.[58] But it reflected, too, the desire of the pope to re-establish control over his inner household, for the chancellor had long ceased to be the personal secretary, in close attendance on the pope, who had emerged in the mid-eleventh century, after Leo IX's wholesale adoption of imperial secretarial methods.[59] The desire to rely on men of humbler status in the administration was not simply a phenomenon of papal government, as the decline of the chancellorship in England after the death of Ralph Neville witnesses.[60] Appointments to head the Chancery under Honorius were made from outside the college of cardinals. The men who were now chosen came, after the bridging appointment of Ranerius, from among the notaries and chancery officials.

Honorius's step may also represent changes in what was required of the head of Chancery. Firstly fewer solemn privileges were now being sought and issued. This meant that the subscriptions of the assembled college of cardinals were not so frequently required. The traditional cancellarial duties of overseeing the writing office and dating the solemn privileges were changing in the light of the kind of documents which were now applied for and their relative number.[61] The vice-chancellor's work was increasingly concerned with the mechanics relating to the issue of the documents and especially with the mandates. The vice-chancellor was present at the reading of the *littere legende* and the most important letters to the pope. He also presided over the public sitting of the Chancery, the *audientia publica*, where chancery pronouncements and all the mandate business was read. The *audientia publica* was crucial to the whole new system of issuing documents and dealing with petitioners. While public audiences of the Chancery were not unheard of before 1198, they were not an integral part of the structure, and the evidence does seem to suggest that it was Innocent III who made the *audientia publica* essential to the changing Chancery. As far as we can follow the work of the chancery officials and the proctors under Honorius, there appear now to be regular sessions of

[58] *Chapters* i 285; and Poole, *Papal Chancery*, 140.
[59] Tout, *Chapters* i 128; and see Poole, *Papal Chancery*, 59–67.
[60] Tout, *Chapters* i 285 speaks of the 'fear of magnate cardinals'. On the suppression of the chancellorship in England, see also B. Wilkinson, *The Chancery under Edward III* (Manchester 1929) 6–8 and App. ii.
[61] See below Chapter 3. Cheney finds only seven original solemn privileges issued by Innocent III for England out of some sixty-five originals of all kinds.

the *audientia publica*. When the papal household left Rome, the Chancery went with it, and the *audientia publica* continued its sittings to make possible the continued issue of letters from Viterbo or Anagni or wherever the curia might be. In this framework the vice-chancellor's duties were increasingly those of a permanent secretary or civil servant, closer to the notaries once more. He was a 'chancery' man and a 'professional', who, if not exactly climbing up from the ranks, had come in three cases out of four from inside the institution, and who had his own particular duties set out for him, as opposed to the wide and general governmental and often ambassadorial ones of the cardinalate.

THE NOTARIES

Traditionally the notaries were seven in number. At some points in the thirteenth century, however, there were only six and it was the opinion of some commentators that they were normally six unless the pope chose to add one.[62] Originally they had been attributed to the seven regions of the city for the purpose of collecting the acts of the martyrs. Theirs was a very ancient office, much older than the chancellor's: according to the *Liber Pontificalis*, they were in existence in the time of Pope Fabian (236–50). By the fourth century, they were clearly discernible when they were organized into a guild or *schola* under the chief notary, the *primicerius*, the forerunner of the vice-chancellor.[63] They were by now secretaries, attending church councils, writing minutes and drawing up acts: they were also associated with the preservation of records as the *scriniarii*, the term being used frequently as an alternative to *notarii*.[64] When the popes 'freed' their Chancery from imperial and more especially from urban Roman influences in the eleventh century, the notaries became papal officers in the true sense. This was one of the reasons for the adoption of the Caroline miniscule. Although the notaries might still come in the main from the Roman families, they were no longer 'civic' officials but papal officials.

The notaries were the seniors of Chancery, approximating to the chancery masters in England.[65] These were the men who were especially skilled in drafting and drawing up acts, in the correct application of the rules of the *cursus* and in letter composition and the collection of forms. They were the confidential secretaries and *dictatores*

[62] Herde, *Beiträge*, 9.
[63] See, in general, Poole, *Papal Chancery*, 12–13.
[64] Ibid., 15–17.
[65] P. Chaplais, *English royal documents* (Oxford 1971) 20–1; Maxwell-Lyte, *Historical notes*, 5–12 and 275; and Tout, 'Household of the Chancery', 53–5.

of Chancery. It is not possible to say in what proportion pope, vice-chancellor and notaries dictated the most important letters. There must always have been some correspondence that was dictated by the pope himself.[66] No medieval head of government hesitated to make policy statements in letter form. This is not to suggest that every word came from the papal mind but that the essence of the letter did. In all likelihood the notaries acted in a similar capacity for the pope, as the abbreviators did for the notaries in the drawing up of the minutes, that is to say they 'took down' the letter. As the notaries were accomplished calligraphers, it was presumably they who, in some cases at least, not only took down the minute but actually wrote the most secret (the letters close) as well as the most elaborate letters (the solemn privileges). Letters which were sent close – unfortunately none survives amongst the originals of Honorius printed below – cannot have been submitted to many eyes and must have been produced in this way. For the great privileges, the dating clause required the hand of the vice-chancellor or a senior clerk of Chancery, usually a notary, if there was no vice-chancellor. The rota (except for the small cross at the top executed by the pope)[67] and the monogram, and the text of such splendid productions, were the personal work of one of the select notarial group or the vice-chancellor himself.[68] The hand of the dating clause (in all the solemn privileges I have examined) is the same as that of the text.[69] As the *per manum* states the author of the dating clause, we are left in no doubt as to the identity of the scribes.

Evidence survives of six papal notaries under Honorius.[70] Willelmus, who dated *per manum* on 12 August 1216, only a few weeks after Honorius's election, became vice-chancellor in 1220, as we have seen, on the resignation of Ranerius, holding the title until 3 April 1222. He must have remained an active notary until 1220. In spite of the common use of the name, I am inclined to think, because of the select number

---

[66] See, however, Cheney's caveat, *Letters*, p. xvii, and 'The letters of Pope Innocent III', *Bulletin of the John Rylands Library* xxxv (1952) 34–41.

[67] For this and for the *subscripsi* symbol of Honorius, see Katterbach and Peitz, 'Unterschriften', plate 5 nos. 67, 68 and 69.

[68] There is one original solemn privilege of Honorius III in Britain at the Scottish Record Office (formerly PRO SC7/18/32; P 5924), reproduced by zincography in Rymer i pt 1 between pp. 152 and 153.

[69] See e.g. *Reg. Hon. III* i, the last plate before p. 1, a document of Ranerius.

[70] In general see Herde, *Beiträge*, 8–11, and C. R. Cheney, *Notaries public in England in the thirteenth and fourteenth centuries* (Oxford 1972) 34, 42. Confusion in the terminology of notaries licensed by the pope and notaries attached to the papal Chancery has led to 'ghosts'. Pressutti, for example (*Reg. Hon. III* no. 1828), has a deacon, Luke, as papal notary, but the register shows that he was not a papal notary but a notary of the archbishop of Rheims.

of the papal notaries and the professionalism of their occupation, that he is the same notary, Willelmus, who had served under Innocent III and who had dated *per manum* on 25 February 1211.[71] Willelmus's successor in the capacity of vice-chancellor was another notary, Master Guido, who served for four years as acting vice-chancellor but never used the title, and who may have continued with some of the other notarial duties although there is no evidence of this in the registers. Master Fortis occurs on two occasions, witnessing business conducted in front of the papal chamberlains, Pandulf and Sinibaldus, on 4 January and 22 April 1217.[72] This suggests that there were some notaries in the Lateran palace, possibly one attached to the Chamber, and there was certainly a notary (Albertinus) and a scribe (W.) of the Chamber under Innocent III.[73] It is interesting to note, however, that neither Master Fortis, nor a papal scribe, wrote the documents in question. One was written by Ricardus, scriniary of the imperial hall, and the other by Iohannes 'Leonis', scriniary of the Holy Roman Church.[74] In 1262 a notary of the *camera* is referred to: he himself wrote a document which was witnessed by Master Martinus de Brixia, 'clerk of the lord pope's *camera*', and by Master Iohannes de Warcino, scribe of the pope.[75] But the position of the scribes and the notaries in the Chamber under Honorius cannot be clarified completely because of the absence of routine records of the Chamber.

The notaries usually had the rank of papal subdeacon.[76] Master Obizo was a papal subdeacon who did well in providing for his nephew or nephews, but not, it seems, for himself. He acted as an arbiter in a case in the last days of Innocent III,[77] and witnessed a codicil to Cardinal Guala's will on 31 May 1227.[78] Master Maximus, another papal subdeacon, had also been a notary of Pope Innocent III, from whom he had received some money payments, and was sent by him on legation to Constantinople in August 1212. He continued as a papal notary under Gregory IX.[79] Master Pandulf, papal subdeacon, acted

---

[71] P 4191.

[72] *Liber Censuum*, ed. Fabre and Duchesne, i nos. 22 cols. 255ᵃ–6ᵃ and 27 cols. 259ᵃ–60ᵃ.

[73] See Denifle, 'Päpstlichen Registerbände', 19 n. 3.

[74] Richard also wrote document no. 20, *Liber Censuum*, ed. Fabre and Duchesne, i col. 254ᵃ⁻ᵇ.   [75] Lunt, *Revenues* i 141 no. 9.

[76] Six out of the eleven notaries of Innocent III were subdeacons: Elze, 'Päpstliche Kapelle', 158, 176–7.

[77] *Liber privilegiorum ecclesiae Ianuensis*, ed. D. Puncuh (Fonti e studi di storia ecclesiastica i, Genoa 1962) nos. 96–8 (pp. 120–5) and no. 100 (pp. 126–8).

[78] Paravicini Bagliani, *Testamenti*, 119–20 (Master Sinibaldus, vice-chancellor, also witnessed this); *Reg. Hon. III* nos. 182, 224 and 5089.

[79] Delisle, *Mémoire*, 3; *Reg. Hon. III* nos. 3990, 4163, 6246; and *Reg. Greg. IX*, ed. Auvray, *sub nomine*.

in the rôle of papal 'peacemaker'. He was virtually the rector of the duchy of Spoleto and was sent as legate to the March of Ancona in 1220, being reappointed, apparently against his will, in July 1224.[80] He appears to be the only one of Honorius's notaries who was entrusted with emissary's powers. It is impossible to say whether he was involved with any of the normal notarial duties within the curia in the early 1220s: it would seem unlikely. He retained, however, his title of notary into the next pontificate, when his arbitrating and conciliatory talents were used on at least one occasion by Pope Gregory IX.[81]

Of the identified notaries of Honorius, three had worked for Innocent III and two continued in Gregory IX's Chancery: Master Maximus served under three popes, Innocent, Honorius and Gregory. Continuity was to be expected in such an exclusive employment. Rewards of bishoprics for their long years of service in the Chancery were not infrequent for notaries, but only Master Pandulf, of Honorius's staff, appears to have made his advancement: he became bishop of Anagni.[82] Notaries were obvious choices as papal nuncios, entrusted with missions requiring tact and secrecy, when they could be spared: only Pandulf, under Honorius, fulfilled this function. The title of master which was accorded to them was probably a 'courtesy' title, not an academic one. There is no evidence that any of the notaries had been at Bologna or any other university. In all probability the title signified that they had junior clerks serving under them.[83] In fact the notary's craft is likely to have been one that had to be learned relatively young. Nothing is revealed about how the notaries were recruited, whether by the pope or by the vice-chancellor. Nor do we know whether they were all Italian. It is possible that Master Maximus may have had previous contacts with Constantinople. There is no certain evidence that any of Honorius's notaries had been scribes but two scribes of Innocent III became notaries: B. Roffridus and Master Bartholomeus, vice-chancellor in 1232.[84] For Master Maximus it would be necessary to go back to Celestine III for whom there is no surviving register or evidence of scribal names on the originals. Willelmus and Guido might be the GUILLMS and G., and Pandulf the PA or P F amongst Innocent's

---

[80] *Reg. Hon. III* nos. 2551, 4402, 4771 and 5092–3. See Waley, *Papal state*, 96, 110, 129–30 and 132.

[81] *Reg. Greg. IX*, ed. Auvray, no. 338.

[82] Ibid., nos. 3747–50; he had an interest in the church of Rheims (? a prebend or canonry), ibid. no. 665. He is not to be confused with Pandulf Masca, legate to England, nor with Masca's nephew. On this, and his provision in England, see below pp. 187–8.

[83] Cf. Tout, 'Household of the Chancery', 54.   [84] Bresslau, *Handbuch* i 270.

The Diplomatic of the Letters

scribes discovered by Delisle,[85] but these identifications are very far from certain.

The so-called chancery institution shows that in the first decades of the thirteenth century the notaries worked for much of their time in the *data* or *recepta communis*, a section of Chancery,[86] where the petitions were received for probably the majority of the documents that were issued by the curia.[87] The work of drawing up petitions in forms that were acceptable to the curia became increasingly the work of proctors during the 1220s and 1230s. Guala's treatise cites the five principal words and forms used in the petition: 'supplicat, insinuat, petit, significat' and 'conqueritur', and advises, though in an extremely delicate way, the use of proctors.[88] From it we can deduce that a large number of petitioners, many of them impecunious,[89] were arriving at the curia, and that they were vague about how to conduct their business and formulate their petitions. The treatise smacks of a manual devised to save the time of the probably overworked chancery officials. If petitions can be cast in their proper form (and, perhaps it suggests, taken to the appropriate persons or place) then the issue of the letters will be speeded up. The petitioner is counselled to be lucid about what he is requesting, be it judges delegate to hear a case or the pope to deliver justice where it had failed, whether on account of negligent or disobedient judges or because of some fraud or contravention of the canonical procedure. The pope is also petitioned to confirm, grant indulgences and privileges, issue *monitoria*, enforce the execution of a mandate and write to the ordinary ordering or empowering him to correct various injustices or to grant certain licences.

If the petition was accepted, it was dated. It was then the notaries' task to arrange for the conversion of the petitions into the minutes or *notae*.[90] This work was committed to the abbreviators (*breviatores*). Later the distributor actually passed the individual petitions to specific abbreviators but there is no evidence of the distributor's office as early

85 *Mémoire*, 31–2.

86 On the *data communis*, see Herde, *Beiträge*, 152–5 and 158; Tangl, *Kanzleiordnungen*, 54 nos. 1, 3 and 10. The text in the *Liber Censuum* calls it *recepta communis*. Delisle regarded this as a separate bureau (*Mémoire*, 3); cf. Herde, *Beiträge*, 180 and 214.

87 On petitions, see Bartoloni, 'Suppliche pontificie', who prints one of 1223 × 1231 on pp. 25–7 (no. 2), but his collection is mainly from the later thirteenth century. See also G. Tessier, 'Du nouveau sur les suppliques', *BEC* cxiv (1956) 186–92, and P. Gasnault, 'Suppliques en matière de justice au xive siècle', *BEC* cxv (1957) 42–57.

88 Guala, *Libellus* (ed. von Heckel) 502 and 509–10.

89 Ibid., 502; 'ad pauperum expeditionem et aliorum omnium litteras in Romana curia impetrare volentium...'.

90 No minutes have been discovered from before the fourteenth century, for which see Barraclough, 'Minutes of papal letters', 109f.

as this. It is not clear whether the abbreviators were drawn from amongst the scribes or whether they were a distinct group, with specific abbreviators attached to individual notaries. As none is known by name, it is impossible to trace their careers. They are mentioned, in what are likely to be the earlier clauses of the so-called chancery constitution, in conjunction with the notaries, the bullators and the scribes, over the promotion of petitions.[91] When the minutes were completed in the appropriate form the notary examined them and passed them to a scribe for engrossment – this again later became the work of the rescribendary – and then presented them, probably arranged in groups, for reading to the pope or, more frequently, to the vice-chancellor.[92] That the abbreviators, notaries, bullators and scribes might take on some proctorial duties in the promotion of petitions on behalf of clients is supported from other, albeit later, sources, but there are no examples of this practice for the notaries, abbreviators and bullators under Honorius III.[93]

THE PROCTORS

In 1924 Rudolf von Heckel, in a seminal article, drew attention to the importance of the proctors in the developments in the Chancery in the early thirteenth century.[94] Since then, and owing to that article, much more work has been done, not only on the activities of the proctors in the curia but also on who they were and whom they represented. The stimulus provided by the availability of increasing numbers of original documents concerning the proctors or made or signed by them has produced much advance in understanding their significance, but the work has been mainly on the later thirteenth century for which the evidence is much better.[95]

For Honorius's pontificate, the evidence must be considered afresh. Firstly there are the institutions of the proctors, giving the terms of their appointments. There were two basic forms of proxy: (1) for the proctor to act during the hearing of the case and (2) for the proctor

---

[91] Tangl, *Kanzleiordnungen*, 54 no. 2.

[92] Herde, *Beiträge*, 156 and 160.

[93] See below pp. 45–6, 47, and for an example of a notary and proctor (Master Iohannes de Sancto Germano) under Innocent IV and Alexander IV, see W. Stelzer in *Römische Historische Mitteilungen* xi (1968–9) 210–21.

[94] 'Das Aufkommen'.

[95] See Herde, *Beiträge*, esp. 125–48; R. Brentano, *Two churches. England and Italy in the thirteenth century* (Princeton 1968) ch. 1; Sayers, 'Canterbury proctors', and in *Proc. of the 3rd International Congress of Medieval Canon Law* (1971) 143–63; Linehan, 'Proctors', and 'Spanish Litigants'; and Stelzer, 'Beiträge', 'Niederaltaicher Prokuratorien' and 'Über Vermerke'.

to impetrate, or apply for documents in the curia, and to contradict or object to the issue of documents which might prejudice his client.[96] An example of a letter of proxy of the first kind is in Guala's formulary. It describes the appointment as one of acting for and defending the proctor's principal, and gives the proctor full powers for this purpose.[97] The second type is represented by an example of 1220 in the appointment of Cistercian proctors at the curia to deal with the Order's business – 'in Curia Romana pro negotiis ordinis ad impetrandum et contradicendum'.[98]

The proctors as they had emerged by the thirteenth century formed no particular corporate group or 'college'. There were proctors or representatives at the curia before Innocent III's accession. They came to conduct particular pieces of business for their employers, often it seems, for their own religious house. Gradually the use of expert proctors became desirable to cope with a more sophisticated system, but well into the thirteenth century monks and canons represented their own institutions and often came to the curia to transact a single piece of business. The religious orders and the rulers of Europe, however, needed more or less permanent spokesmen at the curia, and 'standing' representatives of these powerful interests were probably the first to emerge. By the late thirteenth century, wealthy religious institutions were hiring the best available representatives, increasingly Italians,[99] who knew the system and could be expected to deal with the business undertaken in the *audientia publica*. Like the dealers at auctions, they acted on behalf of more than one client. Such persons made a lucrative profession of procuration. The 'standing' proctors emerge during the early years of the thirteenth century and from then onwards the 'firms' of professionals develop.

Clearly the proctors' activities took place in close association with the officials of the Chancery. The amalgamate chancery ordinance deals mainly with the presentation of petitions in the *data communis*. The obvious additions to the text concern the proctors and the advocates. The first proctorial clause has been commented on by Herde, who assigned it to the pontificate of Honorius III.[100] These four clauses, which may have some affinity, specify firstly that all proctors who had been at the curia for as long as two years were to leave within a month, unless they were actively engaged on transactions on behalf of

[96] Sayers, *Papal judges delegate*, 221.
[97] Guala, *Libellus* (ed. von Heckel) 509 no. 31.
[98] Cited by Stelzer in 'Niederaltaicher Prokuratorien', 295.
[99] Sayers, 'Canterbury proctors', 327–8. [100] *Beiträge*, 128.

themselves or their principals: otherwise, they would not be admitted to impetrate or to contradict or to do anything in somebody else's name. Secondly, no proctor who kept a concubine was to be admitted to impetrate or to contradict. If he had impetrated already the impetration was to be void, and all such misdemeanants were to be excommunicated. Thirdly, proctors of important persons (archbishops, bishops, prelates and magnates) were to present the petitions in person 'secundum statutum nostrum et predecessoris nostri'. Finally, and fourthly, proctors 'ad contradicendum' were to go personally to the audience, unless they had a reasonable excuse; for very important clients, substitute proctors were to be admitted when the principal proctors were unable to go themselves, and for that reason only.[101]

The regulation of the conduct and the activities of the proctors at the curia came under the auditor of the *littere contradicte*. The auditor dealt with the credentials of the proctors. The first clause of the four was aimed clearly at reducing the number of 'hangers-on', increasingly attacked by the popes, who cashed the bonds provided by their principals but were slow in acquiring the desired documents, complaining that they needed more money. This clause could be connected with Honorius's condemnation of 1225, but it could equally have been issued by Innocent III or by Gregory IX, both of whom tried to tidy up the question of fees. The personal behaviour of the proctors became the curia's concern as proctors tended to stay with the papal court for a considerable period of time, while the growth of substitute proctors, who are referred to in clauses 14 and 15, suggests the beginnings of the emergence of the 'firms'. It is not possible to be more precise on these matters: it is advisable to turn for closer scrutiny to what is known about the work of the proctors in the two audiences under Honorius and to examine in particular the *audientia litterarum contradictarum* and its auditors.

THE *AUDIENTIA LITTERARUM CONTRADICTARUM*

It is highly likely that most of the Chancery's work under Honorius concerned the issue of judicial mandates, as was probably the case under Innocent III. There is much that will always remain uncertain about the functioning of the *audientia litterarum contradictarum* at this formative

---

[101] Tangl, *Kanzleiordnungen*, 55 nos. 12–15. Nos. 14, commencing 'Presenti decreto statuimus', and 15, 'procuratores vero...', treated as three and four above, precede 12 and 13, both of which commence with 'item'. There are at least two separate ordinances here, maybe more. See von Heckel, 'Das Aufkommen', 313–14.

period in its history. The sources are meagre and the absence of the evidence before Innocent III's pontificate suggests that it has no formal history.[102] As Herde has shown, both the *audientia publica* and the *audientia litterarum contradictarum*, like the *communis data*, were processes within Chancery rather than separate offices.[103] At this time the Chancery itself was far removed from what can be called a public department. Its activities were still open to direct papal intervention and supervision and, of course, it still moved about with the pope.

In the *audientia publica*, a large number of letters, mainly the mandates which did not have to be seen by the pope, were read out by lectors, who were by Innocent IV's time drawn from the scribes. This session was presided over by the vice-chancellor, and was attended by the notaries, the correctors and the proctors. At least this was the procedure by the mid-thirteenth century.[104] Evidence survives in outline of the reading in the *audientia publica* before the vice-chancellor under Innocent III. With Honorius's pontificate, however, the process can be seen in much greater detail. In 1222 an appeal was made to the apostolic see by the proctor of the count of Blois.[105] This proctor alleged that the judges (the dean of Senlis and his colleagues), who had been entrusted with hearing a case between his master and the abbot and convent of St Denis, had refused to have the acts in the case committed to writing, as required by the Fourth Lateran Council,[106] and, on these grounds, he got a new papal mandate. From what is known about the issue of documents at this time, we can reconstruct the submission of the supplication by the proctor, its receipt and dating in the *data communis*, the drawing up of the minute, its approval by the notary and its engrossment. At this point, and before the sealing, it was read out in the *communis audientia*. By now, however, the abbey's proctor was also in Rome (or a standing proctor had been alerted) and at the reading in the common audience he objected to the letters as they stood. When this happened – and the curia must have been aware of the cases where objections were likely – investigation into the objection became the task of the *auditor litterarum contradictarum*. Before him, the defending proctor put his case, saying that when a day had been assigned to the parties by the judges delegate who were hearing

[102] See above pp. 18–19.
[103] *Beiträge*, 214.   [104] Ibid., 215.
[105] The document recording what follows, Paris Archives Nationales L 240 no. 100, is pd by Rabikauskas, '"Auditor"', 242–4, and described in *BAPP* no. 245, but without any of the details of the contradiction etc.
[106] *Constitutiones concilii quarti Lateranensis*, ed. García y García, cap. 38 (c. 59 X II 28). Cf. below App. 2 no. 28.

the case, it was enquired of the count's proctor whether he wished to allege or say anything. He replied that he did not wish to say or show anything in front of those judges because he held them suspect.[107] The proctor of St Denis continued that the judges had then offered the appointment of arbiters before whom the proctor could prove his suspicion. But the count's proctor had said that he would do neither this nor anything in front of them, renewed his appeal and left the court. The proctor of St Denis therefore asked the *auditor litterarum contradictarum* that the mandate which had been acquired by his opponent should not be sealed and despatched, that the cause should be remitted to the first judges delegate and that the count of Blois should be condemned to pay expenses. This was the normal form of application by the defendant's proctor, but the auditor was unlikely to agree to it as it stood. His duty at this stage, if he found the objection to be sustained, was to bring the parties to agree on a bench of judges. This is indicated in this case by the clause in the new mandate that states that the cause is committed to the abbot of St Lucien, and to the dean and succentor of Beauvais 'de utriusque partis procuratorum assensu...'. Decisions as to the agreement on judges were, by the 1270s, and probably before, recorded in documentary form by the *auditor litterarum contradictarum* and sometimes an agreement was also made as to the place of the hearing.[108] It was usual in such cases for each party to suggest a judge and for the auditor to name the third. Such procedure meant not only that the mandate against which the objection had been made had now to be destroyed, but also that a new mandate needed to be drafted and written.

Besides protestations against the judges, there could also be objections to who was included in the charge. When the mandate was read out in the *audientia publica*, an objection might be made by a third party, or his proctor, who saw a possible threat to his interests, most frequently by the clause 'et quidam alii', which allowed the impetrant to have summoned defendants who were not actually named in the mandate.[109] A sharp and alert proctor, therefore, attended the *audientia publica* and listened carefully to the readings. When an objection of this kind was made, it was transferred for the consideration of the *auditor litterarum*

---

[107] On 'recusatio', see Sayers, *Papal judges delegate*, 104; L. Fowler, '"Recusatio iudicis" in civilian and canonical thought', *Studia Gratiana* xv (1972) 719–85; and c. 61 X II 28.

[108] See for formulary examples of this date, *Die Formularsammlung des Marinus von Eboli*, ed. Schillmann; and for originals of the 1270s, see Sayers, 'Canterbury proctors', 316–24 and 332–6.

[109] Sayers, *Papal judges delegate*, 67–9.

contradictarum (as with the objection against the judges), who required
the proctor of the impetrant to undertake that the letters in question
would not be used against this particular person or institution. By the
1230s, and probably earlier, both the proctor and the *auditor litterarum
contradictarum* drew up 'cautiones' in letters patent which testified to
this and were then kept by the objector in case he should be wrongfully
summoned.[110] It was not necessary for the original mandate to be
redrafted. An instance of the operation of this procedure, which records
the objection and the promise, is to be found in Honorius's register.
Here Master W., proctor of G. de Bourmont, precentor of Toul,
promised that the dean of Metz would not be summoned on the
strength of these papal letters which he had obtained primarily against
the master of the schools of Metz but which included the clause 'et
quidam alii'.[111] It is in this letter that the first mention by name of
an *auditor litterarum contradictarum* is found.

THE *AUDITORES LITTERARUM CONTRADICTARUM*

The *auditor litterarum contradictarum* needed the skill of an arbiter, a
knowledge of chancery procedure and acquaintance with the existing
legal requirements. For this reason, even perhaps before the auditor's
appointment was permanent, he was likely to be chosen from the ranks
of those with legal training who were attached to the papal household,
who were usually young men embarking on their careers.[112] No
auditor litterarum contradictarum is known by name for Innocent's reign,
but for Honorius the succession of officers can be reconstructed: Master
Otto da Tonengo (later legate to England under Gregory IX) until
February 1225, and Master Sinibaldus Fieschi (vice-chancellor under
Gregory IX, and elected pope as Innocent IV in 1243) from November
1226 until the end of the pontificate. That Guido de Sexto was *auditor
litterarum contradictarum* before 1219 is extremely doubtful: the
suggestion rests on a late source and is probably a confusion with his
appointment as an auditor of causes.[113] Master Otto, papal chaplain
and auditor of contradicted letters, was first noticed by Barraclough
in a registered letter of Honorius III that was selected by the compiler
of the *Compilatio Quinta*.[114] The letter as it occurs in the papal register

[110] Sayers, 'Canterbury proctors', nos. vi (after 10 Sept. 1230) and vii (after May 1238).
[111] Rabikauskas, '"Auditor"', 215–16. The text is Reg. Yr. 5 no. 236; *Reg. Hon. III* no.
2854; P 7712 and c. 2 *CQ* I 2.
[112] Sayers, *Papal judges delegate*, 20–1 and 56 n. 3.
[113] Herde, *Audientia* i 75, and Rabikauskas, '"Auditor"', 214–15.
[114] 'Audientia litterarum contradictarum', col. 1390 (text cited as in n. 111).

names him as Master Oct. (or Ott.) and describes him as papal chaplain
as well as *auditor litterarum contradictarum*. The editor of the *Compilatio
Quinta* extended this name to Otto without any hesitation. As the letter
in which he occurs is dated 11 December 1220 and records proceedings
which had taken place before him earlier, Barraclough presumed that
Master Otto may have been auditor earlier, possibly as early as 1216.
Two further occurrences of an O. who is variously described as O.
auditor of contradicted letters and Master O. subdeacon and papal
chaplain, *auditor litterarum contradictarum*, date from 22 December 1222
and 28 February 1225.[115] The argument of Paulius Rabikauskas against
this being one man is unconvincing. It rests on two bases (a) that O.
and Oct. are unlikely to be Otto rather than any other name beginning
with O., and (b) that varieties of description in exact title suggest two
and possibly three different people. But it is unlikely that a person of
Master Otto's promise and standing would disappear completely from
the papal registers in the ensuing years and Rabikauskas's endeavours
to find other likely candidates end with the exclusion of all possibilities
save Otto da Tonengo. Everything about this candidate would fit the
requirements of the office. Paravicini Bagliani has discovered an Otto
de To(h)oneng(u)o, canon of Ivrea, Piedmont (whence Cardinal Otto's
family came), and assessor general to the bishop, who occurs in
documents from 4 April 1214 to 6 March 1219.[116] He almost certainly
had a Bolognese legal training and between September and October
1224 he was one of a delegation from that university, seeking the pope's
approval of the university statutes.[117] During the summer of 1225 he
accompanied Stephen Langton as nuncio to England, arriving in
September. He was perhaps in the Empire on 11 August, when a papal
letter 'Ut ea quae' (dated July 1225), which recited the promise of
Frederick II to serve in the Holy War, was directed to him, ordering
him to press the *crucesignati* to a speedy performance of their duty; and
in France either before that or soon after, probably the latter, when
he met some of Henry III's proctors. Letters concerning his proposed
visit to England (including one of his own to the English royal proctors)
date from late August or early September and suggest that the king
was angry at his coming because of rumours that he would put the

---

[115] Rabikauskas, '"Auditor"', 217–26.
[116] Paravicini Bagliani, *Cardinali*, 80.
[117] *Reg. Hon. III* no. 5120. He might be the Master Oddo who occurs in the chapter of
Bologna on 27 Aug. 1221 (M. Sarti and M. Fattorini, *De claris archigymnasii Bononiensis
professoribus*, ed. C. A. Foroliviensis and C. M. Ravennas, ii (Bologna 1896) no. 15
168–9). In general on the law-school of Bologna at this time, see A. Sorbelli, *Storia
della università di Bologna* i (Bologna 1940) 78–82 and 162f.

case of Fawkes de Breauté and that Fawkes had secured certain letters from the pope.[118] This would explain Otto's last occurrence as *auditor litterarum contradictarum* in February 1225.[119] As the pope's nuncio, he was commissioned to place before English churchmen Honorius's plan for a fixed revenue, outlined in the letter of 28 January 1225.[120] Described as master, subdeacon and papal chaplain on 13 August 1225 he was to be concerned with Langton in the petition of the abbot and convent of Dorchester to translate Birinus's body, and between 1225 and 1226 he certified the vacancy of Stewkley church in the diocese of Lincoln.[121] He left England in April 1226,[122] and was back in Rome by April 1227 when he acted as an auditor of the sacred palace. On 31 May 1227, two months after Honorius's death, he witnessed a codicil to the will of Cardinal Guala Bicchieri, appearing as 'Magister Oddo de Toonengo domini pape capellanus'.[123] He has been identified in all probability with the legate sent to England in 1237.[124]

On 14 November 1226, one year and nine months after Otto's last occurrence as *auditor litterarum contradictarum*, Master Sinibaldus is found in that office, and probably continued as such until Honorius's death in the following March.[125] This is Master Sinibaldus Fieschi (the future Pope Innocent IV) on whom Honorius had conferred a canonry of Parma – a Fieschi stronghold – probably shortly before 5 December 1223, and who is mentioned on this occasion as a papal subdeacon.[126] It is commonly held that Sinibaldus had taught at Bologna before entering the papal service,[127] and that his rise in the curia is to be explained by the patronage of Cardinal Ugolino, the future Pope Gregory IX, to whom, it is said, he was secretary from 1217.[128] If the friendly bantering between Pope Innocent IV and Henry III in 1253, as to which was the elder,[129] is to be taken seriously to the degree that

---

[118] Shirley i no. 223 pp. 270–1, and see nos. 221–2 pp. 264–9, also in *Diplomatic documents*, ed. Chaplais, nos. 182–3, and see nos. 184–5, 190.

[119] *Reg. Yr.* 10 no. 21, *Reg. Hon. III* no. 5601.

[120] P 7350.

[121] *Reg. Hon. III* no. 5601; *Rot. H. Welles*, ed. Phillimore and Davis, ii 68.

[122] *CS* ii pt 1 156.

[123] Paravicini Bagliani, *Testamenti*, 119.

[124] *CS* ii pt 1 155.

[125] P 7610.

[126] *Reg. Hon. III* no. 4592.

[127] See J.-A. Cantini, 'Sinibalde', col. 1030, apparently following von Schulte, *Geschichte* ii 91. On his legal training, see Piergiovanni, 'Sinibaldo dei Fieschi', 125f. and esp. section 6 143f., but Piergiovanni gives no certain dates.

[128] Paravicini Bagliani (*Cardinali*, 64) finds no support for this story.

[129] PRO SC7/21/29; P 15181; Rymer i pt 1 294; and see *Annales monastici*, ed. Luard, i 324.

it confirms that they were much of an age, Sinibaldus would have been not much more than ten years of age in 1217, sixteen when he was made canon of Parma, nineteen as *auditor litterarum contradictarum*, twenty as vice-chancellor and cardinal priest, and pope at thirty-six.[130] That the canon of Parma is to be associated with the *auditor litterarum contradictarum*, and that he remained auditor at least until 5 March 1227, depends on good documentary evidence in the *Regestum Volaterranum*.[131] When the Bolognese period can have taken place is perplexing. It cannot have been before he entered the curia. Honorius's conferment on him of the canonry and the title of papal subdeacon shows that he was already in the curia in 1223. While he may have studied at Bologna at the age of sixteen, he cannot have been a master so young. If we suppose him to have been twenty-two in 1223, the canonical age for ordination as a subdeacon, then he would have been six years older than Henry III, but there is no evidence for this. Nor is it by any means certain that he was the Master S., canon of Parma, who in company with the bishop, Obizo, was ordered by the pope on 16 February 1224 to deal with the citizens of Pavia.[132] During Gregory IX's pontificate he was kept busy as vice-chancellor, cardinal priest (when he relinquished the office of vice-chancellor), papal auditor and, from February 1235 to December 1240, rector of the March of Ancona.[133] The period of his teaching at Bologna, if it took place, would have to fall between 1227 and 1235 or coincide with his activities as *auditor litterarum contradictarum*. His 'De exceptionibus', an *ordo judiciarius*, has been assigned by von Schulte in all probability to the period of his 'stay' at Bologna, and Cantini follows this.[134] The theory that he may have composed this as *auditor litterarum contradictarum* is quite attractive. It is possible, on the other hand, that it was his immense reputation for legal learning that led later to the assumption that he had taught at Bologna.

THE SCRIBES

It is not possible to gauge the exact number of scribes under Honorius. Master Henry, poet of Würzburg, who visited the curia at the time

---

[130] Henry was nine at the time of his first coronation in October 1216; Powicke, *Henry III*, 3–4.

[131] Ed. F. Schneider (Regesta chartarum Italiae i, Rome 1907) 152 no. 431.

[132] *Reg. Hon. III* no. 4776.

[133] Paravicini Bagliani, *Cardinali*, 66–7: that he was bishop of Albenga from 1235 has been dismissed by Paravicini Bagliani, *Cardinali*, 64–5, and by Piergiovanni, 'Sinibaldo dei Fieschi', 149–50.

[134] von Schulte, *Geschichte* ii 93 and Cantini, 'Sinibalde', col. 1031.

of Innocent IV, speaks of some hundred papal scribes, but this figure cannot be taken to be more than an estimate and at that one which suggests that he was amazed at the size of the Chancery.[135] Delisle listed sixteen scribes of Innocent III, and a brief survey of Barbiche's originals provides a further seven.[136] Doubtless a detailed investigation would reveal considerably more. For Honorius's pontificate some sixty to seventy scribes are evident. The sigla of thirty-four to thirty-five of these occur on documents which were either sent to English recipients or concerned matters of English interest. To this number may be added references to a further thirty to thirty-eight in Largiadèr, Barbiche and other sources.[137] As scribes were not selected to write solely for one of the areas of Christendom, the English originals may be regarded as a representative sample on which an analysis may fairly be made. Fourteen per cent carried on from the previous pontificate, and 43 per cent continued under Gregory IX. Two began their careers under Innocent III and appear to have continued working in Innocent IV's Chancery: Master Benedictus of Fratte and Master Scambio of Como. The evidence for Master Benedictus of Fratte shows a career of forty-six years in the papal writing office, and even longer, if Nüske's 'b. f.' is also identified with him.[138] This is difficult to accept. For Master Scambio, on the other hand, whose career spanned three pontificates and who worked for a total of twenty-four years as a papal scribe, the identification is very likely because of his unusual name. He was corrector in Innocent IV's Chancery. Honorius provided him to a canonry of Como: Innocent IV rewarded him with the bishopric of Viterbo.[139]

The first question to resolve is how the scribes entered the Chancery. One possibility might be via the cardinals' households, but apart from Honorius's own chaplain as cardinal, Master Willelmus, who appears to have become a papal scribe early in the reign, there is absolutely no indication of the movement of scribes or notaries from the cardinals' households to the papal Chancery. Willelmus may be identifiable with Master Willelmus de Sancto Germano who was possibly transferred to the household of the legate Guala in England. If that is so the movement was in the opposite direction, as with Master Iacobus, one of Honorius's scribes who became a scribe of the legate Pandulf in or

---

[135] Herde, *Beiträge*, 28.
[136] *Mémoire*, 31–2; *BAPP* i App. i 419–32.
[137] Full details on the scribes are given below App. 1A and 1B. Reference may need to be made to both lists.
[138] *AD* xx (1974) pt 2 no. 39 173–4.   [139] Below pp. 46, 202.

before 1219. He was deprived of the office of papal scribe soon afterwards, for reasons unknown, but was absolved by August 1220, when he was required to make satisfaction to the legate and obey his commands. He signs as a papal scribe again from 1224 and continued under Pope Gregory IX. Two other persons in the legate's household in England, Rusticus and John of London, are incorrectly described as papal scribes in Bliss's Calendar. They occur in the papal register as 'scriptores domini legati' and seem likely, in the case of John of London at least, to have been recruited in England by Pandulf.[140] It is difficult to comment on cancellarial arrangements in the cardinals' households at this time because the sources are as yet inadequately studied. Paravicini Bagliani has suggested that there may be a distinction between the chanceries of the legates and those of the resident curial cardinals. Until a detailed analysis is undertaken, however, it cannot be known whether this is so, or indeed whether these chanceries were influenced more by episcopal examples than by the papal Chancery.[141] In all probability, Master Iacobus was 'seconded' to the legate Pandulf's household, and arrived with him in England in December 1218: he had already been provided by the pope with a prebend of St Omer, though he had not yet secured it, and had been promised a benefice in the diocese of Ely. Pandulf was not a cardinal and so did not have a formally constituted household. Master Iacobus's case suggests that it was the papal Chancery that supplied the legates and nuncios with clerical assistance when required. If the papal scribe, Bobo, is to be identified with Oddo 'Bobonis', beneficed in England in 1222 if not before, he might be associated with the legatine household and the same could apply to Master Azzo.[142]

Where the scribes can be identified with places, they are Italian: Anagni, Asti (?), Città d'Antino, Fratte, Montefiascone, Rieti and San Germano (?). Later many of them came from the papal states, as with the majority of these, and in some cases they were the blood relatives of the pope. None, however, of Honorius's scribes can be shown to be his relatives. The indications are that the aspirant scribe entered the papal service directly and was trained in curial ways from the start. The title of master which is given to the scribes, in most of their occurrences, does not signify an academic attainment, but seems to be a title which

---

[140] Reg. Yr. 4 no. 629 (*CPL* 70) and Reg. Yr. 7 no. 189 (*CPL* 92). The second entry (a copy) adds their full description which Bliss overlooked.

[141] Paravicini Bagliani, *Cardinali*, 474–8.

[142] It is unlikely that Azzo is Master Atto, for whom a prebend of Lincoln was later requested (*Fasti*, ed. Greenway, iii Lincoln, 121, 127).

was commonly applied to the staff of the papal curia.[143] Elze has commented that there were some fifty chaplains under Honorius III (and also under Innocent III) and it is tempting to connect them with the scribes.[144] None, however, is mentioned in this dual rôle, and when Master Willelmus de Sancto Germano is described as papal chaplain he is no longer called papal scribe. But as the sources for many of the scribes are simply their sigla on the *plica*, where one does not expect to find descriptions added to the names, and as details on the personnel of the chaplains are also meagre, no inferences can be drawn about the influence of the papal chapel at this time.

Scribes were not expected to live off their fees for writing.[145] They might look forward to presentation to a benefice somewhere or perhaps to a canonry, neither of which they would be required to serve, as defined in the case of Master Otto, papal scribe and canon of Metz.[146] Master Bartholomeus of Anagni was dispensed in 1222 from the consequences of his illegitimacy which had prevented him from holding *spiritualia*: presumably before this indult he had to make do with chancery fees. Master Constantinus was collated to the living of Alwalton (Hunts.) by Guala; whether as a reward for clerical services to the pope or to the legate it is impossible to say. Master Azzo, papal scribe, was dispensed by Guala to hold two benefices in England and this dispensation was confirmed by the pope. A canonry seems to have been thought an appropriate income. Seven, possibly eight, from the English sample (20–23 per cent) were provided in this way: Master Egidius and Master Scambio both to Como, Master Iacobus to St Omer, Master Otto to St Peter's, Rome, and Metz, Master Petrus of Città d'Antino to Douai, T. to Turin, Master Zacharias to Tivoli and Master Benedictus of Fratte to S. Severina in Calabria. To these may be added seven, possibly eight, from the other sources: Master Andreas to Bourges (a prebend), Master Gentilis to a canonry of Mileto (Calabria), Master Hugo to a canonry of Argos, Master Iohannes of Città d'Antino to a canonry of S. Donatianus, Bruges, Master Nicolaus Scarsus to a canonry of Cambrai, Master R. (? Roffridus of Anagni or Raimundus) to a canonry of S. Gereo, Cologne, and a canonry of Marseilles, and Master Theobaldus to a canonry of Lincoln. With the exception of Master Scambio and Raimundus, provided to the archdeaconry of Lodève, advancement does not seem to have taken place above the rank of canon. The reason is not far to seek, as the

---

[143] Schwarz, *Schreiberkollegien*, 13.
[144] 'Päpstliche Kapelle', 188. [145] 'Gesta' (*PL* ccxiv) col. 80 cap. 41.
[146] c. 14 X III 4 (c. 2 CQ III 3) and Reg. Yr. 6 no. 471 and below n. 147.

latter appointments would have required residence and retirement from active service in the Chancery. Master Otto, papal scribe and canon of St Peter's, Rome, who received a canonry of Metz in 1216, and was apparently the first papal official to be provided to the chapter of Metz, continued as a papal scribe until at least 26 April 1221. It seems very unlikely that this can be the same person as the *auditor litterarum contradictarum*, whom we have identified as Master Otto da Tonengo, and who was involved in the Toul/Metz case before December 1220, probably considerably before, but the possibility cannot be totally ruled out. The inclusion of a papal letter concerning Otto's appointment to Metz in the *Compilatio Quinta* as a canonical ruling may lend weight to the argument that they are one and the same man but a comparison of the signature of the scribe with the subscription of the cardinal certainly does not clinch the matter.[147] The description of Petrus Gregorii as papal scribe, when in receipt of papal mandates while staying at Paris, indicates that the scribes retained their title (although he is not here called master) even if not actively engaged in writing papal letters: no doubt on such visits advantageous contacts could be made with cathedral chapters.

Tout has written of the English Chancery: 'It was not in wages and allowances so much as in fees, perquisites, opportunities for promotion in church and state, pensions for old age, and, above all, facilities for acting as counsel, attorneys, agents, and usurers that the chancery clerk's career had its claim to be considered lucrative as well as dignified.'[148] The so-called chancery ordinance shows that it was permitted for papal scribes to act as proctors. If my identification of the scribe Alexander with Master Alexander of Montefiascone is correct, he is one example of a scribe who also acted as a proctor, representing the bishop of Bagnorea in 1223. Herde cites an example of a scribe under Innocent IV writing the documents in a case where he was also employed as proctor.[149] Barbiche, in examining the originals in the Archives Nationales, has discovered similar connections between the scribes and the recipients of the letters. In one case the scribe and the beneficiary were brothers; in bulls for the friars (both Dominicans and Franciscans) under Innocent IV, the scribe Antonius was concerned; and finally, two particular scribes (P. Set and N. Ver) were associated with papal letters for Philip the Fair's eldest and second sons.[150] No connections of such

[147] See above pp. 38–40 and below p. 200, and C. McCurry, 'Utilia Metensia: local benefices for the papal curia, 1212–*c*. 1370', *Law, church and society*, ed. K. Pennington and R. Somerville (University of Pennsylvania Press 1977) 312 and n. 9.
[148] 'Household of the Chancery', 55.
[149] *Beiträge*, 52, 127 n. 16, and 145.
[150] *BAPP* i p. xcvii.

a kind can be illustrated for Honorius's documents to Henry III, but the presentation of the papal scribe, Cozo, to the church of Lastingham by the abbot and convent of St Mary's York (he was admitted in 1229) suggests some liaison.

THE CORRECTORS

No corrector or correctors are mentioned by name during Honorius's pontificate, but the office was clearly in existence. Master Petrus Marcus, subdeacon, described as 'corrector of our letters', was permitted by Innocent III on 11 September 1212 to become chancellor to Simon de Montfort. This is the first indication of an officer designated corrector.[151] The corrector or correctors were selected from among the scribes. Honorius's scribe Scambio became corrector under Innocent IV. The neatness of his hand and the expert quality of his work as a scribe can be seen in several examples.[152] Correctors' marks appear on the top right of the face of the engrossments, frequently in association with what may be marks of expedition. These will be discussed later.[153] The corrector's duty was to see to the correction of the engrossments, to examine the language and check for scribal error and to return the document, if necessary, to the original scribe for attention. This was doubtless another reason for signing on the *plica*. The drafts were the responsibility of the vice-chancellor, the notaries and the abbreviators, not of the corrector.[154] It is obviously impossible to tell how many engrossments were rewritten rather than corrected. In one case of 1264, a document was ordered to be corrected or rewritten ('corrigenda vel rescribenda'), but rewriting probably remained very much the exception.[155]

Correctors were rewarded with benefices and promotion. Of Innocent IV's correctors, Scambio, as we have seen, became bishop-elect of Viterbo, and Thomas, elect and then bishop of Rieti.[156] Thomas held the church of Heslerton (Yorks. ER) until his election as bishop, when it was surrendered to the papal scribe, Tedisius de Lavania.[157] The possible candidates for the office of corrector under Honorius cannot

---

[151] Delisle, *Mémoire*, 4, and P 4589; Schwarz, 'Corrector', 122–91.

[152] Herde, *Beiträge*, 24, 193 and 206; below App. 1A and App. 2 nos. 8, 17, 27, 38.

[153] See Acht, 'Kanzleikorrekturen auf Papsturkunden'; Herde, *Beiträge*, 176f., and below Chapter 3.

[154] Herde, *Beiträge*, 172, 174–5, 178, and Schwarz, 'Corrector', 122–4.

[155] Herde, *Beiträge*, 292 no. 27; and see PRO SC7/2/28 of 18 Dec. 1257: 'R(?ec) Bar. et fac rescribi' (mid-*plica*).

[156] Herde, *Beiträge*, 24–5.   [157] CPL 275–6.

be shortlisted. There is no sign of Bandinus of Siena, corrector under Gregory IX, in Honorius's Chancery, though Baumgarten lists a B S on 18 January 1222.[158] No successor to Petrus Marcus is known in Innocent's Chancery after September 1212, and the difficulties of establishing the authorship of a hand from a rough and hastily written corrector's note make identification unlikely.[159] There is no indication that the office was held for a short term as was that of the distributor and of the rescribendary.

Little is known about the *bullatores*: this is especially perplexing as their office was an ancient one and their duties originated with the beginning of sealing in the papal Chancery. An early occurrence of the word *bullator* is from the so-called chancery *Institutio*: it occurs, too, in 'Licet ad regimen' of September 1198.[160] The *bullatores* were apparently two in number under Innocent III, if a contemporary satirical poem is to be believed, although only one officiated under Innocent IV.[161] No bullators are known by name under Honorius III. Although it has been held that they were illiterate, this seems unlikely: as Herde has pointed out, there are instances of *bullatores* under Innocent IV, frater Egidius and possibly Iohannes, who acted also on several occasions as proctors.[162] The *bullatores* were present in the *communis data*. As soon as the minutes were accepted they were supposed to be engrossed and the engrossment sealed.[163] The sealing was the occasion, as in most chanceries, of taxing the document, and if the tax was not paid, the *bulla* would not normally be affixed, but no evidence of taxators is found on the engrossments until 1255.[164] The tax on the sealing was the one tax that Honorius proposed should be retained if his scheme to reorganize the curia's finances by seeking endowment from the cathedrals, monasteries and diocesans was accepted.[165] From this money the cost of the parchment, ink, lead, silk and hemp was met, and it has been assumed that, as at

---

[158] Schwarz, 'Corrector', 144; *SB* 657 and P 6767. He seems unlikely to be the B. Se of 1221–3 (*SB* 621, 653, 681) or the Master B. de Sya (*Reg. S. Osmund*, ed. Rich Jones, ii 149, 156) mentioned 13 June 1228.

[159] Herde, *Beiträge*, 205–6.

[160] *Mittellateinischen Wörterbuch*; P 365 and c. 5 X V 20. For the surviving *bullae*, see Chapter 3 below.

[161] Herde, *Beiträge*, 51 n. 447, 283 and App. i 250.

[162] Ibid. 51 n. 447, 134, 283 n. 486.

[163] Tangl, *Kanzleiordnungen*, 54–5 nos. 9–10.

[164] *BAPP* i App. ii 433; and Herde, *Beiträge*, 181.

[165] P 7349–50; *Reg. S. Osmund*, ed. Rich Jones, i 366–9.

a later date, the die for the *bulla* was kept in the Chamber. Herde sees this as the single remaining vestige of Cencio's joining of the Chancery and of the Chamber, which Innocent had brought to an end, except for this one arrangement.[166] As far as I know, there is no evidence for the seal matrix being with the chamberlain under Honorius, and it can only be conjectured that this was the case, as it was for later pontiffs.[167] Whether the *bullatores* had a separate office or chamber is uncertain. Delisle postulated separate offices or bureaux – a bureau for the petitions, a bureau for the drafting, a bureau for the engrossing, a bureau for the sealing (the *bullaria*) and a bureau for registering.[168] There is no evidence for this and it does not seem a likely picture, except, perhaps, for the sealing. There is no indication that the *bulla* was employed in the Chamber or that there were two matrices, as with the Chancery and the Exchequer in England by this time. If the papal chamberlain had custody of the die this must suggest no such clear physical separation between the Chancery and the Chamber as with the English Chancery and Exchequer. When the papal court moved out of Rome, the chamberlain, if he had custody of the seal, would have had to go with it for the documents to be sealed in Viterbo or Anagni or wherever the papal court might be. It is easy to see why the chamberlain was the historic custodian of the *bulla*, but it is not so easy to see why he remained so unless the links between Chancery and Chamber stayed close and we view the peripatetic part of the Chamber as closer to the Wardrobe in England.[169]

To look at the Chancery during Honorius's forty-year career in the curia is to examine the development of long-ranging processes. When Cencio entered the service of Cardinal Giacinto (later Pope Celestine III) in the 1180s, an increasing number of petitioners were arriving at the papal court, seeking privileges, protective documents and judgements. After he attained office under Clement III and then Celestine, his contribution, so far as it can be assessed, was more in the financial department, the Chamber, than in the Chancery, but this deduction is based on the survival of his *Liber Censuum* and also on the lack of any consistent Chancery records at this time to suggest what he may or may not have done as acting chancellor. Honorius is said to have written a life of Celestine III.[170] Had this survived, it might, like

---

[166] Herde, *Beiträge*, 239 & n. 491; and see Lunt, *Revenues* i 143. See also P. M. Baumgarten in *Römische Quartalschrift* xxviii (1914) 183f.
[167] Cf. Fawtier, introduction to *Reg. Boniface VIII* p. xxx.
[168] *Mémoire*, 3; cf. Herde, *Beiträge*, 180.
[169] Tout, *Chapters* i 172 and 231 n. 1.
[170] See Horoy, 'Opera omnia', i introduction.

Innocent III's *Gesta*, have outlined developments of which we have no other evidence. Much of von Heckel's assessment of Innocent III's part in the reform of the administration rests on the so-called chancery ordinance, which can be shown to be a composite document, probably in part pre-dating Innocent's pontificate and certainly post-dating it on into Honorius's and possibly Gregory's reign. Innocent's monolithic reputation as a reformer of Chancery has to undergo certain revision. It is no longer possible to see a sudden and exact date of foundation for the scribes' college, for the court of the *audientia litterarum contradictarum* or for the coming of the standing proctors. They were processes which developed from seeds of change. Nor must the survival of the chancery registers and the large number of original letters blind us into assuming that the administrative changes were Innocent's alone. The Chamber appears a very shadowy institution in the early thirteenth century because of the lack of surviving sources. This apparent removal of the Chamber from the limelight may be far from the truth and may have added to the notion that Innocent definitely separated the two institutions. Innocent's achievement was in rationalizing processes, particularly petitioning, but it cannot be proved that he actually inaugurated offices. Honorius's position as pope in no way denies any of the previous administrative achievements. On the contrary, he clearly built on the petitioning developments, improved the structure and functioning of the *audientia litterarum contradictarum*, and developed the functions of the scribes and proctors. Honorius positively elaborated a legacy that was not entirely Innocent's.

Chapter 2

THE LETTERS

The estimated output of the papal Chancery is a topic that has received much attention. Annual averages of letters for which there is evidence before about 1130 (the accession of Innocent II), based on Jaffé, do not climb beyond the thirties. With Innocent II (1130–43) the annual average rises to seventy-two, with Adrian IV (1154–9) to 130, and with Alexander III (1159–81) to 179.[1] This pronounced curve upwards in the twelfth century appears to reflect both more active government and improved survival of the sources: the two are not unconnected. It has been argued by Alexander Murray that many of Gregory VII's communications were oral.[2] If that be so, a hundred years later there had been a radical transformation from a society that depended on word of mouth and visible ceremony for authentication to one that favoured written testimony. Innocent III's average yearly issue, based on Potthast, amounts to 303.7 letters (total number of letters 5316 in a pontificate of $17\frac{1}{2}$ years), and for Honorius III the average annual issue is 238.7 letters (total issue 2545 in a pontificate of $10\frac{2}{3}$ years). The upward curve in the number of papal letters continues throughout the thirteenth century, being particularly noticeable under Innocent IV and Alexander IV and again under Boniface VIII.

The development of registration and the survival of a continuous series of registers from the early thirteenth century is a marked feature of contemporary Europe in which the papacy led the way. It provides another source for numerical calculation. Innocent III issued 573 letters which were registered in his first year and 276 in the second.[3] If the registers of Honorius are used for this purpose, the average annual issue

---

[1] See R. W. Southern, *Western Society and the Church in the middle ages* (London 1970) 108–9; Clanchy, *Memory to written record*, 43–5; Murray, 'Gregory VII', 149–202, esp. 166 fig. 4, and 202. Using *Italia Pontificia* and *Germania Pontificia* as his sources, Murray estimates that perhaps 26 per cent of the originals issued by Alexander III are extant.

[2] 'Gregory VII', 149–202.

[3] See now *Reg. Inn. III* i & ii, ed. Hageneder *et al.*

rises to 482.5 letters (a total of 5144), and if Pressutti's calendar, which
includes some additional unregistered letters, is employed, the average
annual issue increases to 589.8 (total 6288 letters). There is no doubt
that many letters have perished and there are clear complications in
assessing losses. There is absolutely no doubt, too, that only a
proportion of the total output was registered, although many historians
have written as if a majority of the pope's correspondence was recorded
officially. That is far from the truth. Probably only about one-quarter
of Honorius's letters were registered.[4] If the average annual registered
figure of 482.5 letters is multiplied by four, the issue per annum reaches
1930. This gives a minimum production rate of five letters per day.
On the same basis of calculation Innocent IV's Chancery would have
issued eight letters per day, each scribe writing one letter every six days.
The problem is now partly how many scribes there were in the
Chancery at any one time. Barbiche's suggestion that the scribes
numbered a constant fifty under Boniface VIII (1295–1303) cannot be
tested or substantiated.[5] If, however, it is anywhere near correct, it
would make the scribes' work load only one letter every ten days. This
figure is unacceptably low for a working Chancery. The estimate of
Fawtier, on the other hand, that at the end of the century Boniface
was issuing 50,000 letters a year is very much larger and probably more
realistic.[6] With a Chancery of fifty scribes, each scribe would have
written 1000 letters a year, an average of twenty letters a week and
three a day: this does not seem impossibly high. The total number of
scribes in Honorius III's Chancery comes to sixty-four (minimum) to
seventy-three (maximum). It is quite impossible to deduce from these
by no means certain figures how many would have been working at
once. There are scribes whose names appear in the papal registers but
for whom there is no tangible evidence in the shape of surviving letters
from their hands. This has led Barbiche to suppose that they were purely
honorary.[7] This supposition gains absolutely no support from any of
the sources for Honorius. It seems much more likely that this is merely
a measure of the monumental losses of papal originals. But these scribes
might have been the *registratores*, for whom we have little detailed
evidence and whose activities we must examine later.[8] If the *registratores*
doubled up with the *scriptores*, as Boyle suggests,[9] as well as meeting

[4] See below p. 67.
[5] 'Diplomatique', 121.
[6] *Reg. Boniface VIII* iv pp. v–cvi, esp. c.
[7] 'Diplomatique', 122, citing Herde, *Beiträge* (29, 32) who comments on certain scribes for whom no *sigla* are found.
[8] Below pp. 90, 91.
[9] 'Compilatio quinta', 18, and see below p. 89.

certain extra requirements, such as preparing the ground for Tancred's decretal compilation by copying from the registers, the production rate of five letters a day for say some twenty-five to thirty scribes would seem feasible. Yet it should be stressed that only two factors about the number of letters once issued are certain: the survivors from all sources (originals and copies, registered and unregistered) by no means represent the total issue and to suggest figures by which to multiply them is largely arbitrary. Consequently the exact output of the Chancery will never be gauged with accuracy. The problem, however, may be approached from another angle.

Very few papal letters were issued that were not petitioned for or requested. Inventories and cartularies, therefore, give some indication of the numbers of papal letters once in existence. The Durham fifteenth-century catalogue, the *Repertorium Magnum*, lists sixteen originals of Honorius III.[10] For Bury St Edmunds we have figures for the privileges and for the confirmations from two inventories: in this pontificate they number four.[11] Detailed figures could be compiled for the other five great Benedictine houses: Glastonbury, Westminster, St Albans, Christ Church, Canterbury, and St Augustine's. Taking ten as a mean this would make seventy privileges and confirmations from this source. Such lists do not include the mandates – unless these had particular significance they were destroyed – but confine themselves mainly to the privileges and confirmations. Cartularies, however, include both. Nearly every cartulary incorporates some privileges and some mandates (often in the topographical sections) and Davis in *Medieval Cartularies* lists some 1100 surviving cartularies for the religious institutions. Glastonbury produces at least eight documents from its cartularies for Honorius's pontificate,[12] Battle ten,[13] Abingdon eight[14] and the Augustinian house of St Frideswide, Oxford, fourteen, many of them mandates.[15] Even a smallish house like Broomholm (there were sixteen monks there in 1276) could notch up five letters from Honorius.[16] Furthermore the registers themselves show consid-

[10] Durham 2.1 Pap. 5–20 were their numbers at this time. Earlier Durham inventories (1.1 Pap. 30 and 31 and Misc. Chs. 426 and 7174) show eight to eleven letters from Honorius: the higher total comes from material in other parts of the convent.

[11] BL Harley MSS 638 fols. 119v–20v and 1005 fols. 226–9.

[12] *Glastonbury Chart.*, ed. Watkin, i nos. 15 (p. v) 33 (p. 22), 146 (pp. 93–4), 179 (pp. 131–2) and 191 (pp. 137–8); P 5807; and B fol. 92v.

[13] Battle Cart. fols. 50–2, 73r–v, and abbrev. fol. 23 v (not in Huntington Cart.).

[14] Abingdon Reg. fols. 16, 17v, 18r–v, 27, and *Reg. S. Osmund*, ed. Rich Jones, i 364.

[15] *St Frideswide's Cart.*, ed. Wigram, i nos. 44–7, 209, 468; ii nos. 721, 731, 820 (twice), 826–7, 1020 and 1048.   [16] Broomholm Cart. fols. 9v–10v.

erable numbers of *papalia*: nine for Nostell and three for Guisborough, for example.[17]

The number of religious houses in England and Wales in 1216 was in the region of 1600 at a maximum. Knowles gives 1653 for the period 1216 to 1350. As this figure covers a long period and includes 159 for the friaries – there were only about a dozen in existence before Honorius's death – and 584 for the hospitals, many of which were very impermanent institutions, it is likely to be considerably in excess of actuality and should perhaps be reduced by some three to four hundred.[18] On this basis if each religious house received only one letter from Honorius III a total of some 1200 to 1300 letters is reached. This is almost certainly an underestimate. The evidence suggests that petitioners rarely went to the curia for just one letter. Documents for specific communities frequently bear the same date: on 13 November 1218, for example, St Frideswide's gained a confirmation, a 'Sacrosancta', and a mandate 'Ex litteris abbatis', and the prior and convent of Coventry acquired three documents (and the hospital of St John at Coventry one) all dated 18 December 1221.[19] Abingdon gained confirmations on closely related dates, 19 May, 17 June and 10 July 1220.[20] The occurrence of documents that bear the same date, as a confirmation for Abingdon abbey and a confirmation of an agreement between the nuns of Littlemore and the canons of Oseney, in which the abbot of Abingdon had mediated, suggests that many convents carried on business jointly and probably also shared proctors.[21]

Besides the papal letters for the religious houses, there were also those for the seculars, the hierarchy and the English crown. Two early-sixteenth-century York inventories of the muniments in the Minster list twelve papal letters of Pope Honorius for the dean and chapter and the archbishop of York, some concerning the canonization of St William. There were also letters of Honorius of a contingent interest that had been kept in the various chests, pyxes and cupboards.[22] Ten

[17] *CPL* 42(2), 44, 45, 52(2), 82(3); one original, now at Lambeth, see below App. 2 no. 1. *CPL* 36 and 54(2).
[18] D. Knowles and R. Neville Hadcock, *Medieval religious houses*, 2 edn (London 1971) 488–95.
[19] *St Frideswide's Cart.*, ed. Wigram, i no. 209, ii no. 820. *Reg. Hon. III* nos. 3631–3 and 3635.
[20] Abingdon Reg. fols. 18v and 27.   [21] See below App. 2 nos. 41–2.
[22] York, D. and C. inventories A fols. iv, 7, 7v, 9v, 11, 21, 41v, 52v, and B fol. 1. See K. Longley, 'Towards a history of archive-keeping in the church of York: I. The archbishop's muniments', *Borthwick Institute Bulletin* i no. 2 (1976) 59–74 and 'II. The capitular muniments', ibid. i no. 3 (1977) 103–18.

papalia addressed to the archbishop which are not found in the inventory were copied into Archbishop Walter Gray's register.[23] Ten more, four of them addressed to the archbishop, three of them in company with the dean and chapter of York, and six of a general interest, are to be found in the dean and chapter's *Magnum Registrum Album*.[24] There is no way of ascertaining whether this total of thirty-two letters from Honorius III would have been matched in the other eight English secular cathedrals but there is no reason to suppose that it would not. There is indication that the losses of *papalia* were greater in the secular cathedrals in later centuries and only Hereford and Exeter are represented among the fifty-six originals.[25] Salisbury, Wells and Lincoln are all represented by about ten documents in copies. In most cases it is only from the inseparable nature of many of the archives of the dean and chapter and of the diocesan that we get any idea of the episcopacy's once rich holdings. Figures for the four Welsh foundations and their bishops and for the bishops of the monastic cathedrals would need to be added to this total.

The royal *papalia* in the original number some sixteen documents. Squeezed into the bottom left-hand corner of nine of them, a short series of numbers is discernible running from ii to xii: this system appears to be roughly contemporaneous with the receipt of the letters.[26] Fourteen of the documents carry the mark *Exam(inatur)*. They were examined, presumably in the royal Chancery, and after orders were given for copying, if it was thought appropriate, were endorsed with 'scribitur in libro' or 'Reg' in novo libro'. The 'new book' is mentioned in April 1223 but the old one continued in use throughout the period. Copying, of course, did not remove the necessity of retaining the original document and various finding systems were employed at different times. Two papal letters to the benefit of the Crown, a mandate to the legate Pandulf, ordering that no one in England be allowed to have more than two of the king's castles in his custody, and a mandate to the archbishop of York and his suffragans, directing them to place under interdict the lands in their dioceses

---

[23] *Reg. Gray*, ed. Raine, 137–8, 140–1, 149–58, and 159 n. For the archbishop of Canterbury, ten papal letters of Honorius are recorded in Lambeth MS 1212 (pp. 227–8): they are clearly only a part of the total holding.

[24] Pt 1 fols. 55v–6; pt 2 fols. 12, 82v, 84v, 95 and 100r–v; and pt 3 fols. 4 (pd *Reg. W. Giffard*, ed. Brown, 165–6), 54r–v (pd *Reg. Gray*, ed. Raine, 138–9 and *Reg. Hon. III* no. 3106) and 98v–9 (also 99r–v).

[25] Below App. 2 nos. 8 and 21.

[26] Ibid. nos. 13, 23, 26, 29–30, 33, 38, 44 and 55. ix (38) and x (44) are out of the chronological sequence.

belonging to Llewellyn, prince of Wales, and his followers, have the endorsements A ii and B 2 which indicate their places in the royal presses.[27] L vi also indicates some early archival system, perhaps the same as the above.[28] By the 1260s there was a royal keeper of papal documents, John of St Denis, one of the king's clerks in Chancery.[29]

The list provided by this keeper was unfortunately not a complete schedule of the documents in his custody but a special return made to justify the collection of a tenth based on the Norwich valuation of 1254. It cannot, therefore, be relied on to provide a total view of the contents of the royal archive at this time as the keeper apparently concentrated on the Exchequer collection of *papalia* and the letters of Innocent IV, and made selections, such as 'the privilege of the English' not to be summoned to answer in lawsuits outside England. The same is true of Bishop Stapledon's inventory of *c.* 1323 which listed the papal documents in the Treasury of the Exchequer alone. Stapledon enumerated some 570 papal letters to the Crown, arranged in twenty-six sections, twenty-three of which are distinguished by letters of the alphabet and the remaining three by symbols.[30] Only four are clearly of Honorius III: two in category B, royal privileges, one in M, Scotland, and one in N, privileges of the English prelates.[31] Such a meagre harvest is not surprising after an interval of one hundred years, but the low figure is also explained by the existence of other royal archive repositories besides the Exchequer, namely in the Tower of London and at Chancery Lane in the Rolls chapel. The series now given the prefix 50 is the Tower series of 'Chancery' *papalia*. This included papal letters which were addressed to the king personally, such as those concerning the payment of a pension to Cardinal Stefano de Normandis,[32] and also those to his counsellors (chancellor, justiciar, etc.). Many of these documents were seen by Prynne. There were also 'Chancery' papal documents at the Rolls chapel, but none, so far as I know, is in the collection below.[33]

The Exchequer series (with the prefixes now of 18 and 35) came to include the one surviving original for the legate Guala which was

---

[27] Below App. 2 nos. 13, 33: neither of these marks are Stapledon, see below nn. 30–1.

[28] Below App. 2 no. 23.

[29] Johnson, 'Keeper of papal bulls', 135–8.

[30] *Antient kalendars and inventories of the treasury of his majesty's exchequer*, ed. Sir F. Palgrave, i (London 1836) 4–33.

[31] Ibid. p. 13 no. 40 (below App. 2 no. 19) marked 'Extrahitur de litera B'; p. 14 no. 41 (below no. 44) marked with press mark 'M'; p. 22 no. 92 (backed) and p. 24 no. 107 (below no. 38) marked 'N' also 'L'.

[32] Below App. 2 nos. 34–5.

[33] PRO *Lists and indexes* vol. xlix (1923) pp. iv–v.

registered in 'magno libro'.[34] Those letters directed to Pandulf,[35] like those to Guala, must have found their way from the legates' establishments into the royal archive in the Chapter House. They may have been deposited at the Temple, which was used as a place of deposit for archives and cash, with the Templars acting as the forerunners of the great Italian bankers. Persons of substance and wealth, including the king, treated the Temple as a bank vault. From 1204 the New Temple served fairly regularly as a treasury of the Wardrobe and from 1239 the chancery enrolments were kept there.[36]

Many of the indults that one expects to find for royalty by the early to mid-thirteenth century, such as protections for the royal family against excommunication and against the royal chapel being placed under an interdict, date from the period after the king gained complete control in 1227 and hence were sought from Pope Gregory IX.[37] Henry, however, did obtain in 1226 protection against excommunication for himself and for his brother, Richard of Cornwall.[38] In spite of a possible brake on the issue of letters caused by the king's minority, this may have been overcompensated for by the interest and importance of England to the papacy at this time. While royal archive keeping may have been better than that in the religious houses and in private families, especially in the vulnerable period of the sixteenth century, it is clear that only a proportion of the papal letters addressed to Henry III have survived. Added to the lost *papalia* for royalty must be the papal letters, probably mainly mandates, for lay and ecclesiastical individuals, of which the originals for William, knight of Breauté, and for Roger de Moris, clerk, provide a glimpse.[39]

Accepting the estimate of 1930 letters issued in a year, made on the basis of multiplying the registered figures by four, a total of some 20,573.8 letters may have been sent out during the whole of Honorius III's pontificate. If England is taken as an eleventh part of the area with which the popes corresponded — allowing three parts each for Germania and Italia, one each for Francia, Iberia, and for Anglia, and one for Scotia and Scandinavia, and one for Eastern Europe (Poland, Hungary and Bulgaria) and the eastern Mediterranean — 1800 letters from Honorius III over the whole period of his pontificate for England alone

---

[34] Below App. 2 no. 3.

[35] Below App. 2 nos. 6, 13.

[36] A. Sandys, 'The financial and administrative importance of the London Temple in the thirteenth century', *Essays in medieval history presented to T. F. Tout*, ed. A. G. Little and F. M. Powicke (Manchester 1925) esp. 148–9, 160.

[37] PRO SC 7/15/1, 16.

[38] Below App. 2 no. 55.   [39] Nos. 31 and 47.

would be well within the bounds of possibility and may even be an underestimate.

Out of such a figure only a small fraction of the number of letters issued by Honorius III to English, Welsh and Gascon recipients survives in the original. They total fifty-seven and their survival is largely arbitrary.[40] The papal letters that once formed part of the Crown's archives now number twenty-five. Of these, fourteen were petitioned for,[41] two arrived unsolicited[42] and the remaining nine were either copies of important letters or papal letters that found their way into the royal archives from other sources, such as the letter for Guala, mentioned above, and a letter for the Templars (with the well-known symbol 'T'), both of which may have come from the London Temple during the medieval period.[43] The other thirty-two were for religious institutions. No less than six of the thirty-two were for the priory of Holy Trinity, Aldgate, London. The high rate of survival of letters for this otherwise unexceptional Augustinian house is due to the removal of the Holy Trinity deeds into the records of the Court of Augmentations after the dissolution.[44] (Absorption into the Exchequer archives probably also explains the survival of the papal letters mentioned below for the abbot of Bayham and for St Pancras, Lewes, which were in the Chapter House at Westminster, and are now found in the Public Record Office.)[45] The four originals for the priory of Durham reflect the almost undisturbed survival of the archives of that great religious institution after the creation of the Henrician cathedral foundation.[46] The remaining twenty-two consist of five (one each) for the Augustinian houses of Nostell, Oseney, Newnham, Keynsham and Southwick; four for the Benedictine houses of Thorney, Tynemouth, Bury and Abingdon; two for the Premonstratensians of Bayham and of Dale; two for the Cistercians, one for the Order in general and the other for

---

[40] See below App. 2.

[41] Ibid. nos. 3, 6, 12–13, 19–20, 23–4, 26, 33, 38 (indirectly at the king's instigation), 49 and 54–5.   [42] Nos. 29–30.

[43] Nos. 7, 22, 31–2, 34–5, 44–5 and 47. On copies of letters addressed to other recipients and their circulation, see A. Duggan, *Thomas Becket: a textual history of his letters* (Oxford 1980) 84, and Hilpert, *Kaiser–und Papstbriefe*, ch. 8, esp. 177–81.

[44] Below App. 2 nos. 2, 5, 17, 40, and 50–1. If no. 17 is not Holy Trinity's copy of a document concerning the Augustinian house of St Botolph, Colchester, the total is reduced by one. See *Lists and indexes* vol. xlix pp. iv–v.

[45] Below App. 2 nos. 4 and 56.

[46] Nos. 27–8, 37 and 57 (below); and see W. A. Pantin, *Report on the muniments of the dean and chapter of Durham* (privately pd 1939) esp. 7.

the abbey of Dore; two for the secular cathedrals of Hereford and of Exeter; and one each for the secular college of St Martin le Grand, for the Benedictine alien priory of Totnes in Devon, for the prior of the hospital of SS. James and John at Brackley, for the leper institutions of Clattercote (Oxon.) and Blyth (Notts.), for the Cluniac house of Lewes and for the nuns of Littlemore. The five Lambeth *papalia* (for Nostell, Keynsham, Thorney, Tynemouth and Bury) owe their continued existence to the requirements of the archbishop of Canterbury's Faculty Office in 1536 or to the Court of Augmentations; the latter is the more likely source for those that had nothing to do with dispensations but concerned property.[47] The confirmations for the dean and chapter of Hereford and for the chapter of Exeter were retained by those institutions throughout the archival upheavals of later centuries.[48] Papal documents from certain local religious houses, such as Oseney, Clattercote and Littlemore, went to the Bodleian.[49] Some of the others descended as or with deeds of title, for example the Blyth papal letter to the Mellish family and the prior of Brackley's exemption which passed with other deeds of the house on annexation to Magdalen College, Oxford.[50] Among this collection, over 60 per cent (15) of the papal letters to the Crown and 25 per cent (8) of those to the religious are mandates (or monitions); none is a letter close or a solemn privilege, and only 28–29 per cent (16) were entered in the papal registers. Although this is undeniably a very small sample it is unlikely to be totally misleading statistically. Before considering the implications of papal registration during this pontificate, however, an assessment of the in-letters, the requests for mandates and confirmations and dispensations, must be attempted.

THE IN-LETTERS AND ASSOCIATED CORRESPONDENCE

The relatively large number of surviving papal letters in proportion to those written to the pope has influenced interpretations of the correspondence as a whole. The out-letters have absorbed much attention and rightly so, but what of the in-letters that formed the other part of the correspondence? How many survive and what do they indicate?

---

[47] Below App. 2 nos. 1, 9, 11, 43 and 48; and see Sayers, *Original papal documents*, 2–4.
[48] Below App. 2 nos. 8 and 21.
[49] Ibid. nos. 14, 42; the latter apparently Oseney's copy of the composition between them and Littlemore.
[50] Below App. 2 nos. 39, 53; cf. 10, 36 and 41.

As has already been noticed few letters came from the papacy that were not actively sought and petitioned for. In this process proctors and messengers played a very large part and some of that part was oral. The proctor might be little more than a messenger, one who as Azo says 'takes the place of a letter: he is just like a magpie and the voice of the principal sending him...'.[51] On the other hand, he might be closer to a diplomatic envoy. When in March 1229 Henry III sent messengers to the count of Toulouse he put 'in their mouths' matters that they would disclose more fully.[52] Whereas the magpie could only repeat the voice of his master, the proctor could act in a diplomatic capacity. In either case it is clear that oral communication played a large part in the transaction of business, as it still does. The men who transacted this business in the curia at this period, in particular on behalf of the religious, are shadowy figures. There are few originals and these are not always endorsed with the proctor's name at this early date. There are, however, one or two exceptions that enable us to push the doors of the curia ajar. Master Stephen of Ecton was a royal proctor of King Henry III of the kind that was entrusted with diplomatic business.[53] The fortuitous survival of an original papal confirmation for Holy Trinity, Aldgate, exposes on the dorse that Master Stephen had aided Holy Trinity in acquiring this letter and thus reveals a network of activities that is now almost entirely obscured from view. The initial of Holy Trinity's own proctor, N., presumably Nicholas, active on their behalf in 1217 and 1218, also appears on the dorse of this document.[54] The proctor for the prior and convent of Durham, Master William de Haya, who procured a mandate for them in 1223, was also a proctor of the kind that negotiated settlements and arranged for the issue of letters. Though he may not have had the international experience of Ecton, he accompanied three Durham monks to the curia in 1237–40, no doubt acting as their legal adviser, when the election of Prior Thomas Melsanby as bishop of Durham was referred to the pope. He also witnessed the important agreement (*le convenit*) between the bishop and monks of Durham in 1229.[55] Clearly on arrival at the curia the petitions of the applicants had to be put into the appropriate forms and couched in the accepted language. This we can only surmise for the religious institutions, the majority of which brought no really

[51] Quoted by D. E. Queller in *Speculum* xxxv (1960) 199.
[52] Clanchy, *Memory to written record*, 211.
[53] On Ecton, see K. Major in *EHR* xlviii (1933) 529–53.
[54] Below App. 2 no. 50, and see nos. 2, 5.
[55] Below no. 28; *Durham annals and documents*, ed. F. Barlow (Surtees Soc. clv, 1945) 8; and *Feodarium prioratus Dunelmensis*, ed. W. Greenwell (Surtees Soc. lviii, 1872) 217.

thorny judicial question or problem to the papacy, where the use of trained counsel or a trained envoy, who could reply, inform and argue, was a necessity. Their simple needs and requirements could be catered for without further oral communication.

The main English correspondent of the pope was the Crown. By 1306 and the end of Edward I's reign, the Roman Rolls, registering copies of letters to the pope, had come into existence;[56] before this the material is confined to what was entered on the Close or Patent Rolls, to what has survived among the royal correspondence in draft,[57] and to what the chroniclers deemed sufficiently important to mention. On occasion a stray in-letter might be incorporated in the papal register, as was an important letter of King John, written from Sleaford on 15 October 1216, four days before his death, and concerning the succession. This letter was scooped up apparently by a papal clerk or registrar with the letters of the first year of Honorius III.[58] Such letters to the pope were drafted by the English chancellor himself or by a senior clerk, one of the *dictatores* of the royal Chancery. The negotiations between the English Crown and the papacy over the previous decade must have required a team of specialized clerks in Chancery. On 26 April 1217, from Winchester, the advisers of the king informed the pope of the affair of the canons of Carlisle, who were supporting Alexander, king of Scots, and who had, it was alleged, at that king's instance, elected an excommunicate as their bishop. The letter asked that Honorius should communicate his decision on the affair to the legate: 'Et super hiis voluntatem vestram karissimo amico nostro domino legato significare velitis'.[59] The reply was sent to Guala on 13 July.[60] A year later (24 August 1218) 'Malitia personarum Carleolen'', issued on the petition of the king, the archbishops of Dublin and York and the bishops of London, Winchester, Bath and Worcester, ordered Guala to remove the Augustinian canons and to institute secular canons in their stead, to declare null their election of an excommunicate and to divide the revenues between the bishop and canons.[61] Further royal overtures were made to the pope over the election of the bishop of Carlisle in 1219 and the king's letter was recorded on the Close Rolls, while letters on the same matter were sent

---

[56] See *Guide to the contents of the PRO* (HMSO): they continue to the middle of Edward III's reign.

[57] Many are pd in Shirley i; some in *Diplomatic documents*, ed. Chaplais.

[58] Reg. Yr. 1 no. 147; noted by Bliss, *CPL* 42, but not by Pressutti, *Reg. Hon. III*.

[59] *Patent rolls of the reign of Henry III (1216–25)* (1901) 111, pd Rymer i pt 1 147.

[60] Below App. 2 no. 3.

[61] Reg. Yr. 3 no. 43, *Reg. Hon. III* no. 1596, *CPL* 57.

to all the cardinals and the common form entered on the dorse of the Patent Rolls.[62] Difficulties over the payment of the census had caused Henry III to write to the pope from Westminster on 6 November 1218: the census remained a constant source for the exchange of letters throughout the reign.[63]

In 1219 when the king wrote to the pope on the perfidy of the bishop-elect of Ely, Robert of York, who had supported Louis of France and who had now fled the kingdom, he also wrote 'in eodem modo' to the cardinals.[64] On the occasion when Henry asked the pope to compel Hugh de Lusignan, count of La Marche, to restore his sister Joan, whose marriage had been proposed to the count, he sent his proctor Master William de Sancto Albino to the curia to put the case in detail and despatched a letter, dated 20 June 1220, to the cardinals on the same matter.[65] One papal letter associated with this, 'Intelleximus ex relatione', survives among the royal archive, dated 25 June 1222, when Hugh de Lusignan, who had now married the king's mother, Isabella, was ordered with his wife to restore Joan's dowry to Henry.[66] It would appear to have been initiated for the Crown by Pandulf. Evidence of such negotiations acts as a corrective to the view that most letters were issued of the pope's own volition: on the contrary they proceeded from application. Not infrequently drafts of the petitioning letters, together with the papal originals of the grants, etc., have survived, not because they represent the total surviving archive but simply because they were kept together. A royal letter to the pope on the state of the English realm, dated 19 December 1223, records the sending of proctors, Master Stephen de Lucy and Godfrey de Craucumbe, who were to negotiate on several matters and to seek letters to a long list of magnates and persons who would be named by the king's representatives.[67] Honorius's initial reply may have been 'Gaudemus in domino', a non-committal letter which welcomed the good reports of the king's two diplomatic representatives and urged the king to show himself impartial to his vassals and even to disregard some of the wrongs done to him.[68] The proctors reported their activities in a lengthy letter of 1224. They had awaited brother John

---

[62] *Rot. litt. claus.*, ed. Hardy, i (1833) 405.
[63] Shirley i no. 7. The reply is not Rymer i pt 1 149 as Shirley says. Powicke (*EHR* xxiii (1908) 220–35) has corrected the dating of some of the letters in Shirley.
[64] Rymer i pt 1 155; *Rot. litt. claus.*, ed. Hardy, i 404.
[65] Rymer i pt 1 161; Close rolls 4 Henry III m. 8d; and *Patent rolls (1216–25)*, 261.
[66] Below App. 2 no. 24.
[67] Rymer i pt 1 171; *Rot. litt. claus.*, ed. Hardy, i 630.
[68] Below App. 2 no. 38.

of Bridport at Viterbo, where certain of the cardinals, Raniero (Capocci) and Gil (Torres), and Guala, were staying, before proceeding to Rome, which they had found in a state of some disorder. They had interviewed several of the cardinalate separately and had had a secret talk with the pope. The discussions concerned the count of Toulouse, the French king, Henry III's proposed marriage and Fawkes de Breauté.[69] It is clear that Honorius did not wish yet to declare himself politically. The relationship between the English and French kings was precarious and the pope did not want to be seen to commend an English alliance with Britanny by dispensing Henry III to marry the daughter of the count. Three cardinals were used, however, to intimate to the English proctor, Alexander of Stavensby, that the dispensation was not totally and finally out of the question.[70] Among Henry's many problems, there remained Fawkes de Breauté, who had retained several royal castles. Some time after June 1224 Henry wrote to the pope, apparently in answer to a papal letter of 18 January 1224, 'Sincere fidei et devotionis', which had criticized his behaviour towards the bishop of Winchester, seemingly on the complaint of Peter des Roches that he did not have the king's protection. Henry's letter claimed that he had been misrepresented and went on to claim that Fawkes de Breauté had been condemned on sixteen charges and had then seized one of the judges.[71] The exile of de Breauté, following the capture of Bedford castle, and Henry's justification of his action is referred to in a letter to the king from Egidio, papal subdeacon and chaplain, probably of December 1224, where Henry was assured of Egidio's loyalty and advised to stand firm on the matter of Fawkes. The letter mentions the despatch of Master Fillipo in whom more had been confided.[72]

Quite clearly many of the detailed negotiations and reports that lay behind these letters were oral and were entrusted to proctors and confidential clerks. The payment of pensions and subsidies to cardinals – their 'maintenance' by the English Crown – is reasonably well documented. The surviving letters, such as that of Raniero, cardinal deacon of S. Maria in Cosmedin, who had worked for King John, petitioning for a pension and offering to work for Henry III, and that already mentioned of Egidio, papal subdeacon and chaplain, provide evidence of what was probably a sizeable correspondence.[73] The two papal

[69] Rymer i pt 1 175–6 and Shirley i no. 209.
[70] Rymer i pt 1 174.
[71] Shirley i nos. 194, 199, and see App. 5 nos. 19, the pope's attack on Langton on the matter, and 20, Honorius to Henry again on 17 Aug. 1224. The pope does not seem to have been well informed in this instance.
[72] Ibid. i no. 210.   [73] Rymer i pt 1 167; Shirley i no. 210.

letters, acquired from Honorius III by Cardinal Stefano de Normandis and addressed one to the king and the other to two of the king's counsellors, concerned payment of the large pension of fifty marks yearly for services rendered to the king's father at the curia.[74] Similarly a joint letter to the pope, against traitors returning to England, from nine of the English baronage – Hubert de Burgh, the justiciar, Ranulf, earl of Chester, Fawkes de Breauté, Philip d'Aubigny, William de Cantilupe, Geoffrey de Nevill, Brian de l'Isle, Engelard de Cigogny and Hugh de Vivonia – was probaby not the only one of its kind. Denholm-Young argued that this particular letter, using the papal cursus, originated in Pandulf's household in late 1220/early 1221 and that the barons were put up to sending it.[75]

The letters from the legates in England to the pope are likely to have once constituted a large correspondence. Both Guala and Pandulf may have kept letter-books or registers of their correspondence, as did the legate in Italy from 1219 to 1222, Cardinal Ugolino.[76] Some of Guala's own letters and *acta* and papal letters to him have survived in original and in copy.[77] Guala's importance in every aspect of the administration from May 1216 to December 1218 resulted in numerous letters. Frequently behind a request to the papacy for a confirmation is to be found a licence or dispensation of Guala and behind a mandate an appeal to the Holy See. Guala had allowed the prior and canons of Holy Trinity, Aldgate, to appropriate the church of Braughing (Herts.) and this was confirmed in a 'Sacrosancta' acquired by them on 12 February 1218; and a licence of Guala to Master Azzo to hold two churches was confirmed by the pope, doubtless at Azzo's request, on 10 February 1218.[78] How frequently Guala himself corresponded with the pope is not apparent. Unlike the royal correspondence, many missives which were directed to Guala came probably not as the result of his own reference to the pope, since Guala had plenary powers,[79] but unsolicited or more frequently from the requests of others. The one surviving original followed the king's petition concerning the canons of Carlisle.[80]

74 Below App. 2 nos. 34–5.
75 'A letter from the Council to Pope Honorius III', *EHR* lx (1945) 92; Rymer i pt 1 171.
76 See Sayers, *Papal judges delegate*, 30–1.
77 See ibid. 29–30, 310–11; Richardson, 'Letters', 250–9; *Rot. H. de Welles*, ed. Phillimore and Davis, and *Reg. Hon. III* years 1 and 2 (nine in the first year).
78 Below App. 2 no. 5, and Reg. Yr. 2 no. 902, *Reg. Hon. III* no. 1080, *CPL* 52.
79 *Reg. Hon. III* no. 262, 'Duris nobis rumoribus' of 19 Jan. 1217, refers to his plenary powers; P 5336 and *Reg. Hon. III* no. 45, 'Litteras quas felicis' of 30 Sept. 1216; and see below Chapter 5.
80 Below App. 2 no. 3.

Guala was also ordered to enquire into and examine the petition of the dean and chapter of Salisbury to move the site of their cathedral, to deal with elections, as at Hereford and in the Benedictine nunnery of St Edward, Shaftesbury, to induct and to provide.[81]

A file of Pandulf's letters has survived, addressed to Hubert de Burgh and Ralph Neville and dealing with the administration of the kingdom.[82] Pandulf's appointment was notified to the hierarchy in 'Humane conditionis nature' of 1 September 1218, but was not actually registered until the 12th. It was followed on 4 September by a mandate to the bishops of Winchester, Salisbury and Chichester to revoke certain papal letters, which had been obtained surreptitiously, to Pandulf's prejudice, and the bishops of Salisbury and of Chichester, in letters of the same date, were ordered not to molest Pandulf over benefices which he held in their dioceses and especially not to dispose of them before his consecration. Pandulf's exemption from obedience to the metropolitan, Stephen Langton ('Ut iniuncta tibi') – he was still only bishop-elect of Norwich – was conceded on 5 September.[83] It cannot be doubted that many representations and protestations from Langton and the other bishops lay behind these letters. Of the two surviving original papal letters that were addressed to Pandulf, one was certainly in response to royal overtures, a mandate to him not to allow anyone to have in his keeping more than two of the king's castles. The other, ordering him to inspect the composition made between the late king of Scots and the late king of England and to confirm or annul it, may have been issued at Henry III's request.[84] Pandulf was already in England before his legation, as two mandates of 22 April and 10 June 1218 show: he remained legate until the summer of 1221. During the period mandates reached him from the pope to assign benefices, examine cases, deal with crusaders' vows and induce settlements: a general administration which depended on correspondence. The settlement of the Topcliffe case, proceeding from the mandate of 22 April 1218, was made in the Temple, London, on 31 October 1219, where in the previous September Pandulf and his household had witnessed the submission to the pope of Reginald, king of the Isles.[85] The legate's own correspondence reveals his more or less constant itinerary round

81 See below Chapter 5, pp. 172–3, 176, 180, 181.
82 See Rymer i pt 1 157–8, 162; Shirley i nos. 22, 26–8, 48, 62–70, 85, 92–4, 98–103, 111, 117–19 and 143 (nos. 93–4, 97 and 100–3 belong to May 1219 not 1220); and CS ii pt 1 52 n. 2.
83 Reg. Yr. 3 nos. 54–5, 58–60, *Reg. Hon. III* nos. 1609, 1612–13, 1620–1, *CPL* 58.
84 Below App. 2 nos. 6, 13.
85 York, D. and C. Mag. Reg. Alb. pt 2 fol. 95 and *Glastonbury Chart.*, ed Watkin, i 88 in no. 140. Reg. Yr. 3 nos. 106, 116, 174, 290, 388, *Reg. Hon. III* nos. 1667, 1679–80, 1842 and 1889, *CPL* 59–63, and Shirley i App. 5 no. 7.

the country from the Midlands to the Welsh borders and to the West
Country, through the southern counties and north to Lincoln.[86]

Letters from the bishops to the pope must have been numerous and
would have kept the episcopal chanceries busy. But the texts of only
a few of these now survive, for example the petitions written by some
of the English bishops to the pope to initiate the canonization process
of Hugh of Lincoln.[87] However, many of the pope's communications
to the bishops were sent in answer to requests for advice on all the
problems of the diocese and for the grant of powers to implement the
Lateran decrees.

REGISTRATION

Early popes, using the Imperial Roman Chancery as a model, began
to keep copies of their pronouncements, probably on papyrus rolls, and
there is evidence of registers for at least two fifth-century popes,
Simplicius (468–83) and Gelasius I (492–6). What the principles of
registration were at this time we cannot know but, bearing in mind
that the first original papal document, a fragment, does not pre-date
788 and that there are then only three dozen originals between 788 and
1024, the papal registers are a vital source for the history of government
and administration and for the development of the Chancery and of
letter forms. Our knowledge of Gregory the Great's pontificate
(590–604) and our assessment of it stem from the existence of
registers.[88] The second surviving register is that of John VIII (872–82),[89]
nearly three hundred years later, by whose pontificate originals increase
in number. By this time, too, the notaries, whose primary function was
to collect the acts of the early Christian martyrs in their regions, may
have played some part in the registering of documents and in keeping
copies of the decrees of councils. There is a surviving fragment of the
register of Stephen V (885–8),[90] a register of the anti-pope, Anacletus
II,[91] and then another long gap until Gregory VII's register (1073–85).[92]
It has been argued by Alexander Murray that the 389 letters of Gregory

---

86 See the references to Shirley i, cited above in n. 82.
87 H. Farmer, 'The canonization of St Hugh', *Lincs. Archit. and Archaeol. Soc. Reports and Papers* vi (1956) 86–117 prints the text of the Lincoln dossier, now BL Cotton Roll xiii 27: mm. 1 & 2 include the episcopal letters.
88 See *Gregorii I papae registrum epistolarum*, ed. P. Ewald and L. M. Hartmann, 2 vols. (MGH *Epp.* i, ii, Berlin 1887–99).
89 Ed. E. Caspar in MGH *Epp.* vii (Berlin 1928) 1–333. See also D. Lohrmann, *Das Register Papst Johannes VIII* (Bibliothek des Deutschen Historischen Instituts in Rom, Tübingen 1968).
90 Ed. Caspar in MGH *Epp.* vii 334–53.
91 See P. Ewald in *Neues Archiv* iii (1878) 164–8.
92 Ed. E. Caspar in MGH *Epp.* Selectae ii 2 edn (Berlin 1955).

VII's register (360 were actually outgoing correspondence) represent at least two-thirds of the written output from that pontificate and that a large number of the pope's remaining directives were oral.[93] This view may need some tempering but in general it accords with much that is known about the committing of gifts and grants to writing in other parts of western Europe in the tenth and eleventh centuries.

It is impossible to dogmatize on whether there was an unbroken sequence of registers from Gregory VII's pontificate onwards or not, but it seems highly likely. Urban II (1088–99) may have had registers:[94] his two immediate successors, Paschal II (1099–1118) and Gelasius II (1118–19), certainly did. Their two registers are referred to in a request made to Honorius III in the second year of his pontificate by the archbishop of Toledo for permission to have letters copied. The archbishop also refers to the registers of Lucius II (1144–5), Anastasius IV (1153–4), Adrian IV (1154–9) and Alexander III (1159–81).[95] For Alexander III, indeed, a fragment survives[96] and the references to his registers, which were known to the canonists, as Holtzmann showed,[97] are fairly abundant. In 1170 John of Salisbury requested registration from Alexander, sending him copies for this purpose,[98] and in Honorius III's register for the first year there is a note of the inspection of the register of Alexander for a letter dated at Benevento in his ninth year.[99] Gerald of Wales alludes to the register of Eugenius III (1145–53) and reference is made elsewhere in Honorius's register to that of Lucius III (1181–5), thus confirming an unbroken sequence from 1144 to 1185.[100] In spite of the generally unsettled position of the papacy in the late twelfth century, it is unlikely that some popes did not have registers. There is an increasing number of references to registration and a general burgeoning of archive sources at this time. Nor is there any reason to

---

93 Murray, 'Gregory VII', 149–202. Cf. H. E. J. Cowdrey, *The epistolae vagantes of Pope Gregory VII* (Oxford 1972) p. xx and n. 2, on the question of the number of unregistered letters, accepting Murray's estimate for, at the most, 600 to 750 more (p. 157), but apparently not going with him to the limits of his argument (pp. 163–4), namely that this figure should be much reduced. Cf. also H. Hoffmann in *Deutsches Archiv* xxxii 1 (1976) 86–130, esp. 110–26, who has some criticisms of Murray's thesis and methods.

94 See J. Ramackers in *QFIAB* xxvi (1935–6) 268–76.

95 Reg. Yr. 2 nos. 797–9.

96 Ed. S. Loewenfeld, *Epistolae pontificum Romanorum ineditae* (Leipzig 1885) 149–209.

97 *QFIAB* xxx (1940) 13–87.

98 See *Letters of John of Salisbury* ii, ed. W. J. Millor and C. N. L. Brooke (Oxford 1979) p. lix, and *Materials for the history of Thomas Becket*, ed. J. C. Robertson and J. Brigstocke Sheppard, vii (RS lxvii, 1885) epp. 695, p. 353.

99 Reg. Yr. 1 between nos. 475 and 476.

100 Gerald of Wales, *Opera*, ed. Brewer *et al.* (RS xxi, 1863) iii 180; Reg. Yr. 1 no. 41.

suppose that registers were not commenced for popes whose reigns turned out to be short, such as Urban III (two years) and even Gregory VIII (two months). However it is not until the opening of the thirteenth century that the registers survive in an unbroken sequence, commencing with Innocent III (Reg. Vat. 4–8, including 7A), but for whom there is not a complete series, the most notable loss being the whole of the fourth year.

If under Gregory VII a large proportion of letters was registered, as now seems likely, this had ceased to be the case by the thirteenth century, when only a small fraction found its way into the papal registers. The position has changed totally from one where the register is the prime source to one where it is outstripped and outnumbered by originals and copies recorded in other sources. For the thirteenth century it remains a small, albeit select and important, source. Honorius III's register on its own gives a most defective picture of the writing output of the curia. Out of 440 originals which were examined by Bock he found only eighty to be registered:[101] a proportion of about 20 per cent and comparable with the 28–29 per cent that we find from examining the English originals. Yet, although a deficient source, the register is one that is crucial to our understanding not only of the papal Chancery and its workings but also of papal policy and administration as a whole. If we can assess and appreciate the relationship of the once large number of originals to the small number of registered entries we shall be nearer a genuine picture of thirteenth-century papal government.

There are three main problems of thirteenth-century papal registration on which much has been written[102] and on which we need now to see what the registers of Honorius show. The first problem concerns the moment of registration in the process of the issue of the letter. Did it take place from the draft or from the engrossment and when and why were the originals marked with notes of registration? This is intertwined with the second problem: which letters were registered and which were not and at whose behest? The third group of questions concerns the purpose and the standing of the register. How far was it useful to papal government? Did it in effect protect against fraud and act as a useful memory for political purposes? Was one reason for its compilation to act as a legal memory for the compiler of the official decretal collection of the pontificate, the *Compilatio Quinta*? Where

---

[101] 'Originale und Registereinträge', 105.
[102] On the literature in general, see Hageneder, 'Päpstlichen Register', and Herde, *Beiträge*, 241 n. 500.

were the registers kept, who was entrusted with writing them and were they moved with the papal entourage?

Bock has dispelled the notion that registration took place only from engrossments.[103] Two of the English documents show registration from drafts. The first is a mandate to Geoffrey de Lusignan, ordering him to return to the fealty of Henry III or face censure if he did not do so within a month, which was registered on 8 January 1226, a day before the engrossment was issued.[104] Identical documents were sent to eleven other recipients and registration in this particular instance may have taken place from the copy addressed to Hugh, count of La Marche.[105] It could be argued that registration in this case was in the interests of the curia and for that reason registration from the draft or minute took place. In the second example, six days elapsed between the date of the registration of a document addressed to the legate Guala on 6 July and the date of the issue of the 'original' on 13 July.[106] As the document was a mandate which ordered Guala to settle the affair of the canons of Carlisle, an affair in which the canons had behaved with duplicity towards the English king and with blatant disrespect to the Holy See, it is not surprising that the curial clerks should have seen fit to mark it for registration immediately and without application. No payment would be awaited and for this reason the decision as to registration did not need to wait on final settlement by a petitioner.

With the majority of the documents (twelve out of sixteen) the decision on registration took place at or very soon after the issue, and in every case on the same day. The writing of an engrossment had to be paid for by the applicant and there is every reason to suppose that registration would have required a further payment by the interested party. A papal letter for the prior and canons of Nostell (Augustinian, Yorks. WR) ordered the chapter of York to restore the church of Bramham (Yorks. WR) to them.[107] In the circumstances one would expect registration and that this, coming on the demand of the petitioners, would be ordered as soon as the engrossment was paid for. The privilege for Holy Trinity, Aldgate, 'Sacrosancta Romana ecclesia' of 12 February 1218, took the prior and canons, the place of their

---

103 'Studien', 329–64. Cf. on the registering from drafts in the English royal Chancery, Maxwell-Lyte, *Historical notes*, 359–62, and on episcopal chanceries, C. R. Cheney, *English bishops' chanceries 1100–1250* (Manchester 1950) 103–4.

104 Below App. 2 no. 49; cf. Bock, 'Originale und Registereinträge', 103 no. 13 (132).

105 See P 7515.

106 Below App. 2 no. 3; cf. Bock, 'Originale und Registereinträge', 103 no. 14 (433) and 116 (433) (*Reg. Hon. III* no. 5557; P 7449): there were ten complete days between registration on 14 July and engrossment on 25th. In another instance, the registrar failed to enter the year.   107 Below App. 2 no. 1.

worship and their goods under St Peter's and the pope's protection and confirmed especially the church of Braughing (Herts.) on which issue they appeared sensitive.[108] It was a certain candidate for application for registration by the petitioner. While neither of these documents would have been registered at the command of the pope, it would be in the petitioner's interest to request registration and in the papacy's to assent – but only after the original had been sealed and paid for.

Bock has discussed the large *R scriptum* marks on the dorse of some of the registered originals. He has shown that some documents were registered that do not have these marks – two of Honorius's letters for Durham endorse this[109] – and that some have the marks (sometimes the *R* without the *scriptum* or the *scriptum* without the *R*) but were not registered. The *R* on the dorse and its connection with the actual registration, he has therefore argued, can have no precise bureaucratic connection.[110] What then is its significance? Clearly it was put on by a curial hand, and probably that of the registrar. By the time of Innocent IV, though not in all cases, the sequence number of the document in the register was added together with the pontifical year,[111] and by the pontificate of Alexander IV the mark becomes still more precise, for example 'R script ccccviij capitulo anno primo'.[112] This enabled the document to be found and provided a check that it was registered, but there was no such system under Honorius III. Where registration took place from one of the documents 'in eodem modo', the *R* might be lacking, as in the papal exhortation to Henry III to take part in Frederick II's crusade, where registration was made from a similar letter addressed to Prince Leopold of Austria.[113] If the document was to be sent out in numerous copies it may have been pure chance which one of the group was marked with the *R*. A document addressed to Geoffrey de Lusignan bears an *R script* mark on the dorse. The marginal address, however, of the registered copy reads 'nobili viro comiti Marchie', another recipient of the same document, but whether the count of La Marche's document bore the curial *R* cannot be known without the survival of the original.[114] A letter addressed to the archbishop of York and his suffragans of which the original

---

[108] Ibid. no. 5; Guala's licence is pd Richardson, 'Letters', 258–9.

[109] Below App. 2 nos. 37 and 57.

[110] 'Originale und Registereinträge', 105.

[111] See Hageneder, 'Päpstlichen Register', 69 and n. 118, citing *SB* 512 no. 1986 of 1250 as the earliest.

[112] Lambeth PD no. 54; cf. the plain *R script* of Innocent IV (ibid. no. 39).

[113] Below App. 2 no. 29; cf. Bock, 'Originale und Registereinträge', 104 no. 36.

[114] Below App. 2 no. 49, and Bock, 'Originale und Registereinträge', 103 no. 15.

remains with the *R script* mark was registered under the address of the archbishop of Canterbury and his suffragans.[115] A letter to the king of England, dated 20 June 1224, commending the bishop of Cork who had been postulated by the pope to the archbishopric of Cashel, has the *R* mark although the registered copy was in fact taken from a letter to the archbishop of Canterbury and has some minor variations at the end. The king's letter is mentioned only as 'in eodem modo'.[116] Exactly the same *R* marks are found on documents that were registered from drafts, which must imply that they were put on at whatever point the decision on registration took place. Why some documents received the mark or part of the mark but were not apparently registered at all is more difficult to resolve. It seems only to confirm a lack of system at this date.

Another problematical mark is the *R* with a stroke through the right descender which is found on the face of three documents in the position of top centre to right, all of them registered documents and with the large *R* and the *scriptum* on the dorse.[117] All three, it has been argued, were registered from the engrossment, one probably at the behest of the curia, one at the request of the prior and canons of Holy Trinity, London, and the last probably at the instigation of Stephen Langton. As it occurs sporadically, in three cases out of eleven, its function can only be surmised – possibly it was an indication that the document should be registered, put on as a reminder by a curial officer when a different clerk was involved. The particular place where the mark is found on the face of the document has been associated with curial (not procuratorial) marks and with expedition. One final mark of some difficulty is the word 'scribitur', written under the left *plica*, and hence on the face, of the document which had been dated from Anagni on 13 July 1217 but registered earlier on 6 July. It is in a different ink (and possibly hand) from that of the text and the scribe's name.[118]

A comparison between the surviving originals and their copies in the registers sometimes shows differences of spelling. In the Nostell letter, the diocese of Coventry, *Couentren'* in the original, has become *Conventren'* in the register, a frequent mistake in the curia and one that may suggest copying that was not from the engrossment but perhaps from an apograph or from someone reading the text to the copyist.[119]

[115] Below App. 2 no. 33.
[116] Ibid. no. 44, Reg. Yr. 8 nos. 362, 451a and 486–7, P 7272 (and continuation), *Reg. Hon. III* nos. 5025, 5052, *CPL* 97–8; and see Haskins, 'Two Roman formularies', 281.
[117] Below App. 2 nos. 5, 7 and 38. Cf. *BAPP* nos. 126, 129, 134–5, 144, 147, 154, 173, 236 and 238.
[118] Below App. 2 no. 3.
[119] Below App. 2 no. 1.

In the instances noted by Bock the spellings vary where there are possible variants, e.g. *karissimus* (unusual but found in no. 22 of App. 2, below) for *carissimus*, *Hostiensi* for *Ostiensi*, not because actual errors of spelling have been made.[120] In all these examples there are no differences between the dates of the engrossments and of the registered copies to support the view that they might have been copied at the draft stage. When registration took place the curial clerks abbreviated the documents quite mercilessly and were clearly none too concerned about the spelling. Firstly the address and the greeting were removed, then the document was reduced to shorthand. The form of the document no longer mattered for purposes of verification, simply the gist of the content: 'u(est)re per apostolica scripta mandamus quatinus' became, for example, 'u. p. ap. s: m.ᵃ qᵘ' and 'per censuram eccl(es)iasticam app(e)llatio(n)e postposita compescentes' was shortened to 'p̣ ce: ec. ap. p' cōpescentes' and 'domino sententiam' to 'dño sñam'.[121] Finally the date, which had to follow a precise form in the original, was often heavily abbreviated and might be rendered in the form of *Dat' ut supra* where applicable.

The selective registration which the curia practised under Honorius III would in modern terms be judged naive. To be really effective a register must include the gist if not the text of every communication sent out, however trivial. It must include the requests of all and sundry (regardless of whether they seek registration or not) as well as the contents of despatches issued to persons of status. Only so can a proper check be made for the exact text and for authenticity of issue which could have precluded the not infrequent papal recourse to memory. How could the papal (or chancery) memory be infallible when, at a conservative estimate, the pope or the chancery staff were seeking to recall one particular letter out of literally thousands? Admittedly, in two of the instances referred to,[122] the claims – made in what were very likely forgeries – were extreme enough to produce doubt, but when numerous letters were issued in a year, if the pope in his later years was attempting to recall something issued in his first year, the number would be alarmingly high. Without adequate means of checking, sealed transcripts of the texts of the suspect documents had to be sent to commissions of local judges with instructions to demand the production of the originals. All this work could have been avoided if an inclusive register had been kept. The curia might have kept for

---

[120] 'Originale und Registereinträge', 102.
[121] Below App. 2 no 1, for the full text of the original document.
[122] Reg. Yr. 8 no. 349, Yr. 9 no. 321 (2), *Reg. Hon. III* nos. 4863, 5476, *CPL* 95 and 102.

its own purposes separate books of especially important letters-out,[123] besides the main general registers, as was done under Innocent III, but it must be admitted that there is no indication of a secret or separate register of any kind under Honorius III. From the registering of some of Frederick II's in-letters to the pope in the sequence of the main register,[124] it is clear that the incoming letters were not recorded separately and united with copies of the out-letters, and it seems unlikely that there was ever a separate register of imperial correspondence or indeed of any other specific group of material.

Why then was this administrative machine so selective, despite being in many ways so advanced? The purpose of the register was to act as an official memory, official, that is, to the department it served. There was never any notion that this memory should be complete. It was to harbour and record 'important' letters, primarily those issued on the pope's own volition or at the instigation of curial officers or of political leaders.[125] Judging from the small sample of English registered and unregistered original letters it cannot be held that any obviously important ones (from the point of view of the papal Chancery) were omitted. Provision to the sees of Cashel and of Ardfert took place on the same day, 20 June 1224, but that of the archbishop of Cashel, a postulation after difficulties, was noted, that for the bishop of Ardfert was not.[126] This is understandable. Most of the unregistered documents for the English crown are mandates, and whereas it may be deemed odd that one of these concerning the restoration of Henry III's castles should be registered while another on exactly the same subject should not,[127] and that one admonition to the count of La Marche should be registered and another not,[128] the omissions might simply be explained by the curia's judgement. Notes of consecrations also support the obvious view that the curia noted what was useful for its own purposes.[129] The process of selection by the curia followed curial decisions as to the importance of the matter (or file). Only an intimate knowledge of the way in which the business was conducted (which we do not now possess) would enable us to say whether their judgement was sound.

The issue of registration for the petitioner is a separate matter. From

---

[123] See Bock, 'Sekretregister und Kammerregister'.
[124] e.g. Reg. Yr. 4 nos. 593, 682, 746, Yr. 7 nos. 41–8, 54–5, 64–6, 228–30.
[125] See Gerald of Wales, 'De Invectionibus', ed. Davies, 176–7, and Poole, *Papal Chancery*, 135 n. 2.
[126] Below App. 2 nos. 44–5.
[127] Ibid. nos. 54 (registered) and 12 (only a fragment but no sign of it in the registers).
[128] Below App. 2 nos. 24, 49, and see above pp. 68, 69.
[129] e.g. Reg. Yr. 1, after no. 424, Yr. 4, after no. 549.

the point of view of the petitioner it might seem that registration was usually desirable. If, as seems probable, the letters of Honorius to the English king may be taken as a reliable sample, then a fair proportion of letters to crowned heads were registered, mainly at curial instigation. On 14 March 1224 in 'Gaudemus in domino', cited above, the pope wrote to Henry III that he rejoiced at the good reports of the king's messengers, Master Stephen de Lucy and Godfrey de Craucumbe, and urged the king to show himself impartial towards his vassals, even to ignore some of the wrongs done to him, in order to bring about a settlement.[130] Clearly there was no particular reason why the king of England should wish this letter to be inserted in the papal registers: it looks very much like curial registration. On the other hand, it was definitely in the king's interest that documents which protected his person, property or income in some way should be registered.[131]

For the religious houses, too, registration might seem, on the surface at least, very desirable. Why make the long and arduous journey to Rome only to neglect registration in the last round?[132] Yet numerous documents for the ecclesiastical interest were not registered. Of the original letters to religious institutions, thirty-two in all, twenty-three were privileges or indults and so might be expected to be registered. But only four were: two for the prior and convent of Durham, and one each for the canons of Holy Trinity, London, and for the canons of Nostell (Yorks. WR). The Durham original *papalia* number four: two mandates, an indult, and finally another mandate but concerning the election of Master William Scot, archdeacon of Worcester, to the bishopric of Durham.[133] The last two were registered. The original papal documents of Holy Trinity, London, six in all, break down into four confirmations – each one a good candidate for registration – and two mandates.[134] The sole confirmation chosen for registration confirmed in general terms but mentioned especially the recently appropriated church of Braughing. Why it was preferred for registration to a general confirmation of a year earlier, enumerating all their churches including Braughing, seems to have been on account of a suspicion of weakness in their entitlement to Braughing.[135] The failure to register an indult for the prior not to act as judge delegate, unless special mention was made of this dispensation, may seem foolhardy, although similar indults for the prior of Brackley hospital and for the abbot of

[130] Below App. 2 no. 38.
[131] Ibid. nos. 20, and 54–5.
[132] Cf. Bock, 'Studien', 336.
[133] Below App. 2 nos. 27–8, 37 and 57.
[134] Ibid. nos. 2, 5, 17, 40, 50–1.
[135] Ibid. no. 5.

Bayham were not registered either.[136] The explanation probably lies in the practice whereby the Chancery not unusually required recipients of such exemptions to let it be known throughout their vicinities that they were exempt from service as judges delegate so that petitioners at the curia would not name them. This was doubtless a better protection for this variety of document than registration.[137] For Nostell the position is different. Eight documents in addition to the one original are entered in the papal register.[138] This high proportion of registration can be explained only in the particular circumstances of the house, the seizure of its property, especially the church of Bramham, the outrageous behaviour of the archbishop of York, and the fact that the rich church of Bamburgh, which several of these documents concerned, was in the hands of a curialist.

The chief reason for the low rate of registration in general may have been the cost. Registration is likely to have remained expensive for the petitioner.[139] This must in the main explain why a protective mandate for the Templars, for example, and a grant of exemption from payment of tithes on lands acquired before the council for the Cistercians, both good candidates for registration,[140] remained unregistered, as did so many other *privilegia* both for the orders – where one might have expected a higher rate of registration – and for the separate religious institutions of all kinds. If everything had been registered the papal Chancery would have had to expand beyond recognition. Such an expansion was not in the direct interests of the papal government machine which was already experiencing the high costs of increasing administration. Indeed, its immediate interests were probably to keep the amount of registration down by keeping the costs high. Although in the long term total registration would have eradicated the hazard of forgery, a calculated risk was taken. The machinery which existed for dealing with the forgeries was a cheaper alternative. There is no doubt that the possibility of registration was very attractive for some petitioners, but the register remained a working book of the Chancery, not in essence a record for everyone else's use. The demand of certain

[136] Ibid. no. 51; and see nos. 39 and 56.
[137] Sayers, *Papal judges delegate*, 146–7.
[138] Reg. Yr. 1 nos. 85, 148, 271 bis, 344, Yr. 2 nos. 854–5 and Yr. 5 nos. 632, 634, 663, *Reg. Hon. III* nos. 146, 160, 232, 1041, 1052, 3358, 3373 and 3409, CPL 42(2), 44, 45, all of the first year, 52(2) and 82(3). It is not clear why Reg. Yr. 1 no. 271 bis (*CPL* 44) is cancelled: it is, therefore, unnumbered and does not appear in Pressutti. No. 1 in App. 2 (below) is the original.
[139] On the English royal Chancery's charges, see H. G. Richardson's argument about registration in *Introduction to the Memoranda Roll 1 John* (PRS n.s. xxi, 1943) pp. xxi–l.
[140] Below App. 2 nos. 25, 32.

petitioners for registration was not confined to the papal Chancery. Royal chanceries, including the English, were experiencing the same phenomenon: it was an expression of the general thirteenth-century desire for written record.[141] Central governments had encouraged this but none of them complied totally with its logical results as those results were not directly in their own obvious interests.

The papal Chancery's own interests explain the contents of the registers. In considering the nature of the thirteenth-century papal register one must not lose sight of its purpose in the Chancery. The word register could be used for any authoritative book. It was employed for the work which Innocent III ordered to be consulted on metropolitan sees and their suffragans to clarify the status of St David's. This work was not the *Liber Censuum* (which is also sometimes referred to as a register) but, Poole has argued, an older *Provinciale*.[142] It was also used for the most authoritative book of the pope's own correspondence. Gregory VII refers to the official collection of his letters as a register and Gerald of Wales used the term *registrum* for the register of the correspondence of Eugenius III.[143] Within the Chancery the register was the official record of the papal letters of the particular pontificate. Honorius's papal register provided the texts for the official law-compilation of the reign, the so-called *Compilatio Quinta* (which in turn influenced the composition of the *Decretales*). Clearly it was regarded as the most inclusive and authoritative source for the pope's legal pronouncements. It is a separate matter how far this collection thus influenced the whole law of the Church, and this will be dealt with later, but it has been established that it was Honorius's register that provided the exclusive source for Tancred's *Compilatio Quinta*.[144] The registers were also used by the papal Chancery for formulary purposes.[145] This, however, should not be seen as a *raison d'être* and must have remained incidental to government ends; yet there were occasions when reference to forms was necessary, and naturally the clerks used what was at hand, even possibly consulting registers of previous pontiffs.

---

[141] See V. H. Galbraith, *Studies in the Public Records* (Oxford 1946) 64–77 and *An introduction to the use of the Public Records* (Oxford 1934) 23.

[142] *Papal Chancery*, 150–1, 193–6.

[143] See e.g. Murray, 'Gregory VII', 170 nn. 62–3, and Gerald of Wales, *Opera*, ed. Brewer et al., iii 90, 180.

[144] Boyle, 'Compilatio quinta', identifies 210 letters (214 chapters) behind the 223 chapters of *CQ*. In 1974 Rabikauskas ('"Auditor"', 217, 219) had drawn attention to the crosses in the registers by the entries that were incorporated in *CQ*.

[145] *Letters*, ed. Cheney, p. xviii.

This brings us to the question of the keeping of the registers and the place of custody. The Roman see had a long history of archive keeping and may well have been in advance of other administrations in this matter. The *scriniarii* are found as early as the notaries, and the term seems to have been used interchangeably, with the *primicerius notarius* acting in the joint capacity of archivist and head of the notaries – a distinct indication of the necessary connection between the makers and the keepers of records. Innocent III had an archivist, and reference is made frequently to searching the records, to the recourse to previous archives and registers and to the *Liber Censuum*. On 8 January 1199 Innocent III had charged two legates to take the pallium to the newly elected archbishop of Antivari. It was then discovered from the *Liber Censuum* that Antivari was a suffragan of Ragusa, as the archbishop of Ragusa had alleged – an instance of where the ignorance of the records clerks had clearly let the curia down, resulting in reproof from Innocent.[146] An administration was as good as the clerks who ran its records. There is clear evidence from the compilation of the *Liber Censuum* that Honorius III appreciated that better records could mean better collection of the dues which in many instances had been allowed to lapse.[147] Reference is made during the pontificate to the consultation of previous and current records but no archivists are named.

From the seventh century the papal archives were in the pope's residence at the Lateran palace. Bock, while accentuating the profusion of the records, has maintained that by Innocent III's pontificate the registers were kept in the Chamber.[148] This theory has been regarded by Kempf and Elze as unproven.[149] There is, however, considerable evidence for some, if not all, of the volumes being in the Chamber at various times under Innocent III. When Gerald of Wales was allowed to consult the register of Pope Eugenius III in 1200 he did so under the eagle eye of a clerk of the chamberlain who sat with him and watched over him, as Gerald says 'consedente et totum observante'. Having found and read the required letters, Gerald then sought permission from the chamberlain to have them transcribed.[150] This shows that this particular register was, at least temporarily, in the Chamber and not in the Chancery. It is also possible that there were

---

146 Delisle, *Mémoire*, 4; Fabre, *Étude*, 4, and see P 578. (Tillmann, however, maintains (*Innocent III*, 78 n. 143) that the LC was in fact wrong.)
147 Fabre, *Étude*, 159.
148 'Studien', 350–64.
149 Elze, 'Liber Censuum', 260 n. 2, and citing F. Kempf in *QFIAB* xxxvi (1956) 86–137.
150 *Opera*, ed. Brewer *et al.*, iii 180. See also Poole, *Papal Chancery*, 150, and Hageneder, 'Päpstlichen Register', 74–5. See also Bock, 'Sekretregister und Kammerregister'.

chamber copies of the chancery registers, as is known to have been the case later.[151] Honorius's registers, as we now have them, are all chancery registers,[152] but their existence in no way precludes chamber copies which were perhaps those that Gerald saw. In the English royal Chancery there is evidence of the reverse situation, that is of the chancellor having made for his own use a copy of the Pipe Roll of the Exchequer, known as the Chancellor's Roll. It is by no means certain that only records of a direct fiscal nature were copied for the Chamber. Volumes of privileges are mentioned there, and on the other hand Giusti finds references to 'small books' of Honorius IV and Nicholas IV in the Chancery which were of chamber material.[153] The idea that the previous chancery registers were normally kept in the Chamber – if indeed they were – need not cause too much surprise. The Chancery was first and foremost a writing office, a place that dealt with current and nearly current letters. Apart from the current volumes, or leaves and quaterns, there would be no need to have earlier registers and archives to hand. They needed safe custody and security and the Chamber, which preserved the papal treasure, was the obvious place. The traditional story that Innocent III built a new archive room at St Peter's, for which there seems to be no good evidence, may have a few grains of truth in it, if it is presumed to have been only for documents and volumes required for current business. Throughout Honorius's reign the Lateran palace appears to have remained the main home of the archives, but whether in premises separate from the Chamber or not cannot be said.[154] That some of the records were left in the separate residences outside Rome is not impossible. It is, however, very unlikely that those that were extremely precious, such as the past registers and the early records of the papacy, the *Liber Diurnus* and the *Liber Pontificalis*, for instance, were ever out of the strong room (presumably in the Lateran) for long. Although in the early fourteenth century some at least of the papal archives were at Perugia and then at S. Fridianus in Lucca, it is doubtful whether any other place of deposit could have rivalled the Lateran in the early thirteenth century.[155]

[151] See Boyle, *Survey of the Vatican Archives*, 37–8, referring to Arm. xxxi and xxxv.

[152] Giusti, *Studi sui registri*, 129 and 134.

[153] Ibid.

[154] Poole, *Papal Chancery*, 204, citing G. B. De Rossi, *Codices Palatini Latini Bibliothecae Vaticanae* i (Rome 1886) p. xcix. See F. Ehrle, 'Die Frangipani und der Untergang des Archivs und der Bibliothek der Päpste am Anfang des 13. Jahrhunderts', *Mélanges offerts à M. Emile Chatelain* (1910) 481f.

[155] Denifle, 'Päpstlichen Registerbände', 2 and 46–8; Ehrle, 'Zur Geschichte', esp. 228–316: the archives, including the registers, were at Assisi in 1327 and at Avignon from 1339.

Table 1. Analysis of the registers of Honorius III (Reg. Vat. 9–13)

	(1) Number of leaves and foliation	(2) Measurements: overall (in centimetres)	(3) Measurements of written space	(4) Number of lines (1 column throughout)[d]	(5) Quires	(6) Catchwords and numeration of quires[h]
Reg. Yr. 1	ii + 1–131, + 2 blanks (134, 136) (foliation post-1339)[a]	28.5–29.5 × 38.5–39	15–17 × 23.5–25.6	A B C 43/36/39 i–v/vi–ix/x–xvii	16 in 8s 17th, 5 fols.[f]	Catchwords only for 5, 11–15 All quires numbered
Reg. Yr. 2	137–287 + ii (blanks) ? C14 foliation	28.5–31 × 37.8–39	16.4–22.6 × 25.2–28.5	C D 39/41 i–xi/xii–xviii	18 in 8s	Catchwords for first 10 quires and for number 17 Only first quire numbered
Reg. Yr. 3	16 folios of contents[b] in groups of 10 and 6 (separate letters unnumbered) 1–115 v + fol. lx a	23.7–24 × 31.5–32.9	13.8–14.2 × 22.7–23.1	C 39 i–xiv + ½	14 in 8s + ½ = 4	Catchwords except for 8–10 (clipped) Numbered except for 1–2, 8–10 and 14
Reg. Yr. 4	120(no 116–19)–213 + ii (blanks)	23.7–29 × 31.8–32	13.9–14.6 × 22.1–22.6	B 36 i–xii	12 in 8s	Catchwords except for 4 (blank) Only first 2 quires numbered
Reg. Yr. 5	30 folios of contents (separate letters unnumbered) + 2 duplicate folios (1 & 8 rewritten) 1–154	24.5–25.2 × 32.1–32.2	15.1–17 × 22–22.7	B 36 i–xix	19 in 8s	Catchwords for 1–7, 11 and 18 Only first 2 quires numbered
Reg. Yr. 6	155–265 + 266 (blank) Some of the	24.1–25.1 × 32.1–32.2	15–15.8 × 21.2–22.5	B E 36/30 i–iv/v–xiii	13 in 8s	Catchwords for 4, 6, 8, 11–12 4–6, 8 and 11–12 numbered

9 { (Reg. Yr. 1–2) 10 { (Reg. Yr. 3–4) 11 { (Reg. Yr. 5–6)

	folios					
Reg. Yr. 7	i–ii (blanks) + 1–80 (78, 79 and 80, blanks)	26.5–27.2 × 33.1–33.8	15.4–15.8 × 21–21.3	E 30 i–x	10 in 8s	Catchwords except for 10 (a blank) 1–8 and 10 numbered
Reg. Yr. 8	81–211+ii	26.1–26.8 × 33.5–34	15.4–18.1 × 21.2–25.6	E F G 30/33/38 i–x/xi/xii–xvi+½	16 in 8s +½ = 4	Catchwords only for first 4 quires Only first 3 quires numbered
Reg. Yr. 9	i+1–70+ii (marked 72 & 73) (folio excised between 52v and 53 but probably a blank;c also between 73 and 74)	27 – 28 × 36–36.9	17.9–18.5 × 24.5–26.2	H 37 i–viii	6 in 8s / 1 in 11 / 1 in 8	Catchwords for first 6 quires; for the following 2 they are 3 folios on, but the ultimate is 8 from the previous 1, 3 and 5 numbered
Reg. Yr. 10	74–144+i (marked 145 & lxxii)	26.9–27.7 × 36.1–37	18–18.7 × 24.7–26	H G D 57/38/41 i–vii	4 in 8s / 3 in 10s	Catchwords for first 4 quires; for the following 3 in groups of 10 Quires not numbered
Reg. Yr. 11	146 (lxxiii)–172 (lxxxxiiij) 173–4+i (blank)	26.6–27.6 × 36.5–37	18.3–18.8 × 25.4–25.7	D 41^e i–iii	1 of 10g / 2 of 8	Catchwords for all 3 quires Quires not numbered

(Reg. Yr. 7 and 8 grouped as 12; Reg. Yr. 9 and 10 grouped as 13)

Materials: parchment and ink.

The *folios* are *pricked and ruled*: for the arrangement see Figure 1. *Guide letters for initials* indicated to the rubricator see Figure 1.

a The inventory of 1339 makes it clear that there was then no foliation as the opening and closing words of the first and last folio of each volume are given.

b There is good evidence that the contents lists were made between 1365 and 1367 prior to Urban V's return to Rome. They exist now only for Reg. Vat. 10 and 11.

c The text makes sense without this folio, continuing the last letter on fol. 52v anew on fol. 53.

d The only exception is a double column used for the addressees of a letter 'in eodem modo', Reg. Yr. 1 no. 312.

e The continuation of the use of the same number of lines from the end of one year to another is found in 7 instances. It could be explained by a change in the personnel of those who pricked and lined the quires, changes that did not necessarily correspond with year changes.

f *quatern primi anni* in top left corner of fol. 129 the beginning of the last gathering.

g The quiring in 10 for this and the previous 3 quires might indicate that the same person prepared the parchment.

h The numeration of the quires is sometimes in black, more rarely in red (as in Year 1).

Table 1 *continued*

(7) Arrangement of parchment (fl = flesh; hr = hair)	(8) Hands	(9) Signatures of copyists of Urban V between 1365 and 1367[i]	(10) Colour of rubrics and rubrication changes	(11) Minor initials	(12) Illuminated initials (commencing the annual registers)
fl–hr, hr–fl, fl–hr, hr etc.	Possibly 2–3 hands Change at fol. 129 (quire end) and again at fol. 130?	*Floretus copiavit*	Red ? change of rubricator at fol. 125v[j]	Red until fol. 129 (1 blue) the beginning of the last quire: then red again	M in blue with red decoration (fol. 29 – decorative flower in margin)
fl–hr, hr–fl, fl–hr, hr etc.	Possibly 2 hands Change at fol. 145?		Red	Red and blue alternate From fol. 241 more elaborate	Elaborate blue I with red ornament and at the top a red bird in outline
fl–hr, hr–fl, fl–hr, hr etc.	Possibly only 1 hand	*Rom'*	Red: rubricator may continue with Yr. 4	Red and blue alternate, including decoration in the opposite colour	Superb illuminated E in red and blue, decorated with a leaf pattern
fl–hr, hr–fl, fl–hr, hr etc.	Possibly only 1 hand		Red	Red and blue alternate, including decoration in the opposite colour	Superb illuminated A[k] on a diapered background of red and blue
New fol. 1; fl–hr–fl–hr, hr–fl, fl etc.	Possibly only 1 hand	*Albertus scripsit*	Red	Red and blue alternate, except for fol. 1–1v (red): decoration in the opposite colour	Two fine illuminated capitals: (1) rejected folio – elaborate A[l], but washed out; (2) replacement folio – A in red, comparatively simplem
fl–hr, hr–fl, fl–hr, hr etc.	Probably 2 hands		Red: probably change	Red only	Finely decorated Q in red and green

9
10
11

80

	Hands	Scribe / *Thierricus Thome*	Rubrication		Initial / Decoration
	main part Perhaps change at fol. 73			continue with Yr. 8	decoration outside, perhaps awaiting further colour
12	hr-fl, fl-hr, hr-fl, fl etc.	Possibly 2 hands; I the main part Perhaps change on fol. 162	*Iohannes Noleti* (of the diocese of Chalons-sur-Marne)	Red	Red only	C made with pen but never rubricated or decorated, except small capitals *um* (following the C) lined with red
	hr-fl, fl-hr, hr-fl, fl etc.	Possibly only I hand; but possibly the 'k' hand also		Red: same rubricator throughout year	Red only	Initial L of *Longe*, a dragon ?on its head: never coloured
13	hr-fl, fl-hr, hr-fl, fl etc.	The 'k' hand: fols. 141 (first letter)–144v(end of volume) 2nd hand but change bears no relation to quiring		No rubrication until fol. 106 and then not again until 116–17, 126 and 135v–38 Same rubricator except possibly from 136 onwards, where the capitals cease	Red only	No initial (blank) but indicated
	hr-fl, fl-hr, hr-fl, fl etc.	Probably only I hand ? a change on fol. 157v but no relation to quiring		No rubrication at all	——	No initial (blank)

i The last three are definitely identified as such. The inscription on the board of Reg. Vat. 12 reads: 'liber septimus domini honorii tercii quem scripsit dominus Radulphus Iaquetelli et debet poni cum libro viii eiusdem honorii quem scribit Iohannes Noleti Cathalaun' diocesis'. On the dorse of the first traditional blank folio at the end is written: 'dominus Radulphus Iaquetelli scripsit de isto libro lxxvj folia quolibet continente (lx?) folia que ascendunt ad rationem centum linearum pro folio ad vij flor' et (?vi) gross''; and 'Thierricus Thome scripsit de isto libro (..) folia folium continet lxxvij lineas. Val''. See also Denifle, 'Päpstlichen registerbände', 46–7.

j The *rubrication* was done after the scribe had completed his work. The rubricator corrected one letter in a marginal heading in Yr. 1 on fol. 133, indicating his later part in the production of the manuscript.

k The left-arm is formed by a long green dragon, the right by a pillar, with coiled work inside and feline heads at top and bottom: a man's torso comes out of the cross stroke – he is holding a lance which he spears into the dragon's cheek.

l Formed by a brown dragon on the left (whose long tail ends in a feline head) attacking a leopard on the right: the cross stroke is a dark blue snake. On a background of pale blue, the whole bordered with red decoration.

m The decoration is produced by leaving the parchment white within the letter itself. The A has a long tail that extends three-quarters of the way down the margin.

Table 1 continued

(13) Binding	(14) Peculiarities
Reg. Vat. 9 refurbished in the last century The C18 board and lettered spine are preserved and bound within The registers for the first 2 years are recorded as bound together in cowhide with a silk over-cover or sleeve in the inventory of 1339	*scri tot* written intermittently in the margin by letters until fol. 13 Some very badly written folios Last folio (287v) has note: 'continet folia cciiij'.
Reg. Vat. 10 C18 binding, stamped with gilt ornament and lettering The registers for years 3 and 4 are recorded as bound together in cowhide in 1339	
Reg. Vat. 11 C18 binding, stamped with gilt ornament and lettering The registers for years 5 and 6 are recorded as bound together in cowhide in 1339	The flesh-hair, hair arrangement is upset by the substitution of the new folio
Reg. Vat. 12 C18 binding, stamped with gilt ornament and lettering The registers for years 7 and 8 were bound together in 'antique red leather' in 1339	
Reg. Vat. 13 C18 binding, stamped with gilt ornament and lettering According to the 1339 inventory, the 9th year was as yet separate but years 10 and 11 were bound together Both volumes were in cowhide	Unidentified red numbers: xl, xliii, xxviij and xlii Fol. 112v has only 4 lines and the transcription does not begin again until one-third of the way down fol. 113

Clipping has taken place at some time to allow for uniform binding; probably prior to the C18 renewal.

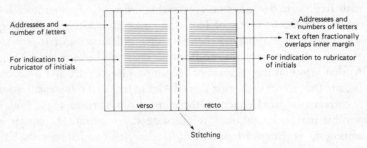

Figure 1 Arrangement of the folios of the registers.

The notes of the inspection of the registers of previous popes that occur in Honorius's registers are all among sequences of Lateran entries with one exception, the reference to the register of Alexander III, which occurs among letters mainly from Anagni.[156] On the other hand, the current material, including the quaterns for the particular year, perhaps even back to the beginning of the pontificate, may have needed different treatment. Did these annual registers or quaterns travel with the pope or did they remain in Rome, awaiting additions when the curia returned there? In order to answer this, it is necessary to look first at the format of the registers.

Honorius's registers (see Table 1) form a remarkably complete series.[157] There is an original and contemporary register in existence for every year from the pope's accession in July 1216 to his death in March 1227. Originally they were in annual format, perhaps in soft parchment covers. The offset made by the blue capital M and by the red incipit line in year 1 suggests this, but the first page of Reg. Yr. 2 is worn, suggesting no such protection. A new quire was commenced for each new year in all cases and binding would not have taken place until the end of the year, probably not until the end of the pontificate. The stages of the compilation of the register from the first cutting of the parchment and arrangement of the quires to the final rubricating of the addresses and illuminating of the capitals can be seen from the details in Table 1 and the accompanying figure. It is made more vivid by the registers for the last two years, where all the details were not completed.

The format shows no change from that of Innocent III's registers. Reg. Vat. 8 for Innocent's last year is not original but a comparison

---

[156] See above p. 66.
[157] For Innocent III only eleven years are covered by original registers. There is none for the fourth year or from the seventeenth year onwards and major gaps in the third.

with Reg. Vat. 5 exhibits no appreciable difference. Furthermore the register for the first year of Honorius's successor, Gregory IX (Reg. Vat. 14), shows no marked changes either. All these registers provide evidence of different hands and Bock has distinguished one hand (Hand A) that wrote in the registers of Honorius, Gregory IX and Innocent IV, and that occurs in the first year of Alexander IV. If this identification is correct, the hand is active, therefore, from 1216 to 1255.[158] It is possible that such continuity might suggest a registrar. Hageneder in editing the registers of Innocent III has detected two hands in the first year and five additional hands in the second year.[159] For Honorius the registers show at most eighteen hands (see Table 1). No change coincides with the quire-changes; some of the hands return. An individualistic hand, forming a curious 'k', occurs in year 10 and possibly it or one very like it in year 9. Apart from this, the hands show much in common. Kempf has identified one hand from Innocent's Chancery (Hand G) that wrote both an original document and register entries, and perhaps two other hands of Innocent's register, one to be found in documents and one in the *Liber Censuum*.[160] None such is clear for Honorius but it may well be so. Such an insufficiency of evidence does not enable us to determine whether there was a distinct registry of select scribes, perhaps notaries or working under the notaries, or whether the scribes of Chancery were used for this purpose. By the time of Boniface VIII there were *registratores* who were papal notaries.[161]

The date order of the registered documents argues strongly against direct registration. Examining the entries for the first year, it can be seen that a rough grouping was made but that this was often broken into. Three letters which were issued from the Lateran in October 1216, on 23, 25 and 24 (Year 1 nos. 67–9) are found in the middle of a November sequence. They are immediately preceded by seven of late November from St Peter's, but this run in turn is upset by one letter

158 Bock, 'Sekretregister und Kammerregister', 35.
159 *Reg. Inn. III*, ed. Hageneder et al., i pp. xix–xxi and ii pp. xii–xiii, and O. Hageneder, 'Die aüsseren Merkmale der Originalregister Innocenz' III', *MIOG* lxv (1957) 303 and 307–8. Cf. Boyle in *Speculum* xlii (1967) 57. F. Kempf, *Die Register Innocenz III eine paläographisch-diplomatische Untersuchung* (Miscellanea Historiae Pontificiae ix, Rome 1945) 17–18, distinguishes seven, two in the *Regestum super negotio Romani imperii* as well.
160 Kempf, *Die Register Innocenz III*, 121, 136–7 and plates 1 and 2.
161 Denifle, 'Päpstlichen Registerbände', 13. It has been argued that Gregory VII's register was written by a notary, Ranerius (see Murray, 'Gregory VII', 174, citing some of the views on this). Boyle, 'Compilatio quinta', 17, favours the chancery scribes under Honorius, and see the argument developed below, pp. 87–9.

of mid-November from the Lateran. Next come forty-seven letters from St Peter's of early to late December and late November all confused in order. The last of these (no. 117) is followed by three from the Lateran of 7 January and 13 and 26 September. Similarly a little group from the Lateran of January, September and October bursts into a mainly December run (one or two of November) from St Peter's (nos. 86–128). On one occasion it looks as if some link was made, with letters for Berengaria (nos. 161–2) and letters with an English interest being found together (nos. 80–5), but this is not sustained. When the pope was constantly at the Lateran in January 1217 odd letters issued at St Peter's in December (between nos. 129 and 211) were spotted about in the sequence. Letters of 13 and 26 September (nos. 119–21), issued at the Lateran, could not possibly have been registered before 7 January, the date of the letter that precedes them (no. 118). Furthermore the last thirty letters at the end of the register for the first year of the pontificate, when the pope was mainly at Anagni and Ferentino, include letters from Narni (no. 512 of 24 August, and hence from the very beginning of the pontifical year), Rome, St Peter's, in December, and the Lateran in February, March, April and November. When the pope was outside Rome at Viterbo in year 4, a group of letters in no strict chronological order follows those from Rieti (no. 573 (2) onwards) but is interrupted by two further letters from Rieti (nos. 576 and 577). By 12 June 1220 the papal court had moved to Orvieto but Viterban letters continue to crop up in the registers until the end of the papal year. The end of the seventh year, from 7 June, was spent at Segni, but earlier Lateran letters of April and May are interspersed amongst them (see nos. 170–87). This is not the pattern of the pope's itinerary but the pattern of the registration. Everything points to registration after the issue.

Table 2 shows the pope's movements in relation to the total number of documents calendared by Pressutti. The pope's movements are reconstructed on the basis of Potthast, with occasional additions from the registers. It shows the curia usually in Rome for an average of nine months in the year, except for the fourth year when, after trouble with the Romans, the papal court moved in June 1219 to Rieti, where it stayed throughout July, August and September, then transferring to Viterbo for eight months until the beginning of June 1220 (6th is the date of the last registered document issued there). By 12 June the pope and his household were at Orvieto, where they remained for the rest of the pontifical year and for the first two months of the fifth year (July to September). The registers, however, show that on 27 June and

Table 2. *Honorius III's movements and the issue of documents*

Annual numbers of letters issued (taken from Pressutti)	Year number	24–31 July	August	September
670	1 (1216–17)	PERUGIA→	12. 22–?31 NARNI.	1–3 ST PETER'S. 4 LATERAN
881	2 (1217–18)	—— FERENTI	NO ——	→ 6. ALATRI →16. 21–30 FERE (15 Casamari, dioc. Veroli)
609	3 (1218–19)	———		LATERAN—
413	4 (1219–20)	———	RIETI———	
937	5 (1220–1)	———O	RVIETO———	
590	6 (1221–2)	———		LATERAN—
348	7 (1222–3)	—— LATERA	N ——	
649	8 (1223–4)	—— SEGNI		→10.
478	9 (1224–5)	———	LATERAN——	
450	10 (1225–6)	——RIETI		
263	11 (1226–7)	———	LATERAN——	

8 July 1220 the pope issued letters from both Viterbo and Orvieto:[162] the distance between the two cities is 45 kilometres (28 miles). Nearly seven months were spent at Rieti again in the tenth year. The court moved there on 23 June 1225, at the end of year nine, and remained in Rieti until 31 January 1226.

Christmas was celebrated in Rome every year except for the fourth year of the pontificate when it was celebrated at Viterbo and the tenth year at Rieti. Similarly Easter was celebrated in Rome on all occasions save two, on 3 April in the sixth year at Veroli and on 29 March in the fourth year at Viterbo. If petitioners arranged their business to coincide with the great festivals of the Church it seems that there was a very good chance of finding the curia in Rome.[163] Nor were the papal

---

[162] Reg. Yr. 4 nos. 783, 814, and 845–6.

[163] The liturgical celebrations for Christmas (the papal masses) took place at the basilica of S. Maria Maggiore and those for Easter at St John Lateran (see Elze, 'Päpstliche Kapelle', 171).

October	November	December	January
RAN ———————→	15. 21 ST PETER'S (10 St Peter's and Lateran) ———→	23. 29 LAT (16 St Peter's and Lateran)	ERAN ———→
———→ 2. ROME. 5 LATERAN ——			
RAN ———————			LATERAN ——→
———→ 1.6 VITERBO ———————		13. 20 VITERBO (17 Civita Castellana,[a] 30 St Peter's)	(3 St Peter's)
TO ——→ 1.5–10 VITERBO. 26 LAT	ERAN —→ 17. 22 ST PETER'S 23 LA	TERAN ———————	———→ LATER-
AN ———————	LATERAN ———————	LATERAN ———————	LATER-
AN ———————	LATERAN ———————		
NAGNI. 23 LATERAN ———————			LATERAN ——→
AN ———————		LATERAN ———————	
——————— RIETI ———————			31.
AN ———————		LATERAN ———————	

[a] Also at the Lateran on the same day according to CUL MS 6845 fols. 11v–12.

towns to which the curia had resort in 1219 to 1220 and in 1225 to 1226, Rieti, Viterbo and Orvieto, too distant for the desperate petitioner, and the standing proctors would have packed their baggage and gone with the curia, as did the scribes and other essential papal officers.

Two of the peak years for the issue (and registration) of documents accord with years when Honorius was in Rome for more than nine months. On the other hand, the lowest year, seven (bar the eleventh year which lasted for eight months only because of the pope's death in March), shows the pope in Rome for nine months. Furthermore, when Honorius was in Rome for $10\frac{1}{4}$ months in the third year the issue was fairly limited. Nevertheless the figures do appear to show some bias towards Rome.

It has been suggested that registration might have been delayed until the pope's return to Rome.[164] This must now be more closely

[164] Boyle, 'Compilatio quinta', 17.

Table 2. (*Cont.*)

February	March	April	May	June–28 July
LATERAN———————————————————			15. 15–31 ANAGNI———— (31 at Lateran also)	→17 July. 19 FEREN (6 July Villamagna dioc. Anagni
LATERAN————————		→26. 27 ST P|ETER'S————————		22. 25 June LATERAN————
LATERAN————————		→11. 20 ST PET|ER'S———————— 31.		11 RIETI————
VITERBO—————————			→2. 3 ORVIETO———— (27 June, 8 July at Viterbo also)	
-AN———→27.	1 LATERAN —			
-AN———→28.	4–31 ANAGNI	3–30 VEROLI. (27 Casamari)	2 ALATRI————————	17. 21 June LATERAN————
→13. 17 FERE|NTINO — 26.		LATERAN———————— 30.		7 SEGNI————
LATERAN—				
LATERAN—		→19. 20 TIVO|LI————————		14. 23 June RIETI————
15 LATERAN			———— LA|TERAN————	
LATERAN———→18.				

investigated for the period and the format of the registers considered in this particular light. Registration was, in the main, sensitive to the pontifical year, and the quaterns were open-ended, like a file. There were, however, some lapses. A letter of year 5 (28 July) found its way into year 4 (no. 853) – it must belong to year 5 because it was dated from Orvieto and the papal court was not there at the beginning of the pope's fourth year. The same mistake was made at the beginning of year 10 where a letter (no. 28) of 15 July, granted at Rieti, appears: this belongs clearly to year 9. At the end of the seventh year (fol. 77v), there is an in-letter from the emperor to the pope dated 29 July which therefore should have been placed at the beginning of the year. Within the pontifical year, as we have seen, the registered documents show no clear chronological order. At some point this material was sorted into the year but the lack of a chronological arrangement rules out immediate registration. The strongest argument that registration did not take place at once is from the apparent muddle which existed whether the curia was in or out of Rome. It might be thought that letters issued outside Rome and so presumably returned in a group would be registered *en bloc*, accepting the argument for registration only in Rome, but then it might be expected, too, that the Roman letters would demonstrate better organization than they do. That there was delay between issue and registration is confirmed by this lack of chronological order as well as the lack of order according to the place of issue. Although differences between registration from draft and registration from engrossment would cause variation in date, it is unlikely to explain differences in date of as much as one or two months. Reg. Year 10, for example, has a letter of 18 September (no. 18) among letters of July to 20 August; register Year 7, a letter of 19 December (no. 80) between letters of 24 and 25 January (all issued at the Lateran), and letters of January and March (nos. 154 and 157, the latter given at Ferentino) in the May sequence. Similarly a letter of 13 May from the Lateran (Reg. Year 1 no. 504) gets between two letters of 14 July granted from Anagni. Six entries before the first of these is 'Tam carissimus in' (no. 497) dated 6 July, of which we have the original engrossment, dated 13 July. The date difference makes it certain that this letter was registered not from the engrossment but from the draft. It is noticeable that the registration from drafts where a considerable time interlude may be involved appears to indicate registration of documents granted outside Rome.[165] To substantiate this thesis it would, of course, be necessary to examine *all* the originals, not only those for England and those noted by Bock, and to compare them with the registered entries. At the present the evidence implies that the work on the registration did not take place until after the curia had returned to Rome bringing the documents with it, as was demonstrably the case in year 10. Boyle has explained the chronological peculiarities of the register in year 10 – discernible for some of the other years but perhaps in a less pronounced fashion – by the calling away of the chancery scribes to make copies for Tancred. The backlog of work, which was inevitable if the curia was away for long, produced the chronologically inconsequential format of the register.

This brings us to the question of what the clerks actually registered from. Obviously registration was not undertaken directly from the engrossment as this would have meant the petitioner waiting more or less indefinitely. It is possible that the registering was done from apographs or *contrabrevia*, made at the time of the application of the

---

[165] See below App. 2 nos. 3 (discussed above n. 106) and 49.

bulla. But if registration was from a copy, it was not from a copy-roll made as soon as the document was issued, for if so the final registration would have been in chronological order. It is also plausible that minutes were marked for registration, when requested and paid for, and that in that case the date of the engrossment was added.[166]

A question of importance is how systematic was this registration. Kempf, Peitz and Hageneder have argued for fairly systematic registration under Innocent III, but Bock has not been inclined to accept this.[167] Moreover he has established that the changes in the hands in Innocent's registers are not related to the movements of the curia.[168] Nothing in Honorius's registers overturns that view. Everything, as argued above, points to the conclusion that registration was not effected outside Rome during this pontificate and that it was not done directly usually, even if the curia was in Rome. It was not highly efficient, for the reasons pointed out, but neither was it chaotic. The registrar or registrars in turn worked at their own particular speeds, registering documents according no doubt to a schedule. There must have been an enormous work load by the autumn of year 5, for the curia had been out of Rome for sixteen months, but we find no signs of this from the register. Indeed, it is only because of Honorius's mandate for the compilation of the *Quinta* and the tight time-schedule that was apparently involved that we have any idea of some of the problems and methods. Nor would the later registers look so very different from the earlier ones if the rubrication and illumination had been completed.

If registration only took place in Rome, could the registers have been compiled in the time available, especially in years where there was a backlog of registration due to the curia's absence from Rome? In an experiment to discover whether the Larger Domesday could have been written by one man in the time available, the calligrapher, Alfred Fairbank, concluded that the scribe might hope to complete three folios or twelve columns in two days, taking into account the preparation of materials and the trimming of quills.[169] This rate would have allowed the completion of the papal register in about ten weeks for most years when roughly one hundred folios was the average number,

---

[166] Barraclough, 'Minutes of papal letters', 116, states that the Cambridge drafts, with one exception, are undated.

[167] See e.g. Hageneder, 'Die aüsseren Merkmale', 296–339, esp. 308. See also H. Feigl in *MIOG* lxv (1957) 242–95, and Haidacher in *Römische historische Mitteilungen* iv (1960/1). [168] Bock, 'Studien', 339.

[169] *Domesday re-bound*, ed. H. Jenkinson (PRO handbooks 2, 1954) 34. A quill might need to be recut after a few lines if it was not a very good one. Its total life would probably be two to three folios. I owe this information to Mr Michael Gullick.

making no allowance for breaks, nor, on the other hand, giving compensation for time saved if someone else did all the preparation – cutting, quiring, pricking and ruling – save the trimming of pens. The registers for years 9 and 10 had only some seventy folios each and 11 (not a full year) twenty-six. This would have reduced the time necessary to complete registration for year 9 or 10 to about seven weeks. One point that is obvious is that not more than one man could actually register at once. In the case of Reg. year 10, when copies were needed for Tancred's purposes,[170] in theory the copyists could get to work as soon as the registration had finished, but the registrar could only go at a certain speed and in practice, of course, the scribes had to wait for Tancred to mark the letters he wanted them to copy. This forced the registrar to halt temporarily and explains the gap in writing but not in material after the first four lines on fol. 112v until one-third of the way down fol. 113r.

It has been suggested for an earlier period that many of the letters issued outside Rome were not registered.[171] Table 3, distribution of registered letters for years 1, 4, 7 and 10 of the pontificate, relates to this question. The relatively large number of letters of the first year is to be explained by the beginning of a new pontificate and the usual resuscitation of business and demand for confirmations. The pope was at the Lateran for the main part of the year and registration was at its highest in January (85) and in the period January to April. All the fourth year was spent out of Rome: at Rieti from July to October, then at Viterbo until the beginning of June and finally at Orvieto. Most of the registered documents are dated from Viterbo in November (36) and more particularly from Orvieto in July (52). In year 7, when the pope was in Rome for most of the year, the total issue was very low. The highest recorded registration was at the Lateran in April and May (36 and 30), but it is noticeable in this year that while he was at Ferentino in February and in March the total number of registrations was only fifteen. For the first six months of the tenth year, from the beginning of his pontifical year in July to 31 January, the pope was at Rieti. During that period 209 letters were marked for registration. For the last six months from February, when Honorius returned to the Lateran, until the end of the pontifical year, the total number of registered letters was 164. The evidence for this year, therefore, does

---

[170] See below pp. 139–40.

[171] Murray, 'Gregory VII', 159, 171–4. The high number of letters issued by a pope for his own family and country/place of origin (e.g. Adrian IV for England) and for the places he visited may be noted (ibid., 201).

Table 3. *Distribution of dated registered letters in years 1, 4, 7 and 10 of the pontificate*

	July 24–31	Aug.	Sept.	Oct.	Nov.	Dec.	Jan.	Feb.	March	April	May	June	July 1–23	Total of dated registered letters for the year
1.	2	9	16	15	37	60	85	73	68	71	36	31	22	525
4.	6	20	12	17	36	18	6	22	19	28	35	33	52	304
7.	0	11	9	13	8	17	30	9	6	36	30	13	29	211
10.	4	33	47	33	29	23	40	25	21	24	44	37	13	373
Totals	12	73	84	78	110	118	161	129	114	159	145	114	116	

Only dated and numbered letters have been included in these calculations, which have been made on the basis of the original papal registers, so that the totals are down if compared with the totals based on other sources.

not show a higher rate of registration for letters issued when the curia was in Rome but rather the opposite. The preponderance of registered letters issued outside Rome implies no impediment to their registration nor any obvious attempt to restrict their numbers more than was usual.

Considering the long history of the papal register, there was an unaccountable slowness in its development. The registration of certain in-letters, especially from Frederick II, the inclusion of the submission of the king of the Isles twice (in years 4 and 7), and the miscellanea, including in year 1 a proctor's constitution by the archbishop of Braga in Portugal (no. 206), shows a fairly primitive registration system. The incoming letters were still not separately sorted and recorded, the material for entry in the registers was not carefully arranged and checked, and miscellaneous and extraneous matter might easily find its way in amongst the official entries. It was not grasped that registration of letters needed to be closely associated with the issue, that it should be strictly chronological and that it should be entirely inclusive. Perhaps we are demanding more of the papal Chancery than it could possibly supply, and in a way the demands are associated with the precociously early development of the papal registers. Their Achilles' heel proved to be that, by the thirteenth century at any rate, they took in registration of the usual range of documents issued when the pope was out of Rome, but did not effect it at once. Thus when the curia returned to Rome the registrars and the clerks had a large backlog of work to attend to: the delayed activity hindered improvements in registration practices and techniques. The detailed endorsements that occur on registered documents by the 1250s show progress towards direct registration but it cannot be seen in the 1220s. The impressionistic *R* mark and the arguments advanced above imply retrospective registration and that the arrangements for year 10 were not exceptional.

The change from an orally based society where few documents were written to government based on the written word caused little by little an archival revolution. The panic period of the production of forgeries in the twelfth century, when it was made clear that original documents were necessary for legal purposes, was matched in the thirteenth century by a general demand for registration, whether in the shape of paying for their official record or of producing one's own copies. The cartularies and registers of the recipients reflected this change as much as the records of the papacy.

Chapter 3

THE FORMS

Letters were the vehicle of the curia's thought. They crystallized curial attitudes and aspirations and provided a bridge between general political ideas and the specific requirements of the particular institution or person. The development of forms in which the letter might be cast mirrored the growth of papal government. While parts of the letter might be very ancient in their form, others were more flexible and could be adapted or shaped to new requirements.

The method of transmitting the contents of a letter to more than one person at a time was by reading aloud.[1] Public readings of some documents at least took place after they were acquired in order to disseminate the contents. An illumination in a Harley manuscript clearly shows Archbishop Arundel reading a sealed document, possibly a papal letter, to an assembled audience.[2] Addresses, such as 'To all the faithful of Christ' and 'To all the faithful of Christ throughout the province of Canterbury', obviously presupposed a reading of the letter in a public place or places: how otherwise were the faithful of Christ to know of the indulgence offered? The translation of St Thomas of Canterbury from his first resting place in the crypt to the superb *corona* or retro-choir of his cathedral was well publicized. Amongst the dossier of papal letters concerning the translation, a letter of January 1219, addressed to all the faithful of Christ, granted an indulgence of forty days of enjoined penance to those visiting the new shrine. It preceded the translation, which took place in July 1220, by no less than eighteen months and was part of a widespread campaign to encourage crowds to come to Christ Church, Canterbury, within the octave of the ceremony, for the veneration of the saint, when they would be invited

---

[1] See H. Fichtenau in *BEC* cxix (1962) 18.
[2] BL Harley MS 1319 fol. 12.

to contribute towards the costs.[3] Another letter with a general address of this kind permitted the collection of contributions towards the repair of the priory church of Southwick (Aug. Hants.). It was not addressed to the prior and convent, who were to benefit from its contents, but to the faithful of the province of Canterbury who were to be informed of the appeal and exhorted to give before the collectors arrived.[4] The task of publicizing such matters was primarily in the hands of the diocesans[5] for proclamation in their cathedral churches but publication must in many cases have percolated down to parochial level and may have formed part of the business of rural chapters. The requirement that the parish clergy should be literate was not an outrageous demand on behalf of an élitist hierarchy but a necessary skill for the dissemination of information. Councils and bishops, such as Robert Grosseteste of Lincoln, strove to make the clergy a useful mouthpiece of ecclesiastical authority for this purpose amongst others.

To be effective, privileges and confirmations had to be made known publicly. Confirmations of gifts of lands and of possessions (some of which gifts may have been oral) were not likely to be respected unless all concerned were aware of the ownership and also of the anathema to be incurred by anyone disputing the possession and preventing the rightful owner's peaceful enjoyment. It seems likely that these confirmations would have been read out in the places to which they related. Often they were acquired simply because the land or tithes or goods had been in dispute and sometimes they were confirmations of those settlements or sentences, as in the case of 'Ea que iudicio', which confirmed an agreement between the nuns of Littlemore and the canons of Oseney over the possession of certain tithes.[6] In all instances it must have been just as desirable to see that all knew to whom the property belonged, and that it had been so donated or confirmed, as it was to ensure that the original deeds of gift and of confirmation were kept safe within the treasury or muniment room.

Within monastic circles, where reading aloud was commonplace, reading of papal documents relating to the house may have been customary, both of newly acquired privileges for the purpose of informing the community and also of older privileges for the reinforcement of common aims and for the benefit of the younger

---

[3] Below App. 2 no. 7. The dossier consists of Reg. Yr. 3 nos. 266, 266a, 267, *Reg. Hon. III* nos. 1830, 1833, 1840–1, P 6528–9, and *CPL* 62.

[4] Below App. 2 no. 52.

[5] See below pp. 114–15.   [6] Below App. 2. no. 42 and cf. no. 50.

recruits whose commitment to the institution would need to be fostered. Reading aloud for instruction was usual among the clergy and, even if literate, they were accustomed to listening rather than to reading by eye. Memory was often the best form of record in the middle ages and was cultivated as such, so that even when, as by the thirteenth century, much was committed to writing, the memory of the community in general was not ignored.

The punctuation indicated the pauses to be made when the document was read aloud. In theory the cursus should substitute for punctuation, but doubtless the reader needed advanced warning of when to raise the pitch and change the rhythm of his voice. Thomas of Capua distinguishes three main punctuation marks, all employed in the documents printed below: firstly the full point, secondly the medial point, used as a colon to indicate a rough equality between the two parts of a sentence, and finally the *punctus elevatus* (⁚) or comma. There is also a weak form of the comma (⁊) like the ⁊.[7] The texts show that the punctuation was added by the papal scribe, in some instances at least, after he had written the letter, the punctuation, in particular the *puncti elevati* and the lesser pauses, being placed very close to the preceding and succeeding words.[8]

The cursus allowed a rhythmic declamation by introducing metrical cadences into the prose. Originating with the sophist, Thrasymachus, it influenced the medieval West through the writings of Cicero and the Fathers.[9] Its complete assimilation into papal chancery techniques was slow – only 56.5 per cent of the letters of Gregory VII (1073–85) fit these patterns[10] but under the influence of John of Gaeta, who was chancellor to Urban II (1088–99) and pope himself from 1118–19, it was employed increasingly by the papal Chancery. Later popes, especially Gregory VIII (1187), Albert of Morra, who had also been chancellor of the Roman Church, fostered the application and perfection of the cursus, which, as used in papal documents, came after him to be known as the *stylus Gregorianus* and to be regarded by some as the 'secret' of papal scribes. The *stylus Gregorianus* was an essential characteristic of all chancery products and the subject of elaborate rules. Not surprisingly chancery officers (chancellors or vice-chancellors and notaries) were drawn to compose treatises not only on the cursus but

---

[7] See the useful survey in *Life of St Anselm...by Eadmer*, ed. R. W. Southern (Oxford repd 1972) pp. xxvii–xxix, who prints Thomas of Capua's definitions (p. xxxi n. 1).

[8] See below App. 2, e.g. nos. 34–5.

[9] See Clark, *Cursus*; and Poole, *Papal Chancery*, ch. 4.

[10] Constable, *Letters and letter-collections*, 36.

also on the whole theory and practice of letter writing, the *dictamen*, of which the cursus was an essential ingredient. The *dictatores* of the Chancery had to be completely versed in its use and there is every indication that they did not fall short of this requirement. 'Possessed by the spell', as Clark says,[11] the *dictatores* employed the cursus in all the original letters of Honorius that are included below. In most instances it was used in set forms which were drawn from the current formularies and files, probably by lesser officials than the notaries or *dictatores*, but 'Iustus dominus in' and 'Gaudemus in domino' are examples of the *dictatores* at work without clear models.[12] Innocent III claimed to be able to tell a forged document by its misuse or neglect of the cursus[13] and Boniface VIII, at the end of the century, had a Chancery capable of producing the sonorous tones of 'Unam sanctam'. Honorius's Chancery appears to have maintained the high standards in the employment of the cursus in chancery products which have come to be associated with the apogee of its use.

The emphasis on listening to the written word encouraged the use of set phrases and forms. The mind was allowed to relax while the familiar formulas were employed. This must have made the special information more obvious and arresting and there is no doubt that the essence of the document would have been retained more easily in the memory. Not only did the informed listener expect set phrases appropriate to the particular type of papal letter but he also expected a formalized procedure or order. An invocation and a benediction were customary at the beginning and at the end of a prose or verse narration in the medieval period: 'Either before or after the usual call for attention the poet invokes a blessing upon the company before him, and he usually closes with a benediction.'[14] Santifaller comments on the modern counterpart of the invocation, the bidding prayer.[15] The invocations 'In nomine dei' etc., used in notarial documents and legal sentences, are not found in letters of grace or in mandates, where the invocation is really the salutation and apostolic greeting of St Peter's successor. The invocation, narration and benediction of the piece of prose or verse corresponded with the threefold form of the letter: initial protocol, text, and final protocol. The initial protocol consisted of the salutation and the *exordium*, or introduction, followed by the text proper, composed of the narration and of the disposition, and culminating in the final protocol or conclusion, embracing the blessing

[11] *Cursus*, 8.
[12] Below App. 2 nos. 29, 38.
[13] Clark, *Cursus*, 16.
[14] Crosby, 'Oral delivery', 108.
[15] 'Über die Verbal-Invokation in Urkunden', 8 and n. 2.

and/or sanction and farewell.[16] Obviously the traditional Latin epistolographical formulas varied according to the particular requirements and the older forms underwent some changes in the mid-twelfth century with the development of the letter of grace. By the thirteenth century the final blessing and the *bene valete* were found only in the great privileges, but the intention remained the same. First of all the audience was addressed, greeted and blessed; then the main message was imparted; finally the company was dispersed with the sanctions (in the letter of grace) or with the closing requirements of the mandate. The 'technique of approach' and the 'technique of withdrawal' were commonplace to all communications. They encased a series of usually stock phrases. With stories and poems these techniques and the 'excessive repetition of stock phrases' are indications of the intention of oral delivery.[17] In all likelihood, in the same way, papal letters were pronounced verbally very frequently, even if security demanded that they should be committed to writing.

The papal letter at this time opened consistently with the pope's name and style, the names of the addressees and the greeting. The pope was styled invariably *episcopus servus servorum dei* from the late sixth century, and the salutation for letters of grace and for mandates was (with exception only for excommunicates and Jews and heretics where 'spiritum consilii sanioris' and 'viam agnoscere veritatis' were substituted) *salutem et apostolicam benedictionem*.[18] The style in which the recipients were addressed followed forms of strict protocol.[19] Crowned heads were always *carissimus in Christo filius illustris*, sometimes with the particular name and title specified, as *Henricus rex Anglor(um)*.[20] Some of the scribes of Honorius's Chancery were not *au courant* with the latest developments in royal style in the English Chancery; in four instances the king was addressed as *Rex Anglie* (correct) and in three as *Rex Anglorum*.[21] Two documents issued on the same day in 1224 but written by different scribes show that S. had it right but that g. did not.[22] Where the king was not the addressee, but was referred to in the course of the document, in a majority of cases he was described

---

[16] Some commentators, e.g. Thomas of Capua, enumerated the parts of the letter as five: salutatio *plus* exordium, narratio *plus* petitio/dispositio, and conclusion; see 'Dictator epistolarum', *Collectio monumentorum veterorum et recentium ineditorum*, ed. S. F. Hahn (Brunswick 1724) i 281, and 'Ars dictandi', ed. Heller, 16.

[17] Crosby, 'Oral delivery', 110.

[18] Thomas of Capua, 'Ars dictandi', ed. Heller, 23–4; and Clark, *Cursus*, 14.

[19] See Constable, 'Structure of medieval society', 253–67.

[20] See below App. 2 nos. 44–5.

[21] Below App. 2 nos. 29–30, 44 and 55; 34, 38 and 45.

[22] Nos. 44–5.

as *Rex Anglorum*, possibly because this is the language of the petitioner or perhaps indicating more variation in the work of royal clerks than is now obvious.[23] Archbishops and bishops were addressed as *venerabiles fratres*.[24] William, whose election to the metropolitan see of Poitiers had not been confirmed and was in some doubt, was called *dictus archiepiscopus Pictavensis diocesis* and addressed as *dilectus filius nobilis vir*, not as 'venerable brother', and similarly Llewellyn, prince of Wales, whose allegiance was suspect, was described as *nobilis vir dictus princeps Norwallie*.[25] The address 'beloved son, the noble man' was employed for nobles such as Hubert de Burgh, William Brewer and Hugh de Lusignan; Hugh's wife, Isabella, Henry III's mother, however, was described simply as Hugh's wife and as 'of the diocese of Poitiers', a distinction common in mandates.[26] Ecclesiastics of all kinds, seculars, such as the chapter of York, as well as regulars, such as the prior and convent of Holy Trinity, London, were called 'beloved sons'; nuns were 'beloved daughters in Christ'; and the two legates simply 'beloved sons'.[27] Any explanation as to why the legates were not addressed at least on a par with the bishops suggests possibly that it was the rank of the cardinal that mattered — Guala was a cardinal priest and therefore 'beloved son' was appropriate.[28] Pandulf, on the other hand, was not a cardinal and he could not be described as 'venerable brother' as he was not yet consecrated as bishop of Norwich. Why the legatine title had not evolved its own exclusive form of address possibly reflects the extreme conservatism of the forms of address, some of which went back to very early formularies and, indeed, without much alteration, to the *Liber Diurnus*, where kings and lay rulers were 'excellent sons' and patriarchs and archbishops 'most reverend and beloved brothers'.[29] The basic assumption was that only archbishops and bishops could be addressed as equals of the bishop of Rome and hence as his brothers. All other important persons, laymen and ecclesiastics, were his sons and daughters. In the wording of mandates the pope does not order a monarch to effect something but 'asks and exhorts' him, and archbishops and bishops usually were 'warned and exhorted' before being ordered.[30] The indications are that the formularies to which the chancery clerks had recourse were clear and

[23] Nos. 3, 10, 13, 20, 22–4, 26, 35 and 49; as opposed to three, nos. 8, 33, 54.
[24] Nos. 19, 31.
[25] Nos. 26, 33.   [26] Nos. 20, 24.
[27] Nos. 1–3, 6, 13 and 42.
[28] See Thomas of Capua, 'Ars dictandi', ed. Heller, 24.
[29] Ed. T. Sickel (Vienna 1889, repd 1966) 1–3.
[30] 'Ars dictandi', ed. Heller, 23–4, and below App. 2 nos. 19, 30.

definite in their regulations and that the clerks were punctilious in their observance of them.

The closing part of the letter of grace, before the date, concluded with the sanction. The blessing, often associated with the sanction in the solemn privileges, had no place in the run-of-the-mill confirmation, protection or concession. However, the penalty clauses commencing 'Nulli ergo' and 'Si quis autem' (settled in form by the thirteenth century) that threatened infringers and contraveners with the indignation of the almighty and the blessed apostles, Peter and Paul, were in reality very close to calling the benediction of God and of the saints on those preserving and accepting the terms of the document. Attention has been drawn to the very fine distinction between interceding with the saints, on the one hand, and swearing by them or calling them to witness on the other.[31] The 'Nulli' and 'Si quis' clauses vary slightly according to the species of the letter: if it was an indult then the infringement of this *concessio* was mentioned.[32] Where the recipients were taken under papal and Petrine protection, as well as having their possessions confirmed, the sanction clause spoke of *protectio* and *confirmatio*, but where no protection was given this term was carefully omitted from the 'Nulli' clause.[33] In a confirmation for the rector and brothers of Blyth, which took them under papal protection, confirmed their possessions and liberties and inhibited anyone from exacting tithes of certain kinds from them, the *protectio*, *confirmatio* and *inhibitio* were all mentioned in the sanction.[34] The form of the document chosen bore no direct relation to these matters; for instance, 'Iustis petentium desideriis' and 'Cum a nobis' were used indiscriminately for plain confirmations and for protections and confirmations, and 'Cum a nobis' was used also for the document that included the tithe inhibition.[35] 'Solet annuere sedes' served both for the plain *concessio* or licence and for another protection, confirmation and inhibition.[36]

Borrowing phrases, especially from the liturgy,[37] was not uncommon in papal documents, but none such is found here. Only two quotations are cited: the Pauline 'Qui parce seminat', which was associated always with a particular kind of indulgence,[38] and a rather commonplace quotation from Persius's *Satires* (perhaps known via Jerome) which occurs in 'Gaudemus in domino'.[39] Presumably dictionaries of quotations were at the service of the chancery *dictatores*.

---

[31] Crosby, 'Oral delivery', 108.
[33] Contrast nos. 46 and 50.
[35] Ibid.
[37] Fichtenau, 'Situation actuelle', 18.
[39] No. 38.

[32] e.g. below App. 2 no. 25.
[34] Below App. 2 no. 53.
[36] Below App. 2 nos. 14, 43.
[38] App. 2 nos. 7 and 52.

An essential part of the extension of the papal bureaucratic machine and the improvement of its techniques was the provision of forms for documents. By the thirteenth century the range of products available for the petitioner stretched from the solemn privilege to the judicial mandate couched in a letter form. The letter form, which had been evolved in the twelfth century, provided for simple confirmations, for indulgences and indults and also for mandates. By Honorius's pontificate, for most mandates and confirmations the abbreviator of the minute needed only to jot down the salient points and once the appropriate form had been chosen the scribe's engrossment presented few problems except of detail. Indeed most of the forms were, from frequent usage, clearly known by heart by the scribes and reference to a model did not need to be made. At a later date the papal Chancery provided forms of a kind in which only the details needed to be inserted, but at this time each document was written for each case as the need arose. For the majority of the documents the issue was very simple where the form had been developed over previous pontificates; in others where the documentary form was less stereotyped the model was in the process of evolution. A generation or two ago it was commonly held and repeated that thirteenth-century papal documents rarely erred from rigid and stereotyped forms. This assertion has been questioned in the last fifteen years and studies on the papal Chancery have shown more variation in chancery practices and products than was supposed. To estimate how far there were forms and deviations from them depends on a minute analysis of the texts. The papal Chancery or writing office has been represented as a very conservative institution. This assessment must now be put to the test in the study of the main forms.

CONFIRMATIONS

'*Sacrosancta Romana ecclesia*'

The form 'Sacrosancta Romana ecclesia...confovere' was commonly used by the thirteenth century for confirming the possessions of religious institutions. Two originals survive in an English context for Honorius's pontificate.[40] The arenga drew attention to the Church's love for its devoted and humble sons. As a 'pious' mother, the Church was there to protect her sons against the molestations of evil men. For this reason the pope agreed to the just requests of his petitioners and took their persons (in the case of religious houses, the place of their worship was usually included), with all their goods, ecclesiastical as well

---

[40] Nos. 5 and 21.

as worldly, which they possessed now or would justly acquire in future, under the protection of St Peter and himself.[41] The arenga, in a primitive form, seems to have been known under Gregory VII, though with much variation, and at first it was not used solely for confirmations.[42] Gregory's document of 6 January 1083, replacing the secular canons at Monk Wearmouth and Jarrow by monks, which appears in this form, is, however, a forgery.[43] 'Sacrosancta' may stem from Gregory VII but its main evolution took place between the 1120s (Honorius II) and the 1150s (Anastasius IV).[44] The taking of the monks and their house under the protection of St Peter is in common use by the pontificate of Innocent III[45] but when it is first found is not clear. The language is redolent of the early-twelfth-century papacy.[46] This common form might, by the thirteenth century, be followed by 'especially the church of X', as in the case of the church of Ilam (Staffs.), confirmed to the abbot and convent of Burton, or by a long list of churches, patronage rights, manors and vills, lands, rents and so forth, down to the last fishpond or mill, as for Great Malvern.[47] Often the donors of the lands and goods are named, as Ralph de Bello Fago and Matilda de Chauz to Shelford (Aug. Notts.), and their charters mentioned and confirmations cited.[48] It is possible that this documentary evidence would have been taken to the curia in the original, or, perhaps more likely, noted on a roll.[49] The abbot and convent of Battle obtained a 'Sacrosancta' from Honorius, which confirmed the liberties and immunities granted to the monastery by William I, and possessions, rents and goods detailed in charters of the Conqueror and of Stigand, bishop of Chichester, thus obtaining a confirmation of some very doubtful grants indeed.[50] In the 'Sacrosancta' which was acquired by the chapter of Exeter, the 'authentic (document)' of H. the late bishop, giving them the church of Colyton, is mentioned: in a similar form for Holy Trinity, London, the legate Guala's licence for the approp-

[41] For the background see J. Fried, *Der päpstliche Schutz für Laien und Fürsten* (Abhandlungen der Heidelberger Akademie 1, 1980).

[42] See JL ii 814–15, cited by Herde; and Herde, *Audientia* i 416 n. 8.

[43] JL 5256, pd *Hist. Dunelm. scriptores tres*, ed. Raine, App. p. vii.

[44] Fichtenau, *Arenga*, 110 (no. 219) and see JL 7231, 7233, 9894.

[45] e.g. *Letters*, ed. Cheney, no. 13.

[46] See Herde, *Audientia* ii Q 9, 2 and 2a.

[47] *Reg. Yr.* 1 no. 397, *Reg. Hon. III* no. 521, *CPL* 46.

[48] *Reg. Yr.* 2 no. 812, *Reg. Hon. III* no. 992, *CPL* 51.

[49] See below pp. 107–8. The Wells proctors in 1242–3 appear to have carried two inspeximuses to Rome, perhaps entered on a roll; see C. M. Church, *Chapters in the early history of the church of Wells* (London 1894) 397–407, and HMC *Wells* ii (1914) 544–5 nos. 39–40.

[50] *Battle Cart.* fol. 50r–v; abbrev. fol. 23.

riation of the church of Braughing is cited.[51] The prior and convent of St Frideswide's referred to confirmatory letters of the diocesans, Bishops Hugh and William of Lincoln, which were mentioned in the papal letter:[52] Bishop William of Blois's charter of 1203 × 1206 had been entered in their cartulary.[53] In instances where no detail or details of the confirmed possession are given, as for the prior and convent of Glastonbury and the prior and convent of Ely, one suspects that the English copyists have omitted the details in their registers.[54] Where confirmations, as for the abbot and convent of Lilleshall and for the abbot and convent of Thorney, spoke of liberties conceded by King John and by Bishops Hervey and Nigel of Ely, presumably these 'liberties' were defined in other documents which could be produced.[55]

The insertion of the details into the common form of 'Sacrosancta Romana ecclesia' would have been an easy operation. Two documents in this form issued for the same house within a period of ten days suggest separate petitions. It might be desirable to have separate documents for specific purposes rather than one great confirmatory sheet of parchment which could not be split into parts. On 2 March 1227 the prior and monks of Durham acquired a 'Sacrosancta' which confirmed the liberties conceded to them by Archbishop Thomas of York and approved by Archbishops Thurstan and Roger. Seven days later, on 9 March, another 'Sacrosancta' was conceded to them, confirming the appropriation of the church of Ellingham for the maintenance of the poor and of the hospice.[56] The prior and convent of Broomholm acquired confirmation of 'the liberties which W. de Glanville, their patron and founder, and Robert of Worstead, knight, had conceded to them, the churches of Paston (Norf.) and Bacton (Norf. or Suff.) and lands, possessions, rents and other goods' in a 'Sacrosancta' of 18 January 1226. Ten days later, on 28 January, lands, possessions and rents in the vill of Bodham and in Westwick, and rents in 'Staldeford', Belaugh (or Bylaugh, Norf.) and 'Litlecros', given them by Ranulf Glanville, and all goods, were confirmed in another 'Sacrosancta'.[57] The separate grants might represent also the submission of separate charters: the above papal letters differentiate between the

---

[51] Below App. 2 nos. 5 and 21.

[52] *St Frideswide's Cart.*, ed. Wigram, i no. 209.   [53] Ibid. no. 43.

[54] e.g. *Glastonbury Chart.*, ed. Watkin, i 140 no. 197 (*Mon. Angl.* i 42 no. 59, and Glastonbury Reg. A fols. 64v–5 and B fol. 91v) and Liber M Ely fols. 8v–9 (pp. 16–17).

[55] Lilleshall Cart. fol. 45v; Thorney Red Bk ii fol. 413r–v.

[56] Durham Loc. III no. 49 (Cart. I fols. 10v–11r: was 2.1 Pap. 13); 1.1 Archid. Northumb., no. 6 (Cart. II fol. 51v: was 2.1 Pap. 6).

[57] Broomholm Cart. fols. 9v–10v.

donors as if the proctors supplicated under single heads, by donor or donors and by place or places. The age of the massive privilege – massive in size and content, as also in its price – was waning fast.

Two special 'Sacrosancta' documents in the papal registers do not concern religious communities but are confirmations to individuals. Savaric de Mauléon received confirmation from the pope in a 'Sacrosancta Romana ecclesia' of 21 September 1216 of the grant made to him by King John, in letters patent, of the lands of Geoffrey de Mandeville and Reginald de Cornhill, in return for the services there defined and saving all rights of churches.[58] When Honorius confirmed and exemplified a deed of Guala, dated at Malvern on 17 March 1218, which instituted the pope's kinsman and *familiarius*, Giovanni de Thebaldo, clerk, in the church of Lambeth on the pope's special order, the form 'Sacrosancta Romana ecclesia' was selected.[59]

'Cum a nobis'

Closely analagous to 'Sacrosancta Romana ecclesia', but at least twice as common, was the form for confirmations, 'Cum a nobis'. Seven originals survive in this form for Honorius.[60] In origin perhaps not as early as 'Sacrosancta' – it is first found in Jaffé in 1184 under Lucius III[61] and may have achieved its final shape under Celestine III – it was used for almost every kind of confirmation. It is difficult to distinguish why it was chosen sometimes rather than 'Sacrosancta' and vice versa. The arenga, 'Cum a nobis...perducatur effectum', led on to the *Eapropter*, the reason for the grant, which mentioned the taking of the petitioners ('personas vestras et locum in quo divino estis obsequio mancipati') under St Peter's and the pope's protection. For Blyth (Hodstock), a leper hospital, for which we have an original, plain *domus* was substituted for *locus* and the rest of the phrase, which was the common form for religious communities, was omitted.[62] A requirement, as expressed in the formulary of the *audientia*, mentioned that for a leper house or hospital 'locum in quo sub communi vita degitis' should be substituted; the simple *domus* seems to be intended to be in line with that.[63] The general protection and confirmation was followed

---

58 Reg. Yr. 1 no. 25, *Reg. Hon. III* no. 37, *CPL* 41. Reg. *etc. usque inclinati.*
59 Reg. Yr. 3 no. 153, *Reg. Hon. III* no. 1663, *CPL* 59. Reg. more traditional: *etc. usque confovere. Eapropter etc.*
60 Below App. 2 nos. 2, 8, 18, 36, 46, 48 and 53. For the form under Innocent III see e.g. *Letters*, ed. Cheney, no. 90, and Sayers in *BIHR* xlix (1976), an original, pd p. 135.   61 JL 15060.
62 Below App. 2 no. 53.   63 Herde, *Audientia* ii Q 9, 2 and 2a.

frequently by a *Specialiter* clause, naming a particular church or churches; the church of St Paul, Bedford, for the prior and convent of Newnham, the church of St John, Mayfield (Staffs.) for the prior and convent of Tutbury, the church of Dalton le Dale for the prior and convent of Durham, and the church of St Alkmund for the abbot and convent of Lilleshall.[64] In some instances these were confirmations of appropriations which were apparently fresh in the petitioners' minds, as the appropriation to Glastonbury of the church of Street with its chapel.[65] General confirmations of property, detailing the vills, as for the Hospitallers in England, or listing the churches, as for Holy Trinity, London, were also issued in this form,[66] as were confirmations of all liberties and immunities, of rents, and of tithes, and of benefices to individuals.[67] This was the form chosen to confirm Aaron, Archbishop Stephen Langton's clerk, in the chapel of St Nicholas, Sevenoaks; by the time of Nicholas III it was commonly used for confirming benefices to clerks.[68] It was also used to confirm that no new church or oratory should be built within the boundaries of the parishes of the prior and convent of Durham, without their consent and that of the diocesan, and to pronounce that the archdeacon should not take procurations when visiting the abbey of Easby unless he had with him only the minimum number of followers as laid down in the decree of the Fourth Lateran Council.[69] It might also be the chosen form for confirming a judicial settlement, usually a composition or arbitration, before judges delegate.[70] This was the form chosen, too, by the curial official when an inhibition was placed against the expenditure of the oblations given to St Edmund on apparently frivolous purposes.[71]

An analysis of the seven originals shows that the Bury confirmation lacks the phrase putting them under the protection of St Peter and of the pope. It proceeds directly from the pope's assenting to their prayers or postulations to the confirmation of Barton Mills (Suff.) with

---

[64] Below App. 2 no. 18; *Tutbury Cart.*, ed. Saltman, no. 2; Durham, Chamberlain's Cart. fol. 4 (Cart. Vet. fol. 37r–v); and Lilleshall Cart. fol. 45v.

[65] *Glastonbury Chart.*, ed. Watkin, i p. v no. 15.

[66] St John of Jerusalem Cart. (detached portion) fols. 145v–6r; cf. Herde, *Audientia* ii Q 12, 1a. Below App. 2 no. 2.

[67] On liberties and immunities, cf. Herde, *Audientia* ii Q 8, 1, 1a, 1b, 1c; on confirmations of rents and of tithes in this form, see e.g. Ely Liber M fol. 8v (p. 16) and Crowland Cart. fol. 96.

[68] Reg. Yr. 2 no. 904, *Reg. Hon. III* no. 998, *CPL* 52. Herde, *Audientia* i 419; ii Q 11, 2b, 3, 6 and 9.

[69] Durham Cart. Vet. fol. 36v; Easby Reg. fol. 317v.

[70] Bradenstoke Cart. fol. 31v; and *St Frideswide's Cart.*, ed. Wigram, i no. 46. Cf. Herde, *Audientia* ii Q 14, 3 and 3a.

[71] *Pinchbeck Reg.*, ed. Hervey, i 31, 43 (ibid.).

liberties, possessions, rents and other appurtenances, which Robert de Hese had given them. Like the Blyth confirmation, which mentions a particular donor, in that case the founder William de Cressy, reference is made to letters in which the grant 'is said to be contained'.[72] In the case of the Hereford document, a general and detailed confirmation, mention is made of gifts of R(ichard) late king of England and of the bishop (of Hereford) and also of liberties and immunities granted by the late King John 'and the princes of England'.[73] The other originals give no indication of documentary evidence, produced or cited, but the copies speak of other charters or name the donors. Confirmation of the church of Whaplode to Crowland abbey defined the grant as set out in the charter of Bishop Hugh of Lincoln.[74] When Waxham church (Norf.) was confirmed to the Augustinians of Hickling the papal letter recited that it had been conceded to them by Archbishop Hubert 'bone memorie'.[75] The diocesan's assent to appropriate or annex is noted; for example, for Glastonbury to appropriate the churches of St John, Glastonbury, and of East Pennard, with their chapels,[76] and for the dean and chapter of Salisbury to annex Melksham church (Wilts.) with the chapel of Earl Stoke.[77] Confirmations to Durham priory specify grants of their bishops and of the archbishops of York.[78] Documents which cite the assent of the diocesans or name the donors, as for example the confirmation to the warden and brothers of the hospital of St Laurence, Canterbury, confirming especially the rents given by Richard de Mare, present as many problems as those which give no details, as the original 'Cum a nobis' for the prior and convent of Totnes which simply states the chapels of Brixham, Broad Clyst and Ashprington (Devon) 'and your other goods'.[79] Are we to imagine a curia issuing documents of confirmation without actually seeing the documentary evidence as to the gifts of the properties or of the assent of the diocesans when required? In some of the confirmations (as with 'Sacrosancta') there are mentions which suggest that if original documents were seen it was at a stage prior to the curia making the grants. But would a wise petitioner have set out for Rome bearing an original charter of King John or an *actum* of Hubert Walter with him? To have lost the original would have been dire. If we are to assume

[72] Below App. 2 nos. 48, 53.
[73] Ibid. no. 8.
[74] Crowland Cart. fols. 79v–80.
[75] Hickling Cart. fol. 45r–v.
[76] Glastonbury Regs. A fol. 30, B fol. 92 (pd *Glastonbury Chart.*, ed. Watkin, i 22 no. 33, and *Mon. Angl.* i 30 no. 21).
[77] Salisbury, D. and C. Reg. Rubrum fol. 137v and see Lib. Evid. C no. 487.
[78] Durham, Cart. Vet. fols. 36v–7.
[79] St Laurence, Canterbury, Cart. fols. 11v–12; and below App. 2 no. 36.

that the curia did not confirm 'blindly' – and that would seem very unlikely – then use must have been made of authenticated copies. The English Chancery would only exemplify its own originals.[80] Did the papal Chancery work on the supposition that if the details proposed were incorrect the petitioner would be unable to uphold his rights anyway or was the word of the proctor, presumably on oath, enough to allow for the issue of the document? With the confirmations of the papal judge-delegate sentences we are on surer ground, for here the papacy, like the English royal Chancery, was confirming its own documents; otherwise acts and originals, or certified copies of them, would surely have been needed. This introduces the question as to whether originals were produced in more than one copy.

When Honorius III confirmed the rights of the abbot and convent of Reading over the priory of Leominster, which the bishop and chapter of Hereford had conceded, it was at the written request of the legate, Guala, who had presumably provided a digest of Reading's case.[81] It is likely that the written assent of the bishop and of the chapter of Hereford was required, at least by Guala, before making his submission, for Reading were to be given the right to regulate and dispose of all that belonged to Leominster. When Thorney sought papal confirmation of their rights over the churches of St James, St Guthlac and Whittlesey, they stated that they had been acquired with the assent of the bishops of Lincoln and of Ely.[82] It is difficult to imagine that the papal curia would not have required tangible evidence of this approval.

Some light is thrown on this matter by the following. In the 1290s a collection of documents was taken to the curia by the bishop of Lincoln's proctor, Robert of Warsop. This collection included not only the *procuratoria* necessary as his credentials and to empower him to appoint proxies and raise loans, but also originals, public or notarial instruments, rolls of processes, authenticated copies, and memoranda concerning documents that had preceded him in the baggage of Master Richard of Willoughby. Mention is also made of a trunk or chest of documents which had been sent previously with another of the bishop's proctors, Master Stephen of Tathwell. Of particular interest are the notes which show that where papal documents were taken to the curia, in each case the other ('alia') was retained at home. 'Pairs' of papal letters are also referred to in a note recording that some of the bishop's documents had been left in a poke or small bag at Theydon Mount.

80 Maxwell-Lyte, *Historical notes*, 218–19.
81 Reading Carts. A fol. 78v and B fol. 65 (pd *Mon. Angl.* iv 57 no. 9), P 6098.
82 Thorney Red Bk ii fol. 414.

Similarly the public instrument of the sentence which this papal letter confirmed went with the proctor to the curia, while a copy remained with the bishop.[83] The impression given is of the existence and circulation of numerous documents and copies. The movement of the originals — and in the case of the papal letters many of them seem to have been in pairs or were duplicated — was not totally circumscribed.[84] Resort to many copies, notes as to the whereabouts of documents and numerous lists or inventories bear witness to the large amount of 'parchment work' which the proctor both generated and needed to take with him. The almost careless abandonment of the papal documents at Theydon Mount, besides the other evidence above, speaks of a world of many copies and authenticated copies, and there seems little doubt that the position was the same with prudent proctors and petitioners before the papal court some seventy years earlier.

Mention has been made above of a 'Sacrosancta' for the prior and monks of Durham which was granted on 2 March 1227 and which confirmed the liberties conceded to them by Archbishop Thomas of York and approved by Archbishops Thurstan and Roger.[85] Some ten years earlier in 1218, a very similar confirmation had been issued to them confirming the dignities and liberties which had been granted to them by Archbishops Thomas and Thurstan in which the form 'Cum a nobis' had been used. On the same day in 1218, Durham acquired another 'Cum a nobis', in which the churches of Aycliffe and Pittington were confirmed to them for the purposes of feeding the poor and entertaining guests.[86] It is obvious why they should have wanted a separate document dealing with separate grants, but it is not obvious why one form should have been chosen rather than the other. Four confirmations for the prior and convent of Broomholm issued on 18, 28 (two) and 29 January 1226 comprise two in the form 'Cum a nobis' and two in the form 'Sacrosancta'.[87] Whether 'Cum a nobis' was used or 'Sacrosancta' seems to have been a matter of no significance, depending no doubt on which form the curial official dealing with the matter chose. Either form was considered appropriate and acceptable in the later formularies. 'Sacrosancta' had developed for this use earlier and possibly now was giving way to the popular 'Cum a nobis', but it certainly tells us nothing important about curial practice. What exactly

---

[83] *Rolls and register of Bishop Oliver Sutton 1280–99* vi (Lincoln Rec. Soc. lxiv, 1969) ed. R. M. T. Hill, 12–14, and see 63–4.

[84] Below App. 2 nos. 7, 19, 23, 25–6, 33, 49 and 54 are all probably duplicates.

[85] Above p. 103.

[86] Durham, Cart. Vet. fols. 36v–7.   [87] Broomholm Cart. fols. 9v–10v.

was confirmed in each particular papal letter was determined conceivably by the proctor's precise petition or supplication which in turn may have been influenced by what particular documents (or certified abstracts of them) he had in front of him.

'Solet annuere sedes'

'Solet annuere sedes' was another form which was appropriate to the confirmation of liberties and immunities, lands, possessions, churches, agreements, rents and appropriations.[88] It might also, but less commonly, take the community and their place of worship and their goods under papal protection and employ the *Specialiter* clause.[89] The arenga 'Solet annuere sedes apostolica piis votis et honestis petentium precibus favorem benivolum impertiri' does not date from as early as the first quarter of the twelfth century and the pontificate of Honorius II, as Jaffé thought: that particular letter belongs to Honorius III.[90] The earliest 'Solet annuere sedes' that has been noted comes from the reign of Innocent II and dates from 1138 × 1143.[91] The form developed further in the second half of the twelfth century. By Innocent III's pontificate, it was common: there are 133 examples in Potthast and 32 in Cheney.[92] The form, as it was preserved in the formulary, was for the confirmation of all liberties and immunities.[93]

Four originals survive for England from Honorius's pontificate. The first, for the abbot and convent of Dore, confirms the land given by John, late king of England, for enlarging the convent's millpond. In common with many Cistercian charters, the bounds and measurements are given, 'the land in wood and field (*planus*) which lies between the river called Dore and the stream called Trivelbroc, in breadth twenty feet of land from the source of the Trivelbroc to the land of the Hospitallers'. King John had granted this land free from all exactions and services as 'in autentico exinde confecto plenius continetur'.[94] The second confirmed specifically an annual rent of twenty marks from the church of Witham to the dean and chapter of the secular college of

---

[88] e.g. Durham Cart. I fol. 9v; Dover Cart. fol. 94; Reg. Yr. 2 no. 1077, *Reg. Hon. III* no. 1295; Durham, Cart. Vet. fols. 36–7v; and *Mon. Angl.* i 137 no. 29.

[89] e.g. the hospital of Hampton (Middx), see St John of Jerusalem Cart. fol. 169; and Battle Cart. fol. 50, abbrev. fol. 23.

[90] JL 7340, pd *Historia et cartularium...S. Petri Gloucestriae*, ed. W. H. Hart (RS xxxiii, 1865) ii no. 500. For this reason it was not included by Holtzmann in his *Papsturkunden in England* (see i 36). See also Herde, *Audientia* i 414 n. 8.

[91] JL 8295α.

[92] See Herde, *Audientia* i 414–15 n. 8 and *Letters*, ed. Cheney, no. 86 etc.

[93] Herde, *Audientia* ii Q 8, 1a, 2, 2a and 2b. [94] Below App. 2 no. 10.

St Martin le Grand, London.[95] The general confirmation in this form for the leper hospital of Clattercote took the prior and brethren and their hospital with all their goods (present and future) under papal protection and confirmed their possessions and rents and added that nobody should attempt to extort tithes of gardens and animals' food from them. In this way it incorporated a papal inhibition.[96] The fourth original is a concession or licence to the abbot and convent of Keynsham (Aug. Som.) to appropriate the church of Burford (Oxon.). The *Eapropter* clause is replaced here by 'Ex parte siquidem...'.[97] Similar forms were used for the bishop of Salisbury's licence to appropriate the prebend of Kingsteignton (in the diocese of Exeter) to the uses of the common fund, for Battle abbey's appropriation of the church of Hailsham (Sussex), and for the confirmation of the appropriation by the abbot and convent of St Augustine's, Canterbury, of the church of Selling and the prebend of Guston to the uses of the chamber.[98] This last letter also added the confirmation of the churches of Lenham and of Chislet to the uses of the refectory and the infirmary as confirmed by popes Urban and Celestine. A confirmation of the church and vill of Shipley (Sussex) to the Knights Templar drew attention to the assent of the bishop and chapter of Chichester;[99] and in the papal confirmation of the churches of Holy Trinity and Oakley with their chapels and appurtenances to the priory of St Frideswide's, Oxford, mention was made of letters of Robert, bishop of Lincoln, 'bone memorie' (entered in the cartulary), and of his chapter.[100] The letters apparently approved possession, not appropriation. A registered 'Solet annuere sedes' for the abbess and convent of St Edward, Shaftesbury, granted on their petition, was an inhibition to them to admit nuns over the number of one hundred as the house was unable to support more.[101]

'*Iustis petentium desideriis*'

The form 'Iustis petentium desideriis dignum est nos facilem prebere consensum et vota que a rationis tramite non discordant effectu

[95] Below App. 2 no. 15.
[96] Ibid. no. 14. Cf. no. 53, for Blyth: both were impecunious leper hospitals and needed protection for their essentials of life.
[97] Below App. 2 no. 43.
[98] Salisbury, Reg. Rubrum fol. 117r–v (pd *Reg. S. Osmund*, ed. Rich Jones, i 365–6) and Exeter Cart. p. 76; Battle Cart. fol. 51r–v (abbrev. fol. 23); and *Mon. Angl.* i 137 no. 29.
[99] St John of Jerusalem Cart. fol. 148r–v.
[100] *St Frideswide's Cart.*, ed. Wigram, i no. 44, and see no. 27.
[101] Reg. Yr. 2 no. 791, *Reg. Hon. III* no. 982, *CPL* 51.

prosequente complere' is found first in a fragment of a letter of Lucius II of 1144 which takes a church under papal protection and confirms its possessions.[102] The arenga did not become invariable until after the middle of the twelfth century but there were many examples. Jaffé lists as many as 489 and after 1198 the number was much greater.[103] The forms as they found their way into the formulary of the *audientia* mainly concerned the confirmation of benefices.[104] Confirmations of churches and of appropriations of churches in this form were common.[105] A slightly variant form of 'Iustis (...loci approbata repugnet)' is found in a letter of Honorius confirming the church of Great Paxton with its chapels to the abbot and convent of Holyrood, which included an indult for Holyrood to establish two of their brethren in the church, one to be presented to the bishop to receive care of souls and to answer to him concerning spiritualities and to the abbot and convent touching temporalities.[106] The form was used also for the confirmation of prebends and for the confirmation to religious houses of cells. The document confirming to the chapter of Lincoln the prebend which had been instituted and endowed in their church by the late Philip de Kyme, whose son S. de Kyme had petitioned the pope, was 'Iustis petentium...complere' and was registered, as was the confirmation to W. Malclerc, canon of Southwell, of a grant made to his prebend of the grove of 'Neuhay' by the archbishop of York to whose income it belonged.[107] In 1219 the dean and chapter of Salisbury petitioned Honorius III that non-residents should forego one-fifth of the revenues of their prebends which amount should go, they said, to the commons of the residents. The form selected was 'Iustis petentium desideriis'.[108] When Peter Sarracenus, a knight of the Roman Empire, received a papal confirmation of a grant by Richard, bishop of Durham, and royal chancellor, of £40 per annum at the Durham exchequer, it was in the form 'Iustis petentium' and may have been a payment in lieu of some other provision for himself or his family.[109] 'Iustis' was chosen also

---

[102] JL 8685.

[103] See Herde, *Audientia* i 419; *Letters*, ed. Cheney, no. 70 etc.

[104] Herde, *Audientia* ii Q 11, 1, 2, 2a, 8 and 9a.

[105] e.g. of the churches of Meldreth, Stetchworth and Witchford to Ely; Liber M fol. 19 (p. 17). Ely already had a 'Sacrosancta' from Innocent III confirming especially the first two named churches and also Impington and Whittlesey (ibid. fol. 8rb).

[106] *Reg. Antiquissimum of...Lincoln*, ed. C. W. Foster (Lincoln Rec. Soc. xxix, 1935) iii no. 820.

[107] Reg. Yr. 3 nos. 7 and 46, *Reg. Hon. III* nos. 1564, 1606 (pd *Reg. Gray*, ed. Raine, 134), CPL 57. Cf. Herde, *Audientia* ii Q 11, 1.

[108] Salisbury, Reg. Rubrum fol. 116v (pd *Reg. S. Osmund*, ed. Rich Jones, i 366).

[109] Reg. Yr. 3 no. 400, *Reg. Hon. III* no. 1876, CPL 62.

The Diplomatic of the Letters

for confirming the cell of Kilburn to the abbot and convent of Westminster and the cell of Wetherall to the abbot and convent of St Mary's, York.[110]

In spite of the formulary's concern with benefices, 'Iustis' could be used much as 'Sacrosancta', 'Cum a nobis' and 'Solet annuere sedes', that is to say it could confirm liberties, immunities, possessions, lands, rents, tithes and sentences,[111] and could take the recipients and their houses under St Peter's and papal protection, as was the case with Hickling, Lilleshall, Leiston, Dunster, Kersey hospital, Abingdon and Thorney.[112] What is more the *Specialiter* clause could be used; 'especially their men in the vill of Stanford and their possessions and other goods' for Thorney, and especially a moiety of the church of Waxham (Norf.), the patronage of Horsey (Norf.), an annual rent of sixteen shillings, homage in Caister (Norf.) and Parham (Suff.) for Hickling.[113]

Of the three originals,[114] Thorney's has the papal and Petrine protection clause before proceeding to the *Specialiter*. The Tynemouth letter omits this section and goes straight on to confirm the appropriation of the church of Woodhorn (Northumb.) and its chapel, which was reported to have taken place with the consent of the diocesan, the bishop of Durham, of his chapter, and of the patron of the church. The third original is a confirmation of a judge-delegate sentence, issued at the request of the prior and canons of Holy Trinity, London, in whose favour the sentence had been given.

As has been noted, papal confirmations of the appropriation of churches were made frequently in this form and there is indication that stringent provisions were laid down by the curia for the provision of adequate portions for the future vicars, in line with the requirements of Lateran IV, before the confirmations were granted.[115] Reference to the consent to appropriations of the diocesans and their chapters, and of the patrons, and to the donors of property when a manor or advowson was confirmed – to Hubert de Burgh, for example, when the manor and advowson of Weston were confirmed to the

---

[110] *Mon. Angl.* iii 427 no. 7 and 586 no. 31.
[111] e.g. Abingdon Reg. fols. 18 (*Reg. S. Osmund* i 364), 18v and 27; Peterborough MS 1 fol. 96v (fol. lxxxiv); and Broomholm Cart. fol. 9v.
[112] Hickling Cart. fol. 45; Lilleshall Cart. fols. 45v–6; *Leiston abbey cart.*, ed. Mortimer no. 5; Somerset RO Dunster Castle MSS Box 16 no. 2; King's College, Cambridge Muns. O 35; Abingdon Reg. fol. 18r–v; and Thorney Red Bk ii fol. 414.
[113] Thorney Red Bk ii fol. 414; Hickling Cart. fol. 45.
[114] Below App. 2 nos. 9, 11 and 50.
[115] Reg. Yr. 2 nos. 1056, 1057, *Reg. Hon. III* nos. 1251, 1264, CPL 54.

112

Templars[116] – suggests contingent documentation. In the case of the confirmation of the advowson of Bamburgh church (Northumb.) to the prior and convent of St Oswald, Nostell, which had been granted them by King John in a charter dated *per manum* by Richard Marsh, the chancellor, on 13 September 1215, a partial exemplification was included in the papal letter.[117] When the church of Holkham (Norf.) was confirmed to the abbot and convent of St Martin al Cimino, Viterbo, King John's grant was quoted.[118] The formulary of the audience also cites an additional use of 'Iustis' for indults concerning the tithes of *novalia*; an example is found in the Easby register.[119]

'Ea que iudicio'

'Ea que iudicio' dates from the beginning of papal delegation. The first instance in Jaffé comes from the pontificate of Alexander III from which time it was in frequent use, occurring later in the formularies of the *audientia* for the confirmation of arbitrations and compositions.[120] A surviving original for the prioress and convent of Littlemore (Ben. nuns, Oxon.) confirmed an agreement with the abbot and convent of Oseney (Aug. Oxon.) over certain tithes, which had been made with the mediation of the abbot of Abingdon and his colleagues, the papal judges delegate.[121] A similar confirmation of a composition was issued to the abbot and convent of Peterborough, following mediation by the legate Niccolò of Tusculum, in a case between them and the parson of Irthlingborough concerning land and other things.[122] Definitive sentences, as the form 'Ea que iudicio' implies, were also confirmed in this way; an annual rent for Binham in 1225, the tithes of the granges of the abbot and convent of Rievaulx, within the parish of Pickering, to Hamo, dean of York, in 1220, and the church of Topcliffe (Yorks. NR) to the dean and chapter of York in 1221.[123]

---

[116] St John of Jerusalem Cart. fol. 136v.

[117] Reg. Yr. 2 no. 854, *Reg. Hon. III* no. 1041, *CPL* 52.

[118] Reg. Yr. 1 no. 278, *Reg. Hon. III* no. 350, *CPL* 45. P 5463.

[119] Herde, *Audientia* ii Q 27, 1; and Easby Reg. fol. 317; cf. below App. 2 no. 41.

[120] Herde, *Audientia* i 429 n. 27, and see 85, 99 and 109, and ii Q 14, 1.

[121] Below App. 2 no. 42, issued on the same day as an indult for Abingdon concerning tithes (see no. 41, below).

[122] Peterborough MS 1 fols. 93v–4 (fols. lxxviiiv–lxxixr).

[123] Binham Cart. fol. 182v; and York, D. and C. Reg. A pt 2 fols. 12 (also in BL Cotton MS Vit. A ii fol. 128v) and 95v–6 (York Minster inventory A fol. 41v).

'Cum omnipotens deus'

'Cum omnipotens deus' confirmed an indulgence of one-quarter of their major sins and one-half of their venial sins, which was conceded by the bishops of Moray, Rochester and (?) Achonry (Architen'), to those visiting the altar of St Mary in the church of St Martin, Dover, on the anniversary of its dedication. The prior and convent of Dover, who requested papal confirmation, had stated that the altar endowment was meagre and could only support one chaplain.[124]

INDULGENCES

'Quoniam ut ait'

'Quoniam ut ait...metet vitam eternam', which cited St Paul's words to the Corinthians: 'Qui parce seminat, parce et metet: et qui seminat in benedictionibus, de benedictionibus et metet', had appeared by the pontificate of Eugenius III (1145–53).[125] A document in this form in favour of Aynho hospital is recorded under Innocent III, and two originals come from Honorius.[126] The first original granted a relaxation of forty days of penance to those visiting the cathedral at Canterbury, within the octave of the translation of St Thomas, and was addressed generally to all the faithful in Christ. The other exhorted 'all Christian faithful of the province of Canterbury' to provide money for the repair of St Mary's priory, Southwick, as the church was in need of repair owing to its antiquity and the ravages of civil war. The document stated the province, as required in a near contemporary formulary of the Chancery, and mentioned the *nuntii* (in the formulary, *questionarii*, or collectors of alms, are specified, unless the letters are for lepers, Cistercians, friars or enclosed nuns) who were to make the collection.[127] When Bishop Gilbert Foliot had appealed for money for the building fund at St Paul's, London, in about 1175, he had used a similar document and quoted the words of the apostle. In this and in other fund-raising examples, messengers were sent to other dioceses and indulgences were issued by the individual diocesans for those who contributed.[128] In 1201, Robert of Shrewsbury, bishop of Bangor, issued an indulgence in the 'Quoniam ut ait' form for those not only in his own diocese who gave alms to St Paul's, London, but also in

[124] Dover Cart. fol. 56v.   [125] Ad Corinthios Secunda, cap. ix c. 6. JL 9639.
[126] Aynho Cart. mm. 2, 3 (ibid.); below App. 2 nos. 7 and 52.
[127] Below App. 2 no. 52. For the formulary entry see Haskins, 'Two Roman formularies', 278.
[128] R. Graham in *Jnl. of the Brit. Archaeol. Assoc.* 3rd ser. x (1945–7) 73–6.

other dioceses whose bishops approved the indulgence.[129] The usual term for the indulgence in both papal and diocesan letters was forty days: the advantage of the papal indulgence, however, was the appeal to a wider public and also the applicability to all the dioceses in the province without the special consent of each bishop. All Christian faithful of the dioceses of London, Lincoln and Rochester were enjoined to support the hospital of St Bartholomew, London, with gifts and contributions in an indulgence granted by Honorius in November 1224,[130] and 'the faithful throughout the whole of England' were addressed in 1218 in a relaxation of forty days' penance to those contributing alms to the Benedictine nuns of St Mary, *De Pratis*, Derby, for the repair of their church and buildings. The copyist of the letter – the original does not survive – apparently misread the word 'Quoniam' and rendered it 'Unde vero'.[131]

INDULTS

'*Religionis vestre promeretur*'

'Religionis vestre promeretur...decimas extorquere presumat' was one of the forms used to exempt the recipients from the payment of tithe on lands acquired before the Fourth Lateran Council which were worked by their own hands or at their expense. The one original in this form exempted the abbot and convent of Abingdon from payment on these lands and also from tithe on meadows, mills and fisheries on which the petitioners declared that they had never paid tithe.[132] On the same day, 15 May 1224, an indult for Abingdon (which had not been used recently) was renewed, exempting them from the payment of tithes from *novalia*, cultivated by their own hands, and of animals' fodder.[133] One of these two indults was doubtless that referred to in the papal register in a mandate of 1 March 1225, when the archdeacon of Berkshire was instructed to end a suit between the rector of Witham (Berks.) and the abbot and convent of Abingdon 'notwithstanding an indult' which the abbey were alleged to have obtained from the curia making no mention of this controversy.[134] In the light of this comment it appears that such indults might be granted without a very

---

[129] *Documents illustrating the history of S. Paul's cathedral*, ed. W. Sparrow Simpson (Camden Soc. n.s. xxvi, 1880–1) no. 1.

[130] St Bartholomew's Cart. i fol. 56v.

[131] BL Wolley Ch. xi 25.

[132] Below App. 2 no. 41.

[133] Abingdon Reg. fol. 17v (pd *Reg. S. Osmund*, ed. Rich Jones, i 362–3).

[134] Reg. Yr. 9 no. 231, *Reg. Hon. III* no. 5353, *CPL* 101.

detailed probe into the veracity of the petitioner's statement, but it must be said that the concessions were made in such wide terms that controversy must have been the not infrequent outcome.

The Abingdon 'Religionis' shows very considerable variations if compared with a 'Religionis' for St Frideswide's which is registered in their cartulary. The St Frideswide's indult immediately diverges from Abingdon's after the initial protocol. Using the *Eapropter* clause, common in letters of grace, it then takes the house under Petrine and papal protection before proceeding to:

Ad hoc vobis auctoritate presencium indulgemus ut de novalibus habitis ante consilium generale, que propriis manibus aut sumptibus colitis, seu de vestrorum animalium nutrimentis aut de ortis, nullus a vobis decimas extorquere presumat.[135]

The variation, which is apparent also in the poem which reads 'Religionis vestre promeretur honestas ut vos graciam sedis apostolice prosequentes postulacionibus vestris quantum cum Deo possumus annuamus', arises from the newness of the form and indicates that where documents do have a rigid and unaltering form it is from long usage. Besides 'Religionis vestre promeretur', 'Vestre religionis honestas' and 'Benignitatis sedis apostolice' were also available for this indult.[136]

'Cum aliquando cogente' was the form used for the other original of this kind, an indult for the Cistercian order in general, exempting them from the payment of tithes on lands which had been acquired before the general council and cultivated by others, if they have been returned to them and are now cultivated by their own hands or at their own expense.[137] Such indults were common for the orders, especially the Cistercians and the Premonstratensians, and were distributed widely to the daughter houses. There is no indication of the original ownership of this document. A 'Cum aliquando cogente' of the same type is copied into the register of St Mary, Newbattle (Scotland) and there are many more examples.[138] Mandates were issued in favour of the orders for enforcement, if necessary; for the Cistercians 'Cum abbates Cisterciensis' and for the Premonstratensians 'Benefaciens dominus bonis' and 'Contingit interdum quod' are found in cartularies of the

---

[135] *St Frideswide's Cart.*, ed. Wigram, i no. 47 (has *nos* for *vos* in the 'Religionis' clause).
[136] Battle Cart. fols. 50v–1 (abbrev. fol. 23v); and Peterborough MS I fol. 97v (fol. lxxxiiv – a later example).
[137] Below App. 2 no. 25.
[138] *Registrum S. Marie de Neubotle*, ed. Cosmo Innes (Bannatyne Club 1849) no. 259, P 7314; and e.g. P 7320 (A. Manrique, *Annales Cistercienses* iv (Lyons 1649) 269).

houses of the orders.[139] The declaration of the Fourth Lateran Council on the *novalia* issue produced this particular indult which remained in its infancy under Honorius III.[140]

'*Petitio vestra nobis*'

On 12 March 1224 Honorius III granted an indult commencing in this way to the prior and convent of Durham, on their petition, that they should not be bound to continue to pay annual pensions to a number of clerks if they refuse benefices when offered.[141] Another form, 'Ex parte vestra', was employed for the abbot and convent of Glastonbury in 1225, when they were released from paying pensions to clerks once they had been provided with churches of an equal value, and for the abbot and convent of Ramsey for the same purpose in 1224.[142] Similarly 'Ex parte tua' was used for the archbishop of York by Gregory IX when he conceded that the archbishop should not be held to provide for clerks who refuse a provision as not substantial enough, unless special mention is made of this indult.[143] In the same genre, in favour of the abbot and convent of Peterborough, is a mandate to the prior of Swavesey and two rural deans of the diocese of Ely ordering them to force clerks of the dioceses of Lincoln, Ely and London who are in receipt of pensions from Peterborough to accept benefices when offered.[144] The interpretation of Bliss that these clerks, in the case of Durham, were clerks of the papal chamber proceeds from a misreading on his part.[145]

'*A nobis humiliter*'

The indult 'A nobis humiliter' and its variants exempted the recipient from service as a judge delegate.[146] 'A nobis humiliter' was one of the more common of the possible forms. Three originals survive: two in

---

[139] *Mon. Angl.* v 536 no. 15, P 7031 from *Reg. S. Marie de Neubotle*, 196, and *Leiston abbey cart.*, ed. Mortimer, nos. 20–1 (P 5991).

[140] Lateran IV can. 55.   [141] Below App. 2 no. 37.

[142] Glastonbury Regs. A fol. 62 and B fol. 92v (pd *Glastonbury Chart.*, ed. Watkin, i 131–2 no. 179, and *Mon. Angl.* i 38 no. 47), P 7479; Reg. Yr. 8 no. 254, *Reg. Hon. III* no. 4767, *CPL* 94.

[143] *Reg. Gray*, ed. Raine, 184.

[144] Peterborough MS 1 fol. 104r (fol. lxxxixr).

[145] See below App. 2 no. 37, ll. 2–5. Bliss misread *de camera vestra* as *de camera nostra*: the phrase surely means that the clerks were being paid out of the monastic chamber. Another confusion has arisen over the Glastonbury indult because the copyist of a late Glastonbury cartulary turned 'quod clerici *ablatis* ecclesiis resignent pensiones' into 'clerici *abbatis*'.

[146] See Sayers, *Papal judges delegate*, 143–4.

this form for the abbot of Bayham and for the prior of Holy Trinity, London, and one 'Cum propter rerum' for the prior of the hospital of SS. James and John at Brackley.[147] None was registered and one specified that those hearings which were in progress should be completed. Other forms of this concession were 'A nobis vestra', 'Cum preter rerum', 'Cum propter cognitiones', 'Cum sicut exhibita', 'Devotionis tue precibus', 'Ex parte tua', 'Tua nobis devocio' and 'Ut indempnitati monasterii'.[148] Examples of indults producing the same effect have been discovered from as early as 1141 (Innocent II) but the very considerable variation of the forms as late as the first quarter of the thirteenth century adds to the likelihood that the indult was still only in the process of acquiring a common form under Honorius III.[149] It may be no more than coincidence but neither original of 'A nobis humiliter' is a good example of papal calligraphy: both have every appearance of hurried execution. In one the scribe omitted one word and in the other he used abbreviations appropriate to the *littere cum filo canapis* and not to the *littere cum serico*.[150] 'Cum propter rerum', on the other hand, is well written, but the 'Nulli ergo' and 'Si quis autem' clauses were omitted and the tironian *et* was incorrectly used for this type of document, suggesting a carelessness.[151] All the examples (originals and copies) state that the exemption will not hold good if special mention is made of the indult notwithstanding.

MANDATES

The original mandates exhibit examples of seven common types: 'Dilecti filii' (or 'Dilectorum filiorum'), 'Ex parte', 'Ex relatione', 'Oblata nobis', 'Rogerus de Moris' (the name of the petitioner), 'Significantibus' and 'Sua nobis'. They all indicate the supplication of the petitioner who had, either himself or by proctor, outlined the case for the preparation of the minute. As to which form of proem was used seems of little significance, probably depending on the form of the original petition. Certainly no particular distinctions can be made

---

[147] Below App. 2 nos. 39, 51 and 56. Other examples of 'A nobis humiliter' are *Leiston abbey cart.*, ed. Mortimer, no. 91 for the abbot and prior of Leiston, and Ely, Liber M fol. 9 (p. 17) for the prior of Ely, pd *Mon. Angl.* i 488 no. 35. It does not occur in this form in *Letters*, ed. Cheney.

[148] Easby Reg. fol. 317; Waltham Cart. fol. 73; Bardney Cart. fol. 23v, St Augustine's Canterbury, Carts. A fol. 25v and B fol. 66v (Reg. Yr. 5 no. 567, *Reg. Hon. III* no. 3291, *CPL* 80); Pinchbeck Reg. (Bury) fol. 17v (pd *Pinchbeck Reg.* i 42); Hickling Cart. fol. 45v; Glastonbury Reg. B fol. 92v; and Peterborough MS 1 fol. 94.

[149] Sayers, *Papal judges delegate*, 144.

[150] Below App. 2 nos. 51, 56.   [151] Ibid. no. 39.

to connect the opening words of the mandate (after the greeting) with the subject of the case. 'Dilecti filii', 'Ex parte', etc. were used indiscriminately: what mattered for the efficacy of the judicial mandate was the description of the case and the terms of the delegation.

The Durham 'Dilectorum filiorum..Prioris et Capituli...precibus inclinati presentium' concerned alienated goods, a variant of the 'ea que de bonis' form which gave the delegate officers wide and general powers of restitution: 'Mandamus quatinus ea que de possessionibus et aliis bonis ecclesie Dunelmen' alienata inveneritis illicite vel distracta ad ius et proprietatem ipsius legitime revocetis', followed by the 'contradictores', 'testes' and 'quod si non omnes' clauses.[152] It is an early use of the 'ea que de bonis' which became common under Innocent IV.[153] The two other 'Dilecti' mandates are made out against named persons: S., T., H. and W. of Chichester and of Winchester dioceses; and R. de Montfichet, knight, R. rector of Hallingbury (Essex) and 'quidam alii', both clerks and laymen of London, Lincoln and Rochester dioceses. The disputes concerned tithes, possessions and 'res alie' in one case, and a certain quantity of hay, tithes and 'res alie' in the other. The usual powers were granted to see that the judges' decision was observed, that witnesses were not suborned and that the commission could function if one of the three judges was unable to undertake the hearing.[154]

'Ex parte' was used in two of the originals: firstly for a mandate to the archdeacon of Worcester and the chancellor and the dean of Oxford, on the petition of the abbot and convent of Oseney, to examine witnesses and record their evidence as to the abbey's rights to tithes in various parishes, and secondly after an appeal by the prior and convent of Durham in the course of the hearing of a delegated suit on the ground that the judges (the dean of York and his colleagues) refused to have the *acta* transcribed according to the requirements of the general council.[155] The hearing of the case was now transferred to the abbots of Rievaulx and Byland and the prior of Newburgh, with instructions to them to declare null and void anything done after appeal and to settle the matter or remit it fully researched to the curia. The case concerned tithes and 'res alie'.

---

[152] Ibid. no. 27; cf. Herde, *Audientia* ii 75–6.
[153] See Herde, *Audientia* i 39, and in *Traditio* xxii (1966) 326 and n. 92, and Marinus nos. 3366 and 3369 in *Die Formularsammlung des Marinus von Eboli*, ed. Schillmann.
[154] Below App. 2 nos. 4 and 40.
[155] Ibid. nos. 16 (cf. Herde, *Audientia* ii Q25 'De testibus') and 28 (cf. Paris, Archives Nationales L 240 no. 100, pd Rabikauskas, '"Auditor"', 242–4, and see above p. 36). 'Ex parte' was also used for indults; see above p. 117.

'Ex relatione' commenced a mandate, addressed to the bishop of
Winchester, and the abbot and prior of Dorchester, in a marriage case
after an appeal. The newly appointed judges were to hear it or return
it to the first judges, in that case condemning the appellant to pay
costs.[156] 'Oblata nobis' ordered the chapter of York to restore to the
prior and convent of Nostell the church of Bramham (Yorks. WR),
which belonged to them by reason of their prebend in York minster.[157]
It may have followed a hearing of which no record now remains.
'Significantibus..Priore' was issued on the complaint of the prior and
convent of Durham that the archbishop of York was delaying in his
examination of the election of Master William Scot, archdeacon of
Worcester, to the see of Durham. He was ordered to proceed within
two months of his receipt of this mandate.[158] 'Sua nobis' dealt with
the question of the obedience of the prior and convent of Holy Trinity,
London, to the prior and convent of St Botolph, Colchester, and
'Rogerus de Moris' initiated a complaint by this clerk against the abbot
of Beeleigh (Essex) and others of the diocese of London over a certain
sum of money 'and other matters'.[159]

Certain mandate forms were restricted to certain uses; for example,
to give protection. 'Postulavit a nobis' was employed to see that
sentences were observed.[160] 'Non absque dolore' was favoured in
mandates ordering the punishment of offenders,[161] and the form
'Quoniam nimis dispendiosum' ordered three ecclesiastics to act,
employing ecclesiastical censures to deal with malefactors whenever
requested by a particular religious house. An example from this
pontificate applied to the Sussex Cistercian house of Robertsbridge.[162]
This last letter is found under Innocent III and like 'Non absque dolore'
was really a letter of protection cast in the mandate form;[163] there are
further examples issued by Gregory IX in the same vein. Finally the
form 'Satis ut accepimus' was used customarily when enabling many
of the English episcopate to forbid hereditary succession to benefices:
it is an example of a mandate of reinforcement where the pope gave
the bishops, on their petition, special power to act in line with previous
papal declarations on the subject.[164]

---

[156] Below App. 2 no. 31.   [157] Ibid. no. 1; cf. *Letters*, ed. Cheney, no. 380.
[158] Below App. 2 no. 57.
[159] Ibid. nos. 17, 47. See Herde, *Audientia* ii K 2 and π 10, 15–16, and 18.
[160] e.g. York D. and C. Reg. B fol. 143 (also in A pt 2 fol. 84v).
[161] Kent Archives Office, De L'Isle and Dudley U 1475 T 264/391 (cf. *Letters*, ed. Cheney,
no. 127).
[162] De L'Isle and Dudley U 1475 T 264/190 (form pd *Letters*, ed. Cheney, no. 619).
[163] See *Letters*, ed. Cheney, p. xv.   [164] See below Chapter 4, p. 146.

PRIVILEGES

'*Religiosam vitam eligentibus*'

'Religiosam vitam eligentibus...eterne pacis inveniant. Amen' has a venerable history stretching back to Pope Gregory the Great, who used the form in January 593 to order Gratiosus, subdeacon, to transfer a house, with gardens and hospices, in the fourth region of Rome near the place called 'Gallinas abbas', to the Abbess Flora for the construction of a monastery.[165] By at least the eleventh century it had become the established form for the solemn privilege, confirming rights and possessions, usually in great detail, to religious communities. Other variants were 'Pie postulatio voluntatis', 'In eminenti apostolice' and 'In eminenti sedis'.[166] It was the aim of most religious institutions in the twelfth century to possess a privilege of this kind. No originals survive for Honorius III to English religious houses, but copies occur in the cartularies, as for example for the Augustinian abbey of Lilleshall in Shropshire.[167] The Benedictine community of St Albans in Hertfordshire, which had acquired many such privileges previously, received a 'Religiosam' from Honorius on 20 February 1218. The reason for the supplication of a 'Religiosam' at this time cannot be determined – it was possibly the desire of a rich house to keep its privileges up to date and in good order. The privilege was registered at the curia and copied assiduously in most of the cartularies of St Albans and of its dependencies, not surprisingly since the cost of a major confirmation of this kind was enormous. In 1218 Cirencester abbey paid sixty-three marks (£43 6s 8d) in obtaining a major privilege, according to a marginal entry against the cartulary copy.[168] Although this sum presumably includes heavy expenses, it indicates that the actual cost of the document was high if compared with the one mark paid by Winchcombe for a 'Solet annuere sedes' in 1217.[169] The 'Religiosam' may have had the added attraction for St Albans that it confirmed the ties of the cells to the mother house.[170] The solemn privilege required the dating *per manum* of the vice-chancellor and the full subscriptions

---

[165] JL 1221.
[166] See e.g. Abingdon Reg. fol. 16; Reg. Yr. 4 no. 820, *CPL* 73, and P 5545.
[167] Lilleshall Cart. fol. 45r–v.
[168] *Cartulary of Cirencester abbey*, ed. C. D. Ross (Oxford 1964) i no. 160/92 p. 160 n.
[169] *Landboc...de Winchelcumba*, ed. D. Royce (Exeter 1892) i 111.
[170] Reg. Yr. 3 no. 291, *Reg. Hon. III* no. 1887, *CPL* 63, P5993; Large Belvoir Cart. fols. 13v–14v; Binham Cart. fols. 33r–5v, whence pd in *Mon. Angl.* ii 232–3 no. 21, where Ranerius is mistakenly given as vice-chamberlain.

of the cardinals, an expensive process and one which became generally in less demand as the scope of the letter of grace developed. The abbot and convent of Lilleshall, it will be recalled, felt the need for a separate confirmation of the church of St Alkmund, and obtained this in a 'Cum a nobis', although they had the great privilege to confirm all, and this was true of other houses and properties.[171] The solemn privilege, as the most sumptuous of the Chancery's products, maintained its own particular prestige although joined by many cheaper and more popular documents on the market. Many of the earlier petitioners for 'Religiosam' were the Benedictine houses. From Honorius's pontificate, however, come 'Religiosam vitam eligentibus' for the Cistercian house of Robertsbridge, for the Augustinian community of Lilleshall and for the Benedictine alien house of Deerhurst (Glos.), which was dependent on St Denis.[172] 'Religiosam' could be seen as the inclusive confirmation, if that was what was wanted, a compendium of rights and immunities, which, as Robertsbridge's 'Religiosam' shows, extended from taking the monastery and its site under St Peter's and the pope's protection to confirming properties, granges, fishponds and meadows, all detailed and given their location. It also included the inhibition that tithes were not to be exacted from the nutriments of their animals and from land which was cultivated with their own hands. Further concessions, concerning laymen and those fleeing from secular justice, were followed by detailed privileges concerning the abbey, the election of the abbot and the arrangements during interdicts. 'Religiosam vitam' continued in use as the major privilege throughout the century: the Augustinians of St Oswald's, Gloucester, obtained one from Innocent IV, and three years after the foundation of the Ashridge Bonshommes by Edmund, earl of Cornwall, in 1283, 'Religiosam' was seen as the appropriate privilege to seek.[173]

FORGERY

In a society that was accustomed to hearing written communications, it is not surprising that Innocent III, when consulted about the authenticity of a papal letter, should have chosen to have the document read to him rather than to read it by eye.[174] The elegant phrases of

[171] See above p. 105.
[172] Kent Archives Office, De L'Isle and Dudley U 1475 T 264/196; Lilleshall Cart. fol. 45r–v; and *Reg. Hon. III* no. 662, P 5580 and F. J. Doublet, *Histoire de l'abbaye de S. Denys en France* (Paris 1625) 550–2.
[173] *Reg....Corbridge*, ed. W. Brown ii (Surtees Soc. cxli, 1928) 47–8; and Salisbury, D. and C. Literae (see HMC *Various Collections* i 382).
[174] Gerald of Wales, *Opera*, ed. Brewer *et al.*, iii 182.

the papal letter and the mysteries of the cursus were what distinguished it from the products of other chanceries. On the other hand, adherence to set forms made the documents easier to forge.

In cases of suspected forgery of documents that were supposed to be papal, the curia asserted its own right to examine and pronounce on the validity. During the course of the quarrel between Bishop Richard Marsh and the prior and convent of Durham, original documents were ordered to be sent to the curia for verification 'cum ad nos pertinet de nostris privilegiis iudicare', but the order was countermanded until the strife between the king of France and the king of England had died down and the danger of losing the originals had receded. The documents in question were privileges and indults granted by the pope and episcopal letters confirming liberties.[175] Supposed papal letters to Tewkesbury abbey in Gloucestershire, of which the tenor was disclosed, were to be denounced as false by a papal commission, consisting of the bishop of Ely and the archdeacons of Bedford and Huntingdon, unless the convent gave sufficient security to produce the originals at the curia within a specified term.[176] Two years later a commission, consisting this time of the bishop of Ely, the abbot of Warden and the archdeacon of Bedford, was ordered to compel the abbot (P.) and others to show them certain letters, including one by which the abbot asserted his right to wear mitre, ring and gloves and to give a solemn benediction after mass, and to see if such letters agree with the accompanying transcript.[177] Clearly the earlier directive had been ignored and the letters sound very suspect indeed. The text of these supposed papal letters for the abbot of Tewkesbury has not survived to compare with similar privileges, such as 'Ut pulcra et decora filia' granted to the abbot of Glastonbury in 1219.[178] But the abbot, in defence, argued that he had not availed himself of these letters (although it was asserted that he had had them recited and published) and that two excommunicate monks had falsified the convent seal and one of them had falsely accused him of collusion with the papal commissioners enquiring into the matter.[179] Another monk of Tewkesbury, H., had obtained in December 1223 false papal letters for R., proctor of the archdeacon of Gloucester, and had obtained them, as he said, in ignorance: in 1224 he petitioned the pope to join the

---

[175] Durham, D. and C. MS IV 24 fol. 104. I owe this reference to the kindness of Dr Meryl Foster.   [176] Reg. Yr. 6 no. 455, *Reg. Hon. III* no. 4067, *CPL* 88.

[177] Reg. Yr. 8 no. 349, *Reg. Hon. III* no. 4863, *CPL* 95 (Bliss's extract is very inaccurate).

[178] See *Glastonbury Chart.*, ed. Watkin, i 137–8 no. 191, *Mon. Angl.* i 41 no. 55, Regs. A fol. 64, B fols. 91v–2, P 6076 and *CPL* 68.

[179] Reg. Yr. 10 no. 294, *Reg. Hon. III* no. 5982, *CPL* 111.

Carthusians.[180] That false letters circulated in considerable numbers
cannot be doubted, but did the recipients always know that they were
false? According to the monk H., he had been deceived by the clerk
in Rome from whom he had bought the letters for the archdeacon's
proctor. The story illustrates the existence of touts at Rome, eager to
take advantage of the uninitiated and unwary who might, indeed, not
recognize a forgery. A clear advantage of the use of a reputable standing
proctor was a certain guarantee for the genuineness of the document.
Simon Pimme, prior of Worcester, was suspended for using forged
papal letters. These were possibly letters acquired in Rome – Pimme
had certainly been in Rome and in 1223 was at Bologna, suffering from
what proved to be a fatal illness – and possibly letters acquired
unwittingly as forgeries.[181] Honorius's register reveals that there were
some forgers at work at the curia between 1220 and 1225 who had
been using a false die (*falsus cimeus*). Following the discovery, the
English archbishops and bishops – apparently the destination of the
letters was England alone – were ordered to request all clerks to
produce for examination any papal letters and indults (especially those
concerning multiple benefices) that they had acquired during this
period; doubtful ones were to be despatched to the curia for scrutiny.[182]
In 1225 the abbot and convent of St Mary's, York, were ordered to
send to the curia for examination all their privileges and indults
exempting them, as they declared, from visitation and correction by
the archbishop of York.[183] It had been noted already that false or
suspected privileges were being used by certain religious in the diocese
of York,[184] and in the following year, 1226, a papal letter addressed
to the archbishop and chapter of York quashed a pretended privilege
and an indult of Celestine III. These allowed the abbot of St Mary's
to excommunicate the *invasores* of the territories of the monastery,
amongst whom, in St Mary's eyes, the archbishop of York was clearly
numbered, and declared that no archbishop, bishop or official might

[180] Reg. Yr. 8 no. 162, *Reg. Hon. III* no. 4642 (and see no. 4648), *CPL* 94.
[181] Reg. Yr. 6 nos. 277, 314, *Reg. Hon. III* nos. 3882, 3890, *CPL* 86. The first of these
letters was cancelled in the register, presumably because of the similarity of the second
letter of four days later. Bliss (*CPL*) totally misread this entry, turning the prior into
the prior of Bologna and the mandate (Reg. Yr. 7 no. 198, *Reg. Hon. III* no. 4413,
CPL 92) did not include the archdeacons of Salisbury and Lincoln as he states. Further
documents in the case are Reg. Yr. 6 nos. 359 and 420, *Reg. Hon. III* nos. 3905, 4020,
CPL 87. For Pimme see *Fasti*, ed. Greenway, ii Monastic cathedrals, 103.
[182] Reg. Yr. 9 no. 321 bis, *Reg. Hon. III* no. 5476, *CPL* 102.
[183] Reg. Yr. 9 no. 305, *Reg. Hon. III* no. 5460, *CPL* 102.
[184] Reg. Yr. 6 no. 428, *Reg. Hon. III* no. 4032, *Reg. Gray*, ed. Raine, 152 n., *CPL* 88.

issue sentences of excommunication, suspension or interdict against St Mary's without a special papal or legatine mandate.[185]

Tests for forgery in all chanceries depended upon detailed scrutiny of the seal: in the papal Chancery this was a minute analysis of the *bulla*. The *bulla* did not change in design after 1116, when Pope Paschal II introduced the heads of the two apostles, Saints Peter and Paul, to the reverse and the pope's name and number in the nominative to the obverse.[186] Innocent III, in his decretal on forgery, insisted on a careful examination of the form of the *bulla* and the way in which it was attached. False dies circulated in the 1220s and the *bulla* would not have been as difficult to forge as a fine wax seal. The reverse of the design of the *bulla* did not change from pontificate to pontificate and the obverse demanded little attention as it consisted only of the pope's name and number, 'HONORIUS PAPA III', for example, so that on the death of Innocent it was necesssary to change only the name: there was no elaborate style as with royal seals. More insidious, of course, was the application of a genuine *bulla* to a forged document. This was not unknown. Not all papal officials were above bribery and the possibility of inserting a forgery in a bundle of genuine documents awaiting bulling is noted in Innocent's register.[187] There was also the possibility of transferring a genuine *bulla* from a defunct document to a false concoction, as the nuns of Wix had done in the late twelfth century, following a disastrous fire which destroyed most of their records.[188] This was the reason for paying attention to the way in which the *bulla* was appended.

THE *BULLE*

Twenty-one *bulle*, four of them detached, survive for Honorius's originals in England.[189] None of them is suspicious, nor any of the

---

[185] Reg. Yr. 10 no. 236, *Reg. Hon. III* no. 5861, *CPL* 109. The papal letter is also in York D. and C. Reg. A pt 3 fols. 99r–v, with date 15 March 1226, and 98v–9r, but with the date 31 March, as in the archiepiscopal cart., fol. 68.

[186] See R. L. Poole, 'Seals and documents', *Studies in chronology and history*, ed. A. L. Poole (Oxford 1934, repd 1969) 90–111, esp. 101, and *Papal Chancery*, 199 no. 3.

[187] *Reg. Inn. III*, ed. Hageneder *et al.*, i no. 349, c. 5 X V 20, and P 365.

[188] See C. N. L. Brooke, 'Approaches to medieval forgery', *Jnl. of Soc. of Archivists* iii no. 8 (1968) 377–86, esp. 381 and the 2 plates, and 'Episcopal charters for Wix priory', *A medieval miscellany for Doris Mary Stenton*, ed. P. Barnes (PRS n.s. xxxvi, 1960) 47–8.

[189] See App. 2 nos. 3–4, 6, 13, 17 (detached), 19, 23, 24 (detached), 26, 29, 30 (detached), 32–3, 38–40, 42, 46, 54 (detached) and 55–6. Nos. 6 and 55 are particularly fine examples. Two further detached *bulle* of Honorius III, which may not have come from English archive sources, are in the Fuller collection of seals in the Palaeography Room, University of London Library.

documents to which they belong, but it is difficult to compare bulls in scattered repositories, some of which are in a poor condition. There is no indication that Honorius used a *demi-bulla* before the new die was ready. The *demi-bulla* was simply the reverse of the *bulla*, leaving the obverse blank. The stamp for the reverse of Honorius's *bulla* was that used by Innocent III on 30 March 1215 and by Gregory IX in May 1227: in use, as Poole has pointed out, from 30 March 1186 to 8 June 1252.[190] The points round the circumference numbered seventy-three, the aureoles round St Paul's head twenty-five and round St Peter's twenty-six. The points composing the hair of St Peter's head came to twenty-five in number and twenty-eight for his beard. There was no variation from this and the identical design confirms that it was the same die. No such similarity is found for the obverse of the *bulla* under Honorius. A comparison of three *bulle*, dating from 1218, 1221 and 1226, shows the use of three different stamps.[191] The placing of the letters in relation to the dots forming the border is not identical. Furthermore the tilt of the letters in (HONO)*RIUS* (l.2) is very obvious in (1), noticeable in (3) but not observable in (2), a much more regular design. Finally the letters themselves are not identical. The H is different in all three, and the O is much more closed up and elongated in (2) than in (1) and (3). Fifty-nine points encircle the obverse of Honorius's *bulla* in an example of 1222 (they are too damaged to count in the three examples cited above): under Innocent the number was forty-eight.[192] The measurements of the obverse of the bulla were *c.* 3.7 cm × 3.7 cm; of the reverse, smaller, *c.* 3.5 cm × 3.5 cm. The significance of the various dies needs further detailed investigation.

CORRECTION

Once the letter was engrossed by the papal scribe, it was conveyed to the corrector. Only one of the fifty-six documents has a correction mark.[193] No entirely satisfactory explanation has been provided as to why this mark appears in the top extreme right-hand corner on the face of some documents, while not on others that show clear signs of

---

[190] See PRO SC 7/19/7 and 46/2. Poole, *Papal Chancery* (following Diekamp) 201.

[191] Below App. 2 nos. 6, 17 and 55. Diekamp originally distinguished three different dies (*MIOG* iii 621–2 and plate nos. 28–30; and see P. M. Baumgarten, *Aus Kanzlei und Kammer*, Freiburg 1907, 157). Probably only one accords with the PRO three, see plate nos. 28–30.

[192] Below App. 2 no. 24. The circumference dots of plate no. 29 in Diekamp, which can clearly be counted, total fifty-nine, not forty-nine, as Diekamp says. For Innocent III, see PRO SC7/19/17; 19/15.   [193] Below App. 2 no. 53.

The Forms

correction. Three documents passed the corrector's examination which should not have done so. All were indults: one omitted the 'Nulli ergo' and 'Si quis autem' clauses and abbreviated the *et*s, the second was incorrectly abbreviated in the manner for *littere cum filo canapis*, and the third omitted a word which has been clumsily added in the margin, perhaps by the hand of the English recipient.[194] We can have no idea either of how many engrossments were scrapped and entirely rewritten. Nor have any completely satisfactory explanations yet been given of the *ad* marks which occur in some documents placed above the corrector's mark, as in the one example below, where *ad bar'* is written: this has been struck through, but whether by the same hand or another is not clear.[195] *Ad* marks occur in four further instances, always followed by a name or names, or initials: Nicolaus, Simon and Ellis (or Willelmus) – this pair twice – and ?f and ?s.[196] *Bar* is presumably a contraction of Bartholomeus. In one further instance, the initials p. B., without the *ad* mark are given in this same top right position. P. B. was the scribe of this document.[197] An explanation of their purpose must lie in whose names these are. There are five possibilities: the corrector, the proctor, the scribe, the bullators, the messengers.

The first possibility that this is the name of the corrector or correctors, as Diekamp thought,[198] and whom Cheney appears to follow,[199] has been put in grave doubt by Herde on the ground that by the mid-thirteenth century, when the notes are more plentiful, not one can be identified with the correctors. Furthermore the *ad* marks appear to be in different hands from the *cor* marks. Numbers 33, 34 and 36 show no obvious signs of correction: no. 21, on the other hand, has been corrected clearly in lines 5 and 8. Baumgarten suggested the second possibility that the marks were associated with the proctors because of the appearance of the word *procuratori* in this position in one case;[200] yet Herde finds only one instance out of thirty-three where the name corresponds with that of the proctor as given on the dorse.[201] No identification can be made of Bartholomew, Nicholas, Simon and Ellis, and f. and s. with proctors of Blyth leper hospital, the archbishop of York, Stefano, cardinal deacon of S. Adriano, and the prior and convent of Durham: the evidence is too insufficient to lead us either

---

[194] Ibid. nos. 39, 51 and 56.
[195] Ibid. no. 53.
[196] Nos. 22, 34–5, 37.
[197] Below App. 2 no. 31.
[198] 'Zum päpstlichen Urkundenwesen von Alexander IV. bis Johann XXII. (1254–1334)', *MIOG* iv (1883) 523.
[199] *ASAR* anno xii (Turin 1973) 11–12.
[200] 'Miscellanea diplomatica iii', *Römische Quartalschrift* xxxii (1924) 76–7.
[201] *Beiträge*, 193–4 and 288.

127

way. The third possibility is that the name might be the scribe's, or somehow associated with him as in the case of P. B. This possibility is demolished by the fact that in some instances there are two names in this position and that in two documents issued on 27 February 1224, one to Henry III and the other to his advisers, both have the *ad* marks to two men, Simon and Ellis, but the scribe was in both cases Petrus Gregorii.[202] That the name or names were those of the bullators has not found much favour. None of the *bullatores* of Honorius is known by name so again the evidence is insufficient for any conclusion. The key to the problem may be found in the last possibility. In the Durham letter, after what are apparently the initials f. and s., comes the word *nun'*, presumably the *nuntii* or messengers, who were now to convey the documents to its last stage, the sealing.[203] The stage of the transfer of the document, when completely engrossed and passed by the corrector (to whom it presumably returned on the second attempt) to await the attachment of the bull, is entirely hazy. This was a dangerous period during which the unscrupulous might insert their own documents amongst those approved by the chancery officials. It would be rash to maintain that the marks were always associated with the messengers (and these might include proctors and scribes) but that the marks are in all cases connected with the expedition of the documents and their movement in the final stage, as Herde has maintained, naming them '*expeditionsvermerke*', is as close as we shall get for the early thirteenth century.[204]

'Mainly an authority to dispense' has been used to describe the fifteenth-century papacy.[205] From an examination of the history and development of the forms of papal documents, broadly three bands or phases may be distinguished. The first phase covers the earliest documents and is the age of the solemn privilege which held sway until the twelfth century, when letters of grace and of justice developed. The second phase is that of the papal confirmation for which the letter of grace was used. The third phase sees the growth to dominance of the indult or dispensation. Where the form had been used over many years, there were few variants, as with the confirmations and solemn privileges. Where, however, variants are found, it is because the form was relatively new and had not yet settled to one usage. This is

[202] Below App. 2 nos. 35, 34.
[203] Ibid. no. 37.
[204] P. A. Linehan, in *AD* xxv (1979) 241 and n. 7 and 249, suggests return to the 'notary, *abbreviator* or *rescribendarius*', but to which one and surely not at this late stage?
[205] R. B. Dobson, *Durham priory 1400–1450* (Cambridge 1973) 207, quoting a remark of K. B. McFarlane.

illustrated in the indults of Honorius concerning tithes and judges delegate where the documents appear to follow the order and to repeat the remarks of the petitioners: they had not yet reached the available formularies in definitive form. There were also the hybrid documents, like the conservatory mandates, which illustrate the changing patterns of the papal Chancery. If the label conservative, used of the papal Chancery, is intended to imply static, it cannot be accepted on the above evidence of the forms. Old forms, some very old indeed, were kept where still acceptable, but the papal Chancery showed itself very sensitive to needs and to its own policy requirements. In the history of documentary forms, Honorius's Chancery stands on the threshold of the major development of the indult or dispensation.

PART II

THE LETTERS IN THEIR LEGAL AND
HISTORICAL CONTEXT

Chapter 4

THE LAW OF THE CHURCH

THE LEGISLATIVE PROCESS

The making and compiling of decretal law under Honorius III has not been investigated fully. Yet how the law was made and collected – and by whom – and how compilation of a decretal collection related to the letters written during the pontificate are essential questions to consider. Of the pope's total correspondence, only a small proportion was selected for preservation for legal purposes. The pope might make many juridical points by letter but only those utterances which were known to and chosen by the canonist collectors had any chance of survival for legal and judicial use. Until the first decade of the thirteenth century collections of decretals were made by canonists for their own private purposes – for teaching and for judicial precedent. There was no notion until 1209–10 of an official collection of the decretals of a particular pontiff. For Honorius no private collections of decretals are known, as they are for his predecessor, Innocent III. The one official law collection, the *Compilatio Quinta*, came towards the end of the pontificate. The compiler, the canonist Tancred, took his texts exclusively from the papal registers of Honorius, as has been demonstrated convincingly.[1] Reliance on this sole source suggests that no previous collections of Honorius's pronouncements were at hand or were known to him, and his method of operation lends further weight to this suggestion. The choice of date for making the collection, 1225–6, rather than waiting for the end of the pontificate, was determined probably by the assumption that a decade of letter writing and of judgements presented a suitable volume of material to be analysed and digested. No collections of the pope's letters – either official or private – made after the date at which the compiler of *Compilatio Quinta* put a stop to his labours, are alluded to or have been found.

---

[1] Boyle has traced all but four decretals ('Compilatio quinta', 12 n. 10). Cironius in his 1645 edition of *CQ* had noted the close association with the registers.

To see the *Compilatio Quinta* in context, it is necessary to look at its immediate predecessors. The direct forerunner of *Compilatio Quinta*, as an official collection, was the compilation known as *Compilatio Tertia*. This had been undertaken by the papal subdeacon and notary, Peter Collivaccinus of Benevento, using the registers of Innocent III up to the twelfth year. It was promulgated officially by the pope probably late in 1209 and was the first collection to receive written papal approval.[2] In his letter of commendation, Innocent stated that all the texts in *Compilatio Tertia* were taken from his registers up to the twelfth year, and that they might be used without any scruple of doubt as much in judgements as in the schools.[3] It was not long before the *Compilatio Tertia* replaced the *Collectio Romana* of Bernard of Compostella in use at Bologna.[4] Although Bernard's work, according to Tancred, was also based on Innocent's registers, it was never approved by the pope.[5] At this time, therefore, the *Compilatio Tertia* represented a new departure in the making of a decretal collection: it had been made under papal sponsorship from the exclusive source of the papal registers.[6]

After the *Compilatio Tertia* was compiled and issued, the law continued to be made and so did collections of decretals, some using the registers directly, some indirectly, and some incorporating other sources.[7] Johannes Teutonicus (besides glossing *Compilatio Tertia*)[8] brought together certain decretals issued between 1210 and 1216, using intermediate collections, and he also included the canons of the Fourth Lateran Council to form the *Compilatio Quarta*. For some reason the pope refused formal approval of the work, and it is reported that John left the curia angrily.[9] *Compilatio Quarta* thus joined the private collections, including the *Compilatio Prima* of Bernard of Pavia, incorporating decretals of Alexander III,[10] and the *Compilatio Secunda*

---

[2] It had been mistakenly presumed that the date of the papal letter of promulgation of *Compilatio Tertia* (P 4157) was the same as that of the previous letter (28 Dec. 1210) until corrected by Kuttner (*Repertorium*, 355).

[3] See Hageneder, 'Papstregister', esp. 319, 336.

[4] Horwitz, 'Reshaping a decretal chapter', 207–8. On Bernard, see S. Kuttner in *Traditio* i (1943) 277–340. [5] Hageneder, 'Papstregister', 334 n. 64.

[6] For the marks on the registers, see O. Hageneder, 'Die aüsseren Merkmale der Original-register Innocenz III', *MIOG* lxv (1957) 314–15, and 'Papstregister und Dekretalenrecht', 339.

[7] See Kuttner, 'Collection in Bamberg', 41–56, and Cheney, 'Three decretal collections', 464–83. [8] Ed. Pennington.

[9] Kuttner, 'Johannes Teutonicus', esp. 625–6, 628.

[10] On *Compilatio Prima*, see G. Fransen in *Proceedings of the Second International Congress of Medieval Canon Law* (Monumenta iuris canonici, Series C, 1, 1975) 55–62. Bernard introduced the five-book arrangement of *iudex, iudicium, clerus, connubium* and *crimen*. Alanus attempted the addition of a sixth (see G. Le Bras, 'Bernard de Pavie', *DDC* ii cols. 782–9).

of John of Wales (of 1210–15), formed from the decretals of Popes Clement III and Celestine III, and other collections, such as those of Rainer of Pomposa (1201), Gilbertus (1202–4) and Alanus (*c.* 1206).[11] But what precise difference did papal approval of a decretal collection make?

Kuttner suggested thirty-five years ago that no particular pre-eminent authority attached in the thirteenth century to the *Compilatio Tertia* and the *Compilatio Quinta* that was not accorded to the three private collections (*Compilationes* I, II and IV) in the usage of the law-schools and of the courts.[12] Pennington has since declared that decretal collections were not primarily collections of papal legislative decrees but reports of cases in ecclesiastical courts or responses to consultations.[13] The texts acted more as guidelines than as binding judgements and the medieval jurists believed that they could not only be discussed and questioned but also amplified. In examining manuscripts of *Compilatio Tertia*, Pennington discovered that there were certain decretals that were not in all of them. He therefore set out to answer why some decretals were added to (or some subtracted from) an official collection and why the readings of some manuscripts correspond more closely to the papal registers. On investigation the expanded version of the *Compilatio Tertia*, including the additional decretals, proves to be a French recension, whose redactor had at his disposal collections or originals no longer known to us. Not only did he add decretals to the compilation, but he also reworked the texts of some of the others. This discovery illustrates forcefully that the French redactor at least did not consider Innocent's *Compilatio Tertia* to be an inviolable text but one that could be supplemented and elaborated with detail. The French recension of *Compilatio Tertia* has impelled a re-evaluation of what an official compilation meant to contemporary canonists. It was certainly not the immutable text of a codex or statute book and the canonists did not distinguish in legal importance between the decretals which were included in such a collection and those which were rejected:

Each genuine papal decretal had an authority of its own even if it was not included in any collection, official or otherwise. The French recension proves that the canonists did not think the collection itself, or Innocent III's sanction of it, added authority to the material within the collection....[14]

---

[11] On Alanus and Gilbertus, see R. von Heckel in *ZRG* lx Kan. Abt. xxix (1940) 116–357, and S. Kuttner, 'The collection of Alanus', *Rivista di Storia del Diritto* xxvi (1953) 37–53: among Alanus's immediate sources appear to have been 'one or another from the group of Anglo-Norman collections' (ibid. 52–3).

[12] 'Quelques observations', 308.

[13] 'French recension', 64.   [14] Ibid. 65.

Exactly the same process of adding and tampering took place after the issue of Honorius III's official compilation. In some manuscripts of *Compilatio Quinta* there are four decretals which were not glossed by Tencararius and Jacobus de Albenga and were not, therefore, part of the original compilation.[15] These four decretals are all found in the registers. A study of the seventeen manuscripts of the *Compilatio Quinta* and a new edition is being undertaken by Professor L. E. Boyle and Dr Giulio Silano of Toronto. Until this is completed it would be premature to make detailed comment. But the additions to *Compilatio Quinta* demonstrate clearly a similar desire on the part of the 'improvers' to augment and touch up an official collection to that exhibited by some of the canonists when confronted with *Compilatio Tertia*. The inclusion of additional decretals also illustrates certain predilections of individual redactors and emphasizes the contemporary attitude towards the official collection as being little different from that towards the unofficial collection. According to the canonists Johannes Teutonicus and Tancred, the Innocentian official collection did not preclude the use of other decretal letters. Furthermore, Raymond of Pennaforte, in compiling his *Liber Extra* for Gregory IX in 1234, used the unofficial collections of the Five Compilations as well as the two approved ones, *Tertia* and *Quinta*. These compendia had not, therefore, in his eyes at least, lost their validity and force. After the compilation of the *Liber Extra*, however, the pope admonished the canonists in 'Rex pacificus' not to use any other collection in future. The question as to whether decretals in earlier compilations might still be cited exercised some canonists' minds. Some commentators thought that they could and, although later canonists may have had a stricter view of codification, as Gregory IX himself, the narrower view was not representative of the early thirteenth century. Any papal decretal, new or old, might be grist to the canonist mill.

What then did an official collection mean to the pope? It appears first of all to have meant that the direct source of the collection was the pope's own register. There were dubious decretals in circulation as Innocent III himself commented to the bishop of Ely in 'Pastoralis'.[16] Official approval could stamp certain collections as authentic. The texts of the registers were reliable and while popes could not vouch for the authenticity of their predecessors' texts they could guarantee the genuineness of their own letters. There would have been no point in

---

[15] Pennington, 'French recension', 67–9.
[16] Pd *Letters*, ed. Cheney, no. 22 p. 77; registered and found in Alanus, Bernard of Compostella, *Compilatio Tertia* and X.

Innocent III confirming the *Compilatio Prima* and the *Compilatio Secunda* because they were collections of the decretals of Alexander III, and of Clement III and Celestine III. He could, however, have approved Bernard's collection of his own decretals to 1208 as well as that of Johannes Teutonicus, covering his decretals for the years 1210 to 1216. He chose not to: in the case of Bernard's compilation, approval was withheld because not all of his selection was deemed suitable for the purposes of a model collection. The authority for this is Tancred, who also comments on the pope's refusal to endorse the collection of Johannes Teutonicus but gives no reasons for that rejection.[17] Apparently the major advantage of the official collection was that it cast out doubt. The *Compilatio Quinta* was recommended in equally vigorous terms as the *Compilatio Tertia*, namely that it should be used without any suspicion of doubt for court judgements and for teaching purposes in the law-schools, with the notable addition that the recipients should cause the collection to be received by others.[18] In the case of doubtful decretals popes and canonists counselled recourse to the registers, but this was not easy for judges at a distance from the authoritative source. If such a search failed to reveal the letter, its style was to be considered and also whether the opinion expressed was consonant with other papal rulings. If it concurred in spirit with *ius commune* it could be accepted; if not, the letter should be referred to a superior judge.[19] The official collection could remove all such suspicion and provide authenticated precedent. The import of the approval of the collections for the use of the law-schools is more difficult to assess. The schools and the commentators had used unofficial collections in the past. Furthermore, after the promulgation of *Compilatio Tertia*, they had exhibited a certain obstinacy over discarding the *Collectio Romana* entirely, shaping and adding to the new texts, as we have seen, and indeed reintroducing some of Bernard of Compostella's decretals that Peter Collivaccinus had rejected.[20]

Even the most casual glance at the *Decretales* shows how heavily Raymond of Pennaforte relied on the sources collected for the Five

[17] Tancred's remarks are from his preface to his apparatus on *Compilatio Tertia*, pd E. Laspeyres, *Bernardi Papiensis Faventini episcopi Summa decretalium* (Regensburg 1860) 356–7. See Horwitz, 'Reshaping a decretal chapter', 207 and n. 6, and Kuttner, 'Johannes Teutonicus', 625–6.

[18] Hageneder, 'Papstregister', 345.

[19] See the gloss of Huguccio on D XIX at *De epistolis*, noted and pd by Duggan, *Twelfth century decretal collections*, 41 n. 1. See also Hageneder, 'Papstregister', 333 nn. 60, 61, and 'Pastoralis' cited above, n. 16.

[20] Pennington, 'French recension', 55–6; Horwitz, 'Reshaping a decretal chapter', 207–8; and see above p. 134.

Compilations. Firstly it must be remembered that Pennaforte's collection did not touch the ancient law, presupposing, as Kuttner has said, that the authority in future was *Decretum* and *Decretales*.[21] His task was not one to discover previously unknown *extravagantes* from a variety of sources but to assemble into order and to classify what was known already. To the sources of the Five Compilations, which accounted for 1771 of the 1971 chapters of *X*, were added 191 decretals for Gregory IX's first six years: only nine decretals came from elsewhere.[22] No more was expected of the undertaking than clarifying and arranging what was available. The vast number of decretals in the archives of the recipients throughout Europe lay unremembered and unrequested for the purpose of codifying the canon law up to 1234.

The part played by the papal curia in the circulation of decretals under Alexander III remains extremely hazy.[23] Under Innocent III the 'common core' of certain decretal collections has suggested to Cheney selection within the Chancery by canonists who had access also to central material outside the registers.[24] Indeed Reg. Vat. 7A itself contains a decretal collection (quire 13), including letters not all of which were registered.[25] For Honorius the sequence of registers is complete, so that the unresolved problem of whether certain letters were taken from that source or not does not arise as it does for Innocent. There is absolutely no evidence of extra-registral activity under Honorius III, nor indeed of canonists working within the curia, and the complete lack of private collections might suggest that they were actively discouraged.

It has been suggested that one of the reasons for making an official register of letters of the pontificate was to form a corpus of legal decisions of a particular pope.[26] This presupposes the existence of a registrar or lawyer, selecting letters that were likely to have some legal significance for inclusion in the quaterns; in other words, a prearranged system for the use of later compilers of collections of canons. The truth might be otherwise. As has been argued above, the purpose behind the compilation of the registers was to provide a record of the important business of the curia.[27] What was included reflected the immediate

[21] 'Quelques observations', 208.
[22] Hanenburg, 'Decretals and decretal collections', 588. Raymond of Pennaforte, like the collector of Bambergensis II, presumably took some decretals of Innocent III, which are not in Comp. IV, directly from the registers; Kuttner, 'Collection in Bamberg', 42.
[23] See W. Holtzmann in *QFIAB* xxx (1940) 13–87, esp. 16–17.
[24] Cheney, 'Three decretal collections', 470–1; Kuttner, 'Collection in Bamberg', 41.
[25] Cheney, 'Three decretal collections', 471–2.
[26] Boyle, 'Compilatio quinta', 19.   [27] See above Chapter 2, pp. 72, 75.

interest of the papal government machine – with certain allowances to the desires of the petitioners – and incorporated an account of its current administration. The registers of Honorius show none of the precision that one would expect if the officials in any way premeditated matters of possible legal interest. The argument would thus run as follows. Once the order was made to begin a collection of decretals, the compiler was given access to the register of the pope's letters. At this point he indicated the letters which he found at first sight to be of some interest and which he wished to have copied. From the copies selection was made by the compiler (the canonist) who then sorted his final choice into the major headings of the five books and into the titles, in the case of *Compilatio Quinta*, ninety-four in number. As has been shown, some 570 letters in the registers of Honorius were marked in this way with the selector's crosses.[28] The second stage was the copying, presumably by the chancery scribes; the third was the final selection which could be undertaken only by a trained canonist. At the end of the process 223 chapters were provided from some 210 letters.[29] Because the whole of the collection thus came from the source of the registers it does not follow that the registers were made with this purpose in mind. Influenced by Raymond of Pennaforte's great collection of the previous law of the Church, instigated and approved by Gregory IX, and circulated in numerous manuscripts, we have come to think, surely mistakenly, of an ordered pattern of development and of numerous skilled lawyers within the curia, concerning themselves with the earmarking of decretals as soon as they left the scribe's pen.

The compiler of the *Compilatio Quinta*, the canonist Tancred, became archdeacon of Bologna on 31 January 1226, succeeding Master Gratian. Soon after 3 February the papal court returned to Rome, following six months' absence in Rieti, bringing with it for registration copies and drafts of the documents that had been issued and despatched during that period. Letters of as late as 30 January 1226 were marked for possible inclusion by Tancred and this cannot have been done until they were registered, which, as has been argued above, did not take place outside Rome.[30] By 2 May the whole undertaking – choice, copying, final selection and arrangement into an ordered collection – was completed and probably promulgated. In March, Tancred is known

---

[28] Boyle, 'Compilatio quinta', 11–13; Hageneder, 'Papstregister', 342; and Rabikauskas, '"Auditor"', 217.

[29] Boyle, 'Compilatio quinta', 12–13.

[30] See above Chapter 2, pp. 87–9. This paragraph is based on Boyle, 'Compilatio quinta' (pp. 16–17). I find no flaw in his argument on the sequence of the compilation but I do not find a letter of 13 Dec. marked with a cross.

to have been in Rome, pleading a cause, and it was perhaps then that he made the final selection, allowing a month to put the finishing touches to the work. As the registration of the Rieti letters was not started until the curia's return to Rome, Tancred's work must have been very speedily pursued as soon as the quaterns were completed. The latest of the Rieti letters included in the register – before there is a distinct and unusual gap – is a letter dated 3 February (no. 180, fol. 109v) which is found as the eleventh letter after the last marked one of 30 January (no. 169, fol. 108).[31] Whether or not the sudden gap in the quaterns is due, as Boyle has suggested, to the temporary removal of the scribes from their task of registration at this particular point, it is clear that this material was available to Tancred while that beginning on the new folio (in the middle) was not. The new section does, however, include a few strays going back to 23 January[32] from Rieti – the final letter – but registration picks up again with a Lateran letter of 9 April and then goes on to record letters mainly of February and March with entries from Rieti of 20 November (no. 215) and 31 January (no. 222), before going on to April, May, June and July, as usual in no clear date order, before terminating in the customary disordered strays which clearly came to light at the last minute – in this case going back to March, April, May and June.

It is obvious that not only the copyists but also Tancred worked extremely hard to finish the compilation in the time between early February and the beginning of May. It is also obvious that no first stage collection was available to him nor indeed other selected sources. Neither does it seem likely that Tancred or anyone else held any official 'legal' post within the Chancery. The method of working denies this. Tancred's brief was to sort out the possibly influential legal decisions incorporated in the letters from the mass of administrative material. This material had not been selected previously for this purpose. The papal register might act as a legal precedent book but it was not compiled to serve as one. Any inclusion of future decretal material was incidental to the register's position as an office book of Chancery.

Exclusive reliance on the register – the failure to discover other sources – proceeded from the demands of the situation. It was not feasible for Tancred or others to visit the archive repositories of Europe. No other respectable sources were so conveniently to hand as the registers. No council had been held in the pontificate – indeed the

---

[31] Boyle, 'Compilatio quinta', 17.

[32] Ibid., citing 11 Feb. (no. 212). There are also, however, letters of 20 Nov. (no. 215) and 31 Jan. (no. 222).

requirements of Lateran IV were still being put into effect. In such a situation the major collection of the pope's pronouncements for the reign, the register, was employed. The selective nature of the thirteenth-century papal register – the fact that only a proportion of the letters written were entered in it, varying from between one-quarter to one-third – presents implications for the whole process of decretal collecting and law-making. If, as we know, Tancred used only the registers, what of the *extravagantes*, possibly on extremely important points, that were not available to him? Did these become of no more than antiquarian interest once they had served their particular purpose? The evidence shows that this is so and that the richness of the local sources was ignored in the general desire for centrally made and approved collections of decretals that were not in doubt.

Several examples from the letters of Honorius to English recipients can illustrate this point. The first concerns *De foro competenti*.[33] On 26 May 1222 the counsellors of Henry III were warned and exhorted by the pope not to concern themselves with a case brought to the king's court by Richard de Percy, knight, against the archbishop of York. The case concerned the church of Dunnington (Yorks. ER) which was a part (*membrum*) of the same prebend of York and both the legates, Guala and Pandulf, had forbidden the king's justices to hear it. Had this monition been registered it must have been a good candidate for inclusion as a clear and precise statement that cases concerning prebends could not be pleaded in a civil court regardless of the parties. The Percy family had an interest in the prebend of Dunnington and Richard de Percy had claimed the advowson against the archbishop as early as 1218–19.[34] The case was postponed indefinitely in the Hilary term of 1220, no doubt following Pandulf's prohibition.[35] In point of fact settlement was made by a final concord in 1225, when Percy acknowledged that the lands were the archbishop's as a free prebend in return for concession of the advowson of the church but not of the prebend.[36] While the Third Lateran Council sought in general terms to establish advowson as a matter for the ecclesiastical court, there were large areas of the subject that remained blurred and unsettled.[37] The above ruling dealt specifically with the lay prebends which, although a minority problem, presented peculiar difficulties (it might, indeed, have

[33] Below App. 2 no. 22. 'De foro competenti' is title 2 of Book II in *X* and in *CQ*.
[34] *Rolls of the justices in eyre...for Yorks...(1218–19)*, ed. D. M. Stenton (Selden Soc. lvi, 1937) no. 1120.
[35] *Curia regis rolls* viii (1938) 183.
[36] See *York minster fasti*, ed. Clay, i 69–71; ii pp. xi, 23–4.
[37] See Sayers, *Papal judges delegate*, 184.

been inserted in *De iure patronatus*).[38] The royal court was proving attractive to the layman, but the ecclesiastics were clear that it was not in line with previous papal rulings that ecclesiastical persons should be summoned before a lay court in cases concerning church endowments and collation. Although the archbishop of York might agree to a lay forum it was not in strict accord with canonist doctrine and might therefore have found its place in a law collection.[39]

In a letter of 1221 it was established that witnesses might be interrogated by the appointed commissioners (the archdeacon of Worcester and the chancellor and the dean of Oxford) for the purpose of drawing up public muniments defining the tithes belonging to the Augustinian canons of Oseney at Oxford. From their depositions a public instrument was to be made by the papal delegates which would have a clear validity in the courts.[40] The papal answer to the request for this commission which sets out the above details might have been included under the title 'De fide instrumentorum' or possibly 'De testibus cogendis' had it been registered.[41] The tithes are described as held 'ab antiquo' and the witnesses as elderly. A similar fate of obscurity befell an appeal concerning documentation. The refusal of the dean of York and his colleagues to have the *acta* transcribed, as required by the Fourth Lateran Council, in a suit between I. rector of Embleton (co. Durham) and the prior and convent of Durham, caused Durham to appeal and led to a redelegation to the abbots of Rievaulx and Byland and the prior of Newburgh. The new commission of judges was to investigate the veracity of the charge and to hear the case if it was as alleged or to return it to the previous judges, condemning the appellants to pay costs.[42] Had the second mandate been registered, it might have been deemed worthy of inclusion in 'De appellationibus'.

Canons concerning residence and prebends occur amongst the titles of the Five Books and in *Compilatio Quinta*.[43] The general drift of the legislation under Honorius was in the direction of establishing that papal officers, canons absent in the bishops' service and those absent for the

---

[38] Title 22 Bk III of *CQ* and 38 of Bk III of *X*.

[39] Another letter concerning 'de foro competenti' (or possibly patronage) comes from March 1226 and therefore would have escaped inclusion in *CQ* as coming after Tancred's search was halted, even if it had been registered; see below pp. 145–7.

[40] Below App. 2 no. 16.

[41] *X* II 22 and *CQ* II 14; or *X* II 21 and *CQ* II 13.

[42] Below App. 2 no. 28.

[43] *CQ* Bk III tit. 3 and 4. All of tit. 3 went into *X* and became Bk III tit. 4 cc. 13–15 'De clericis non residentibus in ecclesia vel prebenda'. Of the five chapters of tit. 4, four were absorbed into *X* (c. 31 *X* I 3, 'De rescriptis', and cc. 32–4 *X* III 5, 'De prebendis et dignitatibus'), one was discarded.

purposes of study might receive the revenues of their prebends or benefices but not the daily distributions.[44] The papal officer involved in the decision incorporated in *Compilatio Quinta* was Master Otto, the pope's scribe, who had been given a canonry of Metz.[45] (Tancred himself had the prebend of Yetminster in Salisbury cathedral.)[46] In part the desire to improve the education of the clergy – in order to offset any possible charges that failure to observe the Lateran decrees was due to inadequate teachers – lay behind the concessionary legislation for clerks to enjoy the fruits of their benefices for five years, while studying, which the canonists found in 'Super specula'.[47] On 26 March 1219 Honorius III had written to the dean and chapter of Salisbury that the non-residents among their number should forego one-fifth of the revenues of their prebends: this sum was to go to the commons of the residents.[48] The establishment of a fixed proportion of the income which the Salisbury non-residents were to pay to the common fund represents a further definition on that aspect of the subject, but as it was not registered it had no chance of incorporation in the contemporary legislation.

Alienation of possessions was the subject of an unregistered mandate to the dean, the penitentiary, and John Romeyn, canon of York. They were ordered to revoke any grants of possessions and goods which had been alienated from the church of Durham. This form of mandate, which was the forerunner of the 'Eaque de bonis' of Innocent IV, clearly gave very wide powers and was in effect the beginning of a precedent for this action.[49] It did not, however, find a place in Tancred's *Compilatio Quinta* under 'De restitutione spoliatorum' or 'De in integrum restitutione' because it had not been recorded in Honorius's register.[50] Numerous other decisions on various matters, from the exaction of pedage to the serving of cells of religious houses,[51] or relating to groups of people, such as the Templars, might have been included but for the limitations of registration and hence of the search

---

[44] cc. 2, 3 *CQ* III 3; and c. 1 tit. 4 (cc. 14, 15 *X* III 4 and c. 32 *X* III 5); cf. Alex. III, c. 7 *X* III 4; *Reg. Gray*, ed. Raine, 154 n.–155 n., and York D. and C. inventory A fol. 9v.

[45] c. 2 *CQ* III 3; see above Chapter 1, pp. 44, 45.

[46] See below Chapter 5, pp. 179, 180.

[47] c. 5 *X* V 5 and *CQ* V 2, un. 'De magistris'.

[48] *Reg. S. Osmund*, ed. Rich Jones, i 366.

[49] Below App. 2 no. 27.

[50] *CQ* II 7 (*X* II 17) and *CQ* I 23 (*X* I 41).

[51] Below App. 2 no. 30, appropriate to 'De censibus et exactionibus'; and Gloucester D. and C. Reg. A fol. 93, pd *Acta Stephani Langton*, ed. Major, 76–7 no. 59, appropriate to *X* III 37 (*CQ* III 21: 'De capellis monachorum et aliorum religiosorum').

for suitable material.[52] A discussion of two more areas, however, will suffice.

Kuttner has pointed out how procedural law is virtually untreated in the *Decretum* and how it is only in the late twelfth century that this large and important gap begins to be filled.[53] Although the sections in *Compilatio Quinta* are ample (forming part of Book II), many important decretals must have slipped through the net because usually mandates were not registered. In the case between Henry, archdeacon of Aquileia (Italy), and the chapter of York about Topcliffe church (Yorks. NR), several commissions of judges delegate were involved, including the legate Pandulf. In the course of the hearing Henry alleged that the prior of Kirkham and his co-judge (the prior of Bridlington) had continued to conduct the suit in spite of a papal concession to him for a stay of proceedings until he had completed some other business. Henry also alleged that letters on this negotiation had already been acquired, addressed to the dean of Lincoln and others, which suppressed his title of archdeacon, and that these judges did not give him time to appear and adjudged possession to the chapter of York.[54] A web of procedural problems was brought to light which amplified the decretal law on the subject: *inducie deliberatorie*, the question of describing the title and status of the defendant in the mandate and the appeal of Henry's proctor that the case had not been heard in the correct time.[55] It also appeared that after the sentence of the priors of Bridlington and Kirkham, Henry and his accomplices, with the help of Richard de Percy, had despoiled the church. Throughout the whole affair the dean and chapter of York alleged Henry's powerful secular connections.[56] When the case had begun in Innocent III's time, Henry was probably only in minor office. The need to detail offices and titles in the mandate was still to be clearly defined in the 1220s: the treasurer of York made the same complaint in 1224.[57] Alexander III had declared in 'De mandatis' that mention was to be made of the order of any religious cited, and Innocent III had declared that the clause 'quidam alii' was not to include more important persons than those actually

[52] App. 2 nos. 23 and 32, which might have found places respectively in 'De consuetudine' and in 'De parochiis et alienis parrochianis'.

[53] *Scritti di Sociologia e Politica in onore di Luigi Sturzo* (Bologna 1953) ii 356–7.

[54] Cheney, *Innocent III and England*, 114, and *Letters*, ed. Cheney, no. 709.

[55] See CQ II 4, 'De dilationibus' (X II 8) and CQ II 16, 'De exceptionibus' (X II 25).

[56] York, D. and C. Reg. A fols. 55v–6; pt 2 fols. 95, and 95v–6. Percy confirmed the church of Topcliffe to the fabric of York minster in 1220; *Early Yorkshire charters* xi, ed. Sir C. T. Clay (Yorks. Archaeol. Soc. Rec. Ser. Extra Ser. ix, 1963) 40.

[57] Sayers, *Papal judges delegate*, 68–9 and 290 no. 63.

mentioned, but no precise point had been made about title.[58] It could have been taken from this case.

The second area where the law was extremely sparse was marriage. Book IV of *Compilatio Quinta* contained only three titles and five chapters. Of these five chapters only two were taken for X, which itself was not overstocked with decisions. Book IV of the *Gregoriana* is the shortest of all the books with only twenty-one titles, as opposed to forty-three (I), thirty (II), fifty (III) and forty-one (V). It seems likely that much of the marriage law vanished and the deficiency cannot be made good by the *extravagantes*. The English material produces very little and what there is does not add significantly to the doctrine or the practice of the law.[59] What then is to be made of this lack of material? One possible explanation is that many decisions were incorporated in mandates and hence were not usually preserved or registered.

The other principal source that was not available to the compiler of the *Compilatio Quinta* was the registered and non-registered material for the last twelve to thirteen months of the pontificate produced after he had completed his search and after the compilation in the Spring of 1226. Among the registered letters of the last year are cases of simony, the shedding of blood, married men petitioning for orders, and clerks with concubines who do not reside in their livings.[60] All these provide elaborations on questions which might have attracted the collectors. The decision that nuns and religious of the diocese of Coventry who had simoniacally entered monasteries were to remain there, it being hard on them to be transferred, refined and simplified the canon which required removal to a stricter house.[61] J. H. Lynch, in his study of simoniacal entry into the religious life, has shown how the papacy upheld in theory the strict law but in practice followed a milder course.[62] The Coventry ruling might have been used to mitigate the harsh effects of the law, whereas a judgement of 6 October 1225, that the canons of Newburgh restore land and money which the donor when dying had seen as involving simony, might have been used to stiffen it.[63] In April 1226 a mandate was sent to Walter Gray, archbishop of

---

[58] c. 6 X I 3. 'Quidam alii' was not restricted in number of persons who could be cited until Innocent IV.

[59] e.g. below App. 2 no. 31. [60] *Reg. Hon. III* nos. 576, 5805, 5816.

[61] Reg. Yr. 11 no. 407. fol. 152v, *Reg. Hon. III* no. 6100, CPL 114, c. 40 X V 3.

[62] *Simoniacal entry into religious life from 1000 to 1260* (Ohio State Univ. Press, Columbus 1976) 208, and see chs. 4, 5 and esp. 8.

[63] Reg. Yr. 10 no. 188 fol. 111, *Reg. Hon. III* no. 5679, CPL 107.

York, requesting him to allow P. of Weaverthorpe (Yorks. ER), who had petitioned the pope, to retain the church there, of which his father who was in minor orders had been incumbent, until another suitable benefice was found for him. P. had occupied the benefice for more than ten years and had been properly instituted at the presentation of the true patron, Nostell, who had received the church from William Fitzherbert, treasurer and later archbishop of York (and canonized as St William) and his brother Herbert. But P. feared the letters which Walter Gray had obtained in 1221 against sons succeeding fathers in benefices.[64] According to a decretal of Honorius, which was selected by Tancred for his *Compilatio Quinta*, only the pope could dispense in a case where a son immediately succeeded his father.[65] The persistence of clerical marriage in England explained the special problem of the hereditary succession of the sons of priests to their fathers' benefices and exposed the danger of the benefice becoming something like a lay fee.[66] Attention has been drawn to the high proportion of English cases concerning the sons of priests in X;[67] but although the problem was conspicuous in England it was by no means confined to this country and further definition that was generally accessible would have been useful.[68] From such requests as that of P. of Weaverthorpe the law was developed, and the qualification that P. was to retain the living until provided for elsewhere could have added further definition to the title 'De filiis presbiterorum', *Compilatio Quinta* I title 11.[69] Furthermore the petitions to the pope of some of the prominent members of the English hierarchy, such as Walter Gray, who were determined to stamp out this abuse, produced the details of individual cases from which the law might have been amplified.[70]

---

[64] Reg. Yr. 10 no. 344 fol. 142v, *Reg. Hon. III* no. 5891, CPL 113, *Reg. Gray*, ed. Raine, 153. Reg. Yr. 6 no. 87, *Reg. Hon. III* no. 3607, CPL 84 (pd CS ii pt 1 99 and *Reg. Gray*, 140–1). See *York minster fasti*, ed. Clay, i 94, ii 134–5 and *Early Yorkshire charters*, ed. W. Farrer (1914) i nos. 26–8.

[65] un. CQ I 11 (c. 17 X I 17); cf. c. 31 X I 17 (Alex. III) sons, especially illegitimate sons, not to follow their fathers.

[66] On clerical marriage before 1200, see Brooke, 'Gregorian reform', 69–99; at this period, see Gibbs and Lang, *Bishops and reform*, 158–60.

[67] 'Gregorian reform', 76 n. 14 (cc. 2–5, 7–11 of X I 17).

[68] See B. Schimmelpfennig in *Studies in medieval and renaissance history* n.s. ii (1979) 37 (graph) and 39.

[69] Clause 31 of Lateran IV was enacted against the sons of canons, especially the illegitimate sons, succeeding their fathers: it became c. 16 of X I 17.

[70] The bishops of Carlisle, Coventry, Durham, Lincoln, London, Salisbury and Worcester all acquired mandates to remove married clerks; in the case of the bishops of Lincoln and Worcester the mandates included powers for action against pluralists (Reg. Yrs. 5 nos. 477, 569, 6 nos. 258, 292, and 7 no. 81, *Reg. Hon. III* nos. 3196, 3304, 3806, 3867 and 4217, CPL 79–80, 85–6, 90–1, and 105; and Gibbs and Lang, *Bishops and reform*, 160).

A case concerning 'De foro competenti' came to light in March 1226, when the dean and chapter of York alleged that the justices 'de Banco' compelled them to litigate in a secular court in a dispute over the hospital of St Leonard, York, which belonged to them in free alms. The dean and precentor of Lincoln and the archdeacon of Stow were ordered to induce and if necessary to compel the justices to stop the case.[71] This decision failed to gain registration and furthermore, as it came after Tancred's collection of material for his compilation had ceased, it was destined to remain a decision that was confined to the one particular instance. A similar fate befell the concession of 3 February 1226 made to the archbishop of York that the four dignitaries, who were allowed to be in occasional attendance on him, should not be forced to continual residence in order to share in the rents, and Honorius's answer to the archbishop and chapter's query of the following December whether absentee student clerks might receive commons as well as rents.[72]

After the promulgation of *Compilatio Quinta* in May 1226 no collector of *extravagantes* apparently came forward to select from the decretals of the end of the pontificate. If there was such a collection or, indeed, earlier collections of *extravagantes* for Honorius (as there had been for Innocent III), no trace has been found of them. Some of Tancred's discarded material, which had been copied from the register, or other selections of decretals may have circulated but this is no more than conjecture. Of the four *extravagantes* occurring in some manuscripts of the *Compilatio Quinta* which were noted by Pennington, two have the cross mark beside them (one was included by Cironius in his edition but was omitted by Friedberg) and one, the letter 'Sapientia', has an oblique stroke by it. 'Exspectavimus' has no mark at all alongside it in the margin. It was not marked for inclusion by Tancred because he did not approve of its tenor,[73] but it was found from some source by others who appended it to *Quinta*. Three out of four of the additions concern Benedictine provincial chapters – two reached *X* under the title 'De statu monachorum' – and the fourth concerned the Benedictines of St Augustine's, Canterbury. These additions await detailed investigation.

It might be supposed that only the decretals of Honorius III that were in *Quinta* were examined for inclusion in the *Liber Extra*. This is in fact

71 York, D. and C. Reg. A pt 2 fol. 82v.
72 *Reg. Gray*, ed. Raine, 157–8; and Reg. Yr. 11 no. 419, *Reg. Hon. III* no. 6114, CPL 114.
73 See below p. 154, and Pennington, 'The canonists and pluralism', 43. This strongly suggests that Tancred did the marking.

not so, for among the letters ascribed to Gregory IX in Friedberg is a canon concerning prebends and dignities which is identifiable as taken from a letter of Honorius, dated 17 February 1227 from the Lateran, and hence far too late to get into *Compilatio Quinta*, and addressed to the prior of S. Fridianus, Lucca.[74] It is unlikely that it was confused with the letters of Gregory IX at the point of its selection, for the registers were distinct entities. Its inclusion in *X* suggests that in order to compile the *Extra*, Raymond of Pennaforte looked through the registers of Honorius from the point where he knew Tancred had left off, presumably combining this entry with those selected for Gregory IX, or that he used a manuscript of *Compilatio Quinta* to which this decretal had been added.

The above survey is in no way intended to suggest what should have been included in the official collection of decretals for the pontificate – only to indicate what was omitted inevitably because of the selectivity of the papal register. The limitations that were imposed on what was registered coloured the collection. Petitioners favoured the registration of confirmations which were useless and uninteresting documents to the compilers of books with a legal and procedural interest. Mandates were not of great import to the papal clerks and yet they could well include curial procedural decisions. It might be argued that most cases, where there was a second or even a third mandate, did not escape the attention of the registrars, who needed at this stage to have documentary evidence to monitor the progress of the suit and for reference if required. At this juncture it was likely that directives and decisions of some legal interest would be found, but if a legal point was made in a first mandate it was likely to be lost. What is noticeably in short supply is secular material, especially on marriage. Aspects of the religious life are well represented; all the dealings of clerks, their ordination, legitimization, revenues and activities attracted much attention and material, a feast on which the selectors could work. The preference of the selectors for letters directed to important and royal persons (e.g. Berengaria, Richard I's queen,[75] and the Emperor Frederick II) and to the Bolognese (eight in total) is also noticeable, taking into account the number of possible addressees. It may reflect a very vigorous papal correspondence with royal persons and with the lawyers of Bologna or simply a predilection for these recipients and their problems.

---

[74] c. 38 *X* III 5 and P 9632 (where it occurs among the undated letters of Gregory IX). Reg. Yr. 11 no. 578 fol. 174 (last folio), *Reg. Hon. III* no. 6244. The entry has an oblique stroke by it, as does no. 576.

[75] See *CQ* c. 1 I 15, c. 1 II 2, c. 1 III 2, and c. 2 V 12.

The excerpts taken from amongst the English registered letters for inclusion in the *Compilatio Quinta* total eleven in number: there is also one each for Ireland and Scotland. They deal with the following subjects: custom (Ireland), the office of the vicar, the office of the judge delegate, admissible delays in the conduct of a suit, the maintenance of the *status quo* while the case was pending, sequestration, appeals (one concerning Scotland), married clerks, prebends, patronage rights, restitution of dowry and clerical privileges. Seven of these pronouncements were incorporated in *X*, including the Scottish decretal and excerpts from two letters directed to Queen Berengaria: six were discarded.

The Irish letter was selected for inclusion in the title 'De consuetudine'. It is found in the register for the fifth year and made the point that if an Englishman accused an Irishman of theft he needed only six Englishmen to support him on oath for the Irishman to be bound to make restitution, although the Irishman is ready to purge himself by thirty or more witnesses: furthermore, the oaths of Irishmen are not supported against English thieves. The legate, Giacomo, was directed by the pope to see that the same ruling was enforced for both parties, regardless of nationality. The ruling was not included in *X*: perhaps it was not considered of wide enough import.[76]

The two decretals, one on the office of the vicar and the other on the office and power of the judge delegate, entered the Church's compendium of 1234. The bishop of Worcester in 1222, following his request for empowerment to deal with married clerks and those who succeeded to hereditary benefices, was instructed to take steps to remove them and replace them by perpetual vicars who would be resident under threat of losing their income.[77] The decretal on the office and power of the judge delegate concerned an appeal by John Sarracenus against summons more than two days' journey from his diocese. The judges (the archbishop of Canterbury and his fellows) ignored the appeal and put Jordan,[78] clerk of Durham diocese, into possession of the church of St Nicholas, Durham, which was in dispute between the parties. John's appeal was dismissed on the ground that he had benefices in the dioceses of Rochester and of Ely, and therefore might be presumed to

---

[76] Reg. Yr. 5 no. 22, *Reg. Hon. III* no. 2606, *CPL* 75, P 6325 and c. 3 *CQ* I 3. Cf. the appeal of an Irish priest from Armagh, who had been asked to purge himself by fifty-eight Irish-speaking priests of that diocese, that he could not find that number (*CPL* 48-9).

[77] Reg. Yr. 6 no. 292 (290), *Reg. Hon. III* no. 3867, *CPL* 86, P 7725 and c. 1 *CQ* I 14 (c. 6 *X* I 28).

[78] Jordan in BL Royal MS 11 C vii; Jolanus in Friedberg *CQ*.

Legal and Historical Context

have a domicile within reach of the diocese of Canterbury. It is not known where the parties were summoned to, but presuming that it was in the south of England, Jordan, unless he too was a pluralist, was a long way distant. In the *Liber Extra* the excerpt was incorporated in 'De rescriptis' to make the point that where there were two rescripts in a case, one in the principal cause, the other concerning an appeal, the principal judge cannot pronounce on the validity of the appeal: that must be left to the judge deputed to hear the appeal.[79]

'De dilationibus' came to include a canon formed from a case between the abbot of St Augustine's, Canterbury, and the archbishop of Canterbury, which had been brought to the notice of Innocent III who had given the parties a fixed time in which to prepare their cases for hearing at the time of the forthcoming Lateran Council. When the parties were reconvened, the archbishop asked for an extension of the *inducie deliberatorie*, pleading the difficulties of conferring with his convent. The proctors of St Augustine's, however, maintained that the archbishop could have consulted Christ Church either by letter or by messenger.[80]

'Ut lite pendente nichil innovetur' included two canons, one of which was extracted from a suit between I., rector of Witham (Berks.) and the abbot and convent of Abingdon about tithes at Witham, in the course of which, as I. alleged, Abingdon procured certain indults from the pope making no mention of the current litigation before the archdeacon of Berkshire acting in his ordinary capacity.[81] The mandate to the archdeacon to resolve the case, now appointing him a judge delegate, was dated 1 March 1225.[82] Abingdon had acquired two concessions on tithes on 15 May of the previous year, 1224, one of which survives in the original. Neither was registered. The indult in question is likely to be the original 'Religionis vestre promeretur', relating generally to Abingdon's exemption from tithes, rather than 'Ex parte vestra', which concerned tithes of *novalia* and of animals' food, although the latter indult did make reference to the fact that it was the restoration of an exemption not recently claimed.[83]

---

79 Reg. Yr. 6 no. 297 (296), *Reg. Hon. III* no. 3873, CPL 86, P 7727, c. 3 CQ I 15 (c. 29 X I 3).
80 Reg. Yr. 1 no. 334, *Reg. Hon. III* no. 435, CPL 45, P 7748, c. 2 CQ II 4 (not included in X).
81 Friedberg prints it under title 8 ('De eo qui mittitur in possessionem causa rei servande') of CQ Bk II, as canon 2 (pp. 163–4), with the footnote that it is found in one manuscript as belonging to the next title, 9, 'Ut lite pendente etc.', which is clearly where it should be.
82 Reg. Yr. 9 no. 231, *Reg. Hon. III* no. 5353, CPL 101, P 7752 (it did not get into X).
83 See above Chapter 3, p. 115; below App. 2 no. 41, also Abingdon Reg. fol. 17v and *Reg. S. Osmund*, ed. Rich Jones, i 363.

Elaboration on the law of sequestration was based on a case between R., rector of Barkway (Herts.), and the abbot and convent of Colchester about the fruits of the church of Barkway, during which the abbot of Sibton (Cist. Suff.) and his colleagues put Colchester into possession *causa custodie*. Until the case was decided, the prior of Bayham, the dean of Dallington and F., canon of St Mary's, Hastings (all in the diocese of Chichester), were ordered by the pope to sequestrate the revenues of Barkway church and to replace what may have been taken.[84]

Both the canons from British sources on the subject of appeals entered the *Liber Extra*. The letter, from which Tancred extracted his first canon, was a mandate to the dean, the chancellor and the precentor of Lincoln, to determine a suit between Croxton abbey (Prem. Leics.) and Newstead priory (Aug. Notts.) about the church of Hucknall Torkard (Notts.).[85] The proctors of both parties had already appeared at Rome and had been heard by Romano, cardinal deacon of S. Angelo. Many commissions of judges delegate, stretching back to Innocent III's pontificate, had been involved in this case, which had also occasioned the seeking of a royal writ of prohibition by the prior and convent of Newstead.[86] The Scottish appeal case of 22 February 1220 concerned expenses incurred and defrayed in a case between the abbot and convent of St Mary's, Dundrennan, in the diocese of Whithorn, and Nicholas, knight.[87]

Book III of the five-book arrangement dealt with the clergy. The complaint of Queen Berengaria, that clerks from her territories left off clerical dress and did not maintain the tonsure so that they could marry and conduct secular business and then resumed the tonsure in order to defraud her of services, exposed a flagrant enough abuse to attract the attention of Tancred.[88] Chapter 2 of title 4, 'De prebendis', was virtually a reproof for Pandulf, bishop-elect of Norwich and legate, who had asked whether an archdeacon might hold a benefice with care of souls without dispensation. In answer it was clearly stated that the archdeacon's business was to act as the eye of the bishop and that a benefice with care of souls required residence.[89] The unusual and

---

[84] Reg. Yr. 5 no. 4, *Reg. Hon. III* no. 2594, *CPL* 74, P 7754, un. *CQ* II 10 (c. 2 *X* II 17).

[85] Not Ault Hucknall (Derbs.) as identified in *Letters*, ed. Cheney; see Newstead Cart. fol. 5r ii.

[86] Reg. Yr. 2 no. 714, *Reg. Hon. III* no. 873, *CPL* 50, P 7772 (without date) and c. 1 *CQ* II 19 (c. 62 *X* II 28).

[87] Reg. Yr. 4 no. 669, *Reg. Hon. III* no. 2337, *CPL* 70, P 6197 and 7774, and c. 2 *CQ* II 19 (c. 64 *X* II 28).

[88] Reg. Yr. 2 no. 1012 (2), Reg. Hon. III no. 1224, *CPL* 53, P 5755, and c. 1 *CQ* III 2 (c. 9 *X* III 3).

[89] Reg. Yr. 4 no. 731, *Reg. Hon. III* no. 2427, *CPL* 71, and c. 2 *CQ* III 4.

unacceptable situation in the kingdom of Man, where the patron, the
king, had not provided an adequate living or land endowment for his
clerical presentees, was revealed to the pope in 1223 and the ensuing
letter caught the eye of Tancred, but it did not find a place in the *Liber
Extra*.[90] Another letter to Berengaria made its appearance in book V,
Crimen, under the title 'De privilegiis et excessibus privilegiatorum'.
It allowed her to punish literates under her rule who put on and off
the clerical dress as it suited them in order to escape punishment.[91]

The brief book IV, *Connubium*, included one ruling on dowry. Henry
III's sister, Joan, had been betrothed to Hugh de Lusignan. Her dowry
consisted of the city of Saintes and the isle of Oléron which Hugh had
received. Hugh's marriage to Joan, however, did not take place. Instead
he married the king's mother, and King John's widow, Isabella, but
the dowry was not restored nor indeed was Joan, who remained the
couple's prisoner for some years. The order for the restitution of dowry
after divorce, which was what the pope decreed, did not make the step
into *X* IV title 20.[92]

It is idle to ponder long on what was not selected by Tancred to
represent Honorius's pontificate. In supplying the collection for the use
of the law-schools, Tancred had provided a textbook with enough
suitable cases for the students to sharpen their teeth on. As for supplying
a compendium for use in the courts, as the papal letter promoting the
collection hoped, judgement must be deferred for the moment.
Roughly one-half of the chapters were omitted by Raymond of
Pennaforte in the *Gregoriana* and so vanished into obscurity for the
purposes of the active law. Their legal life lasted less than a decade.
Six out of the thirteen of our sample failed to make their way into
the Church's corpus of the canon law: they became evidence of
long-forgotten situations and people. That Honorius's legal compilation
was founded on actuality, real people and real situations, is obvious,
but what it meant to those real people, and in particular to those who
were concerned with acquiring a knowledge of or applying the law,
is far from clear. The blinkered way in which the canons were
selected – because of the desire to use only central and approved
sources, the registers – did not reflect the full range of possibilities and
experience which was, theoretically at least, at the Church's disposal.

[90] Reg. Yr. 7 no. 76, *Reg. Hon. III* no. 4207, *CPL* 89, P 6944 and c. 2 CQ III 22.
[91] Reg. Yr. 2 no. 534, *Reg. Hon. III* no. 823, *CPL* 48, P 7848 and c. 2 CQ V 12 (c. 27 X V 33).
[92] Reg. Yr. 9 no. 5, *Reg. Hon. III* no. 5101, Bouquet, *Recueil* xix 757 (dat. 4 Non Aug. (1224)), P 7293. See below App. 2 no. 24.

Law of the Church

The fourth great council of the Lateran which had been held in November 1215 provided judgements and rulings which were to have universal application.[93] The canons of the Council were collected by Johannes Teutonicus and incorporated in his *Compilatio Quarta*, which, as has been noted above, failed to get papal approval, but it was doubtless from this compilation, and from the copies of the canons which were taken home by the bishops, that the separate provinces and dioceses got to know of the positive legislative action which had resulted from the Council's discussions. Lang has commented on the ignorance shown by the English chroniclers of the contents of the Lateran decrees.[94] She has also suggested that the bishops and abbots who were present at the Council were the sole agents for the introduction of the decrees into England.[95] Whether this is so or not, the curia must have been at pains to see that only authorized texts were let out and it cannot have been this part of the *Compilatio Quarta*, although now of course rearranged under appropriate headings, that displeased Innocent III. Dissemination of the texts was essential to the success of the Council: its importance in curial eyes is illustrated by the inclusion of all but two of the seventy chapters (nos. 42 and 49) in Gregory IX's *Liber Extra*. It is clear that there was some legislation that was not applicable in particular localities, for example concerning certain tithe abuses that were unknown in England.[96] There were also areas of the legislation that were in need of further definition and interpretation or were definitely disadvantageous to certain groups of people. In the latter case it was the aim of powerful corporations to temper and restrain the law or where that proved impossible to seek exemption from the law's requirements. The Lateran legislation was part of Honorius III's inheritance. Coming at the end of Innocent III's pontificate, it had an obvious influence over the decade after 1215 before *Compilatio Quinta* was drawn up. The decrees showed how contemporary problems were treated by the assembled ecclesiastics of the Council acting as a body, but there is little on the discussions, and

---

[93] For the text of the canons and the commentaries of the glossators, see *Constitutiones concilii quarti Lateranensis*, ed. García y García; and see also id., 'El Concilio IV de Létran (1215) y sus comentarios', *Traditio* xiv (1958) 484–502.

[94] Gibbs and Lang, *Bishops and reform*, 101–2.

[95] Ibid., 119. For a list of the participants see J. Werner in *Neues Archiv der Gesellschaft für ältere deutsche Geschichtskunde* xxxi (1906) 575–93, 586 for the English; also in Foreville, *Latran I, II, III et Latran IV*, 392; and see *CS* ii pt 1 48.

[96] Gibbs and Lang, *Bishops and reform*, 125.

it is unlikely that the assembly always acted in total agreement with no dissenting voices.[97] Although the decrees were universally binding, there was thus room for some variety of opinion in their application and interpretation. In England there are three contemporary problems which had been considered by Lateran IV that throw light on this process of interpretation and application: they are pluralism, tithes and procurations.

The problem of pluralities had been attacked by the Council but without making any notable advance on the position outlined in the Third Lateran Council of 1179, where it had been stated that normally clerks were not permitted to hold more than one benefice each. The declaration of the Fourth Lateran Council (c. 29), 'De multa', that only one benefice might be held, even if a second did not involve the care of souls, included, however, the proviso that persons of elevation (*sublimes et litterate*) might be dispensed.[98] While for the canonists much of the debate concerned who had the authority to dispense (and whence this authority came), the crux of the matter in practical terms was how far concessions could be made in order to support a trained and upper clergy without endangering the Church's mission. Tancred's own position on pluralities and the power of dispensation was not in line with that of Honorius III.[99] The omission from his collection of 'Exspectavimus' – Honorius's clear declaration that pluralism was not to be tolerated unless a special papal dispensation was obtained – was due to this difference of opinion. Its addition to *Compilatio Quinta* as one of the *extravagantes* represented the Honorine view.[100] It has been suggested that English bishops and later popes gave *de facto* if not *de iure* assent to Tancred's more realistic view.[101] In the long term Tancred's opinion that multiple benefices could be held suited bishops and clergy alike and, perhaps most of all, popes.[102] Only in this way and with a more liberal attitude to dispensation, could many clerks be provided for who were in the episcopal or royal service; men such as Archbishop Stephen Langton's clerk, Aaron of Kent, who petitioned the pope that the archbishop might be allowed to dispense him to hold the chapel of St Nicholas, Sevenoaks, together with another church,[103]

---

97 See Foreville, 'Procédure et débats', 36–7, and Kuttner and García y García, 'A new eyewitness account', 115–78.

98 *Constitutiones*, ed. García y García, 73–4. For the glosses, see 217–21, 324–7, 432–4, 470 and 487.

99 Pennington, 'French recension', 68–9.

100 Ibid. and Pennington, 'Canonists and pluralism', 35–48.

101 Gibbs and Lang, *Bishops and reform*, 16–17 and 172–3.

102 See the judgement of Lang, *Bishops and reform*, 170.

103 Reg. Yr. 2 no. 905, *Reg. Hon. III* no. 1117, *CPL* 53.

and royal clerks, such as Masters Martin of Pattishall and Stephen de Lucy, and Stephen of Ecton and G. de Kauz.[104]

The legate Guala dispensed the papal scribe, Master Azzo, to hold two English benefices and this was confirmed by the pope.[105] According to the registers the pope was the main dispenser – often at the request of the king or of the legate[106] – but that he granted the dispensatory powers to the bishops sometimes is shown by the mandates addressed to the bishop of Hereford and the archbishops of Canterbury and York, frequently for the purposes of paying their own clerks.[107] The indults clearly stated that they were granted notwithstanding the decree of the Fourth Lateran Council.[108] The bishop of Salisbury, Richard Poore, active in implementing the work of Lateran IV, stood out in his request of 1226 for powers to act against pluralists in his diocese, including those with papal dispensations, and a later bishop of Salisbury, Giles of Bridport, was alone in forbidding clerks in his diocese to hold pluralities, even with papal dispensation, unless they also had dispensation for non-residence.[109] Pluralism and non-residence were also connected with bigamous clerks. Robert de Lelleia, clerk of the diocese of York, who had pleaded cases of bloodshedding in the secular court, had three wives and many benefices with care of souls, including Tadcaster.[110] William Dens, vicar of Mundham (Sussex), had more than one wife and probably more than one benefice.[111] These were notorious cases and doubtless provided ammunition for the few determined critics of pluralities.

In view of the general English tolerance of pluralism, Pandulf's query as to whether an archdeacon might hold a benefice with care of souls without dispensation does not seem quite so outrageous.[112] The question was raised in or before May 1220 and might indeed relate to

---

[104] Reg. Yrs. 3 no. 425, 8 no. 354, 9 no. 352 and 10 no. 159 (fol. 106), *Reg. Hon. III* nos. 2024, 4867, 5522, 5790, *CPL* 65, 95, 102 and 105.

[105] Reg. Yr. 2 no. 902, *Reg. Hon. III* no. 1080, *CPL* 52. *CPL* 71 allowed Pandulf to present clerks in his service to more than one benefice.

[106] e.g. *CPL* 76, 95 and 105.

[107] Reg. Yrs. 5 no. 423, 9 no. 236, 10 no. 195, *Reg. Hon. III* nos. 3128, 5386 and 5804, *CPL* 52–3, 55, 79, 80, 101, 108, 113.

[108] e.g. Reg. Yr. 11 nos. 400, 511, *Reg. Hon. III* nos. 6087, 6192, *CPL* 114–15.

[109] Reg. Yr. 10 no. 177 fol. 109, *Reg. Hon. III* no. 5816, *CPL* 105. See Gibbs and Lang, *Bishops and reform*, 117–29.

[110] Reg. Yr. 3 no. 83, *Reg. Hon. III* no. 1646, *CPL* 59.

[111] Shirley i no. 230: more of the text is lost than the editor indicates and he erroneously implies that the vicar was claiming a papal dispensation for bigamy rather than for plurality.

[112] The enquiry raised two questions (1) who could dispense and (2) whether care of souls demanded personal residence: c. 2 *CQ* III 4 and *CPL* 71.

William, archdeacon of Richmond, who in December of that year was dispensed to hold all the benefices which he had before the Lateran Council.[113] The moral question of the rectitude of holding more than one benefice with care of souls could be side-stepped practically by the provision of vicars. It had been stated early on that if the benefice was annexed to a prebend it could be served by a vicar.[114] By the early thirteenth century the number of references to sufficient portions indicates just how frequent these arrangements were.[115] Here the stern requirements of the legislation had to be softened to accord with the social and economic situation. A middle ground had to be found between the individual and flexible solution and the formality which came with a legislative decree.[116]

The law of tithes as left by the Fourth Lateran Council presented another area where from the point of view of the religious, especially the Cistercians, interpretation and adaptation were required. The decree of the Council (clause 55) was far from favourable to them.[117] It stipulated that the Cistercians, as other religious, the *privilegiati* (including the Hospitallers and the Templars, according to one glossator),[118] should pay tithes on lands which they acquired in future (whether they cultivated them themselves or not) to those parish churches which had received the tithe in the past;[119] or they were to compound for the tithes. The papacy was critical of the regulars', particularly the Cistercians', acquisition of property, of their abusing their general privilege of exemption and of their denying tithes to parish churches which were falling into decay – indeed of the general overriding of parochial law by the Cistercians.[120] The Cistercians (and other religious) were now faced with accepting the limitation in an increasingly hostile environment. They might look for loopholes in the legislation and for certainty over what privileges they still possessed.

The decree caused the religious to re-examine their existing privileges.

[113] Reg. Yr. 5 no. 255, *Reg. Hon. III* no. 2828, *CPL* 77 (4 Dec. 1220) and *York minster fasti*, ed. Clay, i 46–7.

[114] c. 30 X III 5.

[115] See *Constitutiones*, ed. García y García, 75–7; Sayers, *Papal judges delegate*, 199–201; and for an example of an appropriation see below App. 2 no. 43.

[116] Horwitz, 'Reshaping a decretal chapter', 210.

[117] *Constitutiones*, 95–9, c. 34 X III 30.

[118] Damasus, Apparatus ad *Constitutiones*, ed. García y García, 452.

[119] The glossators, Damasus and 'Casus Parisiensis' repeat this (*Constitutiones*, ed. García y García, 451 and 473).

[120] The Cistercians had discussed tithes at the General Chapter of 1214 but, as the *Statuta* include nothing on the subject, it may be concluded that they were not of a mind with the pope (see C. R. Cheney in *Cîteaux* xiii (1962) 146–51, esp. 146–7) and perhaps divided among themselves on how to proceed.

Law of the Church

The first re-examination was made in the light of lands acquired before the Council. Although the statement of the Council might seem perfectly clear on this point, it was a precaution to seek reconfirmation. An indult to all the abbots and brothers of the Cistercian order exempting them from payment of tithe on land acquired before the Council and cultivated by others, if it is now returned to them for cultivation, survives in the original and comes most probably from an English Cistercian house: it is not clear which.[121] The Premonstratensians procured a general mandate, addressed to archbishops, bishops and prelates of churches, for the observance of their privilege that they did not pay tithes except on land acquired since the Council: naturally this privilege was entered in the cartularies of the Order.[122] The Benedictine house of Abingdon in Berkshire sought reconfirmation of this kind, drawing attention to the question whether the lands were worked by themselves or at their expense, and squeezing in their 'ancient' (ex antiqua) exemption from tithe on certain meadows, mills and fishponds.[123] The Cistercian exemption of 1220 drew attention to what happened where lands had been cultivated previously and were not being recultivated after an interval.[124]

The law on tithes of novalia presented similar problems of interpretation. Concessions concerning payment of tithe on novalia (new lands where no tithe had been exacted before) followed fast on the Lateran requirement. 'Cum abbates Cisterciensis', addressed to the archbishops of Canterbury and of York and their suffragans, confirmed Cîteaux's privileges and was widely copied into Cistercian cartularies.[125] The Premonstratensians acquired a general exemption in 1219, 'Contingit interdum quod'.[126] The Benedictines' position in acquiring (separately) indults exempting them from the payment of tithes on new lands worked with their own hands (i.e. not leased out) and on the nutriments of animals underlined the threat which the regulars felt from clause 55.[127]

---

[121] Below App. 2 no. 25.
[122] e.g. Leiston abbey cart., ed. Mortimer, no. 20; not however registered.
[123] See below App. 2 no. 41 and above pp. 115–16.
[124] Reg. Holmcultram fol. 152, pd Mon. Angl. v 232 no. 10.
[125] e.g. Reg. S. Marie de Neubotle, 196, P 7031, and Reg. Hon. III no. 4383; Mon. Angl. v 536 no. 15 (Kirkstall) and Reg. Hon. III no. 4053. This is undoubtedly the same privilege: the date, however, has become confused. It is either 7 kal July 6th year (25 June 1222) or 7 kal June 7th year (26 May 1223) from the Lateran.
[126] Leiston abbey cart., ed. Mortimer, no. 21, P 5991, Reg. Hon. III no. 1882.
[127] e.g. Battle Cart. fols. 50v–1, Reg. Yr. 6 no. 290, Reg. Hon. III no. 3858 (Bliss missed this entry). Damasus (Constitutiones, 473) mentions privileges de novalibus for the black monks and canons regular.

Canon 33 of the Fourth Lateran Council repeated the general stipulations of Lateran III that procurations were not to be excessive and were only to be taken when visitation took place in person.[128] Here again there was room for definition and manoeuvre. On 9 July 1225 the abbot and convent of Easby were relieved by papal indult from paying procurations to the archdeacon of York unless he came only with the minimum number of followers as laid down in 1216. This indult was not registered.[129] In March 1226 (too late for inclusion in *Compilatio Quinta*) Honorius wrote to the archbishop of York allowing him to visit the abbey of St Mary, York, for purposes of correction, but not more than once a year and with the accompaniment of only five or six selected canons. The payment of procurations was only to be exacted at the time of the archbishop's consecration when a guest house was to be reserved for him.[130] The popes were in a cleft stick over the question of procurations because they sought to encourage visitation and for this reason payments had to be made available. It was an area of the law best left vague for individual settlements to be effected.

In the application of the law in England between Honorius III's accession and the publication of the *Compilatio Quinta*, the one law-book with definite authority, in the new sense, was the officially approved *Compilatio Tertia* of Peter Collivaccinus. It is difficult to assess the practical influence of the *Compilatio Tertia* in England during this decade. The circulation of legal texts is likely to remain a question of some doubt. There are English manuscripts of *Compilatio Tertia* – not a profusion of them, but enough to illustrate that the collection was known in some circles, doubtless to the prominent members of the hierarchy, to those who had attended the law-schools and the Council, and presumably to the university of Oxford, but whether to a wider group who used it in the courts (as distinct from the schools) is another matter.[131] The *Compilatio Quarta* was in circulation soon after Innocent III's death, but it had no such official approval. Further private collections of decretals are known for Innocent but none for Honorius. There were also, of course, the Lateran decrees.

The registered and the non-registered letters of Honorius's reign bear witness to the continuing reference to Rome in legal matters, perhaps

[128] *Constitutiones*, c. 33, p. 77 (c. 23 X III 39); for the glosses, see pp. 222, 330, 436, 470 and 488; and see Gibbs and Lang, *Bishops and reform*, 157.
[129] Easby Reg. fol. 317v.
[130] York, D. and C. Reg. A pt 3 fol. 99, Reg. Yr. 10 no. 229 fol. 118, *Reg. Hon. III* no. 5850, *CPL* 108.
[131] See Kuttner, *Repertorium*, 361–5; Sayers, *Papal judges delegate*, 35–8.

158

Law of the Church

suggesting either that the sources of the collected law were unknown or that they were inadequate for the particular purposes. The formation of private collections of decretals from sources outside the pope's official register reflected personal interests and particular local situations. According to Cheney, in England under Innocent III, law made from consultation had tended to come from the circles of the bishops.[132] Only if the answers to these individual questions were registered or collected could they survive as judgements that might be used for other cases. Under Honorius there is no hint of any such activity in episcopal circles in England, possibly because of the political situation, possibly because of the depletion of the hierarchy, possibly because of the new and close contact with Rome. The bishops most likely to have attracted collectors and collections were Langton, Walter Gray, Richard Poore, and possibly Hugh of Wells and Alexander Stavensby, but no evidence of such compilations remains.[133] It seems likely, indeed, that local collection was an activity of the past; after all, its uses were extremely limited. The addressees of the letters selected by Tancred (and of the letters in the registers) show no particular predilection for the diocesans, the provincials or even the legates; the commissions of judges were of varied persons, including seculars and regulars, such as the archdeacon of Berkshire, the dean, the chancellor and the precentor of Lincoln, and the prior of Bayham, the dean of Dallington and a canon of Hastings. The spread of the delegate system militated against the old type of episcopally backed collection. The one unifying factor of these letters is their incorporation in the papal register. It is indeed possible that the work of collection had come to be associated exclusively with the university and law-school at Bologna. To make a collection, with any hope of approval after one's labours, one needed to be near the pope. The Bolognese masters not only moulded and shaped the law with their glosses, they also determined what was included.[134]

Honorius's *Compilatio Quinta* shows the way in which the law was now formed. Selection took place from the contents of the papal register. *Extravagantes* and private collections, if they existed for the reign, were not used by Tancred. The law continued to be made mainly from consultation. Kuttner has written that one important aspect of the *Liber Extra* was that it *abolished* law.[135] By weeding out the previous

---

[132] *Innocent III and England*, 34. On twelfth-century collection, see M. G. Cheney, *Roger, bishop of Worcester 1164–79* (Oxford 1980) ch. 5.
[133] On the episcopate, see below Chapter 5.
[134] Pennington, 'French recension', 67, and Horwitz, 'Reshaping a decretal chapter', 217.
[135] 'Quelques observations', 308.

collections, Raymond of Pennaforte made much obsolete. What remained in his book was the old law that was binding: the rest was of no effect. In future, private collections were forbidden: authority and approval became the norm. Authority meant selection from the papal register and approval meant papal promulgation. Approved canons and collections became obligatory. The contrariety of the previous decretal collections with their personal selection and their often differing precedents, which had forced Gregory IX to take action, was at an end.[136] Innocent III, by giving his approval to *Compilatio Tertia* (and withholding it from *Compilatio Quarta*), had decided which of his decretals were to have legislative authority. In so doing he started a new trend in law-making, but until Gregory IX took the ultimate decision to sift out past law and authorize only what was left, as much authority was accorded to the unofficial collections as to the official ones in the usage of the schools and, more important, the courts. New decretals had the force of arguments, not commandments:[137] they were there to produce comment and to be used for purposes of equity. For the scholastic lawyers, to produce comment was no problem, but for the judges in the courts the difficulties of using various precedents explains the relentless reference to the pope. It needed a skilled jurist to establish the wider implications of a decretal. Was it not safer to get an authoritative judgement for the particular case at Rome? Hanenburg sees a complete change in the nature of the law-books after 1234: 'The Gregorian compilation is not just a collection of laws like the older collections were, but a code of law.... It is the formal triumph of new legislation over the old.'[138]

The non-dogmatic quality of much of the canon law before 1234, the lack of one book or codex, the variety of opinion amongst the masters and the commentators – the softening and compromising attitudes of some and the rigid requirements of others – and the tempering of the law in the provinces to allow it to blend with indigenous law or local custom and the stiffening of it by the popes sometimes to hasten reform, all show an underlying flexibility. The view of Bernard of Parma, expressed in his gloss on the words *de iudiciis* in Gregory IX's letter of promulgation, 'Rex pacificus', that anyone reading or using earlier collections should be excommunicated,[139]

---

[136] Horwitz, 'Reshaping a decretal chapter', 212.

[137] Kuttner, 'Quelques observations', 308, 311.

[138] 'Decretals and decretal collections', 588–9.

[139] Cited Pennington, 'French recension', 66 and n. 23. Vincentius Hispanus, however, thought that decretals in earlier obsolete compilations could be cited (ibid. 65–6).

indicates the scale of the change effected in the quarter century after the issue of *Compilatio Tertia*.

Tancred's *Compilatio Quinta*, based on the selection from Honorius's registers, sharpened certain points while neglecting others. Because not everything was registered, the hunt for letters that established precedents or included a judgement on some matter was restricted. For the first year of Innocent III's pontificate one-quarter to one-fifth of the letters in the register got into the *Compilatio Tertia*, and for the second year, between one-fifth and one-sixth:[140] a small part, indeed, of the pope's total correspondence. The exclusion of the old sources, the *extravagantes*, which were, of course, just as selective in their own way, changed the emphasis of the law. Decretals were the precedents: canons were binding.[141] In law-collecting and law-making, Honorius's pontificate lies in the wake of Innocent's notion of an official collection and in the aftermath of Lateran IV. The logical consequence of the elimination of private collections was the compilation of the *Liber Extra* of Gregory IX. In many ways the quarter century between 1210 and 1234 was juristically speaking an interim period.

[140] Hageneder, 'Papstregister', 340. Hageneder estimates that one-tenth of the letters from Reg. Vat. 2 (Gregory VII) became part of the collections (ibid.).
[141] See Fransen, *Les décrétales et les collections des décrétales*, esp. 14, 35.

Chapter 5

CURIAL RELATIONS WITH ENGLAND

Perhaps an action of the greatest diplomatic skill, perhaps a last-ditch attempt to save his Crown, King John's surrender of his kingdom to the pope in 1213 tested Innocent III's exalted claims. These claims were not confined to the spiritual dominion but extended to feudal overlordship. John's manoeuvre, moreover, tried the strength of the papacy in its new role of arbiter of European politics. Yet it was not Innocent who had to re-form the bonds of society, re-establish the peace, end the civil war and restore Angevin government in England. The task had scarcely begun when Innocent died in July 1216. Three months later, King John himself was dead, leaving an heir, a minor. The political complexion had changed considerably.

The text of King John's grant of his kingdom to the pope stated that he granted to 'God, the apostles Peter and Paul, the Holy Roman Church our mother, and to our lord pope Innocent III and his catholic successors the kingdoms of England and Ireland, with all right and appurtenances for the omission of our sins and of all our race (*genus*), living and dead'. In return John received the kingdoms from God and the Roman Church *tanquam feodatarius* in the presence of Pandulf, papal subdeacon and *familiarius*, swearing faith to Innocent and his successors and to the Roman Church. John swore that he would do *homagium ligium* to the pope and pledged his heirs also to fealty. He further granted the Roman Church 1000 marks sterling (700 for England and 300 for Ireland) 'salvis nobis et heredibus nostris justitiis, libertatibus et regalibus nostris'. His oath proclaimed that he would be *adjutor* of the patrimony of St Peter and of the two kingdoms. He pledged this at Dover on 15 May 1213 in the presence of the archbishop of Dublin (Henry of London), the bishop of Norwich (John de Gray), Geoffrey fitzPeter, earl of Essex, the justiciar, William Longespée, earl of Salisbury 'our brother', William the Marshal, earl of Pembroke, Reginald count of Boulogne, William de Warenne, earl of Surrey, Saer de Quincy, earl of Winchester, William d'Aubigny, earl of Arundel, William de Ferrers, earl of Derby, William Brewer, Peter fitzHerbert and Warin fitzGerold.

There is a suggestion that the curia had played some part in the composition of the deed of surrender.[1] However that may be, the text of the first document of 15 May[2] and that of 3 October[3] differ slightly. On the second occasion the pope's legate, Niccolò cardinal bishop of Tusculum, was present. Homage was therefore done to him personally as the pope's viceroy. (On the first occasion, when only a nuncio was present, John had promised homage 'if he should be able to come before the pope'.) The symbolic act of the hands was performed; John's charter was drawn up and sealed with a gold seal, and the tribute for the first year was paid.[4] As a *feodarius* (or *feodatarius*) of the pope, the English king subjected himself to a feudal payment to the papacy which was at all times distinct from the payment of Peter's Pence.[5] To do homage to the pope meant the acceptance of vassalage, the pope granting the kingdom back to the vassal and allowing him to act as the *adjutor* of the patrimony of St Peter. The pope counted numerous feudal vassals among the ruling houses of western Europe but there can be no doubt that the English surrender document added considerably to the pope's claims. Feudal overlordship, conceded by one of the most advanced sovereignties of thirteenth-century Europe, gave the papacy a unique advantage.

It was not a situation that the thirteenth-century popes could afford to ignore. Following John's surrender of the kingdom, Magna Carta was condemned by the pope on 24 August 1215[6] and at the Lateran Council in the following November English affairs were discussed. There were others, besides the pope, who had an interest in England: the powers closest were determined to gain if they could. Accordingly at the Council a claim was made to imperial suzerainty over England by the German archchancellor, Archbishop Siegfried of Mainz.[7] It is unlikely that the imperial party was doing more than register an interest. After the cession of the kingdom of England, with its definite powers and responsibilities, it would have been entirely unrealistic to suppose that Innocent III would have allowed imperial suzerainty to override the pope.

[1] See *CS* ii pt 1 18 n. 3. [2] Ibid. 17–19, trans. Lunt, *Revenues* ii 45–8.
[2] *Selected letters of Pope Innocent III*, ed. Cheney, no. 67.
[4] Ibid., 181 and n. 14.
[5] On *feodum censuale*, see Ullmann, *Growth*, 334.
[6] *Selected letters of Pope Innocent III*, ed. Cheney, no. 82 (P 4990).
[7] Kuttner and García y García, 'Eyewitness account', 158–60, lines 168–78.

But what exactly did the papal fief mean? Other examples of kingdoms brought into this particular relationship with the patrimony of St Peter during the pontificate of Honorius are not hard to find.[8] The kingdoms of Hungary and of Portugal were put under papal protection at this time.[9] The kingdom of Aragon was made a papal fief during the minority of Jaime I and three cardinals were sent to effect the transition.[10] When the conquered lands of Raymond, count of Toulouse, were assigned to Simon de Montfort, he hoped to hold them as a papal fief, thereby gaining direct papal protection.[11] In 1219 Reginald, king of Man, surrendered his kingdom to the pope, commending it and himself with 'a kiss of the feet'.[12] He gave his island, which belonged to him by hereditary right, and for which he was held to do no service to anyone, to the pope. He was to do homage and fealty to the Holy Roman Church, paying annually in perpetuity twelve marks sterling at Furness abbey, and in return was to hold the kingdom in fee. The legate, Pandulf, received the donation and gave the island back to Reginald and his heirs to be held in perpetual fee, investing Reginald with a gold ring. 'Moreover', ran Reginald's letter, 'we petition your holiness that your holiness extend to us that privilege and protection which you grant to other kings and vassals of the Roman Church who pay census.'[13]

An integral part of the bargain was the payment by the liegeman of tribute or census. The oath taken by King John committed both him and his heirs to an annual payment which was a heavy burden.[14] Henry III, who apparently took the oath to pay it at his first coronation,[15] paid faithfully at first, borrowing to keep up the payments, but during the periods of baronial control in Henry's reign it was not rendered and after 1267 even the papacy's most loyal and devoted son began to bridle at the sum. Whenever possible, Edward I avoided making the payment to the papacy. Early in 1273, when Edward was on the return

---

[8] In general, see Ullmann, *Growth*, 331–7. R. L. Benson, *The bishop-elect* (Princeton 1968) 353, comments on Honorius's insistence that laymen should fulfil all their feudal obligations to bishops.

[9] P 5456, 5471, 5663; and 5589 (Cyprus).

[10] P. A. Linehan, *The Spanish Church and the papacy in the thirteenth century* (Cambridge 1971) 189; and see P 5518.

[11] Kuttner and García y García, 'Eyewitness account', 142.

[12] On *proskynesis*, see Ullmann, *Growth*, esp. 315f.

[13] Reg. Yrs. 4 no. 629 and 7 no. 189; pd *Liber Censuum*, ed. Fabre and Duchesne, i 260–1 no. 29, trans. Lunt, *Revenues* ii 48–9.

[14] This paragraph is based on Lunt, *Financial relations of the papacy with England* i 134–72 and ii 66–73, and id., *Revenues* ii 49–54.

[15] Matthew Paris, *Chron. maj.*, ed. Luard, iii 1–2.

journey from Palestine, he stayed at the papal court and was reminded by Gregory X of his liability. Payment was avoided under Innocent V and Adrian V, but John XXI renewed the demand, which was met. The king petitioned Pope Nicholas IV in 1278, and then again fourteen years later in 1292, that the tribute might be paid by the assignment of rents and lands to certain monasteries whose abbots and priors would then render the required amount. It is difficult to see why the request was refused; perhaps the financial wiliness of Nicholas IV sensed that payment would still be avoided and that hostility to the papacy would be transferred from the Crown to the religious. In fact it turned out to be a short-sighted decision, for henceforth Edward I ignored Nicholas's requests for payment. With the election of Clement V in 1305, the king tried to bargain, promising payment in return for the pope's acceding to certain royal requests, but his death intervened and the writ ordering payment was stopped. Edward II was even more remiss than his father in the payment of the tribute: the political dealing of his great-grandfather, transacted nearly one hundred years earlier, could not have seemed binding at this distance of time. Doubts were expressed about John's power to have obligated his successors in this way without the consent of the barons and there is no evidence that later kings took an oath to pay.[16] Edward tried his father's final scheme of bargaining, giving concession for concession, but he did not make the payment again after 1320. The last payment ever rendered was handed over by Edward III in 1333 and thirty-three years later in 1366 parliament repudiated the cession and the papacy's right to this tax. The long history of the payment – it was actually paid for in 78 out of the 120 years – bears witness to the regard for the strength of the oath, for the Crown had long ceased to gain as a vassal. In the years immediately following John's cession and pledge of the tribute, however, there were clear practical returns.

A major advantage of the feudal contract was the protection of minors. As early as 1076 the pope had demonstrated that he might as a feudal monarch protect the widows and children of rulers who had taken an oath of fealty to him.[17] Rulers going on crusade might also put their dependants under papal protection as did Leopold VI, prince of Austria, in respect of his wife, Princess Theodora, and their children.[18] Thus the papacy could be seen as an impartial protector of

[16] It is not found in the coronation oath of 1308, for which see *English constitutional documents 1307–1485*, ed. E. C. Lodge and G. A. Thornton (Cambridge 1935) 10–11.

[17] *Liber Censuum*, ed. Fabre and Duchesne, i 356–7 no. 72.

[18] Cf. H. Hageneder, 'Die Beziehungen der Babenberger zur Kurie in der ersten Hälfte des 13. Jahrhunderts', *MIOG* lxxv (1967) 1–29, esp. 5.

minors and as an upholder of rights of succession in hereditary
monarchies. On 15 October 1216, almost exactly three months after
Honorius's election as pope, King John wrote him a letter. This letter,
'Cum gravi infirmitate', could not possibly have reached the pope
before John died four days later and probably did not arrive much,
if at all, in advance of that fateful news.[19] John's final illness was sudden.
At the end of September he was at Lincoln, encouraging his supporters
against the rebel earl, and from there he rode to the important port
of Lynn where he contracted dysentery.[20] On 11 October he left Lynn
for Wisbech. During this journey the celebrated disaster occurred to
his baggage. Coupled with bad news from the defenders of Dover,
John's spirits seem to have sunk with his failing physical strength. He
stopped briefly to rest at Sleaford on 14–15 October, then forced
himself on to Newark where he finally collapsed and died on 19
October. In the last few days – or perhaps even hours – of his life, he
made a will, a brief and uncomplicated document, appointing as his
executors: Guala, the legate, Peter des Roches, bishop of Winchester,
Richard Poore, bishop of Chichester, Silvester of Evesham, bishop of
Worcester, Brother Amaury of Sainte Maurie, master of the Temple,
William the Marshal, earl of Pembroke, Ranulf earl of Chester, William
de Ferrers, earl of Derby, William Brewer, Walter Lacy, John of
Monmouth, Savary de Mauléon and Fawkes de Breauté. The will
declared that 'not even in health' would the king do anything without
their assent and to them he gave general powers to make satisfaction
for any wrongs he had done, charging them to render assistance to his
sons for the recovery and defence of their inheritance. His body was
to be buried at Worcester in the church of the Blessed Virgin and of
St Wulfstan, to whom the king had a special devotion.[21]

The protection that John was entitled to seek for his heir as a vassal
of the Holy See is at the heart of the Sleaford letter. The maintenance
of the succession would have been fragile, indeed, without the help of
the pope. John recalled the position of his kingdom as the patrimony
of St Peter and of the Roman Church and implored, 'flexis genibus',
the pope's protection for his heir against his and the Roman Church's
enemies. John's final plea for absolution and mercy and the opening
phrase of the letter, drawing attention to his grave and incurable illness,

---

[19] Reg. Yr. 1 no. 147 (noted *CPL* 42): pd *Annales ecclesiastici*, ed. Theiner, xx 359 nos.
31–2.

[20] See *Radulphi de Coggeshall chronicon anglicanum*, ed. J. Stevenson (RS lxvi 1875) 183–4.

[21] W. L. Warren, *King John* (London 1961) 275–6, prints the will; Powicke, *Henry III*,
1 n. 1 (for Wulfstan), 2 and n. 2.

indicate the state of his mind and what was uppermost in it in his last few days – the transfer of the kingdom to the new papal vassal, a minor. Would it be possible to establish the succession with the French occupying part of the country? Much, if not all, depended on the actions of the pope's representative, the legate Guala.

The news of Honorius's election as pope had been received in England, according to one chronicler, with rejoicing by those who stood against the king, thinking and predicting that a new pope would bring changes of policy and would not necessarily 'follow in the footsteps of his predecessor'.[22] Honorius's letter on John's death, 'Duris nobis rumoribus', addressed to the legate Guala, who had now been in the country for five months, was probably written very soon after the pope heard the news. Dated 3 December, it reaffirmed John's position as a vassal of Holy Church and referred to Henry and his brothers as *pupilli*, left in the pope's tutelage, citing the scriptural text 'Pupillo tu eris adjutor' (Psalm X, 14). As the pope's representative, Guala was to protect his wards and was to declare illegal and invalid the oaths taken to the king of France, and more especially to Prince Louis.[23] Two days before, on 1 December, the pope ordered all those who had deserted John to return to loyalty to Henry, 'whose age proves him innocent'.[24] It was not until 20 January 1217, in 'Audito inclyte recordationis', that the pope wrote directly to the young king, Henry III, commiserating with him on the death of his father and exhorting him to be faithful to the Holy See and to obey the counsels of the legate (also including in his exhortation an expression of the hope that the boy would fulfil his father's vow to go to the relief of the Holy Land).[25] Almost certainly the letter followed the pope's receipt of news of the coronation at Gloucester. So far there seems to be no indication of any change in policy. Suddenly, however, the legate's political responsibilities had greatly increased. Tillmann believes that Honorius's letters to Guala indicate a softer line than that taken by Innocent III,[26] but, if that is so, there is no suggestion of a shift on the basic issue of the re-establishment of law and order.

The first step in the re-establishment of order was the coronation of the king, still no more than a child, in his tenth year. This took place

---

[22] *Memoriale fratris Walteri de Coventria* (the so-called 'Barnwell' chronicle) ed. Stubbs, ii 230–1. See ibid., i pp. xxxviii–xlvii and A. Gransden, *Historical writing in England c. 550 to c. 1307* (London 1974) 339–45, who presents arguments for its originating in the Holland area of East Anglia rather than in Cambridgeshire.

[23] Reg. Yr. 1 no. 80, *Reg. Hon. III* no. 142, P 5378.

[24] Reg. Yr. 1 no. 82, *Reg. Hon. III* no. 131, P 5375.

[25] P 5427.   [26] *Die päpstlichen Legaten in England*, 109 n. 54.

on 28 October at Gloucester, in the presence of Guala, of Peter des
Roches, bishop of Winchester, of Jocelin of Wells, bishop of Bath,
of Silvester of Evesham, bishop of Worcester (the diocesan), and of
certain lay barons, abbots and others. Before the high altar of the abbey
church of St Peter, with Bishop Jocelin administering the oath, Henry
swore on the gospels and on many relics, in front of clergy and people,
to maintain the honour of the Church, keep the peace, administer justice
and observe good laws. Henry then did homage to the Holy Roman
Church and the pope for the kingdoms of England and of Ireland and
swore that he would pay the 1000 marks tribute. After the oaths,
Bishops Peter of Winchester and Jocelin of Bath anointed and crowned
him[27] – apparently using the queen mother's circlet, because most of
the English coronation regalia had been lost in the accident in the
Wash.[28] On the next day the king received the homage of his bishops,
earls and barons.[29] The performance of the coronation, away from the
royal abbey church of Westminster which lay in the middle of enemy
territory and carried out by two of Canterbury's suffragans, not by the
archbishop, underlined the urgency of the legate's task on behalf of the
pope. Stephen Langton was abroad and appears to have made no
immediate protest nor to have received any written assurance from the
pope that his rights would not be adversely affected. Later, on 5
November 1218 at Reading, Guala issued a letter which emphasized
that the coronation of Henry III at Gloucester was not to prejudice the
rights of the abbey church of Westminster.[30] In order to rectify the
effects of this unusual step, the king was given a second coronation by
the archbishop of Canterbury at Westminster on 17 May 1220.[31] The
legate Pandulf was still in England but it was Stephen Langton who
performed the coronation. Henry's thirteenth birthday took place
apparently a few months after his second coronation and in the summer

[27] Matthew Paris, *Chron. maj.*, ed. Luard, iii 1–2: two of the manuscripts state that the
bishop of Winchester alone crowned and anointed Henry. Schramm, *English coronation*,
45, sees the bishop of Winchester as acting as a suffragan of Canterbury.
[28] See A. V. Jenkinson in *History* viii (1923–4) 163–6, who shows from the inventories
that very little of the regalia used at Henry's second coronation in 1220 corresponded
with John's.
[29] Matthew Paris, *Chron. maj.*, ed. Luard, iii 1–2. Powicke says that Henry was knighted.
[30] Westminster Abbey Muniments 51111 (an original, written by an English hand). This
letter is wrongly dated (1219) in Powicke, *Henry III*, 4 n. 1, from the copy in the
Speculum of Richard of Cirencester, ed. J. E. B. Mayor (RS xxx 1869) ii 37. Schramm
(*English coronation*, 45 n. 1) also erroneously declared that it was not to prejudice
Langton and that it was addressed to the archbishop. In fact it was not to prejudice
Westminster and was addressed to all Christian faithful. Pandulf had legatine powers
from Sept. 1218 but Guala did not leave until Dec. (*CS* ii pt 1 49).
[31] Schramm, *English coronation*, 164.

of 1221 his tutelage came to an end, but it was not until 1223 that he was declared to be of age for issuing documents under the great seal. Shortly after the first coronation and in order to ensure the settlement the Great Charter had been reissued at Bristol. As the king had no seal it was sealed by his guardians, the legate and William the Marshal.[32] For three years it was the seal of the *rector regis et regni* (the Marshal) and his attestation 'teste comite' that controlled English civil government.[33] In his third year, when Henry was twelve, the first matrix of a great seal was made for him[34] but he was not granted the use of it until 1223, when the pope instructed the vice-chancellor, Ralph Neville, who had the matrix in his custody, not to seal anything in future without the king's approval.[35] The king was still prevented from making grants in perpetuity but was granted powers of disposing freely of his castles, lands and wardships. The famous 'Gaudemus in domino' of 14 March 1224 was virtually a lesson in kingship for the Christian prince, who now had the first taste of direct power. It expressed all the ideals of the papacy concerning monarchical rule. The king was exhorted 'to correct, rule, and govern with care', putting himself above the squabbles of his vassals.[36] Henry's minority did not end entirely until 1227, when he was in his twenty-second year.

The protection afforded the king between 1216 and 1227 included help against the rebellious and excommunicated barons, and against the Welsh, the Scots and the French. Finally a settlement was made for the Church. Resistance to those barons who had deserted John's cause was imperative. There is no doubt that the death of John and the accession of a minor, whom the pope was at pains to point out was of 'innocuous age', made a settlement in some ways easier. Yet there were also acute difficulties in the situation. The seizure of royal castles could obviously not be tolerated: it was a crucial point to settle militarily and there was a fair likelihood that the papal censures would work in favour of the king. Guala's outright success with some of the major barons, especially William the Marshal, must have contributed towards the cession of others whose will was not so determined. The pope was especially concerned over the custody of the castles in the period just before the king's second coronation, no doubt on account

[32] West, *The justiciarship in England*, 224–5.
[33] Tout, *Chapters* i 186–7 and 206. The papal mandate of 3 July 1217 for a seal to be made (Reg. Yr. 1 no. 496, *Reg. Hon. III* no. 643, *CPL* 47–8) may refer to this seal.
[34] *Annales monastici*, ed. Luard, ii 83.
[35] 'Ad hoc in annis' (13 April 1223) in Shirley i no. 358. There is no evidence that Henry had a privy seal before Dec. 1230 (Tout, *Chapters* i 206).
[36] Below App. 2 no. 38.

of reports of messengers from England. On 28 May the legate, Pandulf, was ordered to see that no one had more than two of the king's castles in his custody: a fortnight earlier the English aristocracy had been charged to assist the legate in this matter.[37] As late as 1226 detention of royal castles in Ireland brought forth a papal mandate to the archbishop of Dublin, ordering him to compel restitution, using ecclesiastical censures.[38] In 1221 restoration of the king's wards and escheats was ordered: his counsellors, including the bishop of Winchester, Hubert de Burgh, the justiciar, and Ranulf earl of Chester were to see to this. The letter drew attention to the king's status as an orphan and one who had taken the cross and therefore was entitled to the special protection of the Holy See.[39]

Help was given consistently against the Welsh and Llewellyn, and during the Welsh rebellion of 1223, when in fact the legatine presence had withdrawn, ecclesiastical censures were imposed. On 5 October 1223 the pope ordered the archbishop of York and his suffragans to place under interdict the lands in their dioceses that belonged to Llewellyn, 'so-called' prince of North Wales, and his followers, and to excommunicate him and his supporters and after six months to declare all to be free from allegiance to them.[40] The Scots were an equal problem and from the first the pope and the legate sought to make a political settlement that would maintain Henry and keep the Scots at bay. William, king of Scots, was ordered to return to the allegiance of the English king (as were other rebels) on 17 January 1217 and capital was made of Henry's youth and the change of king.[41] On 10 November 1218 Pandulf was instructed to confirm or annul the composition which had been made between John and William as he thought fit.[42] The border see of Carlisle illustrated in the first few years how important settlement of the Church was to the political issue.[43] Of most immediate moment in 1216 were the French. On 21 April 1217 the pope wrote to Philip Augustus, commanding him to order his son to desist from the English invasion, and describing Henry as *pupillus* and orphan.[44] The peace between Henry and Louis, which Guala had made by the beginning of 1218, was confirmed by the pope on 13 January.[45] Help in labouring

---

[37] Below App. 2 nos. 12, 13. See Powicke, *Henry III*, 59–60.

[38] Below App. 2 no. 54.

[39] Ibid. no. 20.   [40] Ibid. no. 33.

[41] P 5418.

[42] Below App. 2 no. 6, P 5918; and see P 5919 – addressed to the chancellor of the king of Scots.

[43] Below App. 2 no. 3 and pp. 175–6.

[44] P 5528.   [45] P 5668.

for peace in England and supporting the king in the enforcement of his rights against his vassals, including his overseas vassals, the Gascons (especially the Lusignans and their supporters),[46] where again ecclesiastical censures were not eschewed, underlines why papal overlordship had been accepted. This support, moreover, continued after the withdrawal of the legates.

RELATIONS WITH THE CHURCH: *ECCLESIA ROMANA* AND *ECCLESIA ANGLICANA*

It is not meaningful to distinguish too finely between the political and the ecclesiastical settlement. The purpose of Guala's visit in May 1216 was to reinforce John's position as a papal vassal and to provide the necessary ecclesiastical authority, following the suspension of the archbishop of Canterbury, Stephen Langton. One of Honorius's first actions as pope was to confirm Guala's position as legate in England.[47] The powers that Honorius granted him are later made clear in the letter 'Ancxiatur in nobis' of 17 January 1217: full powers (as belonging to the pope) – so that nothing should be lacking which would contribute to the benefit (*utilitas*) of the king and of the kingdom – of imposing interdicts, excommunicating and degrading prelates and others who are rebellious and disobedient, and of appointing to vacant cathedral churches and exempt abbeys.[48]

Guala's immediate task was to deprive the disloyal and although this policy was continued by Pandulf it is best considered first. The deprivations were referred to in 1219, when it appeared that some of the dispossessed were endeavouring to reopen cases without revealing the fact of their deprivation, and Pandulf the new legate was charged to declare invalid letters that hid such facts.[49] It is difficult to gauge the extent of these deprivations. In 1221 a papal letter stated that those who had been loyal to the pope were not to be summoned before those whom Guala had deprived.[50] References to those who were excommunicated at this time occur only by chance: there is no

---

[46] P 5419: to William, archbishop of Bordeaux, to safeguard the young king's lands. Below App. 2 nos. 26 and 49.

[47] P 5319c and see *CS* ii pt 1 49, citing P 5132; Cheney, *Innocent III and England*, esp. 40–1, 391–400; Sayers, *Papal judges delegate*, 16, 29–30 and 31n.; and Powicke, *Henry III*, 4–6 and 45–7.

[48] Reg. Yr. 1 no. 167, *Reg. Hon. III* no. 244 (pd with some errors Shirley App. 5 no. 1), P 5417.

[49] Reg. Yr. 3 no. 436, *Reg. Hon. III* no. 2036, CPL 66.

[50] Reg. Yr. 6 no. 48, *Reg. Hon. III* no. 3566, CPL 83.

complete record. Nor is there any consistent source for the deprivation that resulted from excommunication. Master Gervase of Howbridge was deprived of the office of chancellor of St Paul's and of the church of Lambeth by Guala: furthermore, his election as dean of St Paul's was treated as void by the legate because of his excommunication as one who had openly declared against the king.[51] Brand, canon of St Paul's, had also been excommunicated in the late summer of 1215 for siding with the barons and was consequently deprived by Guala, losing also a moiety of the church of Caddington.[52] Deprivations at St Peter at Pleas, Lincoln, and at Stockton (Lincs.) as well as Caddington, plus at least one other likely instance from the same source, the rolls of Hugh of Wells, bishop of Lincoln,[53] pose the unanswerable question as to what would be the incidence if similar sources had survived for the other sixteen dioceses. There is no reason to suppose, however, that Lincoln was exceptional and it is likely that the legatine activities were equally assiduous elsewhere.

Deprivation led to the exercise of the right of patronage and replacement in the livings by loyalists. Where the patron was excommunicate, the right to present passed to the chief lord of the fee. Numerous examples are found in Hugh of Wells' rolls. To take but two: Joscelin de Aurelian was presented by William the Marshal, chief lord of the fee, to the church of Whitchurch (Bucks.), Robert de Ver, the lord of the fee and the patron being excommunicate; and Joyce, chaplain, was presented by the earl of Chester, chief lord of the fee, to the living of Gayton (le Marsh) (Lincs.), Simon de Sagio (Séez), the lord of the fee and the patron being under sentence of excommunication.[54] The accomplishment of such arrangements depended on the administration of the legate. The legate himself exercised direct patronage, usually only when the 'substitute' patron failed – as witnessed in his presentation to the parsonage of St John the Baptist, Oxford.[55]

Guala's powers included the right of scrutinizing presentations and ordering inductions. Guala had not only to re-establish the English Church but to do so in the light of recent legislation. Accordingly enquiries appear to have been made as to whether the presentee had any other benefice. If the diocesan was active presumably this was done

---

[51] *Fasti*, ed. Greenway, i St Paul's London, 6 and 26, and see below p. 188. See also Richardson, 'Letters', 250–9.

[52] *Rot. H. Welles*, ed. Phillimore and Davis, i 58, and *Fasti*, ed. Greenway, i St Paul's, 27 n. 3, and 29–30.

[53] *Rot. H. Welles*, ed. Phillimore and Davis, i 58, 72, 105, 113.

[54] Ibid. 35, 51.   [55] Ibid. 36.

through the ordinary administration, but if not it was performed by the legate's officers. The legate could decide on custody: moreover, he could dispense if he thought fit. The evidence shows that Guala was concerned with pluralists. The bishop's officers appear to have been ordered to enquire about pluralities before institution. Ralph de Hoby was inducted into Hoby church (Leics.) on the authority of the legate; presumably here the legal patron was loyal, and Hoby had no other benefices, but the officers would have had to ascertain this before induction was ordered. Richard de Taney was given custody of Waddesdon church (Bucks.) on the order of the legate. On one occasion at least Guala used his powers to unite a benefice in deference to Lateran IV. Peter of Southampton, clerk, to whom the legate gave a moiety of the church of Houghton Conquest (Beds.), following a deprivation, was admitted to the other half at the instigation of the legate and at the presentation of Hugh de Hotot.[56]

The legate's right of dispensation does not seem to have been circumscribed. He could and did dispense. Ralph de Verneia, a minor, was allowed to retain the church of Kegworth (Lincs.); presumably he was already in occupation. Gilbert de Innocentibus, rural dean of the city of Lincoln, was permitted to have the church of Edlesborough (Bucks.) on the presentation of the abbot and convent of Bardney; this was presumably a dispensation for plurality. Robert Passelew, presented to Swanbourne (Bucks.) by the prior and convent of Woburn, William of Lincoln, presented to Sutton (Lincs.) by the abbot and convent of Crowland, and Peter, presented to Welton (Lincs.) by the prior and convent of Ormsby, were all dispensed by the legate prior to admission and institution.[57] Most of these dispensations were probably for plurality and indicate that Guala took a tolerant line. The potential for innovatory reform under the legation was obvious, but there is no indication that the sensitive question of married clergy was tackled by the legate.

Pandulf Masca, legate *a latere* from the beginning of September 1218 to July 1221, had already established a close connection with England. He had come as nuncio with Durand in July 1211 with the purpose of persuading the king to accept Langton as archbishop and to receive back the clergy who were abroad. The mission failed and after quashing the election at Coventry/Lichfield the nuncios left England in late September. Pandulf returned in May 1215, in response to the king's overtures to the papal court, and on the day of his landing at Dover

---

[56] Ibid. 26–8, 30–1, 113.   [57] Ibid. 37, 55, 92, 117 and 120.

received John's prepared submission to the pope and two days later the cession of the kingdom.[58] In the summer of 1215 Pandulf was given the bishopric of Norwich on the king's recommendation and was granted the temporalities on 9 August. He attended the Lateran Council in November. So far he is described as papal subdeacon and *familiarius* of Innocent III. His consecration as bishop was delayed at first presumably because of the unsettled state of affairs in England; after 1218 it was delayed purposely to avoid the legate having to make profession of obedience to the archbishop of Canterbury as his provincial. It finally took place on 29 May 1222 after his return to the curia.[59]

Pandulf's background differed markedly from that of Guala. He was not a cardinal and from the beginning of Honorius's reign, certainly by 1217, he was immersed in the business of the papal chamber, where he is found usually in the company of S(inibaldus),[60] canon of S. Maria Maggiore, and also papal chamberlain.[61] Indeed he seems to have been groomed in the papal service much as Honorius himself had been. Guala's petition to be relieved of the office of legate which was made in 1218 was undoubtedly connected with the return of Langton to active administration of his diocese in the May of that year.[62] The situation was difficult. It called for an administrator who was firm but tactful. Pandulf had the advantages that he was known in England and that he understood administrators. Although the main groundwork of establishing a loyal and dependent clergy – by excommunication and deprivation – had been performed by Guala, the machinery of Crown and Church still needed supervision. The settlement of the Church was not complete, the wounds of strife had not been healed and the king was still under tutelage. On the death of the Marshal on 14 May 1219 it was Pandulf who secured the necessary governmental transition, 'captured' the administration and secured the great seal.[63] The despatch

[58] *CS* ii pt 1 12–19, 51–2 and n. 1.

[59] See Powicke, *Henry III*, 47.

[60] There is nothing to indicate that this S. was called Stephen (as Rabikauskas, '"Auditor"', 224 n. 3, says) nor does Stefano, cardinal priest of the basilica of SS. XII Apostoli, occur once as chamberlain under Honorius. The two references (*Reg. Hon. III* nos. 781, 3237) are to past occurrences, and Mansilla, ed., *La documentación pontificia de Honorio III*, 283, mentions an S. papal chamberlain on 13 November 1221 who is in all likelihood the Sinibaldus, canon of S. Maria Maggiore.

[61] *Liber Censuum*, ed. Fabre and Duchesne, i 254–6 nos. 20–2, 258–60 nos. 26–7; *Reg. Hon. III* no. 3074.

[62] *CS* ii pt 1 47, and *Acta Stephani Langton*, ed. Major, 165.

[63] F. M. Powicke, 'The Chancery during the minority of Henry III', *EHR* xxiii (1908) 220–35; and G. J. Turner, 'The minority of Henry III', pt 1 *TRHS* n.s. xviii (1904) 245–95, and pt 2 (3rd ser. i) (1907) 205–62.

of Pandulf to England was an act of diplomatic skill. It confirmed the continuity of papal policy. To have appointed Langton to succeed Guala would have been contrary to normal practice: a legate *a latere* was not normally confused with a *legatus natus*. Moreover it would have been divisive. Langton's position was still equivocal. To have sent another cardinal would have alienated the archbishop still further.

The letter recording Pandulf's appointment as legate speaks of granting *plenariam potestatem* but reveals no details.[64] It was accompanied by the usual letters of commendation requiring obedience to the legate from the English hierarchy and the nobility and also by a specific letter exempting Pandulf from obedience to his metropolitan until his consecration.[65] At roughly the same time a mandate was directed to the bishops of Winchester (Peter des Roches), Salisbury (Richard Poore) and Chichester (Ranulf of Wareham), on Pandulf's representation, ordering them to revoke certain papal letters (of which the contents are unknown) which had been surreptitiously obtained to his prejudice: in this Langton was involved.[66]

The joint influence of the legates on the English bishops and their dioceses indicates a continuous policy directed towards ensuring the security of the kingdom. Of the two provincials, Walter Gray had been translated to York from Worcester after 10 November 1215 and received the temporalities on 19 February 1216. His translation followed the rejection of Simon Langton for the see of York. Gray's two diocesans, Carlisle and Durham, came under the eye of the legate Guala. The see of Carlisle had been used as a political pawn by the Scots who in the period of civil war had put in an excommunicate clerk. The election was quashed in 1218 by Guala who provided Hugh, former abbot of Beaulieu and ambassador of King John. The pope had sought that the regular canons should be replaced by seculars but Guala may have seen more closely the realities of the situation and was unwilling to implement this radical change. (Whether the Victorine observances had ever really been adopted at Carlisle, however, is doubtful.) The arrangements made by Guala and elaborated by Pandulf and his commissioners were as much economic as constitutional, concerning the division of the possessions between the bishop and the cathedral establishment. In the confirmation acquired by Bishop Hugh in 1223, reference was made to the observance of the customs of other bishoprics, but Carlisle, in its isolated position, did not fit neatly into

[64] Reg. Yr. 3 no. 54, *Reg. Hon. III* no. 1621, *CPL* 58. P 5905.
[65] Reg. Yr. 3 nos. 55, 58, *Reg. Hon. III* nos. 1609, 1620, *CPL* 58.
[66] Reg. Yr. 3 no. 59, *Reg. Hon. III* no. 1612.

a papal scheme. A loyalist, however, had been introduced as its bishop.[67] At Durham, Richard Marsh's appointment by the legate Guala brought to an end several vain attempts to secure a suitable candidate. As royal chancellor, it must have been important to accommodate Marsh after his failure to get Winchester and Ely.[68] In the southern province thirteen dioceses (and the four Welsh) were subject to Langton, who was absent until 1218. At Hereford in August 1216 the legate confirmed the election of the dean, Hugh de Mapenor, as bishop.[69] At Bath, where Jocelin of Wells was the bishop, Guala suggested the dissolution of the union between Bath and Glastonbury, which the pope confirmed in 1219, and in 1220 Pandulf was ordered to examine the question of the bishop's title and petition to style himself bishop of Bath and Wells in future.[70] Of the southern bishops, six had attended the Lateran Council, Richard Poore, bishop of Chichester, Simon of Apulia, bishop of Exeter, William of Cornhill, bishop of Coventry, Hugh of Wells, bishop of Lincoln, Benedict of Sawston, bishop of Rochester, and Walter Gray, bishop of Worcester. Also present were the bishops-elect of the two East Anglian sees, Ely (Robert of York) and Norwich (Pandulf). The bishops of Bath (Jocelin of Wells), London (William of Sainte-Mère-Eglise), Salisbury (Herbert Poore) and Winchester (Peter des Roches) did not attend.[71] Appointments which had been made at the end of John's reign were Silvester of Evesham to Worcester to succeed Walter Gray on his translation to York, William of Cornhill (consecrated 1215) to Coventry, Richard Poore to Chichester, and Pandulf to Norwich.[72] The 'continuators' were Hugh of Wells, bishop of Lincoln, consecrated in 1209, Peter des Roches, bishop of Winchester, consecrated in 1205, Jocelin, bishop of Bath, consecrated in 1206, Herbert Poore, consecrated as bishop of Salisbury under Richard I, Walter Gray, consecrated to Worcester in 1214, though now translated to York, and Stephen Langton. The appearance of royal administrators in the episcopate is far from novel but they presented a hard core at this time. Hugh and Jocelin of Wells, the Poores, Richard Marsh,

67 *Fasti*, ed. Greenway, ii Monastic cathedrals, 20; *Patent rolls 1216–25*, 164, 210; below App. 2 no. 3 (P 5578); Reg. Yrs. 3 no. 43, 5 no. 586, and 7 no. 142, *Reg. Hon. III* nos. 1596, 3124 and 4333, *CPL* 57, 81 and 91.
68 *Fasti*, ed. Greenway, ii Monastic cathedrals, 31; *Hist. Dunelm. scriptores tres*, ed. Raine, 35, and *Patent rolls 1216–25*, 81.
69 Reg. Yr. 1 no. 19, *Reg. Hon. III* no. 28, *CPL* 40–1.
70 Reg. Yr. 3 no. 452, *Reg. Hon. III* no. 2069, *CPL* 67, P 6067, and *Mon. Angl.* ii 269 no. 19. Reg. Yr. 4 no. 679, *Reg. Hon. III* no. 2364, *CPL* 70.
71 Cheney, *Innocent III and England*, 397.
72 See *Handbook of British chronology*, ed. Powicke and Fryde, 216, 233, 242 and 261.

Walter Gray and Ralph Neville, appointed to Chichester in 1224, were all from the royal Chancery. Eustace de Fauconberg, appointed to London in 1221, and Thomas de Blundeville, bishop of Norwich from 1226, were connected with the Exchequer. Guala's powers of disposing of bishoprics to men faithful to the king accounted for Richard Poore at Salisbury, William of Blois at Worcester and Ranulf of Wareham at Chichester. Pandulf's position allowed him to confirm Eustace de Fauconberg at London and to quash the election of Robert of York, who had sided with the barons, at Ely, replacing him with the Cistercian, John abbot of Fountains.[73] The stiffening was not clearly in favour of papal men. Even Alexander Stavensby, appointed by the pope to Coventry and Lichfield in 1224, perhaps to monitor Langton's views on Fawkes de Breauté and to mediate,[74] and Pandulf, could not adequately be described in this way. It was a reinforcement of men who could be regarded as loyal to the establishment.

Nor is there any clear influx of papal men into the cathedral chapters. The sources are, however, extremely patchy.[75] Only St Paul's has a medieval catalogue of the prebendaries and only Salisbury has a list of residents and non-residents in the chapter. For the other seven secular cathedrals, York, Lincoln, Exeter, Chichester, Hereford, Bath and Lichfield, details have to be wrung from a variety of sources. With these limitations in mind, the evidence is as follows.

At York, where there were thirty-six prebends, six were filled with Italians in Honorius's reign: two, probably three, had appointees from Innocent III's pontificate. At Langtoft Leonardo Odelini succeeded his uncle, Giovanni (Conti), cardinal deacon of S. Maria in Cosmedin, Innocent III's chancellor and probably his brother, in 1213, and at North Newbald Pietro of Ferentino followed his uncle Stefano of Fossanova, cardinal priest of the basilica of SS. Apostoli, in 1215 on the king's collation.[76] Stefano de Normandis (a Conti), cardinal deacon of S. Adriano, is also likely to have received Laughton from Innocent III.[77] Under Honorius three Italians were provided to York prebends. Gimundo, clerk and relative of Aldebrandino Gaetani, cardinal deacon

---

73 Gibbs and Lang, *Bishops and reform*, 72; *Fasti*, ed. Greenway, ii Monastic cathedrals, 20, 46, and *CPL* 55, 67. Pandulf had custody of the diocese after the quashing of Robert of York's election (see F. Cazel in *PRS* xliv, 46).
74 Gibbs and Lang, *Bishops and reform*, 30–1, 73.
75 See Greenway, 'Ecclesiastical chronology', 53–60. I am very grateful to Dr Greenway for help with this section and for allowing me to use her notes on English cathedral dignitaries.
76 *York minster fasti*, ed. Clay, ii 47, 57–8. Giovanni had the vicarage of Conisbrough on the presentation of the prior and convent of Lewes: his successor in 1213, Tolommeo, was also a kinsman of Innocent III.   77 Ibid. 50.

of S. Eustachio, acquired a papal mandate for his induction to Riccall on 22 March 1217.[78] Rufino of Vercelli received Strensall, probably when his uncle, Guala, was legate, and Master Laurentius de Sancto Nicholao, clerk of Guala, had a prebend, to which Thockrington (Northumb.) was attached, certainly by 1226.[79]

At Lincoln the influence of the Contis was again apparent in the appointment under Innocent III of Stefano de Normandis to Leighton Ecclesia; and the influence of Guala, possibly, in the assignment to Rufino of the prebend of Cropredy and to Master Laurentius de Sancto Nicholao of a canonry.[80] Otherwise Lincoln had only one other Italian in its fifty-six prebends: Master Theobaldus, papal scribe.[81] London (with thirty canons and twelve minor canons in the establishment) seems to have had no more than one, possibly two, foreign occupants of its prebends during the pontificate. Master Petrus de Collemedio, papal chaplain, who occurs as king's clerk and a *socius* of Pandulf in 1219, and who became archbishop of Rouen in 1236, had the prebend of Holborn *c.* 1216 × July 1228[82] and Cinthio the Roman or de Sancto Eustachio may have had Rugmere before 1229.[83] Two canons of St Paul's who were excommunicated in the late summer of 1215, Brand and Master Gervase of Howbridge, were not replaced by Italians.[84] A clerk of Innocent III, Alanus, was prebendary of Chiswick, perhaps holding the prebend into Honorius's reign: it has been suggested that he was the English canonist, Master Alanus.[85] For Lichfield, Hereford and Wells there is no evidence at all of foreign infiltration. For Exeter, Rufino alone is found in a prebend; and for Chichester, the pope himself attempted to get the provision of Blasius Bonnelli, a scholar and the son of Giovanni Bonnelli, a Roman citizen, by mandates to both Ranulf of Wareham and Ralph Neville.[86] This provision and that of Master Theobaldus, papal scribe, at Lincoln are the only two clear instances of Honorius's intervention in the cathedral chapters.

---

[78] Reg. Yr. 1 no. 519, *Reg. Hon. III* no. 458, *CPL* 48; *York minster fasti*, ed. Clay, ii 66: his successor, perhaps not immediate, was Adenulfus Conti.

[79] *York minster fasti*, ed. Clay, ii 72, 74.

[80] *Fasti*, ed. Greenway, iii Lincoln, 64, 80, and see below App. 2 nos. 34, 35. Another Conti succeeded Rufino under Gregory IX.

[81] See above p. 44 and below p. 206.

[82] *Patent rolls 1216–25*, 205; Reg. Yr. 4 no. 629, *CPL* 69; *Fasti*, ed. Greenway, i St Paul's, 54; *Patent rolls 1225–32*, 214, 215; and *Reg. Greg. IX*, ed. Auvray, no. 3281.

[83] *Fasti*, ed. Greenway, i St Paul's, 75. He was instituted to Kirk Ella (patrons the abbot and convent of Selby) in 1234, *Reg. Gray*, ed. Raine, 67.

[84] *Fasti*, ed. Greenway, i St Paul's, 6, 56.

[85] Ibid., 41–2.

[86] Reg. Yr. 7 no. 186, *Reg. Hon. III* no. 4342, *CPL* 92. Giovanni of Colonna had a prebend of Ripon before 1225, *Patent rolls 1216–25*, 531.

Salisbury with fifty-two prebends by 1224 supported six Italians. Master Laurentius de Sancto Nicholao had two prebends, Fordington and Writhlington from 1222 and Preston from 1233. Stefano de Normandis had Lyme and Halstock from at least 1226. The list of residents of 1226 supplies evidence also of Tancred, archdeacon of Bologna (absent) who had the prebend of Yetminster Secunda, Giacomo of Vercelli, likely to be Guala's import, who had Preston, and Reginaldo Sinebaldus who had Major Pars Altaris.[87] Master Martino de Summa, who had acted as a proctor for Glastonbury and held some of their benefices, had the prebend of Chisenbury (Martin) and Chute from 1217; from a Milanese family (and succeeding W. archpriest of Milan) he may have settled in England.[88] It cannot be argued that infiltration was greater where the legate Guala had approved the appointment of the bishop for if so there would not be the sharp contrast between Hereford, say, and Salisbury. Nor can it be shown that the most valuable prebends were secured for papal provisees and the legate's officers. A valuation of the Salisbury prebends was made in 1217. This shows that collectively they were worth 1422 marks. Those held by foreigners were valued as follows: Fordington and Writhlington (Master Laurentius) 30m, Preston (Master Laurentius) 24m, Lyme and Halstock (Stefano de Normandis) 32m, Yetminster Secunda (Tancred) 8m, and Major Pars Altaris (Reginaldo Sinebaldus) and Chisenbury and Chute (Master Martino de Summa) 16m each. They were not therefore of striking value and more than one prebend would have been necessary to support an administrator such as Master Laurentius. In contrast the wealthiest, Ogbourne, was worth 150m, Charminster and the Treasury (including Calne) were both worth 80m, Worth 60m and there were several valued at 50m.[89]

At Salisbury and at York, where most foreign infiltration apparently took place, the numbers of provisions themselves are not impressive. But at both, and to a lesser extent at Lincoln where the evidence is very insufficient, two main influences can be detected, that of Innocent III and that of the legate Guala. Throughout Honorius's pontificate the Contis remained strong in the curia as well as in the provinces and the legates were doubtless able to conserve their inroads into the English prebends. The provisions made by the legate Guala for his own staff and relatives probably did not long outlast their use. For the income

---

[87] *Reg. S. Osmund*, ed. Rich Jones, ii 70–7.
[88] Reg. Yr. 1 no. 407, *Reg. Hon. III* no. 528, *CPL* 47; Cheney, *Innocent III and England*, 91.
[89] W. E. Lunt, *The valuation of Norwich* (Oxford 1926) 17, 525–6.

of a prebend to be worthwhile it was necessary to be on the spot, otherwise the collection of the revenue outweighed the assets. Guala was in a position to put in some of his own men directly: he did not, however, use those powers at St Paul's. Pandulf appears to have exerted little such influence, but may have been responsible for Master Peter de Collemedio's canonry of St Paul's. At Salisbury it is possible that Guala's report, which produced the papal licence for the removal of the cathedral to a new and more convenient site, may have persuaded Richard Poore to accommodate Master Laurentius de Sancto Nicholao and Giacomo of Vercelli.[90] Even Tancred's small pension may have been due to this arrangement. The canonization of St William of York was approved by Honorius in 1226 and may in some way be connected with the foreign infiltration, particularly under Innocent III.[91] York badly needed the cult of a saint to maintain its position and income against those of St John at Beverley and of St Cuthbert at Durham. Undoubtedly the canonization of St William owed much to Archbishop Walter Gray, an active campaigner, but it may also have owed something to the useful influences at the curia of the cardinals Stefano de Normandis, Stefano of Fossanova and Guala. Whether such reciprocal arrangements did take place can only be conjectured. What does seem beyond conjecture, however, is that the provision in English cathedral chapters was minimal, brought little of direct advantage to the central papal administration and made no long-term impact.

Only a few instances refer to the legates exercising any control over monastic appointments. It is recorded that Prior Laurence of Guisborough resigned the priory into the hands of the legate Guala. This undated entry is enigmatic. Was the prior old or in some way incompetent or was he a sympathizer with the king's enemies? He was given the chapel of Hartlepool, so perhaps the first.[92] The next known prior, Michael, who occurs in 1218, is perhaps a presentee of Guala.[93] Guisborough were busy at the curia in 1218 when they petitioned for and acquired three separate confirmations of the churches of Bridekirk (Cumb.), Dearham (Cumb.) and Hessle (Yorks. ER) – Hessle had been

---

[90] See *Reg.* Yrs. 1 no. 345, 2 no. 980, *Reg. Hon. III* nos. 441, 1194, *CPL* 46, 53 and P 5738, and *Reg. S. Osmund*, ed. Rich Jones, ii 5–7.

[91] 'Qui statuit terminos', D. and C. York Reg. A fols. 59–60 (P 7551), pd *Historians of the church of York*, ed. J. Raine, iii (RS lxxi 1894) 127 no. 92; ii 270–91, 388–97 and *Acta sanctorum* June 11 (1968) 136–46 give details of the process so far as known.

[92] *Cartularium prioratus de Gyseburne*, ed. W. Brown, ii (Surtees Soc. lxxxix, 1891) 358, and *Reg. Gray*, ed. Raine, 80–1.

[93] *Heads of religious houses*, ed. Knowles *et al.*, 164.

in the possession of one of Innocent III's notaries, Master Britius.[94]
Could it be that this activity at Rome was in some way connected with
the legate's interest in Guisborough? The evidence is insufficient to say.
The nuns of Shaftesbury petitioned the legate to confirm the election
of their abbess but Guala refused because it appeared that there had
been a dual election and he referred the case to delegates.[95] It cannot
be imagined that the legate scrutinized every monastic election, simply
those brought to his notice, as this one. Pandulf concerned himself on
two occasions with the heads of religious houses. On the first he
restored Roger Norreis to the priorate of Penwortham (Lancs.), a
Benedictine house dependent on Evesham, from which he had been
deposed by the legate, Niccolò bishop of Tusculum, in 1214. Formerly
a monk of Christ Church, Canterbury, and abbot of Evesham,
Norreis's activities had been hair-raising, and it can only be supposed
that his reinstatement by Pandulf followed some negotiations at the
curia of which there is now no evidence.[96] The legate's other appointment was of William to the Benedictine alien house of Cowick
(Devon), dependent on Bec, which took place some time after 20 May
1219, probably following an approach to him.[97]

   The influence of Guala on English benefices has in part been
considered but it is important to see both the legates' activities in a more
general context. The legates and their officers were fully occupied with
administrative duties. No doubt co-operation was encountered from
the first in dioceses where the key offices were filled and the bishop
not absent – the archdeacon of Essex, Theobald de Valognes, for
example, was used by Guala to suspend clergy[98] – but that did not
preclude the need for the legates to have their own administrators. The
question of the support of the legates is crucial to an understanding of
their activities. Legates had a customary and accepted right to their
support and maintenance while on legation. At first the support was
one of bed, board and general hospitality for the legate and his *familia*
(with provision for horses and stabling) while attending to the business

[94] Reg. Yr. 2 nos. 1054–6, *Reg. Hon. III* nos. 1251 and 1262–3, *CPL* 54; and Cheney, *Innocent III and England*, 89.
[95] Reg. Yr. 3 no. 238, *Reg. Hon. III* no. 1810, *CPL* 61–2; and cf. Reg. Yr. 2 no. 607, *Reg. Hon. III* no. 757, *CPL* 49.
[96] *Heads of religious houses*, ed. Knowles et al., 94, and see 34, 48. On Norreis, see D. Knowles, *The monastic order in England* (Cambridge 1950) esp. 321–3, 326, 331–43, 370 and 653.
[97] *Heads of religious houses*, ed. Knowles et al., 102.
[98] Reg. Yr. 4 no. 750, *Reg. Hon. III* no. 2440, *CPL* 71.

of the house or while *en route* to another.[99] This charge in terms of hospitality, clearly the ideal of the early Church, could not often be fairly distributed – there were particular institutions on main routes for example that might suffer greatly from continuous demands. Procuration came therefore to be commuted to a money payment. In any case, by the thirteenth century, the notion of the legation itself had been transformed from one of individual visits to a general visitation. While the curia tried in the main to discourage monetary payments, for example, from Cistercian houses, in practice some procuration in money had to be accepted; in the canon law procuration was increasingly defined as monetary payment owed by all institutions.[100]

Legatine appointments might define what the legate could justifiably receive. Legates were obviously discouraged from making excessive demands on churches and encouraged to live moderately. Honorius's letters of appointment called upon the community to receive the legate *hilariter* and to treat him *honorifice* (or *honeste*) according to his station and rank.[101] Attempts were made through conciliar and decretal legislation to limit the size of the retinue, the number of horses particularly, but the number of attendants, the legate's *familia*, at least at this time does not appear to have been regulated. The maintenance of the legates' households was essential for the conduct of business: the clerks and administrators had to be supported, as well as the domestic officers, for on a long stay the legate needed his own establishment. Innocent III had reiterated that all churches other than those exempt by the Holy See were to pay procurations to legates, whether directly visited or not, and Guala, according to Matthew Paris, took procurations from all cathedrals and religious houses of fifty shillings.[102] Paris goes on to say that Guala sequestrated all the churches of those who had followed Louis which he then 'converted to his and his clerks' uses'. How the legate Pandulf raised the necessary support is not obvious but he is likely to have imposed a general rate of some kind. When the papal nuncio, Otto, came in 1225 with the pope's new financial plan, he took two silver marks from all conventual churches.[103]

Provision for clerks in active service had to be made. Unfortunately we do not have the names of those in Guala's household as we have for Pandulf's in 1219. Guala's clerk, Master Laurentius de Sancto Nicholao, papal subdeacon and chaplain, who was beneficed, perhaps

[99] Berlière, 'Droit de procuration', 509–38.
[100] *Reg. Hon. III* no. 3593, cited by Berlière, 'Droit de procuration', 516; *X* III 39.
[101] Berlière, 'Droit de procuration', 520.
[102] c. 17 *X* III 39; *Chron. maj.*, ed. Luard, ii 663.   [103] *Chron. maj.*, ed. Luard, ii 663.

later, in Salisbury and York cathedrals, had the rectory of Chesterton (Cambs.) and the church of Terrington (Norf.). In 1291 Chesterton was the fifth most profitable living in the diocese of Ely, when the rectory was valued at £53 6s 8d. It was presumably affected by the events of the civil war and its rector probably excommunicated and dispossessed: later Guala granted the church to his new Augustinian foundation of St Andrew at Vercelli. This is the only known example of the legate keeping hold of a church after the first presentation. The church was served by a vicar (Adam of Wisbech, instituted on 17 November 1218) during the tenure of Master Laurentius in accordance with canonical requirements where the rector was an absentee.[104] The other living held by Master Laurentius de Sancto Nicholao, of which there is evidence, was Terrington in the patronage of the bishop of Ely. Robert of York, as bishop-elect of Ely – his election was to be quashed by Pandulf – presented Laurentius, and Guala instituted him at the request of the official of Norwich, Master Ranulf of Wareham. The bishop-elect of Norwich, Pandulf, was not yet consecrated so could not institute. The pope's confirmation of the church, at Guala's request, was probably to set the seal on the settlement, following lay attempts to fill the living.[105] Master Laurentius's activities in 1219 show him to have been high in the legate's chain of command and the indications are that he was Italian.[106] His acquisition of the York prebend does not pre-date 1226 and similarly his holding of the two prebends at Salisbury may not have been due directly to the legate Guala.[107] The small York prebend which had been given him by Archbishop Walter Gray had the church of Thockrington added to it during his tenure; the prebend was alleged to have been insufficient for the maintenance of a canon.[108] Master Laurentius needed a dispensation to hold Thockrington, having other benefices, including the unnamed prebend of Lincoln.[109]

Some of Guala's six or seven nephews may have been members of

[104] *Patent rolls 1216–25*, 76–7; Richardson, 'Letters', 250, and see J. E. Foster, 'The connection of the church of Chesterton with the abbey of Vercelli', *Proc. of the Cambridge Antiquarian Soc.* xiii (n.s. vii, 1908–9) 185–212.

[105] Reg. Yr. 2 no. 901, *Reg. Hon. III* no. 1079, CPL 52.

[106] See e.g. *Rot. H. Welles*, ed. Phillimore and Davis, i, 140–1. CPL 114 provided protection for his properties on his leaving England, and cf. *Reg. Gray*, ed. Raine, 154–6.

[107] See above pp. 178, 179, 180.

[108] See *York minster fasti*, ed. Clay, ii 73–4, CPL 111.

[109] *Fasti*, ed. Greenway, iii Lincoln, 131, 138. The protectors of his property, the abbot of Walden and the prior of Barnwell (CPL 114), suggest possibly an Essex living besides the other East Anglian ones.

his household. Filippo was beneficed in the livings of Alrewas (Staffs.) and Shifnal (Salop).[110] It is tempting to identify the unnamed benefice of St Albans, which J., Guala's nephew, had before 1220, with Woodhorn (Northumb.), over the provision of which there had been some opposition from the abbot of St Albans in 1202 when Innocent III had asked for it to be assigned to a nephew of the cardinal bishop of Albano, then a student at Paris.[111] On 6 May 1220 Tynemouth, dependent on St Albans, was granted the right to appropriate the church of Woodhorn and its chapels, with the consent of the bishop of Durham and the patron, William of Trumpington, abbot of St Albans.[112] There is no mention in the document of a present occupant but this may not signify a vacancy, as appropriation was presumed to be effective on the death of the present incumbent. By 23 July 1220, Guala's nephew, J., was dead and his living – whichever it may have been – reverted to St Albans.[113] Guala's nephew, Rufino, was the most extensively endowed of all the legate's relatives. In 1233 his benefices were said to be worth more than 200 marks (£130), when a papal mandate ordered that he was to be content with this sum from the benefices which did not have care of souls. He was in actual fact deprived of all (unfortunately not named) except the church of Ecclesfield (Yorks.), six marks from a prebend of Exeter, and the rich prebend of Cropredy in Lincoln cathedral.[114] He had already lost the prebend of Strensall in York minster. There is no evidence that his uncle had conferred more than Strensall and possibly Cropredy on him. It seems very unlikely, for many of them clearly had care of souls: if it was so, it was nothing short of scandalous. More probable explanations are that Rufino was involved in his uncle's administration, being endowed with the two prebends, but that others had given him the numerous livings. Three more of the legate's nephews, his namesake, Guala, Martino, and an unnamed one, all enjoyed annual pensions from the Crown: it is likely that they were employed in some way in the English administration.[115]

---

110 *Patent rolls 1216–25*, 299, cited by Richardson, 'Letters', 256 n. 7.

111 Cf. Cheney, *Innocent III and England*, 84–6.

112 See below App. 2 no. 11.

113 Reg. Yr. 4 no. 838, *Reg. Hon. III* no. 2571 (not in *CPL*).

114 *York minster fasti*, ed. Clay, ii 71–2; *Patent rolls 1216–25*, 352; *CPL* 132, 140, 142, 145; *Fasti*, ed. Greenway, iii Lincoln, 64, 72.

115 *Patent rolls 1216–25*, 422, and *Rot. lit. claus.*, ed. Hardy, i 156, 384, 387 and 581b; cited by Richardson, 'Letters', 256 n. 7. The third pension was for only half the amount of the other two (40m) which makes it certain that this is another nephew, for whom Laurentius de Sancto Nicholao acted as proctor. Perhaps yet another nephew was involved in a dispute with a clerk of Pandulf (Reg. Yr. 4 no. 797, *Reg. Hon. III* no. 2508, *CPL* 73).

Giacomo of Vercelli who held the prebend of Preston in Salisbury in 1226 and Giovanni of Vercelli, prebendary of Haydour-cum-Walton in Lincoln, are likely to have been relatives, possibly in his household, one of them perhaps the unnamed nephew.[116]

Thirteen members of Pandulf's household as legate in England are named as witnesses to the submission to the pope of Reginald, king of the Isles, in September 1219.[117] Four or five of them were probably English: Rusticus and John of London, his scribes, Luke de Wytsand, his chaplain[118] and two persons with connections with Chichester, Martin, his steward, and the treasurer of Chichester (?P.).[119] There is little doubt that the last two entered the legate's household through the influence and possibly at the suggestion of Ranulf of Wareham (monk, official and prior of Norwich under Pandulf as bishop-elect) who was elected bishop of Chichester before 17 December 1217 and consecrated early in 1218.[120] It is not clear what the treasurer of Chichester's function was in the household: was he perhaps treasurer of the legate? Another English clerk of the legate, John Bacun, occurs in 1221.[121] The other eight who were present at the submission were clearly Italian, consisting of Pandulf, the legate's nephew, Master Iacobus, papal scribe,[122] Corrado, clerk of Gregorio de Crescentio, cardinal deacon of S. Teodoro,[123] Masters Iohannes of Venafro and Petrus de Babunt' and Master Ardingus of Pavia, papal subdeacon, and probably a lawyer (? a civilian). Master Petrus de Collemedio, papal chaplain and prebendary of Holborn in the cathedral of St Paul, belonged to those immersed in royal, papal and legatine business.[124] Stefano, nephew of Stefano of Fossanova, cardinal priest of the basilica of SS. XII Apostoli (called of Ferentino until the death of his uncle, after which he apparently called himself of Fossanova) had at least two English benefices, Nettleton (Lincs.) to which he had been

[116] *Reg. S. Osmund*, ed. Rich Jones, ii 74, 77; and *Fasti*, ed. Greenway, iii Lincoln, 72.
[117] Reg. Yr. 4 no. 629, CPL 69–70 (not in *Reg. Hon. III*).
[118] He might be the canon of Chichester who occurs 1216 × 1220 (*Reg. S. Osmund*, ed. Rich Jones, i 259).
[119] See *Patent rolls 1216–25*, 260, where P. occurs on 20 Nov. 1220.
[120] For Ranulf, see *Fasti*, ed. Greenway, ii Monastic cathedrals, 60; *Heads of religious houses*, ed. Knowles *et al.*, 58; and *Handbook of British chronology*, ed. Powicke and Fryde, 216. See also *Patent rolls 1216–25*, 130; *Rot. lit. pat.*, ed. Hardy, i 132b–134, 152 bis, 166b, 171b.
[121] *Patent rolls 1216–25*, 296.
[122] See above pp. 42–3, 44 and below pp. 186, 187, 199.
[123] Cecchelli states that Gregorio de Crescentio was related to Honorius III but gives no authority.
[124] *Patent rolls 1216–25*, 205. Elze, 'Päpstliche Kapelle', 188, says that he is the first example of a non-resident chaplain.

preferred by the bishop (presentation due to lapse) and Fishburn (co. Durham) on the resignation of his uncle, presumably in 1214.[125]

The duties of the legate's Italian *familiarii* or associates (Master Petrus de Collemedio is described on another occasion as his *socius*) are likely to have been the usual legal and administrative functions of secular clerks concerned with ecclesiastical administration. The *familia* included a papal chaplain, a papal subdeacon, a (?ex) papal scribe, two masters without title, and therefore presumably university men, and two connected possibly with the cardinals' households. With the exceptions of possibly Petrus de Collemedio, Stefano of Ferentino (whose provisions preceded the legation) and Master Iacobus, papal scribe, there is no evidence of how the other persons in the household were maintained. The sources indicate Pandulf's constant financial difficulties. For two years from 1219 he was allowed to divert the proceeds from non-conventual churches in his diocese and from his manors towards the payment of his debts;[126] and in 1220 Honorius granted Pandulf licence to present clerks in his service to more than one benefice, as the benefices in his gift were few and of small value. Pandulf, however, was charged to do this in moderation and with care so as not to court criticism.[127] Was this a comment on Guala's activities? However that may be, the sources are singularly silent on the provision of benefices and payments to Pandulf's clerks. The only beneficiary of whom we have direct evidence is Master Egidius (Verraclus), his brother, a papal subdeacon and chaplain, who was to be provided to a suitable benefice in the diocese of Norwich, according to a papal mandate of 5 September 1218: whether he got it and whether he was in any way connected with the legate's administration is not clear.[128] Letters of 4 September 1218, at the time of Pandulf's appointment, warned the bishops of Salisbury and Winchester not to molest the legate over certain benefices belonging to him in their dioceses and especially not to dispose of them before the legate's consecration as bishop of Norwich.[129] There is the dual complication that Pandulf also had patronage to use as bishop and an episcopal household to maintain, although this may have been very closely associated with the legatine following.

---

125 *Rot. H. Welles*, ed. Phillimore and Davis, i 124, and *York minster fasti*, ed. Clay, ii 57.
126 Reg. Yr. 4 no. 602, *Reg. Hon. III* no. 2257, *CPL* 68.
127 Reg. Yr. 4 no. 753, *Reg. Hon. III* no. 2463, *CPL* 71.
128 See H. H. Coulson in *Norfolk Archaeology* (Proceedings of the Norwich and Norfolk Archaeol. Soc. xxvi 1938) 330, and Reg. Yr. 3 no. 56, *Reg. Hon. III* no. 1618, *CPL* 58.
129 Reg. Yr. 3 no. 60, *Reg. Hon. III* no. 1613, *CPL* 58.

If we look at the whole of England, only in 21 benefices out of about 9500 – the number recorded in the *Taxatio* of Pope Nicholas IV of 1291 – can foreign occupation be established.[130] Three papal scribes were given English benefices, a papal notary, a papal chaplain, and two relatives of Honorius, and one (?) of Celestine III. Several relatives of Innocent III retained their endowments. The other provisions were those for the support of the legatine households or took place under the legates. Guala presented some of his own clerks and so probably did Pandulf. Guala also dispensed a certain number of these people to hold more than one benefice. Constantinus, papal scribe, was provided to Alwalton (Hunts.) in the patronage of the abbey of Peterborough in 1218 to replace Geoffrey Gibwin who had been excommunicated.[131] In 1239 a chaplain was given possession of it on behalf of G. de Insula, papal subdeacon and chaplain.[132] Clearly the church had remained in papalist hands and it was probably continuously served by a vicar, thus causing little difference to the parishioners. A few months earlier in 1218 the pope had confirmed Guala's dispensation to Master Azzo, papal scribe (who might be identifiable with Master Atto, canon of Lincoln) to hold Wintringham (Hunts.) (or Winteringham, Lincs.) and Stanhope (co. Durham): possibly he held the churches from Innocent III's reign.[133] Again a vicar must have been used. Master Iacobus, papal scribe, who was promised a benefice in the diocese of Ely in 1218, appears in Pandulf's household in 1219.[134] Master Pandulf, papal subdeacon and notary, was granted Exminster because his predecessor, Master Alexander, had resigned the living into the hands of S(inibaldus), the papal chamberlain. He was a papal officer of considerable importance in the 1220s, legate to the March of Ancona and used as a plenipotentiary by Gregory IX.[135] He is not to be confused with either the legate (as Tout thought),[136] who is described always from August 1215 onwards as elect of Norwich and who was never a papal notary, nor with

---

130 See *Taxatio ecclesiastica Angliae et Walliae auctoritate Pape Nicholai IV*, ed. T. Astle, S. Ayscough and J. Caley (Rec. Commission 1802). Cheney (*Innocent III and England*, 84) says that under Innocent III 'between twenty and thirty' Italians held English benefices. For the two benefices not discussed in this chapter, 'Altegnis' (unidentified) and Little Bytham, see Reg. Yr. 4 no. 797, *CPL* 73, and below, App. 1B p. 207.

131 Reg. Yr. 2 no. 1077, *Reg. Hon. III* no. 1295 (not in *CPL*). See above p. 44.

132 *Rotuli Roberti Grosseteste*, ed. Davis, 268; and see 283.

133 Reg. Yr. 2 no. 902, *Reg. Hon. III* no. 1080, *CPL* 52. *Fasti*, ed. Greenway, iii Lincoln, 121 and 127.

134 Reg. Yrs. 2 no. 1065, 3 no. 629, *Reg. Hon. III* no. 1307, and see above pp. 42–3, 44, 186 and below, p. 199.

135 Reg. Yr. 2 no. 1282, *Reg. Hon. III* no. 1525, *CPL* 56–7. See above pp. 30–1.

136 Tout in *DNB* xv 174–9.

Pandulf Masca's nephew, who so far as I know never appears with any other description save that of his relationship to the legate. The mandate for his succession was addressed to Guala, and the bishop of Exeter was ordered to institute him, but his enjoyment of the church was not smooth. The papal chaplain, Master Gratian, laid claim to possession of the church of Kettering, in the patronage of Peterborough abbey.[137] Honorius's relative, Giovanni de Thebaldo, who is described as papal kinsman and *familiarius*, received the church of Lambeth in the archbishop of Canterbury's patronage, on the deprivation by the legate Guala of the excommunicate Master Gervase of Howbridge.[138] Pietro Capocci, another kinsman of Honorius, was in possession of the living of Guilden Morden (Cambs.) by July 1222. The patronage at this time was probably Barnwell's and the name means 'Golden' or 'Rich' or 'Splendid'. Pietro was described as Gregory IX's *hostiarius* on 27 June 1227; by 1243 he had become a canon of St Peter's and in the following year was made cardinal deacon of S. Giorgio in Velabro by Innocent IV.[139] Both these two were clearly in the papal household. Oddo 'Bobonis', papal subdeacon and chaplain, perhaps a descendant of Pope Celestine III,[140] received Felixkirk church, vacated by Ugo de Comite, a papal provisee, in 1222. Oddo's proctor was to be inducted into the living by a York commission, including John Romeyn, canon.[141] The living appears to have been secured in papal hands. In 1244 Corrado, canon and proctor of Ivrea, received it from the legate Otto and was dispensed to hold it with two other benefices, and in 1251 Opizo de Castello had custody, being given leave of absence and appointing a vicar.[142]

Although in some cases livings passed to other papalists, in others the patrons might attempt to reassert their rights, as did Nostell over the church of Bamburgh, to which Stefano of Fossanova had been presented by the Crown. Nostell successfully resecured the church before 1221 and other murmurings of repossession occur elsewhere. The prior and convent of Butley who had promised to make provision for Trasmundus, clerk of Ferentino, were reprimanded in 1227 for having

[137] D. and C. Peterborough, MS 5 fol. 135r–v; 1 fols. 112v–13r (fols. xcviiv–xcviiir).
[138] For Howbridge, see above pp. 172, 178. He had been in Hubert Walter's household, see e.g. Ely Liber M p. 161 and *Mon. Angl.* v 70 no. 7.
[139] Paravicini Bagliani, *Cardinali*, 301; Reg. Yr. 6 no. 474, *Reg. Hon. III* no. 4078, P 11075; *VCH Cambs* viii 107; Eubel, *Hierarchia catholica* i 7; and Matthew Paris, *Chron. maj.*, ed. Luard, iv 250 and v 79.
[140] Pfaff, 'Papst Coelestin III', 110.
[141] Reg. Yr. 6 no. 438, *Reg. Hon. III* no. 3941, CPL 88.
[142] *Reg. W. Giffard*, ed. Brown, 176, 296, and CPL 206.

passed him over for the church of Terling (Essex) and were ordered to find him something else.[143] It is not difficult to imagine how a promise might be made in the hope of some service but that then there were closer and more pressing demands for provision. The number of pensions granted to papal clerks in this pontificate seems very insignificant.[144] Luca, son of Pietro de Iudice, formerly *primicerius* canon of St Peter's, was held to renounce his annual pension of six marks after his provision to the church of Compton (Sussex) by the prior and convent of Lewes. The provision probably took place at the beginning of Gregory IX's reign (close to 1228) as Gregory repeated the mandate of Honorius.[145] There are no indications that papal provision increased during Honorius's pontificate in any significant way.

Throughout the pontificate Langton's position at the curia was influential. This is clear early on from his acquisition of privileges on behalf of English petitioners. The compiler of the Winchcombe Landbook comments on how the cardinal was instrumental in getting a confirmation for his house in 1216, shortly after Innocent III's death.[146] Although Langton had been suspended in 1215, the suspension appears to have been lifted in 1216, possibly before Innocent died. Langton was back in his diocese in May 1218, a few months before the departure of Guala. In Michaelmas 1220 he returned to the curia, where he acquired the important privilege that no further legate should be sent to England during his lifetime.[147] It seems likely that Honorius was growing keen to withdraw the legatine and curial influence in any case, and that this was not simply a successful coup for Langton. Similarly in 1221 Langton is said to have extracted from Honorius the concession that the pope would not replace a clerk of the Roman church or an Italian in an English benefice for the next turn, but allow the presentation to return to the normal patron. This was an assurance to the archbishop that what he regarded as undue interference would be watched.[148] But certainly Honorius was of the view that the clerks in the curia had to be supported provincially. As is well known, his

---

[143] Reg. Yr. 11 no. 502, *Reg. Hon. III* no. 6210, *CPL* 115.

[144] Cf. Cheney, *Innocent III and England*, 94–6.

[145] *Acta Stephani Langton*, ed. Major, 134–5 no. 116. On the de Iudice family, see Gregorovius, *Rome in the middle ages* v (i) 195 n. 1, and *Fasti*, ed. Greenway, iii Lincoln, 75–6. A Giacomo de Iudice is mentioned as nephew of Archbishop John Romeyn of York. The provision of two nephews of Cardinal Ugolino in England appears to have been non-effective; see Reg. Yrs. 2 no. 594, 3 no. 174, 11 no. 546, *Reg. Hon. III* nos. 719, 1667, 6191, *CPL* 49, 61, 116, and *Reg. Gray*, ed. Raine, 12.

[146] *Landboc...de Winchelcumba*, ed. D. Royce (Exeter 1892) i 111.

[147] *CS* ii pt 1 46–7, 52; and *Annales monastici*, ed. Luard, iii 74.

[148] *CS* ii pt 1 96–9; and Powicke, *Henry III*, 274–89.

attempt to rectify a haphazard system by the introduction of a regularly based contribution from the European church was rejected.[149] It is unlikely that the old system ceased nor, indeed, that it could until an alternative source of income was provided for curial clerks. But an analysis of the records does not justify the notion that the curia was excessively greedy. Nor is there reason to suppose that England was supporting more provisees and foreigners than other countries. From the point of view of the parishes and the parishioners 'farming' the benefices in this way was of little moment, as vicars would be appointed to serve. Those who feared the papal right of provision most were the archbishops, bishops and the monasteries who wished to exercise the patronage for their own purposes. Their protest was out of all proportion to what the evidence says about the extent of provision. Honorius's concession, if that is what it was, paved the way for the removal of direct legatine influence.

Two events of 1220 indicate that the pope had this in mind. In May 1220 Langton crowned Henry III in Westminster abbey and the king laid the foundation stone of the new church. Henry's devotion to that church and to the cult of the Confessor was a personal attachment associated with the royal house. While Henry may not have cared to identify himself with his grandfather Henry II, Langton certainly wished to link his own name and office as closely as possible with that of Thomas Becket. If the second coronation of the king served to stress royal claims to maturity and to reinforce Langton's view that the king should be given more powers, the translation of St Thomas was intended to show that *Ecclesia Anglicana* no longer needed direct papal supervision. Langton had already identified himself with Becket's struggle, his refuge at Pontigny accentuating the link.[150] Moreover the year 1220 witnessed the fiftieth jubilee of the martyrdom. It was an opportune moment for a significant event, manoeuvred no doubt to underline the archbishop's role. The cult could be used to weld together the political and religious settlement and to unite the English church and bind it to Rome. It was the cult of St Thomas of Canterbury that came nearest to a national cult in England. The pope's approval was obtained by Langton in January 1219.[151] The translation took place in

---

[149] Powicke, *Henry III*, 346–9, and id., *Stephen Langton*, 83.

[150] Powicke, *Stephen Langton*, 116 ('a man who consciously regarded himself as the successor of St Thomas and the champion of law and order'); see also 18–19, 96 and 104.

[151] On the jubilee and its background, see Foreville, *Le jubilé de Saint Thomas Becket*, esp. 3–10, and doc. no. 1, and below App. 2 no. 7.

July 1220, eighteen months after Honorius's assent, in an *annus bissextilis* which was regarded as an especially favourable augury. On 4 or 5 July Stephen Langton, accompanied by Richard Poore, the bishop of Salisbury, and the Canterbury monks, transferred the body to a new coffin, the archbishop taking certain relics from the corpse, one of which he later conveyed personally to Honorius III,[152] and on the 7th the translation from the crypt tomb to the new shrine was effected, in the presence of twenty cardinals, archbishops and bishops, numerous abbots and priors, the king, the justiciar, several earls and a large audience.[153]

After the withdrawal of the legate in 1221 no papal representative was sent to England again until the summer of 1225 when the nuncio, Otto, arrived to put forward the pope's financial proposal. There is no indication that Honorius wished to maintain the Roman presence in England longer than was necessary. Nor did general policy in the English Church alter after the legate left. There was no sudden change of direction following Pandulf's departure in July 1221, and the English hierarchy strove in general to implement the decrees of the Lateran Council. The same channels of communication, by letter, by messenger, and by visiting the curia, remained. Papal concessions, confirmations and the delegation of cases continued unabated, as witnessed by the letters. Nor did the English Church show itself to be excessively subservient. On the contrary, over the pope's proposal for a fixed income for the curia, it demonstrated a conservatism and lack of imagination, going the way of the other European churches and protecting special and vested interests. Had Honorius's scheme for the central revenue been accepted by the provincial churches, the development of provisions – which so affected the fourteenth-century Church – would have been nipped in the bud with consequences that can only be surmised.

On the main stage of Europe, Anglo-papal relations were of supreme importance during the century. England was still a papal fief and the relations between the two courts reflected this dependence. Tribute was paid. Later the king's brother, Richard of Cornwall, was elected and crowned king of the Romans and senator of the city of Rome, and the king's son, Edmund, was put forward for the crown of Sicily. Had 'the grand design' of Henry III succeeded, the two kingdoms closest to the papal throne, surrounding the papal lands, might have been in English hands in a formative period of Europe's history.

[152] *Memoriale fratris Walteri de Coventria*, ed. Stubbs, ii 249.
[153] Matthew Paris, *Chron. maj.*, ed. Luard, iii 59.

Into what uncharted seas of conjecture we are carried, if we visualize Richard ruling with undisputed sway at Aachen; Edmund firmly established in Palermo; the hegemony of Europe falling to England instead of France; and the royal authority in England magnified to enormous and threatening dimensions. The prosaic actuality was far removed from this glittering dream of Empire. England relapsed into the old interplay of monarchical and baronial power which permitted the emergence of a parliament with more than passive functions.[154]

As it was, and against all precedents, the *genus* of King John turned out to be loyal servants, on the whole, of the thirteenth-century popes. The popes had suffered greatly from the emperors; they were to suffer even more from 'les Rois Maudits'.

[154] C. C. Bayley, *The formation of the German college of electors in the mid-thirteenth century* (University of Toronto, 1949) 195–6.

EPILOGUE

Was Honorius III a continuator or an innovator? The evidence suggests little certain innovation during this pontificate but more a logical, practical and sensible continuation of trends. The end of the old-style chancellorship, the development of the *audientia litterarum contradictarum* in the Chancery, the compilation of an official law collection for the reign, and an application of Innocent III's political programme, in the case of England, and his Church programme, as defined by the Fourth Lateran Council, all illustrate this. Honorius was a capable administrator, able, as perhaps Innocent III might not have been, to implement many of these ideas and intentions. Parallels can be provided in a modern context, in Lyndon B. Johnson's administration following the dynamic and reforming presidency of John F. Kennedy and, indeed, in Paul VI's papacy, coming after and effecting the reforms of the Second Vatican Council and its instigator, John XXIII.

We cannot know Honorius's thought processes and it is impossible to determine what were his personal pronouncements and views, but we do know that he had been steeped in papal administration from his earliest years in Chamber and in Chancery and that he made the administration work. If he was thought to be softer and more accommodating than his predecessor, 'amletico', perhaps, he appears to have preferred compromise to confrontation and the implementation of ideas to theorizing. Even the idea of a fixed income for the curia – which would surely have changed the course of later history – was not his. Had he gained consent for it, however, he would have been able to effect it.

In England the pope's representatives restored the civil and ecclesiastical administration and made it function again on its own. Honorius inherited Guala as legate, Langton as archbishop and Pandulf as bishop. He maintained Guala as legate but allowed him to resign and return to the curia in 1218. Langton he managed to control: his relations with him were good. To Pandulf he gave legatine powers, favouring the appointment of a legate with experience of the country to which he was to be sent. The appointment of men who had had some contact with England as legates continued during the rest of the thirteenth century. The papal nuncio, Otto, who was despatched by Honorius solely to convince the localities of the sense of the pope's financial scheme, was commissioned by Gregory IX as legate to England; and Otto's clerk, Ottobon, who accompanied him on the legation, returned as legate under Clement IV. If Honorius was fortunate in his ' ates and, indeed, in the English episcopate, some of whom had been chosen by the legates, and many of whom were practical reformers like himself, that reflected, at least in part, the strength of the institution that they served.

No pope by the early thirteenth century could divorce himself entirely from the effects of his predecessor's rule. The astonishing growth of the administrative machine made this impossible. This was a movement in which Honorius himself had already been active for the main part of his career before he became pope. Without total dismemberment of the machinery, the curia could not be static. Honorius's attitude towards the friars (whose impact on England lay in the future) is indicative of his priorities. He strove to put their constitutional position in order, wisely entrusting this work to Cardinal Ugolino. Ugolino may have been a Conti and Innocent III's relative but he absorbed much from Honorius III. Honorius's papacy was by no means a weak link in the chain between Innocent III and Gregory IX.

APPENDIXES

Appendix 1 A

SCRIBES OF THE ORIGINAL LETTERS OF HONORIUS III WITH AN ENGLISH INTEREST

* = signs on the left

1. *al'*
1222 *May 26* Alatri (App. 2 no. 22)
Occurs between *1210 June 28* (*BAPP* i no. 88) and *1229 April 10* (Durham 2.1 Pap. 23). Probably to be identified with 2.

2. *alex'*
1216 *Dec. 3* Rome St Peter's (App. 2 no. 1)
Occurs between *1205 Jan. 11* (*BAPP* i no. 59) and *1225 May 23* (*SB* 767). ? = Master Alexander of Montefiascone, papal scribe, who occurs on 27 August 1223 as proctor of the bishop of Bagnorea (Reg. Yr. 8 no. 16; *Reg. Hon. III* no. 4472). Probably not the same as the scribe *alex.* who occurs under Gregory IX and Innocent IV (see *BAPP* i p. 420).

3. *aston*
1224 *Dec. 2* Lateran (App. 2 no. 46). See Schwarz, *Schreiberkollegien*, 65 n. 236.
Occurs from *1216 March 1* (*BAPP* i no. 118) until this date, sometimes as *asten* and as *astan*, ? Asti.

4. *b. a. =*
Master Bartholomeus of Anagni, papal scribe, who was dispensed from the effects of illegitimacy (Reg. Yr. 6 no. 471; *Reg. Hon. III* no. 4090) on 18 July 1222.
1221 *April 29* Lateran (App. 2 no. 19)
1222 *June 26* Lateran (App. 2 no. 25)
Occurs between *1218 May 12* (*PUS* no. 220) and *1224 May 15* (*SB* 730) and possibly is the same as the *b.a.* who occurs *1234 Feb. 17* (PRO SC7/15/33), *1238 May 10* and perhaps on *1244 Sept. 17* (*BAPP* i nos. 412, 504). Nüske finds a *b.a.* to 1283 (*AD* xx (1974) 170 no. 32). A Master Bartholomeus, papal scribe, occurs under Innocent III ('Gesta' col. l), and might be identified with him. On 28 Nov. 1219 he was witness to an arrangement concerning S. Fridianus, Lucca, when

Appendix 1 A

he was described as a papal scribe (*Reg. Yr.* 4 no. 616).

5. *b. f =

Master Benedictus de Fractis (Fratte, Frosinone), papal scribe, who on 8 July 1221 was ordered to be inducted into the prebend in the church of S. Severina in Calabria (diocese of Crotone) which Raniero cardinal deacon of S. Maria in Cosmedin had held and which he had conferred on Benedictus (*Reg. Yr.* 5 no. 756; *Reg. Hon. III* no. 3493).
1220 May 6 Viterbo (App. 2 no. 11)
Occurs from *1208 March 28* (*BAPP* i no. 71) until *1227 Oct. 7* and *1254 July 13* (*BAPP* i nos. 284, 756).

6. B. p.

1221 March 30 Lateran (App. 2 no. 16). Barbiche has a B.P. (*BAPP* i p. 422) but from the 1250s.

7. bl

1224 March 6 Lateran (App. 2 no. 36)
1226 May 30 Lateran (App. 2 no. 56)
Possibly but unlikely to = BS, *1222 Jan. 18* (*SB* 657 and P 6767).

8. bo = ?

Boamundus (Baiamundus), scholar, canon of Asti (*Reg. Yr.* 1 no. 114; *Reg. Hon. III* no. 182) or ? = *Bonomus*, clerk of the apostolic see, who was to be provided to Agde (dep. Hérault, arr. Béziers) (*Reg. Yr.* 1 no. 232; *Reg. Hon. III* no. 221).
1223 April 27 Lateran (App. 2 no. 29)

9. boe

1220 May 28 Viterbo (App. 2 no. 13)
Occurs *1219 Dec. 1* (*SB* 549) and as *bot'* (or *bo'*) *1219 Nov. 21* (*SB* 547).

10. *co

(?*cc*) ? = *Master Constantinus*, papal scribe (*BAPP* i no. 203), who on 7 May 1218 was confirmed in the church of Alwalton (Hunts.), to which he had been collated by Guala (*Reg. Yr.* 2 no. 1077; *Reg. Hon. III* no. 1295), but this is more likely to be the scribe who signs *con'* on the right *plica* (see *1216 Dec. 2* (*SB* 377) and possibly *1216 Oct. 24* (*co9*; *SB* 362), *1217 Feb. 8* (*Con*; *PUS* no. 217), *1219 Nov. 15* (*SB* 546) and *1221 Jan. 9* (*SB* 606), and see below App. 1 B, ?9).
1219 April 20 Rome St Peter's (App. 2 no. 10)

11. coz'

(*cioz, goz', gozo*) = *Cozo*, papal scribe, who was admitted by Archbishop Walter Gray on 28 Jan. 1229 to the church of Lastingham to which he had been presented by the abbot and convent of St Mary's York (*Reg. Gray*, 28).
1226 Jan. 23 Rieti (App. 2 no. 50) apparently as Goz: as Grez (*SB* 779).

198

Occurs between *1220 Dec. 27* (*BAPP* i no. 228) and *1228 May 14* (Durham 2.1 Pap. 27) as Gozo and Goz; also *1225 Dec. 11* (Gocq: *Pont. Hib.* i no. 174: Seine Maritime B 12) and *1236 May 27* (as Goz: *BAPP* i no. 392).

12. *d* (?)   (very small in extreme bottom corner) or *r* (?)
1223 April 27 Lateran (App. 2 no. 30)

13. *eg* = ?   *Master Egidius*, canon of Como. On 5 March 1227 the bishop of Piacenza´ was ordered to warn the chapter of Como to receive him as a canon or to be compelled to do so (Reg. Yr. 11 no. 581; *Reg. Hon. III* no. 6273). Signs as *eg* on *1223 Jan. 28* (*SB* 686) and as *Egidi* on *1223 July 21* (*BAPP* i no. 250), and may be the *er* of *1217 April 24* and *Dec. 21* (*SB* 436 and *BAPP* i no. 172) and *e* of *1220 Oct. 26* (*SB* 588).
1224 March 21 Lateran (as *eg*) (App. 2 no. 39)
1224 May 15 Lateran (*eg*?) (App. 2 no. 41)

     f? or *t*?   see *t*

14. *g* (?)   *1224 June 20* Lateran (App. 2 no. 45); and see below App. 1 B

     goz'   see *coz'*

15. *Iac'* =   *Master Iacobus*, papal scribe, and *familiarius*. On 16 March 1218, the provost of St Omer was ordered to confer a prebend on him (Reg. Yr. 2 no. 1027; *Reg. Hon. III* no. 1159). On 11 May 1218 the bishop-elect of Ely (Robert of York) was required by the pope to provide him to a benefice and the archbishop of Canterbury and the bishops of Rochester and Salisbury were ordered to see that this mandate was effected (Reg. Yr. 2 no. 1065; and *Reg. Hon. III* no. 1307). On 17 April 1219 the dean and chapter of St Omer were warned to admit him as a canon or be compelled to do so (Reg. Yr. 3 no. 463; *Reg. Hon. III* no. 2008). By 22 Sept. 1219 Master Iacobus was in the household of the legate, Pandulf (Reg. Yr. 4 no. 629; *CPL* 70) but appears to have been deprived of office as papal scribe soon afterwards for reasons unknown: he was absolved by 18 August 1220 (Reg. Yr. 5 no. 35; *CPL* 75) when he was required to make satisfaction to the legate and obey his commands.
1217 July 13 Anagni (App. 2 no. 3; this document was addressed to the legate, Guala)
1217 Nov. 28 Lateran (App. 2 no. 4)

He occurs from *1216 Dec. 13* (*BAPP* i nos. 134, 135), throughout *1217*, on *13 Jan. 1218* (*BAPP* i no. 173) and then on *10 June 1224* (*SB* 735), *10 July 1227* (*BAPP* i no. 272) and on *6 April 1228* (Lambeth PD 27).

16. *I.g.*   *1226 Dec. 22* Lateran (App. 2 no. 57)

? the same as *I.G.* who occurs in *1209* on *Jan. 12* (Cheney, *Letters*, no. 828) and *April 17* (*BAPP* i no. 76) and *1214 April 10* and *May 26* (Cheney, *Letters*, nos. 958, 975).

17. *Iord'*   (Io.d, Iode)

1219 Jan. 26 Lateran (App. 2 no. 7)
1221 March 5 Lateran (App. 2 no. 15)
1222 June 23 Lateran (App. 2 no. 23)
Occurs from *1216 Dec. 19* (Io.d) (*SB* 400) on *1 Jan. 1217* (Iord) when signs on the left (*BAPP* i no. 142), on *Feb. 3* (Iod: *SB* 414), and under Gregory IX in a duplicate of *1227 Nov. 9* (PRO SC7/15/21 & 35/29) as respectively Iord' and Iode, and on *3 June 1228* (*BAPP* i no. 315).

18. *l* (?)   *1223 April 3* Lateran (App. 2 no. 28)

? the same as *L*, *1217 Feb. 11* (*BAPP* i no. 151).

19. *n* (?)   *1218 Nov. ?10* Lateran (App. 2 no. 6)

20. *n.f.*   *1226 Jan. 9* Rieti (App. 2 no. 49: *SB* 777, where wrongly dated 8 Jan.)

Occurs from *1224 April 9* (*SB* 721) and under Gregory IX from *1228 Feb. 28* (PRO SC7/15/17) until *1234 April 22* (BL Add. Ch. 17848).

21. *o* (?)   (very small)

1222 July 5 Lateran (App. 2 no. 26)
Occurs *1227 March 29* (*BAPP* i no. 267).

22. *Otto* =   *Master Otto*, papal scribe, and canon of St Peter's. On 15 Nov. 1216, and again on 7 March 1217, the chapter of Metz were ordered to pay him the yearly fruits of his prebend although he may not reside (Reg. Yr. 1 nos. 528 & 528 bis; *Reg. Hon. III* nos. 106, 403).

1217 Jan. 3 Lateran (App. 2 no. 2)
1221 April 26 Lateran (App. 2 no. 18)
Occurs from *1216 Dec. 9* (*BAPP* i no. 130) until *1221 April 26* (as above).

? the *auditor litterarum contradictarum* whom I have identified with Master Otto, papal subdeacon and chaplain (above pp. 38–40, 45).

23. *p.* = ?   *Master Petrus*, papal scribe, and canon of Douai,

who on 19 Dec. 1220 had a prebend of Douai conferred on him, and on which occasion he was called Petrus 'de Civitate Antina' (Città d'Antino, Abruzzi and Molise) (Reg. Yr. 5 no. 336; *Reg. Hon. III* no. 2893).

1224 June 10 Lateran (App. 2 no. 43)

24. *P = ?   *Palmerius Thomasii* of Rieti (Herde, *Beiträge*, 41)

1224 May 15 Lateran (App. 2 no. 42)

1226 March 7 Lateran (App. 2 no. 53)

Occurs *1216 Dec. 12* (*SB* 390) to *1244 Feb. 7* (*BAPP* i no. 458).

25. *p.b.* (*P.B.*)   *1223 May 13* Lateran (P.B.) (App. 2 no. 31)

1223 Oct. 5 Anagni (p.b.) (App. 2 no. 32)

1223 Oct. 5 Anagni (P.B.) (App. 2 no. 33)

1225 Jan. 18 Lateran (p.b.) (App. 2 no. 47)

These may or may not be two separate scribes with *p.b.* appearing from *1219 Dec. 11* to *1233 April 26* (*BAPP* i nos. 205 (*SB* 552) and 360) and *P.B.* from *1218 June 19* (if Baumgarten, *SB* 489, is to be trusted) until *1261 March 26* (*BAPP* i no. 1079) and *1264* (Nüske, *AD*, xxi (1975) 342–3 no. 233).

26. *p.c.*   *1226 Jan. 2* Rieti (App. 2 no. 48)

Occurs from *1217 Feb. 16* (*BAPP* i no. 152) on *13* and *21 Oct. 1239* (Durham 2.1 Pap. 33 & PRO SC7/15/12), on *1 Feb. 1240* (Durham 2.1 Pap. 38) and until *1255 April 9* (*BAPP* i no. 776).

27. *p.g.* =   *Petrus Greg(orii?)*, papal scribe. On 10 Feb. 1222 he was recorded as staying in Paris when he was ordered to effect a papal mandate (Reg. Yr. 6 no. 228; *Reg. Hon. III* no. 3791; and see Reg. Yrs. 6 no. 483 and 7 no. 22; *Reg. Hon. III* nos. 4097, 4125).

1224 Feb. 27 Lateran (App. 2 nos. 34 and 35, a duplicate)

Occurs from *1223 Oct. 6* (*SB* 704) until *1256 June 22* (*BAPP* i no. 859) if the same but probably the latter is Gregory IX's Petrus of Guarcino.

28. *p. po*   *1219 March 31* Lateran (App. 2 no. 9)

1221 Dec. 18 Lateran (App. 2 no. 21)

Occurs *1217 Dec. 4* (*BAPP* i no. 170; *SB* 467) to *1234 July 29* (*BAPP* i no. 381).

29. *Phi(?)* = ?   *Philippus*, nephew of Ranerius, papal vice-chancellor and patriarch of Antioch from 1219 (Reg. Yr. 2 no. 1142; *Reg. Hon. III* no. 1398).

1218 Feb. 12 Lateran (App. 2 no. 5)

    r (?)   see above *d* (?)

30. $\star^{R}_{V}$ *or* $^{N}_{V}$)   (signs to the left of the *bulla* cord)

                                             1224 April 13 Lateran (App. 2 no. 40)

                                             Probably to be identified with the R.V. who occurs *1231 April 14* until *1250 Oct. 14* (*BAPP* i p. 431).

31. $\star$S = ?   *Master Stephanus*, see App. 1 B below

                                               1224 June 20 Lateran (App. 2 no. 44)

                                               1226 May 14 Lateran (App. 2 no. 54)

                                               Occurs *1217 April 29* and, ? another, from *1245–53* (*BAPP* i p. 431).

32. *Sca* =   *Master Scambio*, papal scribe, and canon of Como from 1220 (Reg. Yr. 4 nos. 719, 840; *Reg. Hon. III* nos. 2379, 2487). Active on papal business in the 1220s (Reg. Yrs. 9 no. 316, 11 no. 471; *Reg. Hon. III* nos. 5475, 6161), he held the office of corrector in the Chancery of Pope Innocent IV before 15 June 1245, when he was elected to the see of Viterbo, of which he remained bishop until 1253 (Schwarz, 'Corrector', 144; Herde, *Beiträge*, 24, 193 and 206).

                                               1219 March 11 Lateran (App. 2 no. 8)

                                               1221 April 5 Lateran (App. 2 no. 17)

                                               1223 Feb. 13 Lateran (App. 2 no. 27)

                                               1224 March 14 Lateran (App. 2 no. 38)

                                               Occurs from *1215 Oct. 30* (Sc: *BAPP* i no. 111) until *1239 Oct. 25* (*BAPP* i no. 428).

33. *t*(?) = ?   *T.*, papal scribe, canon of Turin, for whom a canonry and, if vacant, a prebend was requested on 10 Jan. 1221 (Reg. Yr. 5 no. 337; *Reg. Hon. III* no. 2966).

                                               1226 May 15 Lateran (App. 2 no. 55)

                                               Occurs *1224 Dec. 18* (*SB* 745) and *1228 July 11* (*BAPP* i no. 321).

34. *za* (*Za,*   *Master Zacharias*, papal scribe. On 29 May 1219
      zachar) =   he was confirmed as a canon of Tivoli and a prebend was ordered to be assigned to him (Reg. Yr. 3 no. 504; *Reg. Hon. III* nos. 2095–6). On 26 July 1219 he was ordered to enforce (with Master Stephanus, papal scribe) a judgement for the abbot and convent of S. Clemente in Tivoli, following a sentence of the cardinal deacon, Gregorio, against the count and *synodus* of the city of Tivoli (Reg. Yr. 4 no. 537; *Reg. Hon. III* no. 2161).

1222 June 25 Lateran (App. 2 no. 24)

Occurs as a scribe of Honorius III, Gregory IX and Innocent IV between *1218 June 20* (*SB* 490), *1219 May 8* (as Z: *PUS* no. 222) and *1247 Jan. 13* (as z: *BAPP* i no. 602; see Herde, *Beiträge*, 45).

35. -*a*
(who is not b a *or* za)

1226 February 20 Lateran (App. 2 no. 51)

SCRIBES FROM OTHER SOURCES

(the papal registers, *BAPP, PUS, PUZ, Regesta des letras pontificias...de Aragón*)

⋆ = signs on the left	
a	1219 Sept. 30 (*BAPP* i no. 200)
aff	1224 April 8 (*BAPP* i no. 257)
⋆and =	Master Andreas, papal scribe, who has worked long in the service of the church of Bourges in their negotiations with the apostolic see, to be provided to a prebend, 7 Dec. 1216 (Reg. Yr. 1 no. 154; and see *Reg. Hon. III* nos. 29, 235, 811).
	1216 Dec. 13 (*BAPP* i no. 132)
Master Azzo (? = a)	Confirmation of a dispensation granted to him by Guala to hold the churches of 'Winthgeham' (Winteringham, Lincs., or Wintringham, Hunts.) and Stanhope (co. Durham), 1218 Feb. 10 (Reg. Yr. 2 no. 902; *Reg. Hon. III* no. 1080; *CPL* 52).
B ⎫ ? same .B. ⎭	1218 May 17 (*PUS* no. 221) 1221 March 9 (*PUS* no. 229)
b.g.	1223 Dec. 17 (*BAPP* i no. 252) 1226 Dec. 3 (*PUZ* p. 67)
bn.	1216 Oct. 29 (*BAPP* i no. 125)
Bobo	might = Oddo Bobonis (Reg. Yr. 6 no. 438; *Reg. Hon. III* no. 3941; *CPL* 88), papal subdeacon and chaplain, who acquired the church of Felixkirk (diocese of York) on the promotion of Hugh to the archbishopric of Benevento, 8 May 1222. On 16 Jan. 1222 he had been dispensed to hold several benefices (Reg. Yr. 6 no. 185; *Reg. Hon. III* no. 3736).
	1218 Feb. 2, 3 (*BAPP* i nos. 176–7)
? 9	1218 Sept. 26 (*BAPP* i no. 184)
xpi	1223 Oct. 26 (*BAPP* i no. 251)
G	1216 Nov. 28 – 1221 April 17 (*BAPP* i p. 423; and see below Master Gentilis *or* Master Willelmus, possibly)
G R	1223 March 28 (*PUS* no. 233)
G.V.	1216 Dec. 9, 11, 16 (*BAPP* i nos. 129, 131, 138)

Master Gentilis (? G)   1220 Dec. 15; the archbishop of Reggio was ordered to induct his proctor into a canonry of the church of Mileto (Calabria) (Reg. Yr. 5 no. 257; *Reg. Hon. III* no. 2871).

Master Hugo   Occurs as papal scribe and canon of Argos, 1223 Sept. 9 and 1224 Jan. 5 (Reg. Yr. 8 nos. 38, 177; *Reg. Hon. III* nos. 4489, 4654).

?I.   Occurs 1210, 1238–9, possibly not under Honorius III therefore (*BAPP* i p. 424).

.I. tᵃ. =   Master Iohannes of Città d'Antino (Abruzzi and Molise), papal scribe, canon of S. Donatianus, Bruges (Reg. Yrs. 1 no. 531 (bis), 3 no. 269, 4 no. 739, 5 no. 112, 8 no. 509, 9 no. 199 and 10 no. 116; *Reg. Hon. III* nos. 619, 1817, 2452, 2687, 5047, 5333 and 5723).

Occurs 1217 July 17, Nov. 8 and Dec. 3 (*BAPP* i nos. 166, 169 and 186).

Licence granted not to have to reside at Bruges, 1220 May 25 (Reg. Yr. 4 no. 738; *Reg. Hon. III* no. 2451).

m   Occurs 1216–37 (*BAPP* i p. 427).

.m. p.   1217 June 23 (*BAPP* i no. 163)

.n. s. =   Master Nicolaus Scarsus, canon of Cambrai (Reg. Yrs. 3 no. 186, 10 no. 99; *Reg. Hon. III* nos. 1748, 5686).

Occurs 1217 April 29 (*BAPP* i no. 161; see Herde, *Beiträge*, 40–1).

pe.   1217 Jan. 19, Sept. 16 (*BAPP* i nos. 147, 168)

p. n̄.   1226 Dec. 8 (*PUZ* p. 67)

P. Pon   1218 Nov. 29 (*Regesta des letras pontificias...de Aragón* no. 74)

P.T. (p.t.)   1217 April 27 (Ibid. no. 73)

1218 Aug. 11, 1219 Dec. 12 (*BAPP* i nos. 183, 206)

P. V.   1222 June 20 (*BAPP* i no. 242)

Master Pet(rus) Tusci, papal scribe, and clerk of S. Martino de Urbe. On 3 July 1217 an annual rent of £15 was confirmed to him (Reg. Yr. 1 no. 521; *Reg. Hon. III* no. 644). On 26 Feb. 1218, the bishop of Vich was ordered to compel the proctor of the bishop of Gerona to satisfy him over 300s 'Barchinonensis monetae' (Reg. Yr. 2 no. 951; *Reg. Hon. III* no. 1121). It is not clear whether there is any connection with Master Peter 'clerk of our Chancery' who had served the pope long and faithfully and who was to have a prebend in the church of Lille (Reg. Yr.

1 no. 369; *Reg. Hon. III* no. 451).

1218 Feb. 3 (*BAPP* i no. 178)

pmū   1217 Feb. 13 (*PUS* no. 218)

(doubtful, may be a petitioner)

P pd   1220 March 12 (*PUS* no. 224)

q   1226 Dec. 5 (*PUZ* p. 67)

Master R.   papal scribe, canon of S. Gereo, Cologne. On 24 April 1218, as *familiarius* of pope, takes pallium to archbishop of Cologne (Reg. Yr. 2 no. 1046; *Reg. Hon. III* no. 1252).

1216 Dec. 7 and 9, confirmed as a canon of Marseilles (Reg. Yr. 1 nos. 116–17; *Reg. Hon. III* nos. 159, 167).

? = Master Raimundus, papal scribe, and *familiarius*, who was to be given the archdeaconry of Lodève (dep. Hérault, France) (*Reg. Hon. III* no. 216; Reg. Yr. 1 no. 118).

or = Master Roffridus of Anagni, who on 10 Dec. 1216 was dispensed to be promoted to sacred orders although illegitimate (Reg. Yr. 1 no. 105; *Reg. Hon. III* no. 169).

Master Stephanus (? = S *or* *S, see above App. 1 A), papal scribe.

1219 July 26 occurs with Master Zacharias (see above App. 1 A) at Rieti (Reg. Yr. 4 no. 537; *Reg. Hon. III* no. 2161).

.S.   1221 March 5 (*PUS* nos. 227–8)

Sa (? = Sca =   Scambio, see above App. 1 A)

1221 April 20 (*PUS* no. 230)

Master Theobaldus, papal scribe, canon and prebendary of Lincoln. Monition to the bishop and chapter of Lincoln to admit him as one of their canons and give him a prebend, 9 Nov. 1222 (Reg. Yr. 7 no. 31; *Reg. Hon. III* no. 4145; wrongly dated by Bliss, *CPL* 89). Perhaps = Theobald de Berbezeus, who occurs once only as canon on 9 April 1236 (*CPR 1232–47*, 140; *Fasti*, ed. Greenway, iii Lincoln, 145).

Master Willelmus, papal scribe and *familiarius*, formerly (*tunc*) chaplain, when Honorius III was in 'minor' office. Order to the bishop of Pamplona (Navarre) on 14 March 1217 to see that he enjoyed the fruits of the *prestimonium* of Miranda which had been assigned to him (Reg. Yr. 1 no. 316; *Reg. Hon. III* no. 418). It seems likely that he was chaplain to Honorius as cardinal and transferred to the papal chancery. Perhaps to be identified with

Master Willelmus (de Sancto Germano, probably Italy, prov. Aosta, Turin
(two possibilities) or Vicenza), papal scribe, who
had the prebend of Little Bytham (Lincs.) conferred on him after the Fourth Lateran Council
(*Rot. H. Welles*, ed. Phillimore and Davis, i 128).
As clerk and *familiarius* of the pope he was assigned
a prebend of Arrouaise on 17 July 1219 (Reg. Yr.
3 no. 525; *Reg. Hon. III* no. 2150) and ordered the
income on 2 March 1221 (Reg. Yr. 5 no. 426; *Reg.
Hon. III* no. 3136) and again on 30 Sept. 1222,
when described as papal ('now our') chaplain and
called *de Sancto Germano* (Reg. Yr. 7 no. 22; *Reg.
Hon. III* no. 4125). Similarly described on 29 Jan.
1226 when the pope granted him the church of
Rossanclearach (now Rossie, Fife, Scotland) (Reg.
Yr. 10 no. 183 fol. 109v; *Reg. Hon. III* no. 5806;
CPL 106). Called 'Romanus' when a portion of
the Bytham prebend was refilled in 1245–6 (*Rot.
Grosseteste*, ed. Davis, 85). The entry in *Rot. Welles*
suggests that he may have been in England with
Guala and all the evidence suggests that he was not
a papal scribe for long in the pontificate, nor did
he combine that office with papal chaplain.

Appendix 2

TEXTS OF THE ORIGINAL LETTERS OF HONORIUS III WITH AN ENGLISH INTEREST

EDITORIAL TECHNIQUES

Without details of the type listed below, further progress cannot be made in elucidating the practices of the papal Chancery and of the individual scribes who composed this institution. For this reason, it is not satisfactory to reproduce the forms without the details. Nor are the previous editions, such as Rymer and Shirley, or those from cartulary or register sources, suitable for palaeographic and diplomatic study. Details, such as those of abbreviation, spelling, punctuation and form, may not always have immediate significance, but until such minutiae are provided for originals, further advances in the study of papal documents will remain limited.

None of the editions or calendars of these documents, with the exception of the Lambeth catalogue, gives the names of the scribes – a major piece of diplomatic and palaeographical evidence and one that has not been exploited. Hitherto it has been supposed that not every document was initialled or signed as early as this pontificate, but only one document has failed to reveal a *siglum*. Nor do any of the previous editions or calendars indicate line-breaks – information that can contribute towards the evidence necessary for building up the details of a particular hand. For example, in the case of the dating clause, the scribe was supposed to make the break, if it could not be avoided, before *pontificatus*, as can be seen correctly executed in the work of Iacobus and Otto (nos. 3, 4; 2, 18), so that the day and month appeared on one line. The scribe, P. Po, however, whose work is found in nos. 9 and 21, ignored this injunction and split the line at what the Chancery apparently considered the worst possible point. Further examples of P. Po's work can be found in Barbiche's *Actes pontificaux originaux des archives nationales de Paris* (sponsored by the Commission Internationale de Diplomatique) but no comparison can be made because this variety of detail is not included there.

In none of the examples included below has a comparison of hands led to the identification of a scribe, but where the scribal *sigla* have been identified and documents by one man then brought together, further similarities have immediately become obvious. In particular, the use of decoration in the capitals, especially in the initial of the pope's name, but also in the small capitals or enlarged uncials, can be most revealing. Decoration exhibits marked individual characteristics. The initial of the pope's name in nos. 42 and 53 could only be by one hand, that of Palmerius Thomasii of Rieti, and the same is true of the initial capital of Honorius in nos. 36 and 56, the work of bl. Even when the capitals are displayed in a mandate and in an indult, there is no doubt about the similarity of the basic form, as with nos. 19 and 25, where the scribe was Bartholomeus of Anagni. The scribe, Otto, whose work can be seen in nos. 2 and 18, uses elaborate capitals; whereas the scribe Alexander (nos. 1, 22), who incidentally breaks the date before or in the middle of the place, exhibits a hand without much embellishment. Clearly identifications depend usually on more than one feature, however individualistic, and for this reason an attempt has been made to give a general impression of a hand as well as its possible distinctive features. While the individual characteristics of a hand may be important, it is the general impression that is crucial,[1] for the hands of scribes develop and change and the hand of the elderly scribe may not bear a close resemblance to that of his youth. There may be changes, too, not only in the way in which the pen is held but also in the formation of certain letters. On the other hand, it has to be constantly borne in mind when examining these documents that papal scribes received an exclusive training and are likely, therefore, to exhibit many common features in their hands, so that hasty judgements on authorship must not be made. Without the provision of a comprehensive series of plates, the user is obviously at the mercy of the present editor, but it can be stated confidently that the details exposed from the following editorial techniques and from the identification of scribes have revealed certain distinguishing features of hand when compared one with another and will reveal more if such work is done on papal documents in other countries. Roughly two-thirds of the scribes listed above occur only once in documents in this country, but many of them, such as aston, boe, I.g., l and za, occur in other lists, such as those of Barbiche, Largiadèr and the *Schedario Baumgarten*.

Twenty-seven of the fifty-seven documents below have not been printed before and the texts are therefore given in full. Limitation on the space available, however, has not allowed the complete re-editing of originals already published, however inadequately edited. In these instances all the necessary details of the dating clause, address, incipit and variant readings have been given, plus the usual details of whether registered or not, whether in Potthast,[2] whether noted by Baumgarten in the *Schedario* or catalogued elsewhere.[3] Then follow the size of the document, sealing method, condition, and the name of the scribe. Marks on the face and endorsements (cancellarial

---

[1] See R. Vaughan in *Transactions of the Cambridge Bibliographical Soc.* i (1953) 376–94, esp. 385–6 and 388.

[2] Numerous letters of Honorius III are not to be found in Augustus Potthast's *Regesta pontificum Romanorum*. Potthast used certain English sources, such as Rymer and Dugdale, but many of the rich sources, especially the cartulary material, have remained untapped. Limited space has forced the omission of a list of additions to Potthast which it is hoped to publish elsewhere.

[3] All the documents in the Public Record Office, London, are listed in PRO *Lists and Indexes* vol. xlix. Attention has not been drawn to the list on each separate occasion.

and otherwise) and any general comments on the hand have also been given.

EXTENSIONS

Square brackets have been used for all extensions of abbreviations and of contractions, except for *xps* and *ihs* – where these occur they have been silently extended. How the rules of abbreviation were applied can therefore be seen. In principle, letters of grace were not supposed to be much abbreviated, unlike the mandates, and p[ro] and p[er] abbreviations were not acceptable.

The *tironian 'et'* has been extended and enclosed in square brackets.

Pointed brackets have been employed for supplied or suggested readings where the document is torn or illegible and where a reading is provided from another source or can be surmised with a fair certainty. A question mark inside the pointed brackets is used where there is a reasonable doubt.

CAPITALS

The enlarged miniscules of the pope's name in the letters of grace have been printed as capitals but clearly the decoration can be reproduced only by photographic means. In no instances were the principles disregarded concerning the use of the enlarged miniscules for the pope's name in the letters of grace (*cum serico*). In the letters of justice (*cum filo canapis*), only the initial of the pope's name was to be capitalized: this was done in all instances below. Elaborate capitals to introduce clauses have been indicated by an italic. This was a feature of the letter of grace, with the first letter of the first clause after the greeting, *salutem et apostolicam benedictionem*, being made fairly elaborate, followed by those of the other major clauses, terminating with the 'Nulli' and 'Si quis' clauses, as in nos. 48 and 53.

Small capitals. In some cases it has proved extremely difficult to distinguish between small capitals and the lower case equivalent, perhaps slightly enlarged. Here my endeavour has been to convey the intention of the scribe and if the 'a', for example, is distinguishable from the habitual lower case 'a', then I have reproduced it as a capital. Proper names of persons, places, officers and dignities were to have the first letter elevated in all apostolic letters.

REPRODUCED AND NON-REPRODUCED
FEATURES

Ligatures between the 'c' and the 't' and the 's' and the 't', which were required in letters of grace, have been reproduced by a dash.

Tittles, on the other hand, have not been indicated, as the inclusion of these would make the text impossibly overcrowded. Where, however, tittles were employed unusually, as apparently by the scribe, Scambio, who uses them with frequency (often twice in one word, and to abbreviate *cum* (cũ)), this has been noted among the distinctive features of the individual document. Where, too, tittles should have been used but only plain dashes have been employed, as in no. 51, the sole example, this has also been noted among the distinctive features.

The *gemipunctus*, which was expected, and in all cases provided, before names, has been reproduced.

Hyphens have been indicated by a short diagonal line ('). When they occur it is always before the line-break mark (/): it should not, therefore, be confused with the possible punctuation mark(·) (see above p. 96).

Line-breaks have been shown by the symbol /. For the dating clause, in the majority of cases the break was made before *pontificatus* as was required; in some, between the *Dat'* and the place, e.g. *Dat'* / *Lateran* (nos. 25, 56); and in some after the place, e.g. *Dat' Lateran* / *iii*, as in no. 28. Of all the scribes represented here, only P. Po separated the day from the month.

Strictures against *blank spaces* and gaps appear to have been complied with. Often the letters 'e' and 's' have been given long tongues to fill in the line and these have been noted (see below e.g. nos. 11, 16, 32).

Spelling. The spelling of the originals has been retained for two reasons. Firstly this has been thought important for scholars of semantics. Secondly, there are sometimes differences in spelling between the originals and the copies where registered in the papal registers. An attempt has also been made to distinguish between 'c's and 't's and care has been taken to reproduce the use of the 'u' and 'v' as found.

Punctuation (see above p. 96). The punctuation of the originals has been retained. There is, however, the caveat that in some documents in poor condition it may no longer be evident.

I

Mandate to the chapter of York ordering them to restore to the prior and canons of Nostell (Aug. Yorks. WR) the church of Bramham (Yorks. WR). 1216 December 3 Rome, St Peter's

Honorius ep[iscopu]s seruus seruor[um] dei. Dilectis filiis Capitulo Eboracen[si]. Sal[u]t[em] et ap[osto]licam ben[edictionem] (1) Oblata nobis.. (2) Prioris [et] Canonicorum / S[an]c[t]i Oswaldi de Nostle querimonia declarauit. q[uo]d cum iidem olim ante quam ip[s]e prior iter arriperet ad sacrum generale conciliu[m] / ⟨veniendi⟩ (3) se protectioni ap[osto]lice supponentes ne aliquid in ip[s]orum uel eccl[es]iarum suarum preiudicium. ante ip[s]ius Prioris reditum attemp/taretur ab aliquo ad sedem ap[osto]licam appellarint. uos eorum app[e]llatio[n]e contempta non sine ap[osto]lice sedis iniuria prius. quam idem prior ad sua[m] / eccl[es]iam remeasset. ip[s]os eccl[es]ia de Brameham cum pertinentiis suis ad eosdem ratione prebende quam in Eboracen' eccl[es]ia obtinent pertine[n]/tem per uiolentiam spoliastis. alias eis

(4) dampna plurima [et] iniurias irrogand⟨o⟩. Nolentes igitur premissorum prioris [et] canonicorum / grauamen indebitum coniuentibus oculis pertransire. discretioni u[est]re p⟨er apostolica scripta⟩ mandamus quatinus si est ita eccl[es]iam memorata[m] / ⟨cum pertin⟩entiis suis ac fructibus perceptis ex eis sublato cuiuslibet dilationis ac difficultatis obstaculo restituatis eisdem ip[s]is satisfacientes / ⟨co⟩ngrue de d⟨ampn⟩is ac iniuriis irrogatis. Alioquin dilectis filiis.. de Burton' ⟨et de Derleia⟩ Abbatibus [et].. (5) Archid[iacono] de Derbi Couentren[sis] (6) dioc[esis] / ⟨dedimu⟩s in mandatis ut eis restitutis ⟨ad omnia⟩ quibus ip[s]os taliter spoliastis ip[s]is de ⟨dampnis et il⟩latis iniuriis satisfieri faciant competent[er]. / ⟨Contra⟩dictores per censuram eccl[es]iasticam ⟨apostolicam postpo⟩sitam compescentes. Audituri postmodum ⟨si quis⟩ fuerit questionis. [et] si de partium uo/⟨luntate⟩ processerit fine debito decisuri. Alioquin gesta om[n]ia in scriptis redacta sub sigillis suis ad ap[osto]licam remittant examen prefigentes par/tibus terminum competentem quo n[ost]ro se conspectui representent. iustam auctore domino ⟨sententiam⟩ recepture. Dat' Rome / apud s[an]c[tu]m Petrum iii. Non' Decemb'. Pontificat[us] n[ost]ri Anno primo.

Lambeth Palace Library Papal Document no. 20 (cal. Sayers, *Original papal documents*)
Reg. Yr. 1 no. 344, *Reg. Hon. III* no. 146,*CPL* 45–6 Not in P or *SB*
29.7 cm × 26.7 cm: *plica* 2 cm
Hemp strings: no *bulla* surviving
Condition: fair, some holing
Scribe: alex (cf. no. 22, below)
Endorsements: (top centre, inverted) Non est meam (centre to right) R script (papal registration mark) (bottom centre) Bramham / Spoliacio per decanum / abbat' de burton de derley et Derby archid'
(1) The address is omitted in the registered copy.
(2) The gemipunctus is omitted in the registered copy.
(3) Holed: supplied from the registered copy.
(4) *ei* in the registered copy.
(5) The gemipunctus is omitted in the registered copy.
(6) *Conuentren'* in the registered copy.

A clear, unadorned hand, with no embellishments. Capitals plain.

2

Confirmation to the prior and convent of Holy Trinity (Aldgate) (Aug. London) of their possessions, rents, liberties, immunities and goods, especially of the churches of Braughing (Herts.), Tottenham (Middx), Lesnes (Kent), Walthamstow (Essex), Bexley (Kent), Notley (Essex), Broomfield (Essex), Layston (Herts.), St Botolph without Aldgate, All Hallows next the wall and

St Michael before the gate of their monastery, the chapel of Alswick (Herts.) and the hospital of St Katherine on Thames, taking their persons, house and goods under papal protection.

1217 January 3 Lateran

HONORIUS ep[iscopu]s seruus seruor[um] dei. *Dilec–tis filiis..Priori et Conuentui S[an]c[t]e Trinitatis Londonien'/ Sal[u]t[em] et ap[osto]licam ben[edictionem].* Cum a nobis petitur quod ius–tum es–t et hones–tum tam uigor equitatis / quam ordo exigit rationis ut id per sollicitudinem officii nos–tri ad debitum perducatur effectum. *Eapropter/Dilec–ti* in domino filii ues–tris ius–tis pos–tulationibus grato concurrentes assensu. Personas ues–tras / et locum in quo diuino es–tis obsequio mancipati. cum omnibus bonis que impresentiarum rationabiliter possidetis / uel in futurum ius–tis modis pres–tante domino poteritis adipisci sub Beati Petri et nos–tra protec–tione / suscipimus. Specialiter autem de Brackinges. de ⟨Tote⟩ham ⟨de⟩ ⟨Le⟩snes de Welcomes–towe de Bixle de Notoleia de / Brum⟨fild⟩ ⟨?de⟩ Lefs–tanchirch. s[an]c[t]i ⟨Botulfi ... ... (4 to 5 words)⟩ omnium s[an]c[t]orum iuxta murum Londonien' ⟨... (1 word)⟩ / ⟨sancti Michae⟩lis ante portam monas–terii ues–tri eccl[es]ias ⟨... ... ... (3 to 4 words)⟩ Alsewich. et hospital⟨e⟩ ⟨sancte Katerine⟩ / super ⟨Tamesiam?⟩ situm cum pertinentiis suis possessiones redditus ⟨nec non⟩ libertates et immunitates ac ⟨alia bona uestra⟩ / Monas–terio ues–tro pia liberalitate ⟨co⟩ncessa sicut ea omnia ius–te ⟨ac⟩ pacific⟨e⟩ obtinetis ⟨ ... ... (3 to 4 words)⟩ / eidem Monas–terio auc–toritate ap[osto]lica confirmamus et presentis scripti patrocinio communimus. Nulli ergo / omnino hominum liceat hanc paginam nos–tre protec–tionis et confirmationis infringere ⟨uel ei ausu teme⟩/rario contraire. Siquis autem hoc ⟨attemptare presumpserit⟩ indignationem omnipotentis dei et Beatorum Petri / et Pauli ap[osto]lorum eius se nouer⟨it incursurum. Dat'⟩ Lateran' iii. Non' Ianuar / Pontificatus n[ost]ri Anno Primo.,.

PRO SC7/18/24
Not registered, not in P or *SB*
34.2 cm × 29.6 cm: *plica* 2.7 cm
Holes: no *bulla*
Condition: quite good; some mould and one central tear from folding
Scribe: Otto (cf. no. 18, below)
Endorsements: (mid centre) Nyc' (proctor) (lower centre, inverted) Priui-
legium honorii de eccliis (sic) nostris et Hospital' sancte Katerine

This scribe uses elaborate small capitals as in the 'C' of *Conuentui* (first line) and the 'E' of *Eapropter* (l.3) and produces fine ligatures. The snake-like decoration in the stem of the 'H' of *Honorius* is also distinctive to him.

Appendix 2

3

Mandate to G(uala), cardinal priest of S. Martino and papal legate, to settle the affair of the canons of Carlisle who had, at the instance of the king of Scotland, elected a certain excommunicate clerk as bishop, wherefore the king of the English, the archbishops of Dublin and York and the bishops of London, Winchester, Bath, and Worcester sought the canons' removal.

1217 July 13 Anagni (Dat' Anagnie. iij Id' Iulii / Pontificat[us] n[ost]ri Anno Primo;-)

Pd Rymer i pt 1 147
Address: Dilecto filio .G. t[i]t[uli] s[an]c[t]i Martini p[res]b[ite]ro Card[inali]. ap[osto]lice sedis Legato.
Incipit: Tam Carissimus in
Variant readings
l.1 .G. t[i]t[uli] (Rymer l.2 *Gualoni titulo*)
l.2 ..*Dublinen'* (Rymer l.6 *H Dublinen'*)
l.3 *Carleolen'* (Reg. *Karleolen'*)
ll.7 & 8 Rymer ignores the gemipuncti and prints six dots.
l.8 *reg[u]larii* (Rymer l.21 *regulares*)
l.10 *tranquillitati* (Rymer l.27 *tranquilitati*)
l.11 *ac* (Reg. *et*); the *si* after *obesse* inserted with a caret in the registered copy.
l.12 *committendum* (Reg. *comittendum*)
l.14 *iij Id'* (Reg. *ii Non'*)

PRO SC 7/18/3
Reg. Yr. 1 no. 497 (under the date of 2 Non = 6 July), *Reg. Hon. III* no. 650, *CPL* 48 P 5578 *SB* 454
31.2 cm × 22.9 cm: *plica* 2.1 cm
Fine *bulla* on hemp strings
Condition: good
Scribe: Iac' (cf. no. 4, below)
Face: (under left *plica*) scribitur (*SB* scribat') (in a different ink from the text and that of the scribe's name)
Endorsements: (top left) R (top centre) R script (papal registration mark) (mid extreme left) 8 *or* & (bottom left of centre) Bulla Honorii pape iij per quam mand' G. tituli sancti Martini presbitero Card' et Apostolice sedis leg' quod constitueret et ordinaret de canonicis Carliolens' quod melius sibi uiderit expedire ex eo quod celebrauerunt ⟨contra?⟩ excommunicationis inter-dic[t]i sententias et pro eo quod contra pacem R⟨?egis⟩ et regni ueniebant./ Reg' in m' libro.

This scribe uses a simple uncial type 'H' for the 'H' of *Honorius*. He also leaves scarcely any margins.

4

Mandate to the abbot of Stratford Langthorne (Cist. Essex), the prior of
Merton (Aug. Surrey) and the archdeacon of Essex to hear a case between
the prior and monks of Lewes (Clun. Sussex) and S., T., H. and W. of the
dioceses of Chichester and Winchester about tithes, possessions 'et rebus aliis'.
1217 November 28 Lateran

Honorius ep[iscopu]s seruus seruor[um] dei. Dilectis filiis..Abbati d[e]
strafford'..Priori d[e] Mer/ton.' [et]..Archid[iacono] de Essexia Londonien'
[et] Wintonien' dioc[esum] Sal[u]t[em]. [et] ap[osto]licam ben[edictionem].
Dilec/ti filii..Prior [et] monachi Lewen' sua[m] ad nos q[ue]rimonia[m]
destinaru[n]t. q[uo]d. S. T. H. [et] / W. Cicestren' [et] Wintonien' dioc[esum]
sup[er] decimis possessio[n]ib[us] [et] reb[us] aliis iniuriant[ur] eisdem /
Quocirca discretio[n]i u[est]re p[er] ap[osto]lica scripta mandam[us]. q[ua]-
tin[us] partib[us] co[n]uocatis audiatis / ca[usa]m. [et] app[e]ll[ati]one remota
fine canonico t[er]minetis. facientes q[uo]d decreueritis per / censura[m]
eccl[esi]astica[m] firmit[er] obseruari. Testes aut[em] qui fueri[n]t no[m]i[n]ati
si se gr[ati]a odio u[e]l / timore subt[ra]xeri[n]t. censura simili app[e]ll[ati]one
cessante cogatis ueritati testimonium / p[er]hibere. Q[uo]d si no[n] om[ne]s
hiis exequendis potueritis int[er]esse. duo u[est]r[u]m ea nich[il]o/min[us]
exequantur. Dat' Lateran' iiii kl' DecembR' / Pontificat[us] n[ost]ri Anno
Sec[un]do:

PRO SC7/18/11
Not registered, not in P or *SB*
16.2 cm × 13.9 cm: *plica* 1.4 cm
Leaden *bulla* on hemp strings
Condition: good
Scribe: Iac'. (cf. no. 3, above)
Endorsements: (top to left of centre) Vacat (middle left) Lewes (middle centre)
  .ij. (probably all English)

5

Confirmation to the prior and convent of Holy Trinity, London (Aug.) of
their possessions and especially of the church of Braughing (Herts.) which
Guala had given them permission to appropriate.
1218 February 12 Lateran

HONORIUS ep[iscopu]s seruus seruor[um] dei. Dilec–tis filiis..Priori et
Conuentui Canonicor[um] eccl[es]ie s[an]c[t]e Trinitatis / Londonien'. Sal-
[u]t[em] et ap[osto]licam ben[edictionem]. Sacrosanc–ta Romana eccl[es]ia
deuotos [et] humiles filios ex assuete pietatis officio pro/pensius diligere
consueuit. et ne prauor[um] hominum moles–tiis agitentur eos tanquam pia

215

mater sue protec–tio/nis (1) munimine confouere. Eapropter dilec–ti in d[omi]no filii u[est]ris ius–tis pos–tulationibus grato concurren/tes assensu personas ues–tras et locum in quo diuino es–tis obsequio mancipati cum om[n]ibus bonis que / impresentiar[um] rationabiliter possidetis aut in futur[um] ius–tis modis pres–tante d[omi]no poteritis adipisci. sub / beati Petri et nos–tra protec–tione suscipimus. Specialiter autem eccl[es]iam de Brackinges cum pertinentiis (2) / suis ad donationem ues–tram de iure spec–tantem quam dilec–tus filius nos–ter .G. t[i]t[uli]. s[an]c[t]i Martini / p[res]b[ite]r Cardinalis ap[osto]lice sedis legatus considerata fide. deuotione ac obedientia que tempore turbationis. Anglie habuis–tis / ad Roman[am] eccl[es]iam matrem ues–tram in recompensationem dampnor[um] uobis in usus proprios conuertendam prouida / deliberatione concessit. sicut in ins–trumento autentico Cardinalis ip[s]ius exinde confec–to plenius continetur / uobis et per uos eidem eccl[es]ie auc–toritate ap[osto]lica confirmamus. [et] presentis scripti patrocinio communim[us]. / Nulli ergo om[n]ino hominum liceat hanc paginam nos–tre protec–tionis et confirmationis infringere uel / ei ausu temerario contraire. Siquis autem hoc attemptare presumpserit indignationem om[n]ipotentis dei et / beator[um] Petri [et] Pauli ap[osto]l-or[um] eius se nouerit incursurum. Dat'Lateran'ii. Id' FebR'. / Pontificatus n[ost]ri Anno Secundo. ·,

PRO SC7/35/19
Reg. Yr. 2 no. 888, *Reg. Hon. III* no. 1087, *CPL* 52 Not in P *SB* 474
32.9 cm × 30.8 cm: *plica* 2.4 cm
No *bulla* surviving or laces
Condition: good
Scribe: phi
Face: (top right-hand corner) R̃
Endorsements: (middle, left of centre) R script' (papal registration mark) (middle centre) Nycol' (proctor) (underneath the R script') (?) mord. N. (? Holy Trinity mark, late medieval English)
(1) An elongated final 's'.
(2) An elongated final 's'.

An irregular hand with a tendency to slope mainly forwards but sometimes backwards. An elaborately decorated 'H' of *Honorius*.

6

Mandate to P(andulf bishop) elect of Norwich, papal chamberlain and legate, to inspect the composition made between W(illiam I) late king of Scots and J(ohn) late king of England and, as he shall think fit, confirm or annul it. ⟨1218 November ?10 Lateran⟩ ⟨Datum Lateran...Nouembris pontificatus nostri anno tertio⟩

Pd Shirley i no. 13; and Theiner, *Vetera monumenta Hibernorum*, 7 no. 15
Address: Dilecto filio P. Norwicen[si] ⟨e⟩lecto Camerario n[ost]ro ap[osto]lice
   sed⟨is⟩ Legato
Incipit: C⟨arissimu⟩s in christo
Variant readings
l.1 *P.* (Shirley l.2 *Pandulfo*)
l.3 *I* (Shirley l.7 *Johannem*)
l.4 *litteris* (Shirley l.9 *literis*)
l.5 *Sancti* (Shirley l.11 *S.*)

PRO SC7/18/2
Reg. Yr. 3 no. 111 (date as above), *Reg. Hon. III* no. 1673, *CPL* 59–60 P 5918
   Not in *SB*
31.8 cm × 26.7 cm: *plica* 2.6 cm
Bulla on hemp strings
Condition: the document is much decayed and has been mounted but the
   leaden *bulla* is a fine specimen. The date has entirely gone but possibly the
   't' of *tertio* for the year can be detected.
Scribe: (?) n.
Endorsements: (mid left) Alex' (mid left, inverted) bulla missa episcopo
   Norwicensi quod confirmet uel infirmet conuentiones factas inter regem
   Scotie et regem Anglie prout melius uiderit expedire.

7

Relaxation of forty days of enjoined penance to all those visiting the church
of St Thomas the martyr of Canterbury (Christ Church) within the octave
of the translation of the body of the saint proposed by S(tephen Langton),
archbishop of Canterbury and cardinal of the Holy Roman Church.
1219 January 26 Lateran (Dat' Lateran' vii kl' februarii. Pontificat[us] n[ost]ri
Anno Tercio.)

Pd Rymer i pt 1 154, whence pd R. Foreville, *Le jubilé de Saint Thomas Becket*,
   165–6 no. 4.
Address: Vniuersis christi fidelibus ad eccl[es]iam s[an]c[t]i Thome martiris
   Cantuarien' infra diem oc/tauum translationis eiusdem martiris personaliter
   accedentibus.
Incipit: Quoniam ut ait
Variant readings
l.6 *parce* (twice) (Rymer l.11 *pace* (twice))
l.7 *Roman'* (Rymer l.14 *Romane*)
l.9 Foreville inserts *vero* after *uobis*; *quatinus* (Rymer l.17 *quatenus*); *sollempnitatis*
   (Rymer l.17 *solempnitatis*)

Appendix 2

PRO SC7/18/23
Reg. Yr. 3 no. 267, *Reg. Hon. III* no. 1841, *CPL* 62 Not in P *SB* 516
34.5 cm × 29.8 cm: *plica* 2.7 cm
No *bulla* surviving: tears for the lace holes
Condition: good
Scribe: Iord'. (cf. nos. 15, 23, below)
Face: (top: slightly right of centre) |/ (right corner) R̶7̶
Endorsements: (top left) Card', (?) (top centre) R̶7̶ script' (mid right) non.

A hand with distinctive 'd's in which the ascenders go up to the left at 45°
and the hair strokes back sharply at 90°: this is apparent but less marked with
the 'b's and 't's. The tittles also have angular parallel descenders at an angle
of 45° to the left. Decorated capitals. A very elaborate 'H' of *Honorius*. An
elongated final 's' is used on ten occasions, l.2 (3), l.3 (2), l.4 (1), l.8 (1), l.9
(2) and l.10 (1).

8

Confirmation to the dean and chapter of Hereford especially of the churches
of Madley (Heref.), Marden, and Putley (Heref.) with lands, mills, tithes
and all appurtenances, and the chapels of Dinmore and St Mary Magdalene,
Hereford, with mills, tithes and all appurtenances from the gift of King
R(ichard I); land at Donnington (Heref.) and Eggleton (Heref.) with a mill;
assarts near Hay (Heref.), half a hide of land in Huntington (Heref.), a virgate
of land and a rent of 60 *s* in Canon Moor (by Hereford) belonging to the
canons of Llanthony; the mill of Eign in Hereford from the gift of the bishop;
tithes of mills from their demesnes; Woolhope (Heref.), Preston on Wye
(Heref.), Norton Canon (Heref.) and Canon Pyon (Heref.) with their
churches, houses, tithes, lands and all appurtenances; lands in the *burg* of the
church and outside with houses; burgage tithes from the merchants (*negociatores*)
and tithes of Canon Moor with other lesser tithes; the third part of the tithes
from the lordship of Bullinghope (Heref.) of Richard of Cormeilles; two parts
of the tithes from the *fruges* (produce of the fields, pulse, legumes) of all the
land belonging to Bartonsham; liberties and immunities conceded by King
John and the princes of England, and reasonable customs approved for their
church, and all goods; taking their persons, cathedral and goods under papal
protection.
1219 March 11 Lateran (Dat' Lateran.' v Id' Martii. Pontificat[us] n[ost]ri
Anno Tertio.)

Pd Charters and records of Hereford Cathedral, ed. William W. Capes (Cantilupe
    Society 1908) 48–9
Address: Dilec–tis filiis.. Decano et Capitulo Hereforden[sibus]
Incipit: Cum a nobis
Variant readings

l.3 *Eapropter* (Capes l.5 *Quapropter*)

l.5 *Puteleke* (Capes l.11 *Putelehe*)

l.6 *Dunemor* (Capes l.13 *Dunemore*)

l.7 *.R.* (Capes l.15 *Ricardi*); *Duni*[n]*tu*[n] (Capes l.15 *Dunnitune*); *Eglintu*[n] (Capes l.16 *Eglintune*)

ll.7–8 *Hu*[n]*ti*[n]'/*ton*' (Capes l.17 *Huntintone*)

l.10 *negotiatio*[n]*ib*[us] (Capes l.24 *negociatoribus*)

l.11 *Be*[*?r*]*stanesha*[m] (Capes l.28 *Bertanesham*) an open headed 'r' over the first 'e'

l.12 transposition marks to read *consuetudines rationabiles et approbatas* (Capes l.30 *racionabiles consuetudines et approbatas*)

Hereford, Dean and Chapter Charter no. 1850

Not registered, not in P or *SB*

27.5 cm × 32.1 cm: *plica* 2.4 cm

Red and yellow silk: no *bulla* surviving

Condition: good

Scribe: Sca(mbio) (cf. nos. 17, 27 and 38, below)

Endorsements: (top centre) exam' (sixteenth century) (mid to top centre, inverted) Honorius anno domini m^{mo} cc^{mo} xiiij^{mo} super Ecclesias de Mauwardin et putteleye.

The particular quirks of this scribe are the use of the *per* sign, the use of the tittle, often twice in one word, and the open headed 'r' as in *presumpserit* in the 'Si quis' clause; also the use of the tittle for cu[m].

9

Confirmation to the abbot and convent of Thorney (Ben. Cambs.) of their possessions (not listed) particularly in the vill of Wangford (Suff.) or Wansford (Northants.), taking them under the protection of the Holy See.

1219 March 31 Lateran

HONORIUS ep[iscopu]s seruus seruor[um] dei. Dilec–tis filiis.. Abbati et Conuentui de Torneia. Sal[u]t[em] et ap[osto]licam ben[edictionem]. *I*us–tis / petentium desideriis⸍dignum es–t nos facilem prebere consensum et uota que a rationis tramite no[n] discordant⸍effec–tu / prosequente complere. Ea propter dilec–ti in domino filii u[est]ris ius–tis pos–tulationib[us] grato concurrentes (1) / assensu⸍personas u[est]ras et locum in quo diuino es–tis obsequio mancipati cum om[n]ib[us] bonis que impresentiarum rationabiliter / possidet⟨is⟩ aut in futurum ius–tis modis pres–tante domino poterit adipisci sub beati Petri et n[ost]ra protec–tio[n]e / suscipimus (2). Specialiter aut[em] homines quos habetis in Villa d⟨e⟩.... ford possessiones. et alia ⟨b⟩ona u⟨est⟩ra sicut ea om[n]ia⸍ (3) / ius–te ac pacifice possidetis⸍uobis et

Appendix 2

per uos m⟨onas⟩–terio u[est]ro∕auctoritate ap[osto]lica confirmamus. et presentis / scripti patrocinio communimus. (4) Nulli ergo om[n]ino hominum liceat hanc paginam n[ost]re protec–tionis et con'/firmationis infringere. uel ei ausu temerario contraire ⟨S⟩iquis aut[em] hoc attemptare presumpserit∕ indignationem / om[n]ipotentis dei et beatorum Petri et P⟨auli⟩ ap⟨osto⟩-lorum ⟨eius⟩ se nouerit incursurum. Dat' Lateran'. ii. kl'. / Aprilis Pontificat[us] ⟨nostri⟩ Anno Tertio¬

Lambeth Palace Library PD no. 21 (cal. Sayers, *Original papal documents*)
Not registered, not in P or *SB*
29.2 cm × 21.3 cm: *plica* 2 cm
Holes: no *bulla*
Condition: fair
Scribe: p. po. (cf. no. 21, below)
Endorsements: (top centre) (A hand clasping a sword) Caue / (bottom centre)
   Confirmacio bonorum monasterii / 3 /.aaW... / xviij.

(1) The scribe uses an elaborate tongued 's' at the end of the word.
(2) The scribe uses an elaborate tongued 's' at the end of the word.
(3) This dash is not a hyphen but has been provided to fill in the line.
(4) The scribe uses an elaborate tongued 's' at the end of the word.

A clear, open, well executed hand. The 'H' of *Honorius* is distinctly comparable with that of no. 21 below. The scribe uses long and short ligatures, *estis* in line 4 is an example of a short ligature and *protectionis* in line 8 of a long.

10

Confirmation to the abbot and convent of Dore (Cist. Heref.) of land, which King John had given them, 'in bosco et plano' lying between the river (*aqua*) which is called Dore and the brook (*rivulus*) called 'Triuelbroc' and twenty feet of land from the source (*caput*) of the 'Truilbroc' to the land of the Hospitallers, for enlarging the millpond.
1219 April 20 Rome, St Peter's

HONORIUS ep[iscopu]s seruus seruor[um] dei. *Dilec*–tis filiis..Abb[at]i et Conuentui de Dora Cistercien[sis] ordinis. sal[u]t[em] et ap[osto]licam / ben[edictionem]. *S*olet annuere sedes ap[osto]lica piis uotis. et hones–tis petentium precib[us] fauorem beniuolum impertiri. *E*apropter dilec–ti in / d[omi]no filii u[est]ris ius–tis precib[us] inclinati. Terram in bosco et plano que iacet inter aquam que appellatur Dore. [et] riuulum qui'/ appellatur Triuelbroc'∕ et latitudine[m] uiginti pedum terre a capite de Truilbroc' usq[ue] ad terram hospitalarior[um]. ad amplian'/dum s–tagnum molendini quod ibidem habetis∕que clare memorie Ioh[anne]s Rex anglor[um]. ab om[n]i exac–tione ac seruitio / libera in helemosinam uobis contulit perpetuo possidendam sicut ea om[n]ia ius–te ac pacifice possidetis. [et] in autentico ex'/inde confec–to plenius continetur.' uobis [et] per uos monas–terio u[est]ro auctoritate ap[osto]lica confirmamus. [et] presentis (1) / scripti patrocinio co[m]munimus. (2) Nulli ergo om[n]ino hominum liceat hanc paginam n[ost]re confirmationis infrin'/gere. uel ei ausu temerario contraire. Siquis autem hoc attemptare presumpserit.' indignationem om[n]ipotentis / dei. [et] beator[um] Petri et Pauli ap[osto]lor[um] eius se nouerit incursurum. Dat'. Rom' ap[u]d S[an]c[tu]m / Petrum. xii. kl'. Maii. Pontificatus. n[ost]ri Anno Tertio;.

Northamptonshire Record Office I. L. 496
Not registered, not in P or *SB*
30.6 cm × 26.5 cm: *plica* 2.6 cm
Holes: no *bulla*
Condition: good
Scribe: *co
Endorsements: (top centre) Cistercien' (mid centre, running from bottom to top) pro abbate de dora
(1) An elongated final 's'.
(2) An elongated final 's'.

A most distinctive, flowing, large hand, with fine ligatures and elaborate capitals. No margins are left: hair strokes for hyphens.

11

Confirmation to the prior and convent of Tynemouth (Ben. Northumb.) of their appropriation of the church of Woodhorn (Northumb.) and its chapels, with the consent of the diocesan, the bishop of Durham, and W. the patron. 1220 May 6 Viterbo

HONORIUS ep[iscopu]s seruus seruor[um] dei. Dilectis filiis..Priori et Conuentui Monasterii de Tinenie.' / Sal[u]t[em] et ap[osto]licam ben[edic-tionem]. *I*us–tis petentium desideriis dignum es–t nos facilem prebere con-sensum.' et uota / que a rationis (1) tramite non discordant.' effectu prosequente complere. Eapropter dilecti in domino / filii u[est]ris (2) ius–tis pos–tulationibus (3) grato concurrentes assensu.' eccl[es]ia⟨m⟩ de Wodehorn' cum capel'/lis et pertinentiis suis a venerabili fratre n[ost]ro..Ep[iscop]o Dunelmen' diocesan⟨o⟩ loci capituli sui nec'/non Nobilis uiri. W. patroni eiusdem eccl[es]ie accedente consensu Monas–terio u[est]ro pia et pro'/uida liberalitate collatam.' auctoritate ap[osto]lica confirmamus (4) et presentis scripti patrocinio / communimus. Nulli ergo omnino hominum liceat hanc paginam n[ost]re confirmationis (5) / infringere. uel ei ⟨au⟩su temerario contraire. Siquis autem hoc attemptare presumpse'/rit indignationem om[n]ipotentis (6) dei. et beator[um] Petri et Pauli ap⟨ostolo⟩r[um] eius: (7) se no'/uerit incursurum. Dat' Viterbii .ii. Non' Maii. / Pontificatus n[ost]ri Anno Quarto.,

Lambeth Palace Library PD no. 22 (cal. Sayers, *Original papal documents*)
Not registered, not in P or *SB*
28.2 cm × 21.1 cm: *plica* 3 cm
Red and yellow silk strings: no *bulla*
Condition: fairly good
Scribe: *b. f.
Endorsements: (top right) Honorius / (top centre) Confirmatio / Robertus
   Garrard exibuit xxi septembr anno 1537 / Alban' / xij / (mid centre,
   inverted) Honorius. papa. de Ecclesia de Wudhorn'. / Mon' Tineme / 6.
(1)–(7) The scribe uses an elongated 's'.

The scribe also uses a final 'e' with a long tongue.

12
(fragment)

Mandate to—that the earls, barons and castellans and other nobles who are loyal to the king shall assist the legate Pandulf and restore to the king his castles and lordships or be compelled to do so.
[1220] May 14 Viterbo (... / Viterbii. ii. Id' Ma⟨ii⟩ Pontificatus n⟨ostri⟩ ...)

Pd Prynne, *Exact chronological vindication* iii 43
Address and *incipit* lost
Variant readings
l.2 .../ceat (Prynne l.1 *erat*)
l.6 iura (Prynne l.7 *uita*)
l.11 *consoloria* (Prynne l.13 *consolari*)

PRO SC7/50/3
Not registered, not in P or *SB*
Holes: no *bulla*
Condition: fair; fragment, bottom left corner only. The document has
   deteriorated considerably since Prynne saw it.
Endorsements: (mid right, inverted) Quod barones assistant pandulfo legato
   et restituant castra et dominia Regi (English, medieval)

The hand is smallish and regular. There is a very narrow left-hand margin.

13

Mandate to P(andulf bishop) elect of Norwich, papal chamberlain and legate not to allow anyone 'de regno Anglie' to have more than two of the king's castles in his custody.

1220 May 28 Viterbo (Dat' Viterbii v kl' Iunii. / Pontificat[us] n[ost]ri Anno Quarto.)

Pd Shirley i no. 104 and Rymer i pt 1 160
Address: Dilecto filio .P. Norwicen[si] electo. Came/rario n[ost]ro. ap[osto]lice
   sedis Legato
Incipit: Presentium tibi auctori/tate

PRO SC7/18/8
Not registered *Reg. Hon. III* no. 2460 (abstract from Rymer) P 6259 Not in
   SB
16.5 cm × 12.7 cm: *plica* 2.2 cm
Fine *bulla* on hemp strings
Condition: very good
Scribe: boe (not to be identified with bo, no. 29, below)
Endorsements: (top, extreme left corner) R (mid left to centre, inverted) A.ii
   / Scribende quia nullus ⟨custo⟩dire ultra due castra / Scribitur in libro
   (bottom left) Quod nullus de Angl' habeat custod' Castri Angl' plusquam
   de duobus

A neat hand: no hyphens are used, although words are broken.

14

Confirmation of the possessions, rents and other goods (unspecified) of the leper hospital of Clattercote (Oxon.), taking their persons, hospital and goods under papal protection.
1220 July 17 Orvieto

HONORIUS ep[iscopu]s seruus seruor[um] dei Dilec–tis filiis..Priori et Fratribus Hospitalis Leprosor[um] de Clatercotes. (1) / Sal[u]t[em] et ap[-osto]licam ben[edictionem]. Solet annuere sedes ap[osto]lica piis uotis et hones–tis petentium precibus fauorem beniuolum imper/tiri. Eapropter Dilecti in domino filii ves–tris ius–tis pos–tulationibus grato concurrentes assensu personas ues–tras / et hospitale predictum cum omnibus bonis que impresentiarum ⟨ration⟩abiliter possidetis aut in futurum ius–tis modis pres–tante / domino (2) poteritis adipisci sub ⟨beati Petri et⟩ nos–tra protectione ⟨suscipimus⟩... (3). possessiones. redditus ac / alia bona u[est]ra ⟨sicut ea omnia iuste et paci⟩fice possidetis... (4) eid⟨em⟩ hospitali auctoritate ap[osto]lica confirmamus. et / presentis scripti patrocinio communimus ... (5)

223

a uobis de ortis seu de ⟨decim⟩ar[um] (6) animalium nutrimentis / decimas exigere uel extorquere presumat. Nulli ergo ⟨omnino⟩ hominum liceat hanc paginam...(7) inhibitio[n]is / infringere uel ei ausu temerario contraire. Si⟨quis autem hoc at⟩temptare presumpserit indignationem omnipotentis dei et bea/tor[um] Petri et pauli apos–tolor[um] eius se nouerit incursurum. Dat' apud vrbemueterem. / xvj. kl. Aug' Pontificat[us] n[ost]ri Anno Quarto.,

Bodleian Library, Oxford, MS. Chs. Oxon. 147a (listed Major, 'Original papal documents' no. 6)
Not registered, not in P or *SB*
31.5 cm × 21.7 cm: *plica* cut off
Condition: poor. Mounted and trimmed at top and bottom. Considerable wear and holes in the lower part of the right-hand fold. Dorse: signs of repair, and possibly signs of stitching down the sides or prick marks.
Scribe: —.
Endorsements: (top right corner, inverted) ⟨.........'⟩ p[ro]tect (8) loci et p[er]sonar[um] cu[m] po... (9) (? English, C14 or C15)

(1) The 'c' of *dilectis* and the 'f's and the 's's of the first line have an elaborate rope-like decoration.
(2) 's' under the 'n' of *domino*, in a different ink and probably not contemporary.
(3) Three words: the first holed.
(4) Two to three words.
(5) Four words; probably *districtius inhibentes ne quis.*
(6) Probably *decimarum.*
(7) Three to four words. ? *nostre protectionis confirmationis et*; cf. no. 53. Probably omitting *confirmationis.*
(8) Obscured by the mount.
(9) Obscured by the mount.

15
Confirmation to the dean and chapter of St Martin le Grand, London (secular college) especially of an annual rent of 20 marks from the church of Witham (Essex), taking their persons, goods and church under papal protection.
1221 March 5 Lateran

HONORIUS ep[iscopu]s seruus seruor[um] dei. Dilec–tis filiis..Decano et Capitulo s[an]c[t]i Martini Londonien'. sal[u]t[em] et / ap[osto]licam ben-[edictionem]. Solet annuere sedes ap[osto]lica piis uotis. et honestis petentium precibus. fauorem beni/uolum impertiri. Eapropter dilecti in d[omi]no filii u[est]ris ius–tis precibus inclinati. personas u[est]ras et / eccl[es]iam s[an]c[t]i Martini in qua diuino uacatis obsequio' cum om[n]ib[us] bonis que impresentiar[um] rationabiliter / possidetis. aut in futurum prestante d[omi]no ius–tis modis poteritis adipisci.' sub beati Petri et n[ost]ra / protectione suscipimus. Specialit[er] autem annuum redditum viginti marcar[um] u[est]ris usibus deputatum'/ quem obtinetis in eccl[esi]a de Witham sicut illum ius–te ac pacifice possidetis.' uobis auctoritate ap[osto]li/ca confirmamus et presentis scripti patrocinio communimus. Nulli ergo om[n]ino hominum liceat ha[n]c / paginam n[ost]re protectionis et confirmationis infringere.' uel ei ausu temerario contraire. Siquis / aut[em] hoc attemptare presumpserit. indignationem om[n]ipotentis dei. et beator[um] Petri et Pauli ap[osto]lorum / eius.' se nouerit incursurum. Dat' Lateran' .iiij. Non' Martij; / Pontificatus n[ost]ri Anno Quinto;

Westminster Abbey Muniments 13248
Not registered, not in P or *SB*
26.7 cm × 23.7 cm: *plica* 2.8 cm
Plica torn away in centre: no *bulla*
Condition: fairly good
Scribe: Iord'. (cf. nos. 7 above and 23 below)
Endorsements: (left) Confirmacio possessionum sancti martini et ⟨protectio?⟩ cuiusdam xx^{ti} marcarum ecclesie parochie de Witham

16

Mandate to the archdeacon of Worcester and the chancellor and the dean of Oxford, on the petition of the abbot and convent of Oseney (Aug. Oxon.), to conduct enquiries and record evidence about the abbey's rights to tithes in various parishes.

1221 March 30 Lateran (Dat' Lateran' iii kl' Aprilis. / Pontificatus n[ost]ri Anno Quinto.)

Pd Medieval archives of the university of Oxford, ed. H. E. Salter (Oxf. Hist. Soc. lxxx, 1920 for 1917) i no. 6
Address: Dilectis filiis .. Archid[iacono] Wigornien[si] et .. Cancellario. et / Decan[o] Oxonie lincolnien[sis] dioc[esis].
Incipit: Ex parte .. Abb[at]is
Variant readings
l.4 *ualitudinarii* (Salter l.7 *ualetudinarii*)
l.5 *senei* (Salter l.7 *senes*)
l.6 *u⟨estre⟩* and *mandam⟨u⟩s* (Salter l.9) supplied because the document is holed

Oxford University Archives S.E.P./Y/2
Not registered, not in P or *SB*
19.2 cm × 16.1 cm: *plica* 2.3 cm

Appendix 2

Holes: no *bulla*
Condition: fairly good, 2 holes in centre
Scribe: B. p.
Endorsements: (top centre) De Osen' / Honorii 3° 5° a° domini 1221 (centre)
(a device or symbol) (bottom centre) Y.2 / Y. nu.2 / Bull of Pope
Honorius III concerning tithes of Osney abby 1221

Careful 'i's and hair strokes, but the document is cramped (especially in the
last three lines) and not well spaced. An elongated 's' is used to complete
Aprilis (l.11; Salter l.16) and *Pontificatus* (l.12; Salter l. 16).

17

Mandate to the abbot of Langley (Prem. Norf.), the prior of Holy Trinity
and the dean of Norwich to hear the case of the prior and convent of St
Botolph (Colchester) (Aug. Essex) that the prior and convent of Holy Trinity
(Aldgate, London), who are subject to them, refuse obedience.
1221 April 5 Lateran

Honorius ep[iscopu]s seruus seruor[um] dei. Dilectis filiis..Abbati de Langel'
Norwicen[sis] dioc[esis]..Priore / S[an]c[t]e Trinitatis. et..Decan[o] Norwicen[si]⁄ Sal[u]t[em] et ap[osto]licam ben[edictionem]. Sua nobis. . Prior et /
Conuent[us] s[an]c[t]i Botulfi conquestione mo[n]strar[un]t. q[uo]d..Prior et
Conuentus eccl[es]ie s[an]c[t]e Trinitatis / ad eorum eccl[es]iam de iure
spectantis⁄ obedientiam et reuere[n]tiam sibi debitam denega[n]t. exhib[er]e
/ alias graues existentes eisdem pl[ur]imu[m]. [et] molesti. Id[e]oq[ue]
discretioni u[est]re p[er] ap[osto]lica scripta mandam[us] / quatin[us] partib[us]
co[n]uocatis audientiam et appellatio[n]e remota fine debito terminetis.
facientes q[uo]d de/creueritis per censuram eccl[esi]asticam firmiter obseruari.
Testes aut[em] qui fueri[n]t no[m]i[n]ati si se gr[ati]a. odio / uel timore
subtraxerint. censura simili appellatione cessante cogatis ueritati testimo[n]ium
p[er]hib[er]e. Q[uo]d / si no[n] om[n]es hiis exequendis potueritis intere[ss]e.
duo u[est]r[u]m ea nich[il]omin[us] exequantur. Dat' / Lateran'. Non'
April[is]. Pontificat[us] n[ost]ri Anno Quinto;

PRO SC7/18/13
Not registered, not in P or *SB*
29 cm × 12.9 cm: *plica* 2.1 cm
Detached *bulla* on hemp strings
Condition: fairly good
Scribe: Sca(mbio) (cf. no. 8, above, and nos. 27 and 38, below)
Face crossed through
Endorsements: none

226

The scribe breaks the dating clause after *Dat*, where he has lengthened the 't' to fill the line, and before *Lateran*.

18

Confirmation to the prior and canons of Newnham (Aug. Beds.) of their possessions, especially the church of St Paul (Bedford), taking their persons, house and goods under papal protection.
1221 April 26 Lateran

HONORIUS ep[iscopu]s seruus seruor[um] dei. *Dilec*–tis filiis..Priori et Canonicis de Newham. / Sal[u]t[em] et ap[osto]licam ben[edictionem]. *Cum* a nobis petitur quod ius–tum es–t et hones–tum tam uigor / equitatis quam ordo exigit rationis ut id per sollicitudinem officii nos–tri ad debitum perducatur / effectum. *Ea*propter dilec–ti in domino filii ues–tris ius–tis pos–tulationibus grato con/currentes assensu personas u[est]ras et locum in quo diuino es–tis obsequio mancipati cum om[n]ibus / bonis que impresentiarum rationabiliter possidetis aut in futurum ius–tis modis pres–tante d[omi]no / poteritis adipisci sub Beati Petri et nos–tra protec–tione suscipimus. *S*pecialiter autem / Eccl[es]iam s[an]c[t]i Pauli cum pertinentiis suis ac alia bona u[est]ra sicut ea omnia ius–te ac pacifice / possidetis uobis et per uos domui ues–tre auc–toritate ap[osto]lica confirmamus et pre/sentis scripti patrocinio communimus. *N*ulli ergo om[n]ino hominum liceat hanc paginam nos–tre / protec–tionis et confirmationis infringere u[e]l ei ausu temerario contraire. *S*iquis autem hoc / attemptare presumpserit indignationem om[n]ipotentis dei et Beatorum Petri et Pauli Ap[osto]lorum eius / se nouerit incursurum. Dat' Lateran' .vi. Kl' Maii / Pontificatus n[ost]ri Anno Quinto.

BL Harley Ch. 43 A 31 (Bell, 'Original papal bulls' no. 58)
Not registered, not in P or *SB*
22 cm × 21.6 cm: *plica* 2 cm
Holes: no *bulla*
Condition: good
Scribe: Otto (cf. no. 2, above)
Endorsements: (top, extreme left corner) n *or* m (top centre) Iohannes de h(b?).y...(?proctor) / de protectione Priori et Convent' de Newham (English, medieval) (bottom, running from top to bottom) Honorius ...
... ... sancti pauli Bedeford' (English, medieval)

Very pretty, elaborate capitals with snake-like decoration in the main stem of the 'H' of *HONORIUS* and fringe work in some of the letters. The document has been lined.

19

Mandate to the archbishop of York and his suffragans to use their good offices to remove the causes of war in England and to labour to bring about a peace.
1221 April 29 Lateran (Dat' lateran' iii kl' Maii/ Pontificat[us] n[ost]ri Anno Qui[n]to.)

Pd Shirley i no. 151 and Rymer i pt 1 167
Address: Venerabilibus Fratrib[us].. Archiep[iscopo] Eboracen[si]. [et] Suffraganeis eius.
Incipit: Et si / appetenda sit

PRO SC7/18/4
Not registered but cf. *CPL* 80 (to abp of Canterbury under 4 kal May, 28 April) P 6643 Not in *SB*
28 cm × 21.1 cm: *plica* 2.1 cm
Bulla on hemp strings
Condition: very good
Scribe: b. a. (cf. no. 25, below)
Face: (top centre) V
Endorsements: (top centre) REG (top right, inverted) Examinatur (mid right) (other English endorsements) (bottom right) Extrahitur de litera B

This scribe favours the use in this document's first line of small capitals as in *Eboracen*, *Suffraganeis* and *Salutem*. There is an elaborate 'E' beginning *Et si* and this letter is formed from a sphere with dots at top and bottom and a cross stroke leading to an arc (cf. the 'C' in no. 25). There are finely stroked hyphens, fine and careful descenders to the 's's and 'p's, and an elongated final 'e' to *attente* at the end of line 6 and dividing *compe'/scere* lines 9 to 10.

20

Mandate to the bishop of Winchester, H(ubert) de Burgh, justiciar, R(anulf) earl of Chester, William Brewer and other counsellors of H(enry III) king of the English, to cause to be restored to the king such wards and escheats as belong to him but are detained by others. Since the king has taken the cross and is an orphan, he is under the special protection of the holy see; no papal letters to the prejudice of the king are to be regarded as valid.
1221 April 29 Lateran (Dat' Lateran' iii kl' Maii. / Pontificatus n[ost]ri Anno Quinto.)

Pd Rymer i pt 1 167; also Prynne, *Exact Chronological vindication* iii 52–3
Address: Venerabili fratri.. Wintonien[si] Ep[iscop]o. et Dilectis filiis Nobilib[us] uiris .H. de burgo Iustitia/rio .R. Comiti Cestrie. W[i]ll[elm]o. briguere. ac aliis Consiliariis Carissimi in christo filii n[ost]ri .H. Regis Anglor[um] illustris.

Incipit: Cum Carissimus in
Variant readings
l.1 gemipunctus omitted in Rymer; .H. (Rymer l.3 *Huberto*)
l.2 *Carissimi* (Rymer l.4 *charissimi*); .H. (Rymer l.5 *Henrici*)
l.3 *Carissimus* (Rymer l.7 *charissimus*; Reg. *karissimus*)
l.6 *Gaurde* (Rymer l.12 *guardae*); *Eschaete* (Rymer l.13 *escheatae*)
l.8 *Nullis* (Rymer l.17 *Nullius*)

PRO SC7/50/4
Reg. Yr. 5 no. 587, *Reg. Hon. III* no. 3312, *CPL* 81, P 6642, *SB* 626
26.6 cm × 21.9 cm; *plica* 2.6 cm
Holes: no *bulla*
Condition: quite good
Scribe: (symbol like a comma)
Endorsements: (top left to centre) R script (papal registration mark) (top
   centre) REG (bottom right) De restituend' terris et castris regi. / Scribende
   propter(?) ultimum videris / Exam

A clear, definite hand with no slant. Lines 5 and 6 exhibit the weak form of
comma after *nequit* and *occupate*. The scribe uses the long 's' in *litteris* and in
Pontificatus at the end of lines 8 and 10.

21
Confirmation to the chapter of Exeter of their possessions, and especially of
the church of Colyton (*Cvlinton*) (Devon), which bishop H(enry) had
conferred on them, taking their persons and goods (cathedral church not
mentioned) under papal protection.
1221 December 18 Lateran

HONORIUS ep[iscopu]s seruus seruor[um] dei. Dilec–tis filiis. Capitulo
Exonien[si]: sal[u]t[em] et ap[osto]licam ben[edictionem]. Sacro'/sanc–ta
Romana eccl[es]ia deuotos et humiles filios ex assuete pietatis officio propensius
diligere consueuit✓et'/ ne prauorum hominum moles–tiis agitentur eos
tamquam pia mater sue protec–tionis munimine confo'/uere. Eapropter
dilec–ti in domino filii u[est]ris ius–tis pos–tulationibus grato concurrentes
assensu'. / Personas u[est]ras cum om[n]ibus bonis tam eccl[es]ias–ticis quam
mundanis que impresentiarum rationabiliter possidetis / aut in futurum ius–tis
modis pres–tante domino poteritis (1) adipisci : sub beati Petri et n[ost]ra
protec–tione / suscipimus. Specialiter aut[em] ecclesiam de Cvlinton' uobis
a bone memorie .H. Exonien[si] Ep[iscop]o pia liberalite col(2)'/tam sicut
eam ius–te ac pacifice obtinetis et in autentico ip[s]ius ep[iscop]i exinde
confec–to plenius conti'/netur uobis et per uos eccl[es]ie u[est]re auc–toritate
ap[osto]lica confirmamus. et presentis scripti patrocinio com'/munimus. Nulli
ergo om[n]ino hominum liceat hanc paginam n[ost]re protec–tionis et

confirmationis infrin'/gere. uel ei ausu temerario contraire. Siquis aut[em] hoc attemptare presumpserit' indignationem om[n]ipotentis / dei et beatorum Petri et Pauli ap[osto]lor[um] eius se nouerit incursurum. Dat' Lateran'. xv. K[a]l. / Ianuarii. Pontificat[us] n[ost]ri Anno Sexto.,

Exeter, Dean and Chapter Ch. 2087
Not registered, not in P or *SB*
30.3 cm × 27.2 cm: *plica* 3.2 cm
Red and yellow silk: no *bulla*
Condition: very good
Scribe: p. po. (cf. no. 9, above)
Endorsements: (top centre) P g (curial or Italian, with a tittle over the 'g'; possibly a proctor's mark) (upper centre) priuil' octauum / Confirmacio Honorii pape de omnibus possessionibus et precipue de ecclesia de Coleton'. / anno domini mcc xvi^{to} (all English: the first two, probably in one hand of the C14)
(1) The second 't' of *poteritis* thickened, perhaps corrected.
(2) MS sic.

A fine, lined document, with attractive capitals. The scribe, however, in lines 7 to 8 has used *coltam* for the more correct *collatam* and has split the dating clause between *kal* and *Ianuarii*.

22

Warning and exhortation to the counsellors of H(enry), king of the English, not to concern themselves with a case brought to the king's court by Richard de Percy, knight, against the archbishop of York concerning collation to the church of Dunnington, a part (*membrum*) of the same prebend of York, which the legates Guala and Pandulf had forbidden the king's justices to hear. (1) 1222 May 26 Alatri (Dat' / Alatri. Vij. kl' Iunii. Pontificat[us] n[ost]ri Anno Sexto.)

Pd Prynne, *Exact chronological vindication* iii 53
Address: Dilectis filiis Consiliarii[s] k[arissi]mi in christo filii n[ost]ri .H. Regis Anglorum Illustris
Incipit: Venerabilis frat[er] n[oste]r
Variant readings
l.1 *k[arissi]mi* (Pryne l.2 *charissimi*); followed by *in christo*, omitted by Prynne
l.2 *Ricc[ardus]* (Prynne l.4 *Richardus*)
ll.2–3 *Per/ci* (Prynne l.4 *Percy*)
l.4 *t[i]t[uli]* (Prynne l.7 *titulo*); *et* omitted by Prynne after *primo* and before *postmodum*
l.5 *interdixeri[n]t* (Prynne l.8 *interdixit*)
l.6 *nu[n]c* (Prynne l.10 *tamen*); *Dunigthne* (Prynne l.11 *Dunigthue*)

PRO SC7/50/5
Not registered, not in P or *SB*
27.6 cm × 22.3 cm: *plica* 2.1 cm
Holes: no *bulla*
Condition: fairly good
Scribe: al(ex) (cf. no. 1, above)
Face: (top extreme right corner) ? ad..Nicolai
Endorsements: (top centre) Hely (mid left) archiepiscopus b / Scribende quia
ne laicus placitet de prebenda in foro civili (bottom left to centre) Examinat'
(1) See above Chapter 4 p. 141.

There are signs of correction of this document, to the first 'u' in *absurdum*
(l.8, first word) and possibly to the 's' of *usum* (the fourth word in l.5).

23

Mandate to the abbots of la Grâce-Dieu (Cist.), St-Léonard-des-Chaumes
(Cist.) and La Rochelle (*Re*) (diocese of Saintes) to enquire into a complaint
of Henry (III) king of the English against the Knights Templar in La Rochelle
(*Rupella*).
1222 June 23 Lateran (Dat' Lateran' viiii kl' Iulii. Pontificatus n[ost]ri Anno
Sexto;)

Pd Rymer i pt 1 169
Address: Dilectis filiis..de Gratia dei. et..s[an]c[t]i Leonardi de Calmis. et..de
Re Abbatib[us] xanctonen' dioces[is]
Incipit: Carissimus in christo
Variant readings
l.1 *Re* (Rymer l.3 *Rupella*); *xanctonen'* (Rymer l.3 *xantonen'*)
l.3 *xanctonen'* (Rymer l.8 *xantonen'*)

PRO SC7/18/9
Not registered *Reg. Hon. III* no. 4051 (abstract from Rymer). P 6864. Not
in *SB*. See Arcère, *La Rochelle* ii 662. A notarial exemplification of this letter,
dated 1305, is in PRO SC7/36/2.
35.5 cm × 27.4 cm: *plica* 2.5 cm
Bulla on hemp strings
Condition: good
Scribe: Iord' (cf. nos. 7 and 15, above)
Endorsements: (top centre) REG (mid right, inverted) Scribitur in libro
(bottom left corner) .v. (bottom right) L .vi. / Exam' / .iiii. (and further
English endorsements)

A small, closely packed and spiked hand, with flamboyant 'd's, exaggerated
ascenders and backward hooks to some of the final 's's.

Appendix 2

24

Warning and mandate to Hugh de Lusignan (*Leziniaco*), count of La Marche, and Isabella, (1) his wife, to restore to Henry, king of the English, before the feast of St Andrew (30 November) next, the dowry of the king's sister, which, when the betrothal was broken, the count had failed to return, and also the castles of Cognac and Merpins, or face sentence.

1222 June 25 Lateran (Dat' Lateran' vii. kl' Iulii. Pontificatus n[ost]ri Anno Sexto;)

Pd Rymer i pt 1 169: also Bouquet, *Recueil* xix 726
Address: Dilecto filio nobili uiro Hugoni de Leziniaco Comiti Marchie. et Isabelle uxori eius Pictauen' dioc[esis]
Incipit: Intelleximus ex relatione
Variant readings
l.5 Rymer (ll.13–14) ignores the *gemipuncti*.

PRO SC7/18/28
Not registered *Reg. Hon. III* no. 4054 (abstract from Rymer). P 6866. Not in *SB*
36.3 cm × 34.8 cm: *plica* 3.1 cm
Detached *bulla* on hemp strings
Condition: good
Scribe: za
Face: (top centre, extending to right) the same / In   Comiti Comiti Uxori eius Bene placet
Endorsements: (top centre) Reg (mid centre) Mandat papa comiti Marchie quod restituat quedam castra Regi Angl' alioquin quod (?)quedam iudices ipsos ad hoc per excommunicationis sententiam coherceant et compellant (bottom centre) Examinatur
(1) The king's mother, who married Hugh de Lusignan as her second husband in 1220. Hugh had been betrothed to Isabella's daughter and the king's sister, Joan, who was later married to Alexander II, king of Scots (see Powicke, *Henry III*, 172).

A thin, upright hand with no particular embellishments, except for the 'v' in the 'vii' of the date which is given a rounded ascender from the top of the left limb. The scribe uses a long final 's' in *infestares* at the end of l.7.

25

Indult to all the abbots and brothers of the Cistercian order from the payment of tithes on lands which were acquired before the General Council and were cultivated by others if they have been returned to them and are now cultivated by their own hands or at their own expense.

1222 June 26 Lateran

HONORIUS ep[iscopu]s seruus seruor[um] dei. Dilec–tis filiis Vniuersis Abbatibus et fratribus / Cis–tercien' ordinis. Sal[u]t[em] et ap[osto]licam ben[edictionem]. Cum aliquando cogente necessitate uel utilitate / propria requirente terras u[est]ras ante generale concilium acquisitas concesseritis aliis exco'/lendas ne pro eo q[uo]d de possessionibus pos–t idem concilium acquisitis decimas / soluitis si ad manus u[est]ras taliter concesse redierint a quoquam uexari possitis ut / nullus a uobis de ip[s]is terris quas propriis manibus aut sumptibus colitis / occasione concilii memorati decimas exigere uel extorquere presumat auc–to'/ritate uobis presentium indulgemus. Nulli ergo omnino hominum liceat / hanc paginam nos–tre concessionis infringere uel ei ausu temerario / contraire. Siquis autem hoc attemptare presumpserit⟩ indignationem omnipoten'/ tis dei et beator[um] Petri ⟨et⟩ (1) Pauli ap[osto]lor[um] eius se nouerit incursurum. Dat' / Lateran' vi kl' Iulii Pontificat[us] n[ost]ri Anno Sexto.;

BL Add. Ch. 19805 (Bell, 'Original papal bulls' no. 59)
Not registered, not in P, but see P 7314 and P 7320, two indults of 1224 to the Cistercians in general (the first from the register of St Mary, Newbattle, Scotland) SB 670
24.4 cm × 20.4 cm: *plica* 2.8 cm
Red and yellow silk: no *bulla* surviving
Condition: good, apart from some wear into holes at the bottom left
Scribe: b. a. (cf. no. 19, above)
Endorsements: (top centre) M *or* N (cf. no. 40, below) Honorius de decimis (followed by late C15, early C16 description) (bottom centre) HONORIUS x (bottom right) De decimis ... . ante concilium etc. (bottom left corner) xi
(1) Hole: ⟨ ⟩ supplied.

Fine hyphens. Point marks for the lines. Compare the dot on the back of the stem of the 'N' in *Nulli* with that on the back in the centre of the stem of the 'H' in *Honorius* (in no. 19) and the straight serif from the left foot in both these capital letters.

26

Warning, exhortation and mandate to William, called (*dictus*) archbishop of Poitiers, one of the supporters of H(ugh) de Lusignan (*Leziniaco*), count of La Marche, to make satisfaction to H(enry), king of the English, before the feast of St Andrew (30 November) next, for the injuries inflicted on the king and his subjects. The abbots of Talmont and St-Michel-en-l'Herm (both diocese of Poitiers) and the dean of Poitiers had already promulgated sentences against William.
1222 July 5 Lateran (Dat' Lateran' / iii Non' Iulii. Pontificat[us] n[ost]ri anno Sexto.)

Pd Rymer i pt 1 169; also in Bouquet, *Recueil* xix 727
Address: Dilecto filio Nobili uiro W[i]ll[elm]o dicto Archiep[iscop]o Pictauen'
    diocesis
Incipit: Carissimus in christo
Variant readings
l.1 .*H.* (Rymer l.4 *Henricus*)
l.2 Rymer (ll.6, 7) prints three and six dots for the *gemipuncti*.
l.6 *treugua* (Rymer l.16 *treuga*)

PRO SC7/18/31
Not registered *Reg. Hon. III* no. 4072 (abstract from Rymer). P 6871. Not
    in *SB*
43.1 cm × 32.8 cm: *plica* 4 cm
Bulla on hemp strings
Condition: very good
Scribe: (?)o
Endorsements: (top centre) REG (bottom left corner) vi (bottom left to centre,
    inverted) examinatur (bottom left to centre) (further English Chancery
    endorsements)

A well-spaced and regular hand. The scribe uses two distinct types of 's', a
long hooked 's' and a neat square 's' to complete words. The use of the long
'i' is also distinctive in line 10 *difficultatis* and *mandauerit*, in line 12 *sententiis*.

27

Mandate to the dean, G(odard) the penitentiary and I. Romanus, canons of
York, to revoke any grants of possessions and goods, which have been
alienated from the church of Durham.
1223 February 13 Lateran

Honorius ep[iscopu]s seruus seruorum dei. Dilectis filiis..Decano. G. peni-
tentiario et / .I. Roman' canonicis Eboracen[sibus] Sal[u]t[em] et ap[osto]licam
ben[edictionem]. Dilector[um] filior[um] . . Prioris et / Capit[u]li Dunelmen-
[sis] precibus inclinati'presentium uobis auctoritate mandamus. / quatin[us]
ea que de possessionib[us] et aliis bonis eccl[es]ie Dunelmen[sis] alienata
inueneritis / illicite uel distracta ad ius et proprietatem ip[s]ius legitime
reuocetis. Contradictores / per ce[n]suram eccl[es]iasticam app[e]ll[ati]one
postposita compescendo. Testes aut[em] qui fueri[n]t no[m]i[n]ati / si˙se
gr[ati]a. odio u[e]l timore subtraxerint˙ censura simili app[e]ll[ati]one cessante
cogatis ueritati / testimo[n]ium p[er]hib[er]e. Q[uo]d si no[n] om[n]es hiis
exequendis potueritis intere[ss]e˙ duo u[est]r[u]m ea nich[il]o/min[us]
exequantur. Dat' Lateran'. Id' febR̸. Pontificat[us] n[ost]ri Anno Septim[o].

Durham, Dean and Chapter Muniments (Prior's Kitchen) 2.1 Pap. 14 (copied
   into Cart. III fol. 155v)
Not registered, not in P or *SB*
16.1 cm × 11.4 cm: *plica* 1.2 cm
Holes: no *bulla*
Condition: fairly good; some damp staining
Scribe: Sca(mbio) (cf. nos. 8 and 17 above, and 38 below)
Endorsements: (top centre) (an elaborate ?) M (mid centre, inverted) super
   alienatis ✠

The small, neat hand of Scambio, showing only one deviation from the
mandate form in that *seruorum* in line 1 is not abbreviated to *seruor[um]*.

28

Mandate to the abbots of Rievaulx and Byland (Cist. Yorks. NR) and the
prior of Newburgh (Aug. Yorks. NR) to hear the appeal by the prior and
convent of Durham against I. rector of Embleton (co. Durham) concerning
tithes. Durham represent that I. summoned them before the abbot of St
Agatha's (Easby) (Prem. Yorks. NR) and other judges delegate and then
before the dean of York and his colleagues, from whom the prior and convent
appealed because the judges refused to have the *acta* transcribed as required
by the Fourth Lateran Council.
1223 April 3 Lateran

Honorius ep[iscopu]s seruus seruor[um] dei. Dilectis filiis..de Riuallis. [et]..de
Beiland' Abb[at]ib[us]. [et]..priori de Nouo / burgo Eboracen[sis] dioc[esis].
Sal[u]t[em] [et] ap[osto]licam ben[edictionem]. Ex parte..prioris [et] Conuent[us] Dunelmen' fuit propositum cora[m] nob[is]. / q[uo]d cum ip[s]i .I.
Rectorem eccl[es]ie de Emeldon' Dunelmen' dioc[esis] coram..abb[at]e
s[an]c[t]e Agathe dioc[esis] Eboracen' [et] co[n]iudicib[us] / suis sup[er]
quib[us]dam decimis [et] reb[us] aliis auctoritate ap[osto]lica co[n]uenissent.
idem Rector ad audie[n]tiam n[ost]ram ap/pellans..decan[o] Eboracen' [et]
collegis ip[s]ius n[ost]ras sup[er] hoc obtinuit litt[er]as destinari. a quib[us] ip[s]i
quia iudicii acta / conscribi contra iustitiam facere denegabant humilit[er]
requisiti, s[e]c[un]d[u]m statuta concilii generalis n[ost]ram audie[n]tiam /
appellarunt. Id[e]oq[ue] discretioni u[est]re p[er] ap[osto]lica scripta mandam-
[us]. quatinus siest ita reuocato in statum debitum quic/quid post app[e]-
ll[ati]onem hui[us]modi temere inuen[er]itis atte[m]ptatum. audiatis ca[usa]m
app[e]ll[ati]one remota fine debito t[er]/minetis. facie[n]tes q[uo]d decreu[er]-
itis p[er] censuram eccl[es]iasticam firmit[er] obs[er]uari. Alioquin partes ad
ei[us]dem decan[i] [et] / collegor[um] suor[um] remittatis examen. app[e]ll-
antes in expensis legitimis conde[m]pnando. Testes aut[em] qui fu[er]int
no[m]inati / sise gr[ati]a odio u[e]l timore subtrax[er]int. p[er] censuram

Appendix 2

eandem app[e]ll[ati]one cessante cogatis u[er]itati testimonium p[er]hib[er]e. / Q[uo]d sinon om[n]es hiis exequendis potu[er]itis intere[ss]e. duo u[est]r[u]m ea nich[il]omin[us] exequant[ur]. Dat' Lateran' / iii. Non' April'. Pontificatus n[ost]ri Anno Septimo.

Durham, Dean and Chapter Muniments (Prior's Kitchen) 2.1 Pap. 17 (copied into Cart. III fol. 156r)
Not registered, not in P or *SB*
23.4 cm × 19 cm: *plica* 2.4 cm
Holes: no *bulla*
Condition: good; some damp staining and mould on lower left side and along folds
Scribe: (?)l
Endorsements: (top centre) ✠ W de Haya et 3A (bottom centre). Ad aud' ⟨querelam?⟩ inter Rectorem de Emyldon' et priorem et capitulum Dunelm'. (?C14) / honorius tercius (?C13)

A fine, flowing hand, although the writing rises on the right-hand side from line 2 to 6, where it is particularly noticeable: the penultimate line is cramped.

29
Exhortation to the king of England to take part in the crusade to be undertaken by the Emperor Frederick II.
1223 April 27 Lateran (Dat'. Lateran.' v. kl'. Maii. / Pontificat[us] n[ost]ri Anno Septimo.,.)

Pd Rymer i pt 1 172–3
Address: Carissimo in christo filio..Illustri Regi Anglie
Incipit: Iustus d[omi]n[u]s in
Variant readings
ll.1, 10, 11 Rymer (ll.2 and 45–8) ignores the *gemipuncti* and prints nine to eighteen dots (four occasions).
l.3 co[n]fund[er]et (Rymer l.15 *confundent*)
l.4 *potentia* (Rymer ll.16–17 *potentiae*); p[ro]tend[er]et (Rymer l.18 *protendent*); q[u]asi has an open-headed 'a'
l.5 *nomen* (Rymer l.20 *nominis*)
l.6 t[em]p[or]is (Rymer l.27 *ipsis*)
l.7 aliq[ua]n[do]: MS aliqñ (Rymer l.29 *alioquin*)
l.8 S[et], S plus the tironian *et*
l.9 The tironian *et* used to terminate iudic[et]
l.11 Ier[usa]litan': MS Ierl'itan'; Bethleemitan' (Rymer l.47 *Bethleemetan'*)
l.12 bapth[ist]e (Rymer l.52 *baptistae*)
l.15 *sumi* (Rymer l.64 *summi*)

PRO SC7/18/14
Not registered (but see Bock, 'Originale und Registereinträge', 104 no. 36,
Reg. Yr. 7 no. 181, *Reg. Hon. III* no. 4330, to Prince Leopold of Austria)
P 7003 Not in *SB*
54.1 cm × 38.8 cm: *plica* 3.5 cm
Bulla on hemp strings
Condition: good
Scribe: bo
Endorsements: (bottom left corner) viii (bottom centre to right) Examinat'
/ Registrata in nouo libro

A small, cramped hand. Lines 10, 12 and 13, especially the last words and the
words towards the ends of the lines, are very irregular, and the letters lean
in all directions.

30

Request and exhortation to the king of England not to permit the exaction
of pedage from crusaders or from those who carry their supplies (*necessaria*)
but to enact that each house shall pay monthly for at least three years a
contribution of 1 (penny) *Tournois* or the equivalent for the relief of the Holy
Land.
1223 April 27 Lateran (⟨Dat' Lateran'⟩ v kl' ⟨Maii⟩ / Pontificat[us] n[ost]ri
anno septimo.)

Pd Rymer i pt 1 173
Address: Carissimo in christo filio..Illustri Regi Anglie
Incipit: Cum sit nonsolum
Variant readings
l.1 Rymer (l.2) ignores the *gemipunctus* and prints nine dots.
l.13 *terre...Lateran'* and *Maii* supplied from Rymer (ll.23–5) who prints
Laterani.

PRO SC7/18/10
Not registered *Reg. Hon. III* no. 4331 (abstract from Rymer). P 7004. Not
in *SB*
22 cm × 21.6 cm: *plica* 1.9 cm
Detached *bulla* on hemp strings
Condition: fair; bottom two lines obscured by gall in the centre
Scribe: d? or r?
Endorsements: (top left to centre, inverted) quod non extorquantur pedagia
.... in Angl' / Scribende / .vj. ✠ (mid left to centre) scribitur
in libro (bottom left corner) .vij.

Appendix 2

A slightly microscopic and fussy hand, fitted into a square document. The document has been lined and there are small, neat hyphens. A distinctive lower case 's' is used at the end of words, which 'fades away' and has no clear return stroke, and a long final 'e' occurs in 'siue' at the end of line 5.

31

Mandate to the bishop of Winchester and the abbot and prior of Dorchester (Aug. Oxon.) to hear the case of William, knight of Breauté, (1) who had appealed to the pope in a matrimonial suit brought before the bishop of Lincoln and other judges delegate by W. Talbot (*Taleboth*), layman of the diocese of Salisbury, against A. de Merlai, William's wife, or to remit the case to the former judges, condemning the appellant to pay costs.

1223 May 13 Lateran (Dat' Lateran' iij Id' Maii. / Pontificat[us] n[ost]ri Anno Septimo.)

Pd Prynne, *Exact chronological vindication* iii 53–4
Address: Venerabili fratri..Ep[iscop]o Wintonien[si] [et] Dilectis filiis..Abb-[at]i et..Priori de Dorke/cestre Lincolnien[sis] dioc[esis]
Incipit: Ex relatione Will[elm]i
Variant readings
ll.1, 3 Prynne omits the *gemipunctus* before titles.
ll. 1–2 *Dorke/cestre* (Prynne l.2 *Dorkcestre*)
l.2 *Will[elm]i* (Prynne l.3 *Willielmi*)
l.3 *.W.* (Prynne l.4 *Will.*); *Saresberien[sis]* (Prynne l.4 *Sarisburien'.*); *.A.* (omitted by Prynne, before *de Merlai*, l.4)
l.4 *lincolnien[si]* (Prynne l.5 *Lincoln.*)
l.9 *statuatis* (Prynne l.12 *statutis*)
l.13 *Id'* (Prynne l.18 *kal.*)

PRO SC7/50/7
Not registered, not in P. *SB* 692
20.2 cm × 15 cm: *plica* 1.8 cm
Holes: no *bulla*
Condition: quite good
Scribe: P. B. (cf. nos. 32, 33 and 47, below)
Face: (top extreme right corner) p. B.
Endorsements: (top centre, inverted) (English) Iudicibus super quodam matrimonio (Prynne) (mid centre) Examinat'
(1) William de Breauté, brother of Fawkes. The mandate precedes his activities in the summer of 1224, on behalf of his brother, in kidnapping one of the king's justices, Henry de Braybrooke, and imprisoning him in Bedford castle, leading to its siege. Fawkes's occupation of the castle had been regarded as a case of 'novel disseisin' (see Powicke, *Henry III*, 62–4).

Texts of the Original Letters

A clear, rounded hand, with only one word break (at the end of line 1, where no hyphen is used).

32

Mandate to all archbishops, bishops, abbots, priors, deans, provosts, archdeacons and 'other prelates of churches' to show justice to the brethren of the knighthood of the Temple when complaints are made about their parishioners.
1223 October 5 Anagni (Dat' Anagnie iii Non' OctobR̃. / Pontificatus n[ost]ri Anno Octauo.)

Pd Shirley i no. 190
Address: Venerabilibus fratribus Archiep[iscop]is et Ep[iscop]is. et Dilectis
   filiis Abbatibus. Priori/bus. Decanis. Prepositis. Archidiaconis. et aliis
   eccl[es]iar[um] Prelatis ad quos littere iste p[er]uenerint
Incipit. Cum a reli/giosorum
Variant readings:
l.7 *supponitis* (Shirley l.16 *imponitis*)
l.9 *attemptatur* (Shirley l.19 *attentatur*)
l.13 *dampna* (Shirley l.27 *damna*)

PRO SC7/18/29
Not registered (but cf. *CPL* 93, another privilege for the English Templars
   issued on the same day) Not in P or *SB*
26.5 cm × 21.4 cm: *plica* 2.2 cm
Bulla on red and yellow silk threads
Condition: very good
Scribe: p.b. (cf. no. 31 above, and nos. 33 and 47 below)
Face: (bottom right) ✠ (before the *Octauo* of the date)
Endorsements: (top extreme left corner) w (top left to centre) (?)C (top centre)
   T (proctorial) cum a religiosorum uirorum (mid right, inverted) Ne
   sententia data relaxetur fratribus ignorantibus

A clear, rounded hand, with rounded ascenders of the 'd's and rounded descenders of the 'p's. The scribe uses a long 'e' and a long 's' at the end of lines 4 and 9 in *corrigere* and *precipimus* and also for the final letters of *districtius* and *adimplere* in lines 13 and 14.

33

Mandate to the archbishop of York and his suffragans to place under interdict the lands in their dioceses belonging to Llewellyn, called (*dictus*) prince of North Wales, and his followers, and to excommunicate him and his supporters and after six months to declare all to be free from allegiance to them unless they go personally to the apostolic see for absolution.
1223 October 5 Anagni (Dat' Anagnie iii Non' OctobR̃. Pontificat[us] n[ost]ri Anno. Octauo.,.)

Pd Shirley i no. 191 and Rymer i pt 1 180

Address: Venerabilib[us] fratrib[us]..Archiep[iscop]o Eboracen[si] et suffraganeis eius

Incipit: Frequens sicut intellexim[us]

Variant readings

l.1 ..*Archiep[iscop]o* (Shirley l.2 *archiepiscopo*..)

l.2 *dampnationem* (Shirley l.6 *damnationem*)

l.3 *k[arissi]m[u]s* (Shirley l.9 *carissimus*)

l.5 *set* (Shirley l.16 *sed*); *t[i]t[uli]* (Shirley l.19 *titulo*)

l.9 *hiis* (Shirley l.32 *his*)

l.12 *Baliuo* (Shirley l.43 *ballivo*)

l.14 *iniuncxeram[us]* (Shirley l.52 *injunxerimus*)

l.15 *cohercere[n]t* (Shirley l.54 *coercerent*); *extitit* (Shirley l.56 *exstitit*)

l.19 *nuntiati* (Shirley l.70 *nunciati*); *subiacere* (Shirley l.71 *subjicere*)

l.21 *ar⟨t⟩issimo* (Shirley l.76 *arctissimo*)

l.23 *uos* (Shirley l.86 *nos*)

PRO SC7/18/6

Not registered (but cf. Reg. Yr. 8 no. 66, *Reg. Hon. III* no. 4517, *CPL* 93, to abp. of Canterbury) *Reg. Hon. III* no. 4518 (abstract from Rymer) P 7083 *SB* 702

Bulla on hemp strings

Condition: good

Scribe: P. B. (see nos. 31–2, above, and no. 47, below)

Face: (top extreme right corner) (?)s

Endorsements: (top left to centre) ꝑ̄ (mid centre) (?papal registration mark reported; now obscured by backing) (bottom far left) De Lewelyno Wall' Principe excommunicata et terris suis interdicend' pro guerra quam fecit H. R. Angl' / 7 Bulla Honorii pape iij / directa Archiepiscopo Ebor' et suffraganeis suis / .xj.

The document has been lined.

34

Request, admonition and exhortation to the king of the English to cause to be paid to Stefano, cardinal deacon of S. Adriano (1), the annual rent of 50 marks which had been granted to him when he was in minor office by the king's father, and which the present king has withheld, or the pope will be compelled to proceed against him.

1224 February 27 Lateran

Honorius ep[iscopu]s seruus seruor[um] dei. Carissimo in christo (2) filio.. Illustri Regi Anglor[um]. Sal[u]t[em]. [et] ap[osto]licam / ben[edictionem]. Et si beneficior[um] collatio principaliter de gr[ati]a prouenire habeat liberali'. gr[ati]a tamen in iustitiam transeun/te'. nequeunt reuocari collata quin utraq[ue] manifeste ledatur. Quare honori suo consulit liberalis cum donata / munifice nulla patiens penitudine deformari ea soluit ilariter et libenter. cum non nunqua[m] affectus effectui prefera/tur. Sane dilectus filius n[oste]r. Stephanus s[an]c[t]i Adriani Diacon[us] Cardinal[is] exposuit coram nobis q[uo]d cum clare memo/rie.. Pater tuus ei ad huc in minori officio constituto annuum redditum quinquaginta Marcarum contulerit. / tu eum sibi q[uo]d non decuit hactenus subtraxisti et licet ut eum sibi exolueres te rogantes pl[ur]ies et monentes etiam per aliu[m] / fecerimus co[m]moneri'. nichil tamen nobis exinde respondere curasti. qui si beneficia que felicis recordationis Innocentius papa / predecessor n[oste]r patruus eius patri tue co[n]tulit recoleres ut deceret'. et attend[er]es grata obsequia que tibi dictus Card[inalis] impendit / et potest impendere in futurum'. multo maiora sibi deberes offerre ne dum q[uo]d debitum subtraheres requisit[us]. q[uo]d sine turpatione / gr[ati]e precede[n]tis. [et] turbatione subsequentis iustitie'. nec non absq[ue] offensa n[ostr]a non poteris retinere. Vt igitur ex iteratione precum / expressius agnoscas precantis affectum'. Serenitate[m] tuam rogam[us]. monem[us]. [et] hortamur sicut iterum sic attentius. quatin[us] / prudenter aduertens q[uo]d dona et gr[ati]e sine penitentia debent e[ss]e'. dicto Card[inali] subtractum redditum facias sine aliqua diffi/cultate persolui. ita q[uo]d de iustitia gr[ati]am sibi faciens'. ip[su]m ad deuotione[m] tuam redd⟨a⟩s merito pro[m]ptiorem. [et] nos tua[m] debeam[us] / munificentia[m] co[m]mendare. Alioquin preter id q[uo]d ip[su]m a tua deuotione proturbans'. rem a[m]mittes [et] meritum. nos qui eide[m] / in suo iure deesse non possum[us] cui potius uolum[us] gra[tia]m impertiri'. aliter exinde co[n]tra te procedere co[m]pellemur. [et] potuissem[us] / procedere. nisi nuntii tui nunc apud sedem ap[osto]licam existentes'. aliud suasissent. Dat' Lateran'. / iiij. kl' Martii. Pontificatus n[ost]ri Anno Octauo.,.

PRO SC7/50/9
Not registered, not in P, *SB* 714 records as a duplicate of SC7/50/8
22.6 cm × 19.5 cm: *plica* 1.6 cm
No *bulla*: holes
Condition: fairly good
Scribe: p.g. (cf. no. 35, below)
Face: (top, extreme right corner) ad Sy W(?) (struck through: ? in same hand and ink as the text)
Endorsements: (top centre) Card (mid centre to right) Scribende quia pro redditu annuo Stephani de Sancto Adriano / non R̸ (? English) / (a flourish) / Examinat'
(1) Stefano dei Conti, nephew of Innocent III, prebendary of Lincoln, probably of Leighton Ecclesia (*Fasti*, ed. Greenway, iii Lincoln, 80); also called Stefano de Normandis.
(2) xp̄o.

Appendix 2

A rounded hand which writes the words very closely. The document has been ruled and it is written close to the edges. No hyphens are used and there are no apparent signs of correction.

35

Mandate to Hubert de Burgh, justiciar, and William Brewer, counsellor of the king of the English, to cause to be paid to Stefano, cardinal deacon of S. Adriano, the annual rent of 50 marks which had been granted to him by the king's father and which the present king has withheld, or the pope will be compelled to proceed against him.

1224 February 27 Lateran

Honorius ep[iscopu]s seruus seruor[um] dei. Dilectis filiis Nobilib[us] uiris Vberto de Burc Iustitiario [et] Will[elm]o Briguer Consi/liario Illustris Regis Anglor[um] Sal[u]t[em] [et] ap[osto]licam ben[edictionem]. Et si beneficior-[um] collatio pri[n]cipaliter de gr[ati]a prouenire / habeat liberali. gr[ati]a tamen in iustitia[m] transeunte. nequeunt reuocari c⟨o⟩llata. quin utraq[ue] manifeste ledatur / Quare honori suo co[n]sulit liberalis cum donata munifice nulla pat⟨iens⟩ ⟨pen⟩itudine deformari. ea soluit ilariter / [et] libent[er]. cum non nu[n]quam affectus effectui preferat[ur]. Sane dilectus filius n[oste]r. Stephanus s[an]c[t]i Adriani diacon[us] / Cardinal[is] exposuit coram nob[is]. q[uo]d cum clare memorie..pater Carissimi in christo (1) filii n[ost]ri. Illustris Regis / Anglor[um] ei adhuc in minori officio co[n]stituto annuu[m] redditum quinquaginta marcar[um] contulerit. idem Rex / eum q[uo]d no[n] decuit hac-ten[us] subtraxerit eidem. [et] licet ut eum sibi exolueret ip[su]m rogantes pl[ur]ies [et] ⟨mo⟩nent⟨es⟩ etiam p[er] / alium fec[er]im[us] co[m]moueri. nichil tamen nobis exinde respondere curauit. qui si beneficia que felicis record-atio[n]is In/nocentius papa predecessor n[oste]r ⟨patr⟩uus eius patri suo co[n]tulit recoleret ut deceret. [et] attenderet grata obseq[ui]a que / sibi dict[us] Card[inalis] impendit [et] potest imp⟨en⟩dere in futuru[m] multo maiora sibi deberet offerre ne du[m] q[uo]d debitu[m] subtraheret / re[qui]situs. q[uo]d sine turpatio[n]e gr[ati]e p[re]c⟨ede⟩ntis [et] turbatio[n]e subseque[n]tis iustitie. nec no[n] absq[ue] offensa n[ost]ra no[n] poterit retinere. Vt / igit[ur] ex iteratio[n]e precu[m] expressi⟨us⟩ a⟨gno⟩scat preca[n]tis affectu[m]. Sere-nitate[m] sua[m] rogam[us]. monem[us]. [et] hortamur sicut iteru[m] sic at/tentius ut prudent[er] aduerte[n]s q[uo]d ⟨dona⟩ [et] gr[ati]e sine peniten-tia debent e[ss]e. dicto Card[inali] subtractu[m] redditu[m] faciat sine aliqua dif/ficultate p[er]solui. ita q[uo]d de iustiti⟨a⟩ gra[tia]m sibi faciens. ip[su]m ad deuotione[m] suam redd⟨at⟩ ⟨m⟩erito pro[m]ptiore[m]. [et] nos suam debea/mus munificentia[m] co[m]mendare. Alioquin pret[er] id q[uo]d ip-[su]m a sua deuotio[n]e ⟨proturbans⟩ rem a[m]mitt⟨et⟩ [et] meritu[m]. nos qui ei/dem in suo iure deesse no[n] possum[us] cui potius uolum[us] gra[tia]m impertiri. alit[er] ex⟨in⟩de contra eu[m] procedere co[m]pellemur. et po/tuissem[us] procedere. nisi nuntii s⟨ui⟩ nu[n]c apud sedem ap[osto]licam existentes aliud s⟨ua⟩sissent. Quocirca Nobilitati u[est]re per / ap[osto]lica scripta mandam[us]'. quatin[us] dictum Regem ad hoc moneatis attentius [et] efficacit[er] inducere procuretis. Dat' / Lateran' .iiij. kl' Martii Pontificat[us] n[ost]ri Anno Octauo.

PRO SC7/50/8
Not registered, not in P *SB* 714
22.8 cm × 19.8 cm: *plica* 1.7 cm
Holes: no *bulla*
Condition: fairly good
Scribe: p.g. (cf. no. 34, above)
Face: (top extreme right corner) ad Simon ⟨et?⟩ ⟨?Hlys⟩ (struck through: possibly in the same hand and ink as the text)
Endorsements: (top centre) (?) pro P.f. / Card' ✠ (mid centre, inverted) pro Steph' sancti Adriani redditu / Examinat
(1) *xp̄o*.

This letter may have been corrected. In it hyphens are used and the break in the dating clause is made between *Dat* and *Lateran*.

36

Confirmation to the prior and convent of Totnes (Ben. al. Devon) of their possessions, especially the chapels of Brixham, Broad Clyst and Ashprington (all Devon), taking their persons, house and goods under papal protection.
1224 March 6 Lateran

HONORIUS ep[iscopu]s seruus seruor[um] dei. *Dilec*–tis filiis. .Priori et Conuentui de Tortan'. / Sal[u]t[em] et ap[osto]licam ben[edictionem]. *Cum* anobis petitur quod ius–tum es–t et hones–tum tam / uigor equitatis quam ordo exigit rationis ut id per sollicitudinem officii n[ost]ri ad debitum / perducatur effec–tum. *Ea* propter dilecte in domino filii u[est]ris ius–tis pos–tulatio/nibus grato concurrentes assensu. personas u[est]ras et locum in quo diuino es–tis / obsequio mancipati cum om[n]ibus bonis que impresentiar[um] rationabiliter possidetis / ⟨uel in⟩ futurum ius–tis modis pres–tante domino poteritis adipisci sub beati / Petri et n[ost]ra protectione suscipimus. *Specialiter* autem de Brichham. et olistun' / et de Aspingunt Capellas. ac alia bona u[est]ra sicut ea om[n]ia ius–te canonice pos/sidetis uobis et per uos eccl[es]ie u[est]re auctoritate ap[osto]lica confirmamus et presentis / scripti patrocinio communim[us]. Nulli ergo om[n]ino hominum liceat hanc paginam / n[ost]re protectionis et confirmationis infringere uel ei ausu temerario contraire. / Siquis autem hoc attemptare presumpserit indignationem om[n]ipotentis dei et bea/tor[um] Petri et Pauli ap[osto]lor[um] eius se nouerit incursurum. Dat' Lateran' .ij. Non'. martii. / Pontificat[us] n[ost]ri Anno Octauo.,.

243

Appendix 2

Exeter, Devon Record Office 312 M/TY 54
Not registered, not in P or *SB*
18.4 cm × 15.5 cm: *plica* 1.2 cm
Holes: no *bulla*
Condition: quite good; some coloured mould in centre
Scribe: bl (*or* bs – partly obscured by red ink archive no. lxx) (cf. no. 56 below)
Endorsements: (top extreme left corner) R (top centre) (possibly a proctorial
  device, but now illegible) (mid centre, inverted) Priori de Tort (English,
  medieval)

The document is ill-spaced in the dating clause where at the end of the penultimate line the words have been squeezed in so as to make the break before
pontificatus. The names for Totnes, Broad Clyst and Ashprington have been
garbled.

37

Indult to the prior and convent of Durham that they shall not be held to continue
to pay annual pensions to clerks awaiting benefices if they refuse those offered.
1224 March 12 Lateran

HONORIUS ep[iscopu]s seruus seruor[um] dei. Dilec–tis filiis.. Priori et Conuentui Dunelmen' Sal[u]t[em] / et ap[osto]licam ben[edictionem]. Petitio u[e-
st]ra nobis exhibita continebat. q[uo]d cum quampl[ur]ibus Cl[er]icis de
camera u[est]ra te/neamini annuas soluere pensiones. donec ip[s]is per uos in
eccl[es]ias–ticis beneficiis sit prouisum quidam / ex illis parrochiales eccl[es]ias
obtine[n]tes'. beneficia habentia curam animarum annexam nolunt a uobis (1)
/ recipere pensionibus inherendo. Vnde nobis humiliter supplicas–tis. ut uobis
super hoc consulere / misericorditer dignaremur. Nos igitur u[est]ris
grauaminib⟨us⟩ prouidere uolentes'auc–toritate (2) / uobis presentium
ind⟨ulgemus⟩ ⟨ut⟩ (3) ⟨h⟩uiusmodi Cl[er]icis qui a ⟨uobis⟩ ⟨eccles⟩ias
parrochiales sibi oblat⟨as⟩ / recipere recusarint' decetero non teneamini
promissas soluere pensiones. Nulli ergo om[n]ino homi/num liceat hanc
paginam n[ost]re concessionis infringere uel ei ausu temerario contraire. Siquis
/ autem hoc attemptare presumpserit indignationem om[n]ipotentis dei et
beator[um] Petri et Pauli ap[osto]lo/rum eius se nouerit incursurum. Dat'
Lateran' iiii Id' Martii. / Pontificat[us] n[ost]ri Anno Octauo;

Durham, Dean and Chapter Muniments (Prior's Kitchen) 2.1 Pap. 5 (copied
  into Cart. III fol. 154v)
Reg. Yr. 8 no. 340, *Reg. Hon. III* no. 4854, *CPL* 95 Not in P or *SB*
25.1 cm × 19 cm: *plica* 2.2 cm   Holes: no *bulla*
Condition: poor; coloured mould and two central holes from the folds
Scribe: – (there is no indication of a scribal mark)
Face: (top extreme right corner) ad ⟨? f, ? s⟩ nun' (struck through)

Endorsements: (top left (?) a *or* Sy *or* n (top centre) (an illegible mark
?proctorial) / Honorius tercius (?C13) / ad prouidend' cleric' ...de beneficiis cessanti in pensionibus (?C14)
(1) The upper stroke of the final 's' is elongated to fill the line.
(2) The tongue of the 'e' is elongated to fill the line.
(3) Document holed.

The document is neatly written. There are no signs of correction but the
parchment is worn, holed and stained.

38

Rejoices at the good reports of Master Stephen de Lucy and G(odfrey) de
Craucumbe, the king's messengers, and requests the king to show himself
impartial towards his vassals and even to ignore wrongs done to him.
1224 March 14 Lateran (Dat' Lateran'. ii Id' Martii. Pontificat[us] n[ost]ri Anno
Octauo:)

Pd Rymer i pt 1 177 and Shirley i 540–1 no. 16
Address: Carissimo in christo filio Henrico Regi Anglor[um] illustri
Incipit: Gaudemus in domino
Variant readings
l.5 *et* inserted by Rymer (ll.15–16) after *uno* (the end of the quotation: Persius,
   Satire V ll.52–3) at the end of the line
l.13 *possent* (Rymer l.32 *possunt*)
l.16 *ac* (before *regni*) (Rymer l.42 *et*)
l.18 *quibuscu[m]q[ue]* (Rymer l.45 *quibuscunque*)

PRO SC7/18/7
Reg. Yr. 8 no. 356, *Reg. Hon. III* no. 4866, *CPL* 95. P 7193a. *SB* 715
40 cm × 24.5 cm: *plica* 1.8 cm
Bulla on hemp strings
Condition: good
Scribe: Sca(mbio) (Cf. nos. 8, 17 and 27, above)
Face: (top centre) R̄
Endorsements: (top centre) R scriptum (papal registration mark) / .L. (mid
   right, inverted) Exortatorie quod Rex bene se habeat penes suos uassallos
   / N / Examinat' / Quod Rex Angl' prudenter se habeat erga suos uassallos
   (bottom left) Registr' in nouo libro / .ix.

The scribe, Scambio, uses a tittle on two occasions (l.3 in *om[n]ibus* and l.18
in *n[ost]ri*) where normally a plain abbreviation mark would be found. The
hand is very regular, well formed and well spaced. There is a long 's' in *actiones*
at the end of line 1.

Appendix 2

39

Indult to the prior of the hospital of SS. James and John, Brackley (Aug. Northants.), not to be bound to hear delegated cases in future unless special mention is made of this indult.

1224 March 21 Lateran

HONORIUS ep[iscopu]s seruus seruor[um] dei. *D*ilec–to filio..Priori Hospital[is] S[an]c[t]or[um] Apo'/s–tolorum Iacobi [et] Iohannis de Brachele. Sal[-u]t[em] et ap[osto]licam ben[edictionem]. *C*um propter rerum / dispendia [et] Labores quos in persona propria oportet multotiens te subire propter multi'/plicitatem causarum que tibi a sede ap[osto]lica delegantur et quies tui ordinis perturbetur / et graue Hospitali tibi commisso immineat detrimentum⁄ nobis humiliter supplica'/s–ti. ut tibi [et] hospitali super hoc prouidere de benignitate sedis ap[osto]lice dignarem[ur]. / *N*os igitur tuis pos–tulationib[us] inclinati⁄ auc–toritate tibi presentium duxim[us] / indulgendum. ut auc–toritate litterarum n[ost]rarum de causis aliquibus cognosce'/re in pos–terum non cogaris⁄que specialem non fecerint de hac indulgentia mentio'/nem. Dat'. Lateran'. xii. k[a]l' April'. Pontificat[us] n[ost]ri Anno Octauo.

Magdalen College, Oxford, Brackley 106 D
Not registered, not in P or *SB*
20.3 cm × 13.3 cm: *plica* 2.2 cm
Bulla on red and yellow silk threads (the lead for the impression is very misshapen)
Condition: good
Scribe: eg (very small) (cf. no. 41, below)
Endorsements: (top centre) Guill[elmu]s (proctor)

The similarities of this hand and that of no. 40 (below) are apparent especially in the 'g's, the ligatures and the 's's, although the 's' with the long straight descender is not used. The document is unusual in not having the *Nulli ergo* and *Si quis autem* clauses (cf. nos. 51 and 56 below) and, although an indult, the *ets* are abbreviated.

40

Mandate to the dean, archdeacon and chancellor of London to hear the case of the prior and convent of Holy Trinity, Aldgate, against R. de Montfichet, knight, R. rector of Hallingbury (Essex) 'et quidam alii', both clerks and laymen of London, Lincoln and Rochester dioceses, about a certain quantity of hay, tithes 'et res alie'.

1224 April 13 Lateran

Honorius ep[iscopu]s seruus seruor[um] dei. Dilectis filiis..Decan[o]..Archid[iacono]. et..Can/cellario Londonien'⁄Sal[u]t[em] et ap[osto]licam ben-

[edictionem]. Dilecti filii..Prior. et Conuent[us] / s[an]c[t]e Trinitatis Londonien' nobis co[n]querendo monstrarunt q[uo]d. Nobil[is] uir. / .R. de Montfichet miles .R. Rector eccl[es]ie de Hallingeb[er]y. et quidam alii / cl[er]ici et laici Londonien'. Lincolnien'. et Roffen' dioc[esum]. sup[er] quadam quantita/te feni. decimis. et reb[us] aliis iniuriant[ur] ei[s]dem. Id[e]oq[ue] discretio[n]i u[est]re p[er] ap[osto]lica scrip/ta mandam[us]⸍ quatin[us] part-ib[us] co[n]uocatis audiatis ca[usa]m et app[e]ll[ati]one remota⸍fine de/bito terminetis. facientes q[uo]d statu[er]itis p[er] censura[m] eccl[es]iasticam firmit[er] obs[er]uari. / Testes aut[em] qui fueri[n]t no[m]i[n]ati si se gr[ati]a odio u[e]l timore subtraxerint per / censura[m] eandem cessante app[e]ll[ati]one cogatis u[er]itati testimonium p[er]hibere. / Q[uo]d si no[n] om[ne]s hiis exequendis potu[er]itis int[er]e[ss]e⸍ duo u[est]r[u]m ea nich[il]omin[us] exe/quant[ur]. Dat' Lateran' Id' April'. Pontificat[us] n[ost]ri Anno Octauo;

PRO SC7/18/5
Not registered, not in P or SB
14.7 cm × 13.9 cm: *plica* 1.2 cm
Bulla on hemp strings
Condition: very good
Scribe: (left of the *bulla*) *R̶/V̶ (? N̶/V̶)
Endorsements: (top left) .ff (bottom left, inverted) apud sanctum trinitatem
  lon (top right, from bottom to top) de decimis feni de ecclesia (*ellīa*) de
  Halyngb⟨u⟩ry

A hand in which there are very pronounced backward curves on the descenders, particularly noticeable with the 'p's, 'f's and 's's, and in some cases with the capital and final 'i's.

41

Indult to the abbot and convent of Abingdon (Ben. Berks.) that they need not pay tithes on lands, which they held before the General Council and which they cultivate with their own hands or at their expense, and also on meadows, mills and fisheries on which they have never paid tithe.

1224 May 15 Lateran (Dat'. lateran'. Id' Maii. Pontificat[us] n[ost]ri Anno Octauo.)

Pd Reg. S. Osmund i, ed. Rich Jones, 362–3 (from Diocesan Registry, Salisbury,
  Reg. S. Osmund fol. 54)
Address: Dilec–tis filiis. .Abbati [et] Conuentui Monas–terii de/habendon'.
Incipit: Religionis ues–tre promeretur
Variant readings
ll.1–2 *seruus...ben[edictionem]* omitted in Rich Jones l.1
l.4 *benedic–tione* (Rich Jones l.5 *benedictionibus*); *preuenire* (ibid. *provenire*)
l.7 *exoluis–tis* (Rich Jones ll.10–11 *exsolvistis*)

Northamptonshire Record Office I.L. 186

Not registered (but cf. *CPL* 101, 1 March 1225, reference to this indult) Not in P or *SB*

23.3 cm × 17.6 cm: *plica* 1.8 cm

Red and yellow silk threads: no *bulla*

Condition: good

Scribe: eg(?) (cf. no. 39, above)

Endorsements: (mid centre, inverted) viᵃ (mid to bottom centre) confirmacio fact' abbati de abendon' pro decimis suis non soluendis (?C16) / de terris ante Consilium datis quas propriis ... ex⟨h⟩ibit' (C16)

A stylish hand with very elaborate capitals and neat ligatures. Because the capitals are elaborate, they are sometimes divorced from the word as in *R eligionis* (l.2) and *S iquis* (l.9). The scribe uses a very characteristic final 's' with a long straight descender: l.3 *foueamus*, l.5 *indulgemus* and l.6 *colitis*.

42

Confirmation to the prioress and convent of Littlemore (Ben. Oxon.) of the agreement between them and the abbot and convent of Oseney (Aug. Oxon.) over tithes, made after mediation by the abbot of Abingdon and his colleagues (unnamed).

1224 May 15 Lateran

HONORIUS ep[iscopu]s seruus seruor[um] dei. Dilec–tis in christo (1) filiabus.. Priorisse et Conuentui de / Littlemor'. sal[u]t[em] et ap[osto]licam ben[edictionem]. Ea que iudicio uel concordia terminantur˙firma debent / et illibata persis–tere. et ne in recidiue contentionis scrupulum relabantur˙conuenit / ap[osto]lico presidio communiri. Eapropter dilec–te in d[omi]no filie u[est]ris ius–tis precib[us] / inclinati'. compositionem inter uos ex parte una'. et.. Abb[ate]m et Conuentum de Oxeneia / Lincolnien[sis] dioc[esis] ex altera super quib[us]dam decimis mediantibus dilectis filiis.. Abb[at]e de / Abendon' et eius collegis amicabiliter initam. sicut rite sine prauitate prouide facta / est et ab utraq[ue] parte sponte recepta'. et hactenus pacifice obseruata auc–toritate / ap[osto]lica confirmamus et presentis scripti patrocinio communimus. Nulli ergo om[n]ino / hominum liceat hanc paginam n[ost]re confirmationis infringere uel ei ausu temerario / contraire. Siquis aut[em] hoc attemptare presumpserit'. indignationem om[n]ipotentis dei / et beator[um] Petri et Pauli ap[osto]lor[um] eius se nouerit incursur[um]. Dat'. Lateran' Id'. Maii. / Pontificat[us] n[ost]ri Anno Octauo.

Bodleian Library, Oxford, MS Chs. Oxon. Oseney 5b (Major, 'Original papal documents' no. 7, where it is incorrectly dated 8 id' May = 8 May)

Not registered, not in P or *SB*

22.1 cm × 18.6 cm: *plica* 1.9 cm

Bulla on red and yellow silk threads
Condition: good
Scribe: ★P (cf. no. 53, below)
Endorsements: (top centre) M / Confirmatio Honorii pape tercii super decimis
 prati inter Abbatem Osoneye et priorissam et conuentum de Littlemor
 in forma communi (English ?C13)
(1) xp̄o.

A fine, definite, well-formed hand, with rounded qualities which are shown
particularly with the capital 'E's and 'S's where the scribe conceives of the
letters as spheres to which he adds the necessary distinguishing embellishments.
The capital 'H' of *HONORIUS* is distinctly comparable with that of no. 53.
The document has been ruled.

43

Licence to the abbot and convent of Keynsham (Aug. Som.) allowing them
to appropriate the church of Burford (Oxon.).
1224 June 10 Lateran

HONORIUS ep[iscopu]s seruus seruor[um] dei. Dilec–tis filiis..Abbati et
conuentui de Kainesham ordinis / s[an]c[t]i Augustini. sal[u]t[em] et ap[os-
to]licam ben[edictionem]. Solet annuere sedes ap[osto]lica piis uotis et hones–tis
peten/tium precibus fauorem ben⟨iuo⟩lum impertiri. Ex parte siquidem
u[est]ra fuit nobis humiliter sup/plicatum. ut cum eccl[es]ia de Bureford ad
uos pertineat pleno iure. ne occasione.⟨ . . . ⟩ (1) ip[s]ius vica/rii . . . . . tin' in
poster⟨um⟩ obnubilari contingat ip[s]⟨?a⟩m cum pertinentiis suis in usus
p[ro]prios ad / ... ... (2) seruandam ⟨ . . . . ⟩ ⟨?vicario⟩ memorat⟨?o⟩
diocesan⟨i⟩ Ep[iscop]i et ip[s]ius Officialem... (3) / ⟨saluo⟩ ⟨retinere⟩ ...
... (4) per... ... (5). Nos igitur u[est]ris deuoti⟨s⟩ ⟨?precibus⟩ inclinati
/ auctoritate uobis presentium ⟨? conce⟩dimus postulata dummodo ... ...
... ... (6) / per vicarium idoneum deseruiri. Nulli ergo ⟨omnino
hominum liceat hanc paginam nostre conces⟩/sionis infringere uel ei ausu
temerario contraire. Siquis autem hoc attemptare presump/serit indignationem
om[n]ipotentis dei et beatorum Petri et Pauli ⟨apostolorum⟩ eius se nouerit
in/cursurum. Dat' Lateran' iiii Id' I⟨unii⟩ / Pontificat[us] n[ost]ri Anno
Octauo.

Lambeth PD no. 23 (cal. Sayers, *Original papal documents*)
Not registered, not in P or *SB*
20.3 cm × 19.6 cm: *plica* 1.8 cm
Red and yellow strings: no *bulla*
Condition: poor. The document has much faded
Scribe: p.
Endorsements: (top right, from top to bottom) .I. de Staunford' dd' H de

Appendix 2

hemesby (bottom left to centre) De Buref' / introducta nomine Abbatis et et conuentus de Keynsham per Wm Say xxii Septembr' anno 1537/ii/7.
(1) One word washed right out or a space?
(2) Two words lacking.
(3) One word lacking.
(4) Two to three words lacking.
(5) One word lacking.
(6) Five to six words lacking.

44

Request and exhortation to the king of England to give his assent to the provision of the bishop of Cork to the archbishopric of Cashel. (1) 1224 June 20 Lateran (Dat' Lateran' xii kl' Iulii / Pontificat[us] n[ost]ri Anno Octauo.)

Pd *Pontificia Hibernica* i, ed. Sheehy, no. 168
Address: ⟨Carissimo in christo⟩ filio..Illustri Regi Anglie
Incipit: Cum olim Venerabilis
Variant reading l.14 *Dat' Lateran'* (Sheehy l.23 *Datum Laterani*)

PRO SC7/35/18
Reg. Yr. 8 no. 487, *Reg. Hon. III* no. 5053, *CPL* 98 (addressed to the archbishop of Canterbury and 'in eodem modo' to the king of England) (2) *SB* 737
18.9 cm × 17.6 cm: *plica* 1.8 cm
Holes: no *bulla*
Condition: poor
Scribe: *S (cf. no. 54, below)
Endorsements (top mid) R scriptum (papal registration mark) (mid left) M̃ examinatur (mid centre) (?) Taurus (bottom left corner) Quod postulacionibus Episcoporum adhiberi debet requiri assensus R. / .x. (bottom right) Domino Regi / Scribende totaliter quia prolat quod postulato debet preberi Reg' assensus Argun' / Scribitur in libro.
(1) The catalogue description in PRO *Lists and Indexes* vol. xlix (p. 225), which states that it is a request to the king to assent to the provision of Master M. to the bishopric of Cork, vacant from the translation of the former bishop to the archbishopric of Cashel, is totally incorrect.
(2) Reg. Yr. 8 no. 486 (*Reg. Hon. III* no. 5052, *CPL* 97–8, P 7272), which precedes it, addressed to the newly elected archbishop of Cashel, late bishop of Cork, bids him seek the approval of the king of England, erroneously designated J. The mistake presumably proceeds from the mention in no. 487 of the king's father (King John) having approved the election of this man as bishop of Cork.

45

Request and exhortation to Henry, king of the English, not to impede nor to allow his subjects to impede G. bishop of Ardfert in the peaceable possession of his see, the pope having ordered the archbishop of Dublin to put him into possession, removing John a priest, who had caused himself to be consecrated bishop of Ardfert and who had refused to go to the pope to answer for his action.

1224 June 20 Lateran (Dat' Lateran'. xii. kl' Iulii. / Pontificatus n[ost]ri Anno Octauo.)

Pd Prynne, *Exact chronological vindication* iii 60
Address: Carissimo i[n] christo filio Henrico Regi Anglor[um] Illustri:
Incipit: Cum Ioh[anne]s p[res]b[ite]r
Variant readings
l.1 *Carissimo* (Prynne l.1 *charissimo*)
l.5 *Arferten'* (Prynne l.7 *Arfercen.*)
l.6 *epi[scopat]i* (Prynne l.8 *episcopatus*)
ll.7–8 *roga[n]/dam* (Prynne l.10 *rogandum*)
l.8 *n[ost]ra* (Prynne l.11 *uestra*)
l.10 *Lateran'* (Prynne l.14 *Laterani*)

PRO SC7/50/6
Not registered (but see *CPL* 98, to archbishop of Dublin of 14 kal' July) Not
   in P or *SB*
21.3 cm × 14.3 cm: *plica* 1.6 cm
Holes: no *bulla*
Condition: quite good except for a hole in the middle to the left
Scribe: (?) g
Endorsements: (top centre) Brandus (mid centre) .G./Scribende pro Iohanne
   Affercensi Episcopo / Exam'

A regular hand with no very distinctive qualities

46

Confirmation to the abbot and convent of Dale (Prem. Derbs.) of their possessions, especially of Ockbrook, Stanley and Depedale (all Derbs.), taking them, their house and goods under papal protection.
1224 December 2 Lateran

HONORIUS ep[iscopu]s seruus seruor[um] dei. Dilectis filiis..Abbati et Conuentui de Parco Stanleie pre'/monstraten' ordinis Sal[u]t[em] et ap[osto]-licam ben[edictionem]. Cum a nobis petitur quod iustum est et honestum tam / uigor equitatis quam ordo exigit rationis ut id per sollicitudinem officii n[ost]ri ad debitum perducatur / effectum. Eapropter dilecti in d[omi]no filii u[est]ris iustis precibus inclinati personas u[est]ras [et] locum in quo / diuino estis obsequio mancipati cum om[n]ib[us] bonis que impresentiarum ration-abiliter possidet aut in/futurum iustis modis prestante d[omi]no poterit adipisci sub beati Petri et n[ost]ra protectione su'/scipimus. Specialiter aut[em] de Okebro⟨c⟩. de Stanl' [et] de Depedal' possessiones et terras cum perti'/nentiis ear[un]dem ac alia bona u[est]ra sicut ea om[n]ia iuste canonice ac pacifice possidetis uobis et per / uos monasterio u[est]ro auctoritate ap[osto]lica confirmamus et presentis scripti patrocinio communi/mus. Nulli ergo om[-n]ino hominum liceat hanc paginam n[ost]re protectionis et confirmatio'/nis infringere uel ei ausu temerario contraire. Siquis aut[em] hoc attemptare presump'/serit indignationem om[n]ipotentis dei et beator[um] Petri et Pauli ap[osto]lor[um] eius se nouerit / incursurum. Dat' Lateran' iiii non' Decemb'. / Pontificat[us] n[ost]ri Anno Nono.

BL Wolley Ch. x 32 (Bell, 'Original papal bulls' no. 60)
Not registered, not in P or *SB*
22.5 cm × 16 cm: *plica* 1.5 cm
Bulla on red and yellow silk threads
Condition: very good, although the leaden *bulla* has deteriorated
Scribe: aston
No medieval endorsements

A fine, clear hand which is well spaced. There are elaborate small capitals and long ascenders, particularly in the first line; hair-stroke hyphens.

47

Mandate to the priors of Dunstable (Aug. Beds.) and St Albans (Ben. Herts.) and the dean of Luton (rural deanery, Lincoln diocese) to hear the case of Roger de Moris, clerk, against the abbot of Beeleigh (Prem. Essex) 'et quidam alii' of London diocese over a certain sum of money 'et res alie'.
1225 January 18 Lateran

Honorius ep[iscopu]s seruus seruor[um] dei. Dilectis filiis..de Dunestabul'. [et]..s[an]c[t]i Al/bani Priorib[us]. [et]..Decan[o] de Loui[n]ton' Lincolnien' dioc[esis]. Sal[u]t[em] [et] ap[osto]licam ben[edictionem]. Ro/gerus de Moris cl[er]icus nob[is] co[n]querendo mostrauit (sic). q[uo]d..Abbas de Bileya. [et] qui/dam alii Londonien' dioc[esis]'. sup[er] quadam pecunie su[m]ma [et] reb[us] aliis iniuria[n]t[ur] / eidem. Ideoq[ue] discretioni u[est]re per ap[os-to]lica scripta mandamus. quatin[us] partibus / co[n]uocatis audiatis ca[usa]m. [et] app[e]ll[ati]one remota usuris cessantib[us] fine debito ter/minetis. Facientes quod decreueritis per censura[m] eccl[es]iasticam firmit[er] obs[er-] /uari. Testes aut[em] qui fueri[n]t no[m]i[n]ati si se gr[ati]a. odio. u[e]l timore subtraxe'/rint. p[er] censura[m] eandem app[e]ll[ati]one cessante cogatis ueritati testimoniu[m] / perhibere. Q[uo]d si non om[ne]s hiis exeq[ue]ndis potu[er]itis intere[ss]e. duo u[est]r[u]m ea / nich[il]omin[us] exequant[ur]. Dat' Lateran' xv kl' Februarii. / Pontificat[us] n[ost]ri Anno Nono.

PRO SC7/50/11
Not registered, not in P *SB* 751
13.9 cm × 12.3 cm: *plica* 1.6 cm
Holes: no *bulla*
Condition: good
Scribe: p.b. (cf. nos. 31–3, above)
No endorsements

The distinctive 'n' in the last word *Nono* compares with that letter in no. 33, above. The document is somewhat roughly or speedily written. From the capital 'H' of *Honorius* used in the mandate form, it can be seen how the scribe develops this letter for the privilege form.

48

Confirmation to the abbot and convent of Bury St Edmunds (Ben. Suff.) of the vill of Barton Mills (Suff.) with liberties, possessions, rents and other appurtenances which Robert de Hese has given them.
1226 January 2 Rieti (Dat' Reate ⟨ii⟩ij Non' Ianuarii. / Pontificat[us] n[ost]ri ⟨Anno⟩ Decimo;')

Pd Pinchbeck Register i, ed. Hervey, 42–3 (from CUL MS Ee 3.60)
Address: Dilec–tis Filiis Abbati et Conuentui s[an]c[t]i'/ Edmundi Norwicen' dioc[esis]
Incipit: Cum a nobis
Variant readings
l.1 Hervey (l.1) adds *iij* after *HONORIUS*.
l.6 Hervey (l.7) omits *Nobilis* before *uir*.
l.7 Hervey (l.8) omits *ac* between *ius–te* and *pacifice*.
l.10 Hervey (l.12) prints *Si quis etc.*, omitting the rest of the clause.

Lambeth Palace Library, PD no. 24 (cal. Sayers, *Original papal documents*)
Not registered, not in P or *SB*
21.6 cm × 17.5 cm: *plica* 1.5 cm
Red and yellow silk threads: no *bulla*
Condition: fairly good
Scribe: p.c.
Endorsements: (top centre) Honorius tercius / abbati / G (?) 7 / Confirmacio Bertune parve / h 7 perpetua

A large, open hand, which slopes backwards towards the left. There are very elaborate capitals.

49

Mandate to Geoffrey de Lusignan (*Lesiniaco*) to return to the fealty of Henry, king of the English, or face censure from the bishops of Dax and Bazas and the archdeacon of Bazas, if he does not do so within a month.

1226 January 9 Rieti (Dat' Reat' .v. Id' IanuaRȳ. Pontificat[us] n[ost]ri Anno Decimo . . ;)

Pd Rymer i pt 1 181; also Bouquet, *Recueil* xix 769–70
Address: Dilecto filio Nobili uiro Galfrido de Lesiniaco
Incipit: Fidelitatis uincul[u]m quo
Variant readings
l.1 *Lesiniaco* (Rymer l.2 *Liziniaco*)
ll.1–2 *uas/salus* (Rymer l.4 *vassallus*)
l.3 *extimetur* (Rymer l.7 *aestimetur*)
l.4 *istorias* (Rymer l.9 *historias*)
l.5 *Carissimo* (Rymer l.12 *charissimo*)
l.8 *astricxeras* (Rymer l.17 *astrixeras*); *peieres* (Rymer l.18 *pecces*)
l.11 *quatin[us]* (Rymer l.23 *quatenus*)
l.18 .v. (Rymer l.37 *quint'*)

PRO SC7/50/10
Reg. Yr. 10 no. 157 fol. 105v (under 6 Id Jan = 8 Jan), *Reg. Hon. III* no. 5776, *CPL* 104–5. P 7515. *SB* 777
23.9 cm × 19.8 cm: *plica* 1.7 cm
Holes: no *bulla* surviving
Condition: fairly good
Scribe: n.f.
Endorsements: (top centre) ⟨?l⟩ex *or* ⟨?r⟩ex (top centre to right) R script (papal registration mark) (mid right, inverted) Examinat' / G. de Leziniaco quod reuertatur ad fidelitatem Regis.

A rounded hand, on the large side, with a slight backward tilt to some of the ascenders of 'l' and 'b'.

50

Confirmation of the sentence passed by the dean of London and his co-judges (unnamed) against Richard and I., priests, and Robert de Rokell', knight, and certain others of Lincoln, London and Rochester dioceses in a suit with the prior and convent of Holy Trinity, London, over tithes and other things.
1226 January 23 Rieti

HONORIUS ep[iscopu]s seruus seruor[um] dei. *Dilec*–tis filiis . . Priori et Canonicis (1) / s[an]c[t]e Trinitatis Londonien'. Sal[u]t[em] et ap[osto]licam ben[edictionem]. *Ius*–tis petentium desideriis dignum / es–t nos facilem prebere consensum. [et] *uota* que a rationis tramite non discordant / effec–tu prosequente complere. *Eaprop*t[er] dilec–ti in domino filii u[est]ris ius–tis (2) / pos–tulationib[us] grato concurrentes assensu. diffinitiuam sententiam quam . . Decan[us] / Londonien' et Coniudices sui delegati a nobis contra Ricc'. et. I. p[res]b[ite]ros. Rob[er]tum de / Rokell' militem. [et] quosdam alios Lincolnien'. Londonien'. et Roffen' d[iocesum]. sup[er] decimis et rebus / aliis cognitis cause meritis promulgarunt. sicut es–t ius–ta nec legitima prouocatione sus/pensa auc–toritate ap[osto]lica confirmam[us]. et presentis (3) scripti patrocinio communimus. / Nulli ergo om[n]ino hominum liceat hanc paginam n[ost]re confirmationis infringere. / uel ei ausu temerario contraire. Siquis autem hoc attemptare presumpserit / indignationem om[n]ipotentis dei. et beator[um] Petri et Pauli ap[osto]lor[um] eius. se / nouerit incursurum. Dat'. Reate . x. kl'. februaR'. / Pontificat[us] n[ost]ri Anno Decimo.

PRO SC7/35/17
Not registered, not in P *SB* 779
19.1 cm × 16.3 cm: *plica* 1.7 cm
Holes: no *bulla*
Condition: very good
Scribe: Goz (SB reads as Grez)
Endorsements: (top centre) N (proctorial mark) (right centre, upside down)
    Littere prioris et canonicorum sancte Trinitatis london' facte per magistrum
    Stephanum de Elieton' (? *Eketon'*)
(1)–(3) Terminates in a long 's'.

51

Indult to the prior of Holy Trinity (Aldgate) London (Aug.) not to be bound to hear delegated cases in future, unless special mention is made of this indult; those cases in progress to be completed.
1226 February 20 Lateran (Dat' Lateran' / x. kl' Martii. Pontificatus n[ost]ri Anno Decimo;)

Pd Rymer i pt 1 184
Address: Dilec–to filio . . Priori s[an]c[t]e Trinitatis Londonien
Incipit: *A* nobis humiliter
Variant readings
Rymer (l.2) ignores the *gemipunctus* in line 1 and prints twelve dots.
l.4 end *annue[n]tes* (Rymer l.8 *anuentes*)

PRO SC7/18/27
Not registered *Reg. Hon. III* no. 5838 (abstract from Rymer), P 7535. Not in *SB*
18.9 cm × 14.9 cm: *plica* 1.9 cm

Appendix 2

Holes: no *bulla*
Condition: good
Scribe: (?) – a (not apparently b a *or* za)
Endorsements: (one English endorsement obscured by gall) (bottom centre to right) Tang⟨i⟩t priorem trinitatis(?) quod non tenetur procedere ad causas sibi committendas

Although the document is an indult, no tittles are used in the abbreviations, only plain dashes. There are no hyphens. The document has been ruled. A long 's' concludes *tenearis* at the end of line 6 and a long 'e' terminates *contraire* at the end of line 8.

52

Exhortation to the faithful of the province of Canterbury to subscribe towards the repair of the priory church of St Mary, Southwick (Aug. Hants.).
1226 February 26 Lateran

HONORIUS ep[iscopu]s seruus seruor[um] dei. Uniuersis christi (1) fidelibus per Cantuarien' prouinciam cons–titu'/tis ad quos littere is–te peruenerint.' Sal[u]tem et ap[osto]licam ben[edictionem]. Quoniam ut ait ap[osto]l[u]s om[ne]s s–tabimus ante tri'/bunal christi (2) recepturi prout in corpore gessimus siue bonum siue malum oportet nos diem messionis extreme mi[sericordi]e / operibus preuenire. et eternorum intuitu seminare in terris q[uo]d reddente domino cum multiplicato fruc–tu/ recolligere debeamus in celis. firmam spem fiduc⟨iam⟩q[ue] tenentes quoniam qui parce seminat parce et metet. et / qui seminat in benedic–tionibus de bened⟨ic–tio⟩nib[us] et m⟨etet⟩ uitam et⟨ern⟩am. Cum igitur sicut di/lec–ti filii . . Prior et Conuentus eccl[es]ie sanc–te marie de Suw . . . (3) ordinis sanc–ti Augus–ti/ni transmissa nobis petitione mons–trarunt.' eadem eccl[es]ia cum . . . . ⟨?gu⟩erra–⟨ru⟩m (4) discrimina tum etiam / propter uetus–tatem qua consumpta es–t reparatione indigeat et ad reparandam illam proprie sibi no[n] / suppetant facultates. Vniuersitatem ues–tram monemus et exhortamur in domino ac in remissionem uob[is] / iniungimus peccatorum quatin[us] cum eiusdem eccl[es]ie nuntii ad uos accesserint propter hoc beneficia petituri.' / de bonis uobis a deo pres–titis pias elemosinas et grata eis subsidia erogetis. ut uos per hec et alia bona / que domino inspirante feceritis.' ad eterne possitis felicitatis gaudia peruenire. Dat' Lateran.' / iiij kl' martii. Pontificat[us] n[ost]ri Anno Decimo.

BL Harley Ch. 43 A 32 (Bell, 'Original papal bulls' no. 61; who wrongly assigns to St Mary, Southwark); Southwick Cart. (Hants. Rec. Office) iii fol. 10v
Not registered, not in P or *SB*
22.2 cm × 16.9 cm: no *plica*
Bulla lost; holes in centre

Condition: document repaired at the foot
Endorsements: (middle centre) XVII$_7$ (archival mark) (top centre) (a bird's
head) / PP n° 28° (top centre, inverted) Exhortacio Honorii pape
Indulgentia super ... de Suwic

(1) *xpi* with tittle.
(2) *xpi* with a tittle.
(3) The document is holed here: probably three letters missing.
(4) The document very worn and rubbed; probably two words illegible.

The document is ruled and the dating clause is separated after Lateran. The
hand is neat and well executed. The capital 'H' of *HONORIUS* is delicately
and attractively ornamented. At the ends of lines 1, 2 and 12, the final letters
(u, i and a) have been given ascending tails to indicate hyphens.

53

Confirmation to the rector and brothers of the hospital of lepers of St John
the evangelist outside Blyth (*alias* Hodstock by Blyth, Notts.) of the liberties,
immunities and lands (unnamed) conceded to them by the prior of Blyth, with
the consent of the convent (Ben. al. Notts.), and by W(illiam I) de Cressy,
their founder, taking their persons, house and goods under papal protection,
and forbidding anyone to exact tithes from their gardens and copses (*virgulta*)
or from the feed of animals.
1226 March 7 Lateran (Dat'. Lateran'. Non'. Ma[r]tii. / Pontificat[us] n[ost]ri
Anno Deci[m]o.)

Pd The cartulary of Blyth priory ii, ed. Timson, no. 499, and *Mon. Angl.* iv 625
no. 7.
Address: Dilec–tis filiis..Rec–tori et fratrib[us] domus Leprosor[um] s[an]c[t]i
/ Ioh[ann]is euang[e]lis–te extra Blidam
Incipit: Cum a nobis
Variant readings
l.3 *sollicitudinem* (Timson l.5 *solicitudinem*)
l.5 *possi⟨detis⟩* MS holed (Timson l.7 incorrectly *possideant*: Dugdale has it
correctly)
l.11 *districtius* (Timson l.15 *districti*)
l.12 *pres⟨u⟩mat* MS holed
l.13 *⟨in⟩hibitionis* MS holed

Nottingham University Library, Mellish collection, Me D 1/4
Not registered P 7544 (whence *Reg. Hon. III* no. 5851) Not in *SB*
18.8 cm × 17.2 cm: *plica* 1.6 cm
Holes: no *bulla*

Condition: good, apart from two small holes, bottom left
Scribe: *P (cf. no. 42, above)
Face: (top extreme right corner) ad bar' (struck through) (slightly to the left of this, and not struck through) cor
Endorsements: (top extreme left corner) p. (top centre) (a device) ⚓ (? proctorial) (bottom centre, inverted) A Confermacion from Honorius (C16 or C17, English)

The hand displays the same features as no. 42, above. The note *cor* at the top right indicates correction. The abbreviation mark to indicate the 'r' in 'Ma[r]tii' in the dating clause is unusual: it is not a tittle.

54

Mandate to the archbishop of Dublin to admonish and, if necessary, compel by ecclesiastical censure those who unlawfully detain certain castles belonging to the domain (*ad demanium*) of the king of England in Ireland to restore them to the king.
1226 May 14 Lateran (Dat' Lat⟨eran⟩ ii Id' Maii. Pontificat[us] n[ost]ri Anno Decimo)

Pd Pontificia Hibernica i, ed. Sheehy, no. 180, and Theiner, *Vetera Monumenta Hibernorum* 26 no. 63 (Variants not given below)
Address: Venerabili fratri . . Archiep[iscop]o Dubli/nen'
Incipit: Cum Castra quedam
Variant readings
l.7 *simonitis* (Sheehy l.9 *si monitis*)
l.9 *Dat'Lat⟨eran⟩* (Sheehy l.11 *Datum Laterani*)

PRO SC7/50/1
Reg. Yr. 10 no. 272 fol. 127v, *Reg. Hon. III* no. 5932, *CPL* 111 P 7572 *SB* 791
14.7 cm × 10 cm: *plica* 1.3 cm
Detached *bulla* on hemp strings
Condition: fairly good
Scribe: *S (cf. no. 44, above)
Endorsements: (top left) H (top right) R̷ script (papal registration mark) (top extreme right corner) (?) ⱴ (mid right) ad Dublinensis compellat detentores castrorum in hybern' (bottom right) Exam'

There are no hyphens where words are broken.

55

Intimation to the king of England that he has ordered R(omano Bonaventura) (1) cardinal deacon of S. Angelo, papal legate, not to proceed to publication of any sentence of excommunication, general or special, against the king or R(ichard of Cornwall) count of Poitou, his brother, without the pope's special order.

1226 May 15 Lateran (Dat'. Lateran'. / Id' Maii. Pontificat[us] n[ost]ri Anno Decimo)

Pd Rymer i pt 1 185
Address: Carissimo in christo filio ⟨..?⟩ Illustri Regi An'/glie
Incipit: *U*olentes in quib[us]
Variant readings
Rymer (l.2) ignores the *gemipunctus* in line 1 and prints nine dots.
l.5 *aut special[is] (seu) sententie: seu* (deleted with dots) *specialis siue* (Reg.)
l.8 *oporteat* (Rymer l.12 *oporteret*)

PRO SC7/18/12
Reg. Yr. 10 no. 270 fol. 127v, *Reg. Hon. III* no. 5938, *CPL* 110 P 7573 *SB* 792
15.8 cm × 10.2 cm: *plica* 1.4 cm
Bulla on hemp strings
Condition: very good
Scribe: (?) t *or* f
Endorsements: (top left of centre) H (top right of centre) ℞ script (papal registration mark) (mid centre, inverted) Scribende (mid right) examinatur (bottom extreme left corner) .xij. (bottom centre) Scribitur in libro / De non proferendo sententiam interdicti aut excommunicationis in personas domini Regis et R. fratris sui de non denuntiando (bottom right) .iij.
(1) Eubel, *Hierarchia* i 4. He was made cardinal bishop of Porto in 1238; he died by 1243.

There is an uncorrected mistake in the first word of the fifth line, 'denuntia*ti*ationem'.

56

Indult to the abbot of Bayham (Prem. Sussex) not to be bound to hear delegated cases in future unless special mention is made of this indult.
1226 May 30 Lateran (Dat'/ Lateran' iii kl' Iunii Pontificat[us] n[ost]ri Anno Decim[o].,)

Pd Rymer i pt 1 185
Address: Dilec–to filio..Abbati de Begham
Incipit: *A* nobis humiliter

Appendix 2

Variant readings
l.1 *gemipunctus* omitted in Rymer
l.2 Rymer (l.5) supplies *per* at the end of the line, omitting the *propter* (clearly in a different hand) written in the margin to the left between the lines, which is acceptable for this form of document (cf. no. 51, above), but there are no signs of correction by the corrector.

PRO SC7/18/1
Not registered *Reg. Hon. III* no. 5965 (abstract from Rymer) P 7579 Not in *SB*
17.3 cm × 12.2 cm: *plica* 1.3 cm
Bulla on red and yellow silk threads
Condition: very good
Scribe: bl (cf. no. 36, above)
Endorsements: (top centre) de Be (mid left) (?) Bayham (English endorsement) priuilegium quod Abbas de Beg' non tenetur esse delegatus in causis per litteras apostolicas contra sui assensum et uoluntatem.

This document is not well written. The letters are not of a uniform size and they slope in various directions. The ink of the 'A' of *A nobis* and of the 'N' of *Nulli* has run. In comparison with no. 36, note the backward slope of the letters 's' and 'f', the hooked descenders of the 'p's, the triangular 'D' in *Dat'* and the similar decoration of the stem of the 'H' of the pope's name.

57

Mandate to the archbishop of York, on the complaint of the prior and convent of Durham, to examine the election of Master W(illiam Scot), archdeacon of Worcester, to the see of Durham, within two months of the receipt of this mandate, or else to send the form and process of the election to the pope.
1226 December 22 Lateran (Dat' Lateran' xi kl' Ianuarii. Pontificatus n[ost]ri anno Vndeci[m]o)

Pd Reg. Gray, ed. Raine, 156–7 no. 31 (from BL Add. MS 15353, 363)
Address: Venerabili fr[atr]i .. Archiep[iscop]o Eboracen[si]
Incipit: Significa[n]/tibus .. Priore ac
Variant readings
l.1 *Honorius ep[iscopu]s seruus seruor[um] dei. Venerabili fr[atr]i .. Archiep[iscop]o Eboracen[si]* (Raine l.1 *Honorius, etc., archiepiscopo Ebor.*)
l.2 *ac* (Raine l.1 *et*)
l.5 *conpositione* (Raine l.7 *compositione*); *elegerunt* (Raine l.8 *elegerant*)
l.9 *dampnosa* (Raine l.13 *damnosa*)
l.14 *Dat' Lateran xi kl' Ianuarii. Pontificatus n[ost]ri anno Vndeci[m]o* (Raine ll.20–1 *Datum Laterani, xj kalendas Januarii, anno decimo primo.*)

260

Texts of the Original Letters

Durham, D. and C. muniments (Prior's Kitchen) 2.1 Pap. 18 (copied into Cart.
 III fol. 156v)
Reg. Yr. 11 no. 456, *Reg. Hon. III* no. 6119, *CPL* 114–15 Not in P or *SB*
20.4 cm × 17 cm: *plica* 1.9 cm
No *bulla* surviving
Condition: fair (damage where the *bulla* has been torn away at the bottom
 centre of the document)
Scribe: I.g.
Endorsements: (bottom centre) Secunda

BIBLIOGRAPHY

A. UNPRINTED SOURCES

Printed with the kind permission of the owners. Particular acknowledgements, where requested, are given in brackets.

1 *Original Papal Letters of Honorius III*

Devon Record Office, Exeter, 312 M/TY 54
Durham, Prior's Kitchen (the Dean and Chapter of Durham), D. and C. Muniments 2.1 Pap. nos. 5, 14, 17–18
Exeter Cathedral Library, D. and C. Muniments 2087
Hereford Cathedral Library, D. and C. Muniments 1850
London,
    British Library, Add. Ch. 19805, Harley Chs. 43 A 31–2, Wolley Ch. x 32
    Lambeth Palace Library, Papal Documents nos. 20–4
    Public Record Office, SC7/18/1–14, 23–4, 27–9, 31; SC7/35/17–19; SC7/50/1, 3–11
    Westminster Abbey, D. and C. Muniments 13248
Northamptonshire Record Office (the Trustees of the late Sir Gyles Isham, Bart), I. L. 186, 496
Nottingham University Library, Mellish Collection ME D 1/4
Oxford,
    Bodleian Library (the Curators of the Bodleian Library),
        MS Chs. Oxon. 147a; MS Chs. Oxon. (Oseney) 5b
        Oxford University Archives Y 2
    Magdalen College (the President and Fellows of Magdalen College), Brackley Ch. 106 D

2 *Original Papal Registers of Honorius III*

Archivio Segreto Vaticano, Reg. Vat. 9–13

3 *Other Manuscripts Cited*

Abingdon Reg., Bodleian MS Lyell 15
Aynho Cart. (roll format), Magdalen College, Oxford, 137/1
Bardney Cart., BL Cotton MS Vespasian E xx

Bibliography

Battle Cart.,
  Huntington Library, San Marino, California, Battle Abbey Papers vol. 29
  (abbrev.) London, Lincoln's Inn Hale MS 87
Belvoir Cart. (large), Duke of Rutland, Belvoir Castle, Add. MS 98
Binham Cart., BL Cotton MS Claudius D xiii
Bradenstoke Cart., BL Stowe MS 925
Bridlington Cart., BL Add. MS 40008
Broomholm Cart., CUL MS Mm 2. 20
Burton Cart., BL MS Loans 30
Bury (Pinchbeck Reg.), CUL MS Ee 3. 60
Cambridge, King's College, Muns. O 35
Canterbury,
  archiepiscopal cart., London, Lambeth Palace Library, MS 1212
  St Augustine's Cart.,
    (A) BL Cotton MS Claudius D x
    (B) BL Cotton MS Julius D ii
  St Laurence Cart., CUL Add. MS 6845
Crowland Cart., Spalding Gentlemen's Society
Dover Cart., London, Lambeth Palace Library MS 241
Durham,
  D. & C. MS iv 24
  Prior's Kitchen 1.1 Archid. Northumb.; Cart. I, II, III; Cart. Vet.; Cham-
    berlain's Cart.; Loc. III no. 49; 2.1 Pap. 23, 27, 33, 38
Easby Reg., BL Egerton MS 2827
Ely Liber M, CUL EDR G 3. 28
Exeter Cart., D. & C. 3672
Eye Cart., Essex Record Office D/D By Q 19
Glastonbury Reg.,
  (A) Bodleian MS Wood empt. 1
  (B) Cambridge, Trinity College MS R 5. 33
Gloucester Reg., D. & C. Reg. A
Hickling Cart., Bodleian MS Tanner 425
Kent Archives Office, De L'Isle & Dudley U 1475 T 264/190, 196, 391
Lilleshall Cart., BL Add. MS 50121
London,
  British Library, Add. Ch. 17848, Wolley Ch. xi 25, Harley MS 1319
  Lambeth Palace Library PD no. 27
  Public Record Office SC7/2/28; 15/12, 21; 19/3; 35/29
  Westminster Abbey, D. and C. Muniments 51111
Newstead Cart., London, College of Arms, Arundel MS 60
Peterborough, D. & C. MSS 1, 5 (deposited CUL)
Reading Cart.,
  (A) CUL MS Dd 9. 38
  (B) BL Cotton MS Domitian A iii
St Bartholomew's Cart., St Bartholomew's Hospital, Smithfield, Cok's
    Cartulary

Bibliography

St John of Jerusalem Cart. BL Cotton MS Nero E vi, (detached portion) BL
  Cotton MS Nero C ix
Salisbury, D. & C. Liber Evidentiarum C; Literae
  Diocesan Registry, Registrum Rubrum
Somerset Record Office, Dunster Castle MSS Box 16 no. 2
Thorney Red Bk ii, CUL Add. MS 3021
Waltham Cart., BL Cotton MS Tiberius C ix
Westminster Cart., BL Cotton MS Faustina A iii
York,
  archiepiscopal cart., BL Lansdowne MS 402
  D. & C. registers,
      (A) York Minster Mag. Reg. Alb. pts 2 & 3
      (B) BL Cotton MS Vitellius A xii
  (inventories)
      (A) York Minster muns. M2/2a
      (B) York Minster muns. M2/2b

B. SELECTED PRINTED MATERIAL

Acht, P., 'Kanzleikorrekturen auf Papsturkunden des 13 und 14 Jahrhunderts',
  Folia diplomatica i (Brno, 1971) 9–22.
'Annales Cavenses', MGH SS iii (1839) 185–97.
'Annales Ceccanenses', MGH SS xix (1866) 275–302.
'Annales Sancti Rudberti Salisburgenses', MGH SS ix (1851) 758–810.
Arcère, L. E., Histoire de la ville de La Rochelle et du pays d'Aulnis, 2 vols. (La
  Rochelle, 1756–7).
Auvray, L., ed., Les registres de Grégoire IX, 4 vols. Bibliothèque des écoles
  françaises d'Athènes et de Rome (Paris, 1896–1910).
Barbiche, B., Les actes pontificaux originaux des Archives Nationales de Paris, 2 vols.
  (1198–1261 & 1261–1304) (Città del Vaticano, 1975–8).
  'Diplomatique et histoire sociale: les "scriptores" de la chancellerie apostolique
  au xiiie siècle', ASAR anno xii 1–2 (1973) 117–29.
Barraclough, G., 'Audientia litterarum contradictarum', DDC i (1935) cols.
  1387–99.
  'Minutes of papal letters (1316–1317)', Miscellanea archivistica Angelo Mercati,
  Studi e testi clxv (1952) 109–27 with 2 plates.
Bartoloni, F., 'Suppliche pontificie dei secoli xiii e xiv', Bulletino dell' Istituto
  storico Italiano per il medio evo e archivio Muratoriano lxvii (Rome, 1955) 1–188
  with plates.
Battelli, G., '"Membra disiecta" di registri pontifici dei secoli xiii e xiv',
  Mélanges Eugène Tisserant iv, Studi e testi ccxxxiv (Città del Vaticano, 1964)
  1–34.
  and see Baumgarten
Baumgarten, P. M., 'Miscellanea diplomatica I', Römische Quartalschrift xxvii
  (1913) 102–15; II, xxviii (1914) 87–129 & 169–98; and III, xxxii (1924)
  37–81.
  Schedario Baumgarten. Descrizione diplomatica di bolle e brevi originali da Innocenzio
  III a Pio IX, ed. G. Batelli, i (1198–1254) (Città del Vaticano, 1965).

Bibliography

Bell, H. I., 'A list of the original papal bulls and briefs in the department of manuscripts, British Museum', *EHR* xxxvi (1921) 393–419 and 556–83.

Berlière, U., 'Le droit de procuration ou de gîte. Papes et légats', *Académie Royale de Belgique. Bulletins de la classe des lettres et des sciences morales et politiques* (Brussels, 1919) 509–38.

'Honorius III et les monastères bénédictins 1216–27', *Revue Belge de philologie et d'histoire* ii (Brussels, 1923) 237–65 and 461–84.

Bock, F., 'Originale und Registereinträge zur Zeit Honorius III', *Bulletino dell' archivio paleografico Italiano* n.s. ii (1956) 101–16.

'Päpstliche Sekretregister und Kammerregister, Überblick und erganzung fruherer Studien zum Registerwesen des Spatmittelalters', *Archivalische Zeitschrift* lix (1963) 30–58.

'Studien zu den original Registern Innocenz' III. (Reg. Vat. 4–7A)', *Archivalische Zeitschrift* l/li (1955) 329–64.

Bouquet, M., *Recueil des historiens des Gaules et de la France...*, new edn by L. Delisle, 24 vols. (Paris, 1869–1904).

Boyle, L. E., 'The compilatio quinta and the registers of Honorius III', *BMCL* n.s. viii (1978) 9–19.

A survey of the Vatican archives and its medieval holdings, Pontifical Institute of Medieval Studies, Subsidia Mediaevalia i (Toronto, 1972).

Bresslau, H., *Handbuch der Urkundenlehre für Deutschland und Italien*, 2nd edn 2 vols. (Leipzig and Berlin, 1912–31).

Brewer, J. S., Dimock, J. F., and Warner, G. F., ed., Gerald of Wales *Opera*, 8 vols. RS xxi (London, 1861–91).

Brooke, C. N. L., 'Gregorian reform in action: clerical marriage in England, 1050–1200', *Medieval church and society* (London, 1971) 69–99.

Brown, W., ed., *The register of Walter Giffard, lord archbishop of York 1266–1279*, Surtees Society cix (1904).

Calendar of entries in the papal registers illustrating the history of Great Britain and Ireland, ed. W. H. Bliss and others (HMSO London, 1893–).

Calendar of the patent rolls 1232–47 (HMSO London, 1906).

Cantini, J.-A., 'Sinibalde dei Fieschi' pts 1–3, *DDC* vii (1965) cols. 1029–39.

Capasso, R., 'Un contributo allo studio delle suppliche pontificie nel secolo xiii', *Bulletino dell' archivio paleografico Italiano* n.s. ii–iii pt 1 (1956–7) 169–73 + plate.

'Catalogus pontificum et imperatorum Romanorum Casinensis', *MGH SS* xxii (1872) 359–67.

'Catalogus pontificum Romanorum Viterbiensis', *MGH SS* xxii (1872) 349–52.

Chaplais, P., ed., *Diplomatic documents*, i (1101–1272) (HMSO London, 1964).

Cheney, C. R., *Pope Innocent III and England*, Päpste und Papsttum ix (Stuttgart, 1976).

The study of the medieval papal chancery, 2nd Edwards lecture (University of Glasgow, 1966).

'Three decretal collections before Compilatio IV: Pragensis, Palatina I, and Abrincensis II', *Traditio* xv (1959) 464–83.

ed., *Handbook of dates for students of English history*, Royal Historical Society guides and handbooks no. iv (London, 1955).

Bibliography

Cheney, C. R., ed., and Semple, W. H., trans., *Selected letters of Pope Innocent III concerning England (1198–1216)*, Nelson Medieval Texts (London, 1953).

and Cheney, Mary G., cal. and ed., *The letters of Pope Innocent III (1198–1216) concerning England and Wales* (Oxford, 1967).

And see Powicke.

'Chronica minor auctore minorita Erphordiensi', MGH SS xxiv (1879) 172–204.

Ciaconius, A., *Vitae et res gestae pontificum Romanorum et S.R.E. cardinalium* ii (Rome, 1677).

Clanchy, M. T., *From memory to written record* (London, 1979).

Clark, A. C., *The cursus in mediaeval and vulgar Latin*. A paper read to the Oxford Philological Society on Feb. 18, 1910 (Oxford, 1910).

Clausen, J., *Papst Honorius III (1216–1227)* (Bonn, 1895).

Clay, Sir C. T., ed., *York minster fasti*, 2 vols. Yorkshire Archaeological Society Record Series cxxiii–cxxiv (1958 and 1959).

Constable, Giles, *Letters and letter-collections*. Typologie des sources du moyen âge occidental, fasc. xvii (Turnhout, 1976).

'The structure of medieval society according to the *dictatores* of the twelfth century', *Law, church and society. Essays in honor of Stephan Kuttner*, ed. K. Pennington and R. Somerville (University of Pennsylvania Press, 1977) 253–67.

Crosby, Ruth, 'Oral delivery in the middle ages', *Speculum* xi (1936) 88–110.

Davies, W. S., ed., Gerald of Wales, 'De invectionibus', *Y Cymmrodor* xxx (1920).

Davis, F. N., ed., *Rotuli Roberti Grosseteste*, Lincoln Record Society xi (1914).

Davis, G. R. C., *Medieval cartularies of Great Britain. A short catalogue* (London, 1958).

Delisle, L., *Mémoire sur les actes d'Innocent III suivi de l'itinéraire de ce pontife* (Paris, 1857).

Denifle, H., 'Die päpstlichen Registerbände des 13 Jhs. und das Inventar derselben vom Jahre 1339', *Archiv für Litteratur und Kirchengeschichte des Mittelalters* ii (1886) 1–105.

Dugdale, Sir William, *Monasticon Anglicanum*, ed. J. Caley, H. Ellis and Bulkeley Bandinel, 6 vols. (London, 1846).

Duggan, C., *Twelfth century decretal collections and their importance in English history* (University of London, Athlone Press, 1963).

Ehrle, F., 'Zur Geschichte des Schatzes, der Bibliothek und des Archivs der Päpste im vierzehnten Jahrhundert', *Archiv für Litteratur und Kirchengeschichte des Mittelalters* i (1885) 1–48 and 228–364.

Elze, R., 'Der Liber Censuum des Cencius (Cod. Vat. Lat. 8486) von 1192 bis 1228', *Bulletino dell' archivio paleografico Italiano* n.s. ii (1956) 251–70.

'Die päpstliche Kapelle im 12. und 13. Jahrhundert', *ZRG* lxvii (Kan. Abt. xxxvi, 1950) 145–204.

Eubel, C., *Hierarchia catholica medii aevi* i (Munster, 1913).

Fabre, P., *Étude sur le Liber Censuum de l'Église Romaine*. Bibliothèque des écoles françaises d'Athènes et de Rome, fasc. lxii (1892).

and Duchesne, L., ed., *Le Liber Censuum de l'Église Romaine*. Bibliothèque des écoles françaises d'Athènes et de Rome, 2 ser. vi, 3 vols. (Paris, 1905–10).

Bibliography

Fawtier, R., ed., *Les registres de Boniface VIII*, 4 vols. Bibliothèque des écoles françaises d'Athènes et de Rome, 2 ser. (Paris, 1939).

Fichtenau, H., *Arenga. Spätantike und Mittelalter im Spiegel von Urkundenformeln* (Graz, 1957).

'La situation actuelle des études de diplomatique en Autriche', *BEC* cxix (1962) 5–20.

Foreville, R., *Le jubilé de Saint Thomas Becket du xiiie au xve siècle (1220–1470)* (Paris, 1958).

Latran I, II, III et Latran IV. Histoire des conciles oecumeniques vi (Paris, 1965).

'Procédure et débats dans les conciles médiévaux du Latran (1123–1215)', *Rivista di storia della Chiesa in Italia* xix (1965) 21–37.

Fransen, G., *Les décrétales et les collections des décrétales.* Typologie des sources du moyen âge occidental, fasc. ii (Turnhout, 1972).

Friedberg, E., ed., 'Decretales' in *Corpus iuris canonici* ii (Leipzig, 1881).

ed., *Quinque compilationes antiquae* (Leipzig, 1882, repd Graz, 1956).

García y García, A., ed., *Constitutiones concilii quarti Lateranensis una cum commentariis glossatorum.* Monumenta iuris canonici ser. A: Corpus glossatorum ii (Città del Vaticano, 1981).

'Gesta', *PL* ccxiv (Paris, 1890) cols. 17–227.

Gibbs, M. and Lang, J., *Bishops and reform 1215–1272 with special reference to the Lateran Council of 1215* (Oxford, 1934).

Giusti, M., *Studi sui registri di bolle papali.* Collectanea Archivi Vaticani i (Città del Vaticano, Archivio Vaticano, 1968).

Göller, E., *Die päpstlichen Pönitentiarie von ihrem Ursprung bis zu ihrer Umgestaltung unter Pius V*, 2 vols. Bibliothek des königl. Preussischen Historischen Instituts in Rom iii, vii (Rome, 1907–11).

Gottlob, A., *Die Servitientaxe im 13. Jahrhundert*, Kirchenrectliche Abhandlungen i pt 2 (Stuttgart, 1903).

Greenway, D. E., 'Ecclesiastical chronology: Fasti 1066–1300', *Studies in Church History* xi, ed. D. Baker (Cambridge, 1975) 53–60.

ed., *Fasti ecclesiae Anglicanae 1066–1300*, i St Paul's London, ii Monastic cathedrals, iii Lincoln (London, 1968–77).

Gregorovius, F., *History of the city of Rome in the middle ages*, trans. from 4th German edn by Annie Hamilton, v pt 1 (London, 1897).

Guala, *see* Richardson; von Heckel.

Hageneder, O., 'Die päpstlichen Register des 13. und 14. Jahrhunderts', *ASAR* anno xii (Turin, 1973) 45–76.

'Papstregister und Dekretalenrecht', *Recht und Schrift in Mittelalter*, ed. P. Classen, Vorträge und Forschungen Konstanzer Arbeitskreis für mittelalterliche Geschichte xxii (Sigmaringen, 1977) 319–47.

Haidacher, A., Maleczek, W. and Strnad, Alfred, A., ed., *Die Register Innocenz' III*, 2 vols. Publikationen des Osterreichischen Kulturinstituts in Rom (Graz–Köln, Rom–Wien, 1964–79).

Hanenburg, Jacoba J. H. M., 'Decretals and decretal collections in the second half of the twelfth century', *Tijdschrift voor Rechtsgeschiedenis* xxxiv (1966) 552–99.

Bibliography

Hardy, T. D., ed., *Rotuli litterarum clausarum*, 2 vols. (Record Commission, London, 1833–44).

Rotuli litterarum patentium, i pt 1 (1201–1216) (Record Commission, London, 1835).

Haskins, C. H., 'Two Roman formularies in Philadelphia', Miscellanea Francesco Ehrle iv, *Studi e Testi* xl (Rome, 1924) 275–86.

Heller, E., ed., 'Die ars dictandi des Thomas von Capua', *Sitzungsberichte der Heidelberger Akademie der Wissenschaften*, Phil.-hist. Klasse Abhandlung iv (Heidelberg, 1928/9) 1–59.

Herde, P., *Audientia litterarum contradictarum*, 2 vols. Bibliothek des Deutschen Historischen Instituts im Rom xxxi–xxxii (Rome, 1970).

Beiträge zum päpstlichen Kanzlei und Urkundenwesen im dreizehnten Jahrhundert, 2 edn, Münchener Historische Studien i (Kallmünz, 1967).

'Papal formularies for letters of justice (13th-16th centuries)', *Proceedings of the Second International Congress of Medieval Canon Law*. Monumenta iuris canonici ser. C, i (1975) 321–45.

Hervey, Lord Francis, ed., *The Pinchbeck register*, 2 vols. (privately printed Farncombe's, Brighton, 1925).

Hilpert, H.-E., *Kaiser-und Papstbriefe in den Chronica majora des Matthaeus Paris*, Publications of the German Historical Institute London ix (1981).

Horoy, C., ed., 'Honorii III opera omnia', *Medii aevi Bibliotheca Patristica ab anno 1217 usque ad Concilii Tridentini tempora* i–ii (Paris, 1879–80).

Horwitz, S., 'Reshaping a decretal chapter: *Tua nobis* and the canonists', *Law, church and society*, ed. K. Pennington and R. Somerville (University of Pennsylvania Press, 1977) 207–21.

Innes, Cosmo, ed., *Registrum S. Mariae de Neubotle*, Bannatyne Club (1849).

Jaffé, P., ed., *Regesta pontificum Romanorum ad 1198*, revsd S. Loewenfeld, F. Kaltenbrunner and P. Ewald, 2 vols. (Leipzig, 1885–8).

Johnson, Charles, 'The keeper of papal bulls', *Essays in medieval history presented to Thomas Frederick Tout*, ed. A. G. Little and F. M. Powicke (Manchester, 1925) 135–8.

Katterbach, B., and Peitz, W., 'Die Unterschriften der Päpste und Kardinäle in den "Bullae maiores" vom 11. bis 14. Jahrhundert', Miscellanea Francesco Ehrle iv, *Studi e Testi* xl (Rome, 1924) 177–274+6 plates.

Knowles, David, Brooke, C. N. L., and London, Vera C. M., ed., *The heads of religious houses England and Wales 940–1216* (Cambridge, 1972).

Krautheimer, Richard, *Rome. Profile of a city, 313–1308* (Princeton University Press, 1980).

Kuttner, S., 'A collection of decretal letters of Innocent III in Bamberg', *Medievalia et humanistica* n.s. i (1970) 41–56.

'Johannes Teutonicus, das Vierte Laterankonzil und die Compilatio Quarta', Miscellanea Giovanni Mercati v, *Studi e Testi* cxxv (1946) 608–34.

'Quelques observations sur l'autorité des collections canoniques dans le droit classique de l'Église', *Actes du congrès de droit canonique Paris 22–26 avril 1947* (Paris, 1950) 305–12.

Repertorium der Kanonistik (1140–1234). Prodromus Corporis Glossarum i, *Studi e Testi* lxxi (1937).

Bibliography

and García y García, A., 'A new eyewitness account of the Fourth Lateran Council', *Traditio* xx (1964) 115–78.

Ladner, G. B., *Die Papstbildnisse des Altertums und des Mittelalters*, ii, Innocenz II. zu Benedikt XI. Monumenti di Antichità Cristiana pubblicati del Pontificio Istituto di Archaeologia Cristiana 2 ser., iv (Città del Vaticano, 1970).

Largiadèr, A., ed., *Die Papsturkunden der Schweiz von Innocenz III bis Martin V ohne Zürich*, 2 vols. (Zürich, 1968–70).

Die Papsturkunden des Staatsarchivs Zürich von Innocenz III bis Martin V (Zürich, 1963).

Lea, H. C., *A formulary of the papal penitentiary in the thirteenth century* (Philadelphia, 1892).

Liber Censuum, see Fabre and Duchesne.

Linehan, P. A., 'Proctors representing Spanish interests at the papal court, 1216–1305', *AHP* xvii (1979) 69–123.

'Spanish litigants and their agents at the thirteenth-century papal curia', *Proceedings of the Fifth International Congress of Medieval Canon Law* (Città del Vaticano, 1980) 487–501.

Litta, Pompeo, *Famiglie celebri Italiane*, 10 vols. (Milan, 1819–99, 1902–23); vol. x dispensa 167–8 'Savelli di Roma' by Luigi Passerini (Milan, 1872).

Luard, H. R., ed., *Annales monastici*, 5 vols. RS xxxvi (London, 1864–9).

ed., *Chronica majora*, 7 vols. RS lvii (London, 1872–3).

Lunt, W. E., *Financial relations of the papacy with England to 1354*, 2 vols. Studies in Anglo-papal relations during the middle ages. The Medieval Academy of America nos. xxxiii, lxxiv (Cambridge, Mass., 1939–62).

Papal revenues in the middle ages, 2 vols. (Columbia, New York, 1934).

Major, Kathleen, 'Original papal documents in the Bodleian Library', *Bodleian Library Record* iii (1951) 242–56.

ed., *Acta Stephani Langton*, Canterbury and York Society l (London, 1950).

Mansilla, Demetrio, ed., *La documentacíon pontificia de Honorio III (1216–1227)*, Istituto Español de Historia Ecclesiastica, Monumenta Hispaniae Vaticana Sección: Registros II (Rome, 1965).

Maxwell-Lyte, H. C., *Historical notes on the use of the Great Seal of England* (London, 1926).

Mengozzi, N., *Papa Onorio III e le sue relazioni col regno di Inghilterra* (Siena, 1911).

Miquel Rosell, F. J., ed., *Regesta des letras pontificias del Archivo de la Corona de Aragón* (Madrid, 1948).

Mortimer, R., ed., *Leiston abbey cartulary and Butley priory charters*, Suffolk Record Society, Suffolk Charters i (Ipswich, 1979).

Muratori, L. A., ed., 'Vita Honorii III', *Rerum Italicarum scriptores* iii(2) (Milan, 1734) 387–92.

Murray, Alexander, 'Pope Gregory VII and his letters', *Traditio* xxii (1966) 149–202.

Nüske, G. F., 'Untersuchungen über das Personal der päpstlichen Kanzlei 1254–1304', *AD* xx (1974) 39–240 and xxi (1975) 249–431.

Panvinius, O., *Epitome pontificum Romanorum* (Venice, 1657).

Paravicini Bagliani, A., *Cardinali di curia e 'familiae' cardinalizie dal 1227 al 1254*, 2 vols. Italia Sacra xviii & xix (Padua, 1972).

Bibliography

Paravicini Bagliani, A., *I testamenti dei cardinali del duecento*. Miscellanea della Società Romana di storia patria xxv (Rome, 1980).

Partner, Peter, *The lands of St Peter* (London, 1972).

Passerini, *see* Litta.

Patent rolls of the reign of Henry III 1216–25 (HMSO London, 1901).

Patent rolls of the reign of Henry III 1225–32 (HMSO London, 1903).

Peitz, *see* Katterbach.

Pennington, K., 'The canonists and pluralism in the thirteenth century', *Speculum* li (1) (1976) 35–48.

'The French recension of Compilatio Tertia', *BMCL* v (1975) 53–71.

ed., *Johannes Teutonicus apparatus glossarum in compilationem tertiam* i Monumenta iuris canonici ser. A: Corpus glossatorum iii (Città del Vaticano, 1981).

Pfaff, V., 'Die Kardinäle unter Papst Coelestin III. (1191–1198) (I)', *ZRG* lxxii (Kan. Abt. xli, 1955) 58–94.

'Die Kardinäle unter Papst Coelestin III. (1191–1198) (II), Beurkundunglisten', *ZRG* lxxxiii (Kan. Abt. lii, 1966) 332–69.

'Papst Coelestin III', *ZRG* lxxviii (Kan. Abt. xlvii, 1961) 109–28.

'Papst Clemens III. (1187–1191) mit einer Liste der Kardinalsunterschriften', *ZRG* xcvii (Kan. Abt. lxvi, 1980) 261–216.

Phillimore, W., and Davis, F. N., ed., *Rotuli Hugonis de Welles episcopi Lincolniensis, A.D. 1209–1235*, 3 vols. Canterbury and York Society i, iii & iv (1907–9).

Piergiovanni, V., 'Sinibaldo dei Fieschi decretalista. Ricerche sulla vita', Collectanea Stephan Kuttner iv, *Studia Gratiana* xiv (1967) 127–54.

Poole, R. L., *Lectures on the history of the papal Chancery down to the time of Innocent III* (Cambridge, 1915).

Potthast, A., ed., *Regesta pontificum Romanorum 1198–1304*, 2 vols. (repd Graz, 1957).

Powicke, F. M., *King Henry III and the Lord Edward* (repd Oxford, 1966).

Stephen Langton (Oxford, 1928).

and Cheney, C. R., ed., *Councils and synods*, 2 vols. ii pts 1 and 2 (Oxford, 1964).

and Fryde, E. B., *Handbook of British chronology*, Royal Historical Society guides and handbooks no. ii, 2 edn (London, 1961).

Pressutti, P., cal., *Regesta Honorii III*, 2 vols. (Rome, 1888–95).

Prou, M., ed., *Les registres d'Honorius IV*. Bibliothèque des écoles françaises d'Athènes et de Rome, 2 ser. (Paris, 1888).

Prynne, W., *The third tome of an exact chronological vindication...of the supreme ecclesiastical jurisdiction of our...English kings* (1668).

Public Record Office, *Lists and Indexes* xlix (HMSO London, 1923).

Rabikauskas, P., '"Auditor litterarum contradictarum" et commissions des juges délégués sous le pontificat d'Honorius III', *BEC* cxxxii (1975) 213–44.

Raine, J., ed., *Historiae Dunelmensis scriptores tres*, Surtees Society ix (1839).

ed., *The register or rolls of Walter Gray, lord archbishop of York*, Surtees Society lvi (1872 for 1870).

Rainer, 'Annales', *MGH SS* xvi (1859) 651–80.

Raynaldus, *see* Theiner.

Bibliography

Rich Jones, W. H., ed., *The register of S. Osmund*, 2 vols. RS lxxviii (1883–4).

Richardson, H. G., 'Letters of the legate Guala', *EHR* xlviii (1933) 250–9.

Rusch, B., *Die Behörden und Hofbeamten der papstlichen Kurie des 13. Jahrhunderts*, Schriften der Albertus-Universität, Geistwissenschaftl. Reihe iii (Königsberg, 1936).

Rymer, Thomas, and Sanderson, Robert, *Foedera, conventiones, litterae...*, ed. A. Clarke and F. Holbrooke, 3 vols. in 6 (Record Commission, London, 1816–30).

Saltman, A., ed., *The cartulary of Tutbury priory*, HMC JP and Staffordshire Record Society (1962).

Santifaller, Leo, 'Über die Verbal-Invokation in Urkunden', *Sitzungsberichte der oesterreichische Akademie der Wissenschaften* Phil.-hist. Klasse ccxxxvii (2) (1961) 1–20.

Sayers, Jane E., 'Canterbury proctors at the court of the *audiencia litterarum contradictarum*', *Traditio* xxii (1966) 311–45.

Original papal documents in the Lambeth Palace Library, Bulletin of the Institute of Historical Research, Special Supplement vi (1967).

Papal judges delegate in the province of Canterbury 1198–1254 (Oxford, 1971).

'Proctors representing British interests at the papal court, 1198–1415', *Proceedings of the Third International Congress of Medieval Canon Law*, Monumenta iuris canonici ser. C: Subsidia iv (Città del Vaticano, 1971) 143–63.

Schillmann, F., ed., *Die Formularsammlung des Marinus von Eboli*, Bibliothek des Preussischen Historischen Instituts in Rom xvi (Rome, 1929).

Schramm, P., *A history of the English coronation*, trans. L. G. Wickham Legg (Oxford, 1937).

Schwarz, B., 'Der corrector litterarum apostolicarum', *QFIAB* liv (1974) 122–91.

Die Organisation kurialer Schreiberkollegien von ihrer Entstehung bis zur Mitte des 15. Jahrhunderts, Bibliothek des Deutschen Historischen Instituts in Rom xxxvii (Tübingen, 1972).

Sheehy, Maurice P., ed., *Pontificia Hibernica* (Medieval Papal Chancery documents concerning Ireland 640–1261), i (Dublin, 1962).

Shirley, W. W., ed., *Royal and other historical letters... of the reign of Henry III from the originals in the Public Record Office*, 2 vols., RS xxvii (1862–6).

Stelzer, W., 'Beiträge zur Geschichte der Kurienprokuratoren im 13. Jahrhundert', *AHP* viii (1970) 113–38.

'Niederaltaicher Prokuratorien. Zur Geschichte der Impetrationsvollmachten für die päpstliche Kurie im 13. Jahrhundert', *MIOG* lxxvii (1969) 291–313.

'Über Vermerke der beiden Audientie auf Päpsturkunden in der zweiten Hälfte des 13. Jahrhunderts', *MIOG* lxxviii (1970) 308–22.

Stubbs, W., ed., *Memoriale fratris Walteri de Coventria*, 2 vols. RS lviii (1872–3).

Tangl, M., *Die päpstlichen Kanzleiordnungen von 1200–1500* (Innsbruck, 1894).

Tessier, G., 'Note sur un manuel à l'usage d'un officier de la cour pontificale (xiiiᵉ siècle)', *Études d'histoire du droit dédiées à Gabriel Le Bras* i (Paris, 1965).

Theiner, A., *Vetera monumenta Hibernorum et Scotorum historiam illustrantia* (Rome, 1864).

Bibliography

Theiner, A., ed., Caesar Cardinal Baronius, Odoricus Raynaldus and Jacobus Laderchius, *Annales ecclesiastici*, vol. xx (1198–1228) (Bar-le-Duc, 1870).

Tillmann, H., *Die päpstlichen Legaten in England bis zur Beendigung der Legation Gualas (1218)* (Bonn, 1926).

Pope Innocent III, trans. W. Sax (Amsterdam, New York, Oxford, 1980).

Timson, R. T., ed., *The cartulary of Blyth priory*, 2 vols. Thoroton Society xxvii–xxviii for 1968 & 1969, and HMC JP xvii (1973).

Tout, T. F., *Chapters in administrative history*, 6 vols. (Manchester, 1920–33).

'The household of the Chancery and its disintegration', *Essays in history presented to R. L. Poole*, ed. H. W. C. Davis (Oxford, 1927).

Ullmann, Walter, *The growth of papal government in the middle ages* (London, 1955).

von Heckel, R., 'Das Aufkommen der ständigen Prokuratoren an der päpstlichen Kurie im 13. Jahrhundert', Miscellanea Francesco Ehrle ii, *Studi e Testi* xxxviii (Rome, 1924) 290–321.

'Das päpstliche und sicilische Registerwesen', *Archiv für Urkundenforschung* i (Leipzig, 1908) 371–510; edits Guala's 'Libellus petitionum', 502–10.

'Studien über die Kanzleiordnung Innocenz' III', *Historisches Jahrbuch* lvii (1937) 258–89.

von Schulte, J. F., *Geschichte der Quellen und der Literatur des kanonischen Rechts von Gratian bis auf die Gegenwart*, 3 vols. (Stuttgart, 1875–80).

Waley, Daniel, *The papal state in the thirteenth century* (London, 1961).

Watkin, A., ed., *The great chartulary of Glastonbury*, 3 vols. Somerset Record Society lix, lxiii–lxiv (1947–52).

West, Francis, *The justiciarship in England 1066–1232* (Cambridge, 1966).

Wigram, S. R., ed., *The cartulary of the monastery of St Frideswide at Oxford*, 2 vols. Oxford Historical Society xxviii, xxxi (1895–6).

Winkelmann, E., 'Zwölf Papstbriefe zur Geschichte Friedrichs II und seiner Nachkommen', *Forschungen zur deutschen Geschichte* xv (Göttingen, 1875) 373–89.

INDEX

(1) The counties given are those used before the reorganization of 1974.
(2) Incipits are given under the opening letter, e.g. 'A nobis humiliter' under A.
(3) Abbreviations used (in addition to those on pp. xi–xii) are as follows:
abb. = abbot; abp = archbishop; a.l.c. = *auditor litterarum contradictarum*; archdcn = archdeacon; bp = bishop; c. = chapter; can(s). = canon(s); cath. = cathedral; cdnl (bp, dcn, pst) = cardinal (bishop, deacon, priest); ch. = church; chamb. = chamberlain; chanc. = chancellor; chapl. = chaplain; cl. = clerk; d. = dean; dcn = deacon; hosp. = hospital; knt = knight; Mag. = Magister, Master; not(s). = notary, notaries; pr. = prior; preb. = prebendary; proc(s). = proctor(s); pst = priest; subdcn = subdeacon; v.-c. = vice-chancellor

a, papal scribe, 204
'A nobis humiliter', 117–18, 255, 259
'A nobis vestra', 118
Aaron *see* Kent, Aaron of
abbeys, exempt (appointments to), 171
abbots: election of, 122; privileges of, 123
abbreviators (*breviatores*), 22, 29, 32–3, 46
Abingdon (Berks.), Ben. abbey, 52, 53, 57, 112, 115–16, 150, 157, 247; abb. of, 53, 113, 248
Achonry? (Architen'), bp of, 114
acta (court) *see* Lateran Council, Fourth, canons
'Ad hoc in annis', 169 n. 35
ad marks, 127–8
Adrian IV, pope (1154–9), register of, 66
Adrian V, pope (1276), 165
advocates, 20 and n. 26, 34
advowson, 141–2
aff, papal scribe, 204
Agde (France), 198
Alanus (Anglicus), canonist, 20; collection of, 134 n. 10, 135, 136 n. 16, *and see the following*
Alanus, preb. of London (? Alanus (Anglicus) the canonist), 178
Albenga, Jacobus de, 136
Albertinus, papal not., 30
Albertus, copyist of Urban V, 80
Alexander, 217
Alexander II, king of Scots, 60; Joan, wife of, 232

Alexander, Mag., 187
Alexander, papal scribe, *see* Montefiascone, Mag. Alexander of
Alexander III, pope (1159–81), 19, 50, 113; decretals of, 134, 137, 138, 144; register of, 66, 83
alms, free, 147
Alrewas (Staffs.), ch., 184
Alswick (Herts.), chapel, 213
'Altegnis', ch., 187 n. 130
Altisodoreus, Peter, emperor of Constantinople, 8
Alwalton (Hunts.), ch., 44, 187, 198
Anacletus II, anti-pope (1130–8), register of, 65
Anagni (Italy), bp of, *see* Pandulf, Mag.
Anagni, Mag. Bartholomeus of (b. a), papal scribe, 44, 197–8, 209, 228, 233
Anagni, Mag. Roffridus of, papal scribe, 206
Anastasius IV, pope (1153–4), register of, 66
'Ancxiatur in nobis', 171
Andreas, Mag. (and), papal scribe, preb. of Bourges, 44, 204
Antioch, patriarch of, *see* Ranerius, papal v.-c.
Antivari (Yugoslavia), abp of, 76
Antonius, papal scribe, 45
apographs *see contrabrevia*
apostolic see, absolution of, 239
appeals, 22, 119–20, 142, 151, 235

273

Index

Index

Beverley (Yorks. ER), 180
Bexley (Kent), ch., 212
Bicchieri, Cdnl Guala, see Guala
Binham (Norf.), Ben. priory, 113
Birinus, St, 40
bishops: appointments of, 175–7; archives
  of diocese, 54; legal enquiries from,
  159; petition for powers, 120, 155
bl, papal scribe, 198, 209, 244, 260
Blasius, papal not., 26 n. 53
Bliss, W. H., 117
Blois, count of, 36–7; proc. of, 36–7
Blois, William of, as bp of Lincoln, 103;
  as bp of Worcester, 177
bloodshed, 145, 155
Blundeville, Thomas de, bp of Norwich,
  177
Blyth (Notts.), St John, leper hosp., 58,
  100, 104, 106, 127, 257
bn., papal scribe, 204
Boamundus, scholar and can. of Asti (?
  bo, papal scribe), 198, 237
Bobo, papal scribe, 43, 204
Bobone, Giacinto, cdnl dcn of S. Maria
  in Cosmedin, see Celestine III
Bobone family, 2 n. 12
'Bobonis', Oddo, papal subdcn and
  chapl., 43, 188, 204
Bock, F., on registers, (in the Chamber)
  76, (hands of) 84; on registration, 67,
  68, 69, 71, 89–90
Bodham (Norf.), 103
boe, papal scribe, 198, 209, 223
Bologna (Italy), archdcn of, see Gratian;
  Tancred
Bologna (Italy), university of, 39, 40–1,
  134, 159
Bolognese, letters to, 148
Bonaventura, Romano, cdnl dcn of
  S. Angelo, 151, 259
Bonnelli, Blasius, scholar, 178
Bonomus, papal cl., 198
Bordeaux (France), abp of, see William
Boulogne, count of, see Reginald
Bourges (France) cath., preb. of, see
  Andreas, Mag.
Boyle, L. E., 51, 89, 133 n. 1, 136, 140
Brackley (Northants.), SS. James and
  John, Aug. hosp., pr of, 58, 73, 118,
  246
Braga (Portugal), abp of, 93
Bramham (Yorks. WR), ch., 68, 74, 120,
  211
Brand, can. of London (St Paul's), 172, 178

Brandus, proc., 251
Braughing (Herts.), ch., 63, 69, 73, 103,
  212, 215
Braybrooke, Henry de, 238
Breauté, Fawkes de, 40, 62, 63, 166, 177,
  238
Breauté, William, knt of, 56, 238
Bresslau, H., 20
Brewer, William, 99, 163, 166, 228,
  242
Bridekirk (Cumb.), ch., 180
Bridport, Mag. Giles of, bp of Salisbury,
  155
Bridport, Brother John of, 61–2
Britius, Mag., papal not., 181
Brixham (Devon), chapel, 106, 243
Brixia, Mag. Martinus de, 30
Broad Clyst (Devon), chapel, 106, 243
Broomfield (Essex), ch., 212
Broomholm (Norf.), Clun. priory, 52,
  103, 108
Bruges (Belgium) cath., can. of, see Città
  d'Antino, Mag. Iohannes of
building funds, 114–15
bulla, 47–8, 89–90, 125–6. See also die
bullatores (bullators), 17, 33, 47–8, 127,
  128
bulling, 19
Bullinghope (Heref.), lordship of, 218
Buoncambio, Giacomo, papal v.-c., 24
Burford (Oxon.), ch., 110, 249
Burgh, Hubert de, justiciar, 63, 64, 99,
  112, 170, 228, 242
Burton (Staffs.), Ben. abbey, 102; abb. of,
  212
Bury St Edmunds (Suff.), Ben. abbey, 52,
  57–8, 105, 253; oblations given to St
  Edmund, 105
Butley (Suff.), Aug. priory, 188
Byland (Yorks. NR), Cist. abbey, abb. of,
  119, 235
Bylaugh (or Belaugh, Norf.), 103
Bytham, Little (Lincs.), prebend of, 187
  n. 130, 207

Caddington (Beds.), ch., 172
Caister (Norf.), 112
Calixtus III, anti-pope (1168–78), 25
Cambrai (France) cath., can. of, see
  Scarsus, Mag. Nicolaus
Camera see Chamber
Canon Pyon (Heref.), 218
canonization processes, 53, 65
canonries, as scribal income, 44

275

Index

Canterbury, abp of, 54 n. 23, 150, 174, 188, 199, 240 *and see* Arundel, Thomas; Becket; Langton, Stephen; Walter, Hubert

Canterbury, abp of, faculty office of, 58

Canterbury (Kent), cath. priory (Ben.), 94–5, 114, 150, 217; St Augustine's, Ben. abbey, 110, 147, (abb. of) 150, (procs. of) 150; St Laurence hosp., 106

Cantilupe, William de, 63

Cantini, J.-A., 41

Capocci, Pietro, 5, 188; Raniero, cdnl dcn of S. Maria in Cosmedin, 5, 62, 198

Capocci family, 5

Capua, Thomas of, cdnl pst of S. Sabina and papal chanc., 5, 24, 25, 96, 98 n. 16

cardinals: chanceries of, 43; increase in number of, 3; payment of pensions to, 62; subscriptions of, 45

'Carissimus in christo', 216–17, 231, 233–4

Carlisle, bp of, *see* Hugh; election and see of, 60, 170, 175, 214

Carlisle, cath. priory (Aug.), cans. of, 60, 63, 68, 175, 214

Carmelites, 8

Caroline miniscule, 28

Carthusians, 124

Casamari (Italy), 9

Cashel, archbishopric of, 70, 72, 250

Cashel, elect of, 23 n. 37

Castello, Opizo de, 188

castles, royal, 54, 62, 64, 72, 169–70, 223; in Ireland, 258; and lordships, 222

'Casus Parisiensis', glossator, 156 n. 119

cathedrals, English secular, archives of, 54

Celestine III, pope (1191–8) (Giacinto Bobone), 2–4, 11, 25, 48, 104, 124; as Cdnl Giacinto, 2, 10, 48; decretals of, 135, 137

cells, serving of, 143

Cencio Savelli *see* Honorius III

censures, ecclesiastical, 170, 171

census (tribute), 61, 163, 164–5, 168

Chamber, papal, 15–16, 30, 48–9, 76–7; chamberlain of, 48 *and see* Pandulf; Sinibaldus; clerk of, 76, *and see* Brixia; Rofio

Chamber, papal, unification with Chancery, 16

chanceries, episcopal, 68 n. 103

Chancery, English royal, 28, 45, 60, 74 n. 139, 77; archives of, 54–6, 57, keeper of papal documents *see* St Denis, John

of; bishops from, 176–7; chancellorship, 27; and Exchequer, 48; registration from draft, 68 n. 103; Roman rolls, 60; royal style, 98–9

Chancery, Imperial Roman, 65

Chancery, papal, 15–49, 96–8, 101, 208–9; number of scribes in, 51–2; ordinance ('Institutio'), 18, 19–21, 32, 33, 34–5, 45, 47, 49; records of, 76–7, 138. *See also audientia litterarum contradictarum; audientia publica; data communis;* formularies

Chancery, papal, chancellors, *see* Capua, Thomas of; Egidio; Gaeta; Giovanni, cdnl dcn of S. Maria in Cosmedin; Giovanni, cdnl dcn of S. Maria in Via Lata; Honorius III; Morra. *See also* vice-chancellors

Chancery, papal, chancellorship, suppression of, 26

chapel, papal, 16–17, 44

Charminster, prebend of Salisbury, 179

Chartres, bp of, *see* Salisbury, John of

Chauz, Matilda de, 102

Cheney, C. R., 127, 138, 159

Chesney, Robert, bp of Lincoln, 110

Chester, earl of, *see* Ranulf

Chesterton (Cambs.), ch., 183

Chichester, bp of, *see* Neville; Poore, Richard; Stigand; Wareham

Chichester, bp and c. of, 110

Chichester (Sussex) cath., c. of, 178; can. of, 185 n. 118; treasurer of (P.?), 185

Chisenbury (Martin) and Chute, prebend of Salisbury, 179; preb. of, *see* Summa; W. archpriest of Milan

Chislet (Kent), ch., 110

Chiswick, prebend of London (St Paul's), 178; preb. of, *see* Alanus

Cigogny, Engelard de, 63

Cinthius, cdnl pst of S. Lorenzo in Lucina, 16 n. 7

Cirencester (Glos.), Aug. abbey, 121

Cironius, 133 n. 1

Cistercians, 9, 57, 109, 114, 116, 156–7, 232

Cîteaux, abb. of, *see* Urach

Città d'Antino, Mag. Iohannes of, papal scribe, can. of Bruges, 44, 205; Mag. Petrus of (p.), papal scribe, can. of Douai, 44, 200–1, 249

Clattercote (Oxon.), leper hosp., 58, 110, 223

276

Index

Clement III, pope (1187–91) (Paolo Scolari), 2, 3, 10, 11; decretals of, 135, 137

Clement V, pope (1305–14), 165

clergy: absent for study, 142–3; bigamous, 155; dress and tonsure, 151; married (sons succeeding to benefices), 146, 149, 173; non-resident, 145; suspension of, 181

clerks, provision of, 117

co, papal scribe, *see* Constantinus, Mag.

Cognac (France), castle of, 232

Colchester (Essex), Ben. abbey, 151; St Botolph, Aug. priory, 57 n. 44, 120, 226

Collectio Romana, 134, 137

Collemedio, Mag. Petrus de, 178, 180, 186

Collivaccinus, Peter, of Benevento, 134, 137, 158

Cologne (Germany) cath., abp of, 206; can. of, *see* R., Mag.

Colonna, Giovanni, preb. of Ripon, 178 n. 86

Colonna family, 5 n. 28

Colyton (Devon), ch., 102, 229

Comite, Ugo de, 188

communis audientia see *audientia publica*

communis data see *data communis*

Como (Italy) cath., c. of, 199; cans. of, *see* Como, Mag. Scambio of; Egidius, Mag.

Como, Mag. Scambio of, can. of Como, bp of Viterbo, 42, 44, 46; as papal scribe, 202, 206, 210, 219, 226, 235, 245

Compilatio Prima, 134, 137

Compilatio Quarta, 134, 153, 158, 160

Compilatio Quinta, 9, 45, 67, 75, 90, 133–41, 142–52, 154

Compilatio Secunda, 135–6, 137

Compilatio Tertia, 134–6, 137, 158, 160, 161

Compostella, Bernard of, 134, 136 n. 16, 137

Compton (Sussex), ch., 189

concubines (of clergy), 145

Conisbrough (Yorks. WR), vicarage, 177 n. 76

Constantinople, legation to, 30

Constantinus, Mag. (co), papal scribe, 44, 187, 198, 221

Conti, Adenulfus, preb. of York, 178 n. 78; Giovanni, cdnl dcn of S. Maria in Cosmedin, papal chanc., preb. of

York, 177; Giovanni, vicar of Conisbrough, 177 n. 76; Ugolino, *see* Gregory IX

Conti family, 1, 177, 179

'Contingit interdum quod', 116, 157

contrabrevia (apographs), 89–90

Cork (Ireland), bp of, 70, *and see* Marianus

Cormeilles, Richard of, 218

Cornhill, Reginald de, 104

Cornhill, William of, bp of Coventry, 176

Cornwall, Edmund earl of, 122; Richard earl of, 56, 191, 259

coronation (English), oath, 165 n. 16; regalia, 168

Corrado, can. and proc. of Ivrea, 188

Corrado, cl. of cdnl dcn of S. Teodoro, 185

correctors, papal, 17, 36, 46–7; correction by, 126–7

costs: of appeal, 238; in case, 37, 120, 151; of papal administration, 74

courts, English royal, 141–2, 155, 230; justices of, 141, 147, 230, 238

Coventry (and Lichfield), bp of, *see* Cornhill, William of; Stavensby; election of, 173

Coventry (Warw.), cath. priory (Ben.), 53; hosp. of St John, 53

Cowick (Devon), Ben. priory, pr. of, *see* William

Cozo (Goz), papal scribe, 46, 198, 255

Craucumbe, Godfrey de, 61, 73, 245

Crescenzi family, 1 n. 1

Cressy, William (I) de, 106, 257

Cropredy, prebend of Lincoln, 178, 184; preb. of, *see* Vercelli, Rufino of

Crowland (Lincs.), Ben. abbey, 173

Crown, pensions from, 184

Croxton (Leics.), Prem. abbey, 151

crusade, fifth, 10, 12, 236

crusaders, 237

crusading vow, 167

'Cum a nobis', 100, 104–9, 112, 122, 213, 218, 227, 243, 251, 253, 257

'Cum a religiosorum', 239

'Cum abbates Cisterciensis', 116, 157

'Cum aliquando cogente', 116, 233

'Cum carissimo in', 229

'Cum castra quedam', 258

'Cum gravi infirmitate', 166

'Cum Iohannes presbiter', 251

'Cum olim venerabilis', 250

277

Index

'Cum omnipotens deus', 114
'Cum preter rerum', 118
'Cum propter cognitiones', 118
'Cum propter rerum', 118, 246
'Cum sicut exhibita', 118
'Cum sit nonsolum', 237
curia (papal), finances of, 47, 189–90,
    191; income of in late twelfth century,
    3; movements of, 86–8
cursus, 28, 63, 96–7, 123

d (?), papal scribe, 199, 237
Dale (Derbs.), Prem. abbey, 57, 251
Dalton le Dale (co. Durham), ch., 105
Damasus, glossator, 156 n. 119, 157
    n. 127
Damietta (Jordan), captured by
    Christians, 8
Darley (Derbs.), Aug. abbey, abb. of, 212
data communis (or *communis data* or *recepta
    communis*), 32, 34, 36, 47
Dax (France), bp of, 254
Dearham (Cumb.), ch., 180
decretal collections: 133–52; official *see*
    Compilatio Quinta; *Compilatio Tertia*;
    unofficial (or private) *see Compilatio
    Prima*; *Compilatio Quarta*; *Compilatio
    Secunda*
Decretales (Gregoriana, Liber Extra), 75,
    136, 137–8, 145, 148, 150, 151, 152,
    153, 159, 160–1
Decretum, 138, 144
Deerhurst (Glos.), Ben. priory, 122
Delisle, L., 32 and n. 86, 42, 48
demi-bulla, 126. *See also bulla*
Denholm-Young, N., 63
Denis, St, 10
Dens, William, 155
Depedale (Derbs.), 251
deprivations (of clergy), 171–2, 173
Derby, archdcn of, 212; earl of, *see*
    Ferrers
Derby (Derbs.), St Mary de Pratis, Ben.
    priory, 115
'Devotionis tue precibus', 118
dictamen, 97
dictatores, 28–9, 97, 100
die, false, 124, 125
Diekamp, W., 127
'Dilecti filii . . prior', 215, 246–7
'Dilectorum filiorum . . prioris', 234
Dinmore (Heref.), chapel, 218
dispensation, 44, 154–6, 173, 206, *and see*
    indults

distributor, 32, 47
documents: engrossment of, 17, 18;
    produced or cited, 102, 106–9;
    publicizing of, 94–6; taxation of, 17, 47
Domesday, Larger, 90
Dominicans, 8
donations, collection of, 95, 114
Donnington (Heref.), 218
Dorchester (Oxon.), Aug. abbey, 40; abb.
    and pr. of, 120, 238
Dore (Heref.), Cist. abbey, 58, 109, 220
Dore (Heref.), river, 109, 220
Douai (France) cath., can. of, *see* Cività
    d'Antino, Mag. Petrus of
Dover (Kent), Ben. priory, 114
dowry, 152, 232
drafts, 46; registration from, 67, 68 and
    n. 103, 89
Dublin, abp of, 170, 214, 251, 258, *and see*
    London, Henry of
Dundrennan (Scotland), St Mary's, Cist.
    abbey, 151
Dunnington (Yorks. ER), ch. and
    prebend of, 141, 230
Dunstable (Beds.), Aug. priory, pr. of,
    252
Dunster (Som.), Ben. priory, 112
duplicates (and copies) of papal letters,
    108
Durand, papal nuncio, 173
Durham, bp of, 106, 112, 184, 221, *and
    see* Marsh; (election of) 59, 73, 120,
    260, (*le convenit*) 59
Durham cath. priory (Ben.), c. of, 59,
    112; cult of St Cuthbert at, 180; as
    litigants, 123, 142, 235, 260; papal
    letters for, 57, 73, 105, 106, 108, 119,
    120, 128, (indults) 117, 244; parishes of,
    105; possessions of, 143, 234; pr. of, *see*
    Melsanby; procs. of, 127
Durham, St Nicholas ch., 149
'Duris nobis rumoribus', 63 n. 79, 167

'Ea que iudicio', 95, 113, 248
Earl Stoke (Wilts.), chapel, 106
Easby (Yorks. NR), St Agatha's Prem.
    abbey, 105, 113, 158; abb. of, 235
Ecclesfield (Yorks. WR), ch., 184
Ecton (Eketon), Mag. Stephen of, 59,
    155, 255
Edlesborough (Bucks.), ch., 173
Edmund, son of Henry III, 191
Edward I (1272–1307), 165
Edward II (1307–27), 165

278

Index

Edward III (1327–77), 165
Edward the Confessor, cult of, 190
eg, papal scribe, *see* Egidius, Mag.
Eggleton (Heref.), 218
Egidio, cdnl dcn of S. Niccolò in Carcere, papal chanc., 15
Egidio, papal subdcn and chapl., 62
Egidius, *frater, bullator* under Innocent IV, 47
Egidius, Mag. (eg), papal scribe, can. of Como, 44, 199, 246, 248
elections, 64; use of lots in, 9
Ellingham (Northumb.), ch., 103
Ellis (Hlys) (or Willelmus), 127–8, 243
Ely, bp of, 107, 123, 136, 183, *and see* Fountains; Hervey; Nigel; see of, 176–7
Ely, bp elect of, *see* York, Robert of
Ely (Cambs.) cath. priory (Ben.), 103, 111 n. 105; pr. of, 118 n. 147
Ely, diocese, rural ds. of, 117
Elze, R., 16, 44, 76
Embleton (co. Durham), I. rector of, 142, 235
England, French invasion of, 8, 12, 167, 170; kingdom of, 162; number of benefices in, 187; war in, 228
engrossments (engrossing), 33, 46, 47–8, 90, 127; payment for, 68
envoys, 59–60
Erfurt (E. Germany), chronicle of, 9
Essex, archdcn of, 215, *and see* Valognes
Essex, earl of, *see* fitzPeter
'Etsi appetenda sit', 228
'Etsi beneficiorum collatio', 240–1, 242
Eugenius III, pope (1145–53), 114; register of, 66, 75, 76
Evesham (Worcs.), Ben. abbey, abb. of, *see* Norreis
Evesham, Silvester of, bp of Worcester, 166, 168, 176
'Ex litteris abbatis', 53
'Ex parte..abbatis', 225
'Ex parte..prioris', 235
'Ex parte tua', 117, 118
'Ex parte vestra', 117, 150
'Ex relatione Willelmi', 238
Exchequer, English royal, 48; archives of, 57, (of court of Augmentations) 57, 58; bishops from, 177
excommunicates, 98
excommunication, 125, 171–2, 174, 239, 259
executors, papal, negligent, 22

Exeter, bp of, 188, *and see* Apulia; Henry (Marshal)
Exeter, bp and cath., archives of, 54, 58
Exeter (Devon) cath., c. of, 102, 229; preb. of, *see* Vercelli, Rufino of
Exminster (Devon), ch., 187
expedition marks (*expeditionsvermerke*), 46, 128
expenses (in case) *see* costs
'Exspectavimus', 147, 154
extravagantes, 138, 141, 145, 147, 159

Fairbank, Alfred, 90
Fauconberg, Eustace de, bp of London, 177
Fawtier, R., 51
fees (of proctors), 35
Felixkirk (Yorks. NR), ch., 188, 204
Ferentino, Pietro of, preb. of York, 177; Stefano of, 185–6
Ferrers, William de, earl of Derby, 163, 166
'Fidelitatis vinculum quo', 254
Fieschi, Mag. Sinibaldus, *see* Innocent IV
Filippo, bp of Viterbo, 9
Filippo, Mag., envoy, 62
Filippo, nephew of Guala, 184
Fishburn (co. Durham), ch., 186
fitzGerold, Warin, 163
Fitzherbert, Herbert, 146; William *see* York, St William of
fitzHerbert, Peter, 163
fitzPeter, Geoffrey, earl of Essex, 162
Flora, abbess, 121
Floretus, copyist of Urban V, 80
Foliot, Gilbert, bp of London, 114
Fordington and Writhlington, prebend of Salisbury, 179; preb. of, *see* Sancto Nicholao
forgery, 19, 74, 93, 97, 102, 122–5
formularies, 22–3, 99, 104, 108, 109, 111–12, 113, 114
formulary of Guala *see* Guala
Fortis, Mag., papal not., 30
Fossanova, Stefano of, cdnl pst of the basilica of SS. XII Apostoli, preb. of York, 174 n. 60, 177, 180, 185, 188
Fountains, John of, abb. of Fountains, bp of Ely, 177
France, king of, 62, *and see* Philip Augustus; Philip the Fair
Franciscans, 8
Fratte, Mag. Benedictus of (b. f.), papal scribe, can. of S. Severina, Calabria, 42, 44, 198, 222

Index

fraud, 20, 32
Frederick II, emperor, coronation of, 8, 12; crusade of, 69, 236; letters to and from pope, 72, 93, 148; in pope's *tutela*, 16 n. 7
'Frequens sicut intelleximus', 240
Friars, 45, 114
Furness (Lancs.), Cist. abbey, 164

g (?), papal scribe, 98, 199, 251
G., papal scribe, 31–2, 204
G R, papal scribe, 204
G. V., papal scribe, 204
Gaeta, John of, papal chanc. (later Pope Gelasius II), 96
Gaetani, Aldebrandino, cdnl dcn of S. Eustachio, 177–8
Garrard, Robert, 222
'Gaudemus in domino', 61, 97, 100, 169, 245
Gayton le Marsh (Lincs.), 172
Gelasius I, pope (492–6), 65
Gelasius II, pope (1118–19), register of, 66, *and see* Gaeta
Gentilis, Mag., papal scribe, can. of Mileto, 44, 205
Gerona (Spain), bp of, proc. of, 205
Giacomo, legate to Ireland, 149
Gibwin, Geoffrey, 187
Gilbert, bp of Ardfert, 251
Gilbertus, canonist, collection of, 135
Gimundo, cl., preb. of York, 177–8
Giovanni, cdnl dcn of S. Maria in Cosmedin, papal chanc., 25
Giovanni, cdnl dcn of S. Maria in Via Lata, papal chanc., 25
Giusti, M., 77
Glanville, Ranulf, 103
Glanville, W. de, 103
Glastonbury (Som.) Ben. abbey, abb. of, 123; benefices of, 179; papal letters for, 52, 105, 106, 117 and n. 145; pr. and convent of, 103; proc. of, *see* Summa
Glastonbury, St John's ch., 106
Gloucester, archdcn of, R. proc. of, 123
Gloucester, St Oswald's, Aug. priory, 122; St Peter's, Ben. abbey, 168
Godard, penitentiary of York, 234
Goz, papal scribe, *see* Cozo
Gratian, Mag., archdcn of Bologna, 139
Gratian, Mag., papal chapl., 188
Gratiosus, subdcn, 121
Gray, John de, bp of Norwich, 162
Gray, Walter, abp of York, 145–6, 159,

183, 198; and canonization of St William, 180; from Chancery, 177; register of, 54; translated from Worcester, 175, 176
Gregoriana see *Decretales*
Gregorii, Petrus (p. g.), papal scribe, 45, 128, 201, 241, 243
Gregorio, cdnl dcn, 202
Gregory I, the Great, pope (590–604), 65, 121
Gregory VII, pope (1073–85), communications of, 50; letters of, 96, 102; register of, 66, 75, 84 n. 161, 161 n. 140; registration under, 67
Gregory VIII, pope (1118–21), 25, *and see* Morra
Gregory IX, pope (1227–41) (Ugolino Conti), as cdnl, 6–7, 40, 63, (nephews of) 189 n. 145; as pope, 84, 117, 120, 126, 189; *hostiarius* of, *see* Capocci, Pietro. *See also Decretales*
Gregory X, pope (1272–6), 165
Guala (Bicchieri), cdnl pst of S. Martino, legate to England, action on death of John, 167–9; absent from Innocent III's funeral, 7; and Carlisle affair, 60, 175; correspondence of and to, 55, 57, 63–4, 104, 199, 214; deprivations by, 188; dispensations by, 44, 155, 187; disposal of bishoprics by, 176, 177; exacts procurations, 182; executor of King John, 166; forbids king's justices to proceed, 141, 230; formulary (*libellus*) of, 21–2, 23, 32, 34; household of as legate, 42, 182–5, 207; influence on English clerical appointments, 179–81, 186, 187; licences granted by, 79 n. 108, 102–3, 215; makes peace with Scots, 170; nephews of, 184; powers of, 171–3; and Reading case, 107; reports on removal of Salisbury cathedral, 180; sequestrates churches, 182; staying at Viterbo, 62; style of address of, 99; visits England in 1216, 171; will of, 30, 40; withdraws, 174, 189
Guala, nephew of the legate Guala, 184
Guarcino, Petrus of, papal scribe, 201
Guido, Mag., papal chapl. and not., 30, 31–2
Guilden Morden (Cambs.), ch., 188
Guillelmus, papal scribe, 31–2
Guisborough (Yorks. NR), Aug. priory, 53, 180–1; prs. of, 180

280

Index

'In eminenti sedis', 121
inducie deliberatorie, 144, 150
indulgences, 22, 32, 94, 100, 114–15
indults, 22, 73–4, 115–18, 150, 155–6, 158. *See also* dispensation
Innocent II, pope (1130–43), 109
Innocent III, pope (1198–1216) (Lothario dei Conti di Segni), archivist of, 76; and chancery organization, 15–20, 25, 26–7; death of, 6–7; decretals and decretal collections, 134, 136–7, 138, 144–5, 158, 160; dream of, 11; on forgery, 97, 122, 125; forms of documents under, 104 n. 60, 109, 114, 120; *Gesta* of, 17, 49; nephew of, *see* Normandis; notaries under, 30–2; number of letters issued by, 50; policy to England, 167; on procurations to legates, 182; provisions under, 177–80, 184; registers of, 67, 83–4 and n. 157, 90, (used by canonists) 134, 138 n. 22, 161; and submission of John, 162–3; work at S. Paolo, 6
Innocent IV, pope (1243–54) (Sinibaldus Fieschi), as can. of Parma, a.l.c. and v.-c., 24, 26, 30 n. 78, 38, 40–1; legal training of, 40
Innocent IV as pope, Chancery of, 42, 51; forms of documents under, 119, 122, 143, 145 n. 58
Innocent V, pope (1276), 165
Innocentibus, Gilbert de, 173
Insula, G. de, papal subdcn and chapl., 187
'Intelleximus ex relatione', 61, 232
interdict, sentences of, 54, 122, 171, 239
Iohannes, *bullator*, 47
Iohannes de h(b?).y..., proc., 227
Iohannes 'Leonis', 30
Iohannes of Città d'Antino *see* Città d'Antino
Iord', papal scribe, 200, 218, 225, 231
Ireland, kingdom of, 162, 170
Irishmen, oaths of, 149
Irthlingborough (Northants.), parson of, 113
Isabella, Queen, *see* Lusignan
Isles, king of the, *see* Reginald; kingdom of, *see* Man
Italians in English cathedrals, 177–80
itinerary of Honorius III *see* curia, movements of
Iudice, Giacomo de, 189 n. 145
'Iustus dominus in', 97, 236

'Iustis petentium desideriis', 100, 110–13, 219, 221, 255

J., nephew of Guala, 184
Jaime I, king of Aragon, 164
Jarrow (co. Durham), Ben. priory, 102
Jerusalem, 11
Jews, 98
Joan, sister of Henry III, 61, 152, 232
John, bp of Ardfert, 251
John, king of England (1199–1216), approves election at Cork, 250; death of, 8, 166–7; gifts and grants of, 103, 104, 106, 109, 113, 218, 220, 240, 242; gives kingdom to pope, 162–6, 171, 174; letter to pope, 60, 166; retains cdnls at curia, 62; treaty with Scots, 170, 216
John VIII, pope (872–82), register of, 65
John XXI, pope (1276–7), 165
Jordan, cl. of Durham diocese, 149–50
Joyce, chapl., 172
judges delegate, papal, application for and appointment of, 21 and n. 30, 32, 37–8; exemptions from service, 117; negligent and suspect, 22, 32, 36–7

Kauz, G. de, 155
Kegworth (Lincs.), ch., 173
Kempf, F., 76, 84, 90
Kent, Aaron of, 105, 154
Kersey (Suff.), Aug. hosp., 112
Kettering (Northants.), ch., 188
Keynsham (Som.), Aug. abbey, 57–8, 110, 249
Kilburn (Middx.), Ben. priory, 112
Kingsteignton (Devon), prebend of, 110
Kirk Ella (Yorks. ER), 178 n. 83
Knowles, D., 53
Kuttner, S. G., 134 n. 2, 135, 138, 144, 159
Kyme, S. de, son of Philip, 111

l (?), papal scribe, 200, 209, 236
La Grâce-Dieu (France), abb. of, 231
La Marche, count of, *see* Lusignan
La Rochelle (France), 231
Lacy, Walter, 166
Lambeth (Surrey), ch., 104, 172, 188
Lang, J., 153
Langley (Norf.), Prem. abbey, abb. of, 226
Langtoft, prebend of York, 177; preb. of, *see* Conti, Giovanni; Odelini

Index

littere legende, 27
Littlemore (Oxon.), Ben. priory, 53, 58, 95, 113, 248
liturgical celebrations, 86 n. 163
Llanthony (Mon.), Aug. priory, cans. of, 218
Llewellyn, prince of North Wales, 55, 99, 170, 239
Lodève (France), archdcn of, *see* Raimundus, Mag.
London, archdcn of, 246
London, bp of, 214, *and see* Fauconberg; Foliot; Sainte-Mère-Église
London cath. (St Paul's), building fund, 114; c. of, 177, 178, 180; cans. of, *see* Brand; Howbridge; chanc. of, 246, *and see* Howbridge; d. of, 246, 254; prebends of, 178
London, churches, All Hallows next the wall, ch., 212; St Botolph without Aldgate, ch., 212; St Michael's Aldgate, ch., 213
London, religious houses, Holy Trinity Aldgate, Aug. priory, archives of, 57; as litigants, 226, 246, 254; obedience to St Botolph's Colchester, 120, 226; papal letters for, 63, 68–9, 73, 102, 105, 112, 212, 215; pr. of, 73, 118, 255; procs. of, 59, 213, 216; St Bartholomew's hosp., 115; St Katherine (on Thames) hosp., 213
London, St Martin le Grand, secular college, d. and c. of, 58, 109–10, 224
London, Temple, 56, 57
London, Henry of, abp of Dublin, 162; John of, 43, 185
Longespée, William, earl of Salisbury, 162
Louis, prince of France (later Louis VIII), 61, 167, 170, 182
Luca, son of Pietro de Iudice, 189
Lucca (Italy), St Fridianus, 197; pr. of, 148, *and see* Ranerius
Lucius II, pope (1144–5), 66, 111
Lucius III, pope (1181–5), 66, 104
Lucy, Mag. Stephen de, 61, 73, 155, 245
Luke, dcn, not. of the abp of Rheims, 29 n. 70
Lusignan, Geoffrey de, 68, 69, 254
Lusignan, Hugh de, count of La Marche, 68, 69, 72, 233; and Isabella, his wife, 61, 99, 152, 232
Lusignans, 171
Luton, rural d. of, 252

Lyme and Halstock, prebend of Salisbury, 179; preb. of, *see* Normandis

m, papal scribe, 205
m. p., papal scribe, 205
Madley (Heref.), ch., 218
Magna Carta, 163, 169
Mainz, abp of, *see* Siegfried
Major Pars Altaris, prebend of Salisbury, 179; preb. of, *see* Sinebaldus
Malclerc, W., can. of Southwell, 111
Malvern, Great (Worcs.), Ben. priory, 102
Man (the Isles), king of, *see* Reginald; kingdom of, 152, 164
mandates, papal (*littere cum filo canapis*), 52, 58, 143, 210; clauses of, 37–8, 119, 144, ('et quidam alii') 246, 252; forms, 118–20; legal points in, 145, 148; petition for in formularies, 21, 118; petition to pope for execution, 32; rarely registered, 143, 145; read in *audientia publica*, 18–19, 27, 36–7; wording of, 99
Mandeville, Geoffrey de, 104
Mapenor, Hugh de, d. and bp of Hereford, 176
Marcus, Mag. Petrus, 46, 47
Marden (Heref.), ch., 218
Mare, Richard de, 106
Marianus, bp of Cork and abp of Cashel, 70, 250
Marlborough, Thomas of, 18
marriage case, 120, 238
Marseilles (France) cath., can. of, *see* R., Mag.
Marsh, Richard, royal chanc. and bp of Durham, 111, 113, 123, 176
Martin, steward of Pandulf, 185
Martino, nephew of Guala, 184
Mauléon, Savaric de, 104, 166
Maximus, Mag., papal subdcn and not., 30, 31
Mayfield (Staffs.), St John's ch., 105
Meldreth (Cambs.), ch., 111 n. 105
Melksham (Wilts.), ch., 106
Melsanby, Thomas, pr. of Durham, 59
Merlai, A. de, wife of W. Talbot, 238
Merpins (France), castle of, 232
Merton (Surrey), Aug. priory, pr. of, 215
messengers *see* nuntii
Metz (France) cath., c. of, 45, 200; can. of, *see* Otto, Mag.; d. and master of schools of, 38, prebend of, 200

Index

Mileto (Calabria) cath., can. of, *see* Gentilis
minutes (*notae*), 29, 32, 36, 47, 90, 118
Miranda (Spain), *prestimonium* of, 206
monitoria (letters of warning), 32
Monk Wearmouth (co. Durham), Ben. priory, 102
Monmouth, John of, 166
monogram, papal, *see* privileges
Monte Cassino (Italy), 26
Montefiascone, Mag. Alexander of, papal scribe, 45, 197, 209, 212, 231
Montfichet, R. de, knt, 119, 246
Montfort, Simon de, 164; chanc. of, *see* Marcus
Moray (Scotland), bp of, 114
Moris, Roger de, cl., 56, 120, 252
Morra, Albert of, papal chanc. (later Pope Gregory VIII), 96
Moyses, papal chapl., 20
Mundham (Sussex), vicar of, *see* Dens
muniments (public), 142
Murray, Alexander, 50 and n. 1, 65

n (?), papal scribe, 200, 217
N., proc., 255
n. f., papal scribe, 200, 254
Nettleton (Lincs.), ch., 185
'Neuhay', 111
Nevill, Geoffrey de, 63
Neville, Ralph, royal v.-c. and bp of Chichester, 64, 169, 177, 178
Newbald, North, prebend of York, 177; preb. of, *see* Ferentino, Pietro of; Fossanova
Newbattle (Scotland), St Mary's, Cist. abbey, 116
Newburgh (Yorks. NR), Aug. priory, cans. of, 145; pr. of, 119, 235
Newnham (Beds.), Aug. priory, 57, 105, 227
Newstead (Notts.), Aug. priory, 151
Niccolò, cdnl bp of Tusculum, 163
Nicholas, knt, 151
Nicholas (Nyc', Nycol'), proc., 213, 216
Nicholas III, pope (1277–80), 105
Nicholas IV, pope (1288–92), 165; *Taxatio* of, 187
Nicolaus, 127, 231
Nigel, bp of Ely, 103
Noleti, Iohannes, 81
'Non absque dolore', 120
non-residence, 155, 205

Normandis, Stefano de (dei Conti), cdnl dcn of S. Adriano, preb. of Lincoln, Salisbury and York, influence at curia, 180; pension of, 55, 63, 240, 242; as preb., 177, 178, 179; proc. of, 127
Norreis, Roger, 181
Norton Canon (Heref.), 218
Norwich, bp of, *see* Blundeville; Gray, John de; Pandulf (Masca)
Norwich (Norf.) cath. priory (Ben.), pr. of, 226
Norwich, rural d. of, 226
Nostell (Yorks. WR), St Oswald's, Aug. priory, papal letters for, 53, 57, 68, 73, 74, (Bamburgh ch.) 113, (Bramham ch.) 68, 120, 211; as patrons, 146, 188
notae see minutes
notaries, papal, 28–33; as archivists, 76; in *audientia publica*, 36; in Chamber, 30; in chancery 'ordinance', 20; early, 65; *primicerius notarius*, 76; as *registratores*, 84; supervise drafts, 46; treatises of, 96; and v.-c.s, 26, 27
Notley (Essex), ch., 212
novel disseisin, 238
nuncios, papal, 43
nuns, enclosed, 114; and simony, 145
nuntii (messengers), 59, 114, 128
Nüske, G., 42

o (?), papal scribe, 200, 234
Oakley (Bucks.), ch., 110
Obizo, bp of Parma, 41
Obizo, Mag., papal subdcn and not., 30
'Oblata nobis..prioris', 211
Ockbrook (Derbs.), 251
Odelini, Leonardo, preb. of York, 177
Ogbourne, prebend of Salisbury, 179
Oléron (France), isle of, 152
oral communication, 50, 59, 62, 66
oral delivery, 94–8
ordeal, 9
orders, petition for, 145
Ordo Romanus XII, 7
Ormsby, North (Lincs.), Gilb. priory, 173
Orsini family, 1, 2 n. 12, 4
Oseney (Oxon.), Aug. abbey, 53, 57, 58, 95, 113, 119, 142, 225, 248
Otto, Mag., papal scribe, can. of Metz and of St Peter's, 44, 45, 143, 200, 208, 209, 213, 227
Otto, Mag., papal subdcn, chapl. and a.l.c., *see* Tonengo
Oxford, d. of, 119, 142, 225

Index

Index

Salisbury, earl of, *see* Longespée
Salisbury, John of, bp of Chartres, 66
Sancto Albino, Mag. William de, 61
Sancto Eustachio, Cinthio de (the Roman), preb. of London, 178
Sancto Germano, Mag. Iohannes de, papal not. and proc., 33 n. 93; Mag. Willelmus de, papal scribe, chapl. and preb. of Arrouaise, 42, 44, 207
Sancto Nicholao, Mag. Laurentius de, papal subdcn, chapl., can. of Lincoln, preb. of Salisbury and of York, 178, 179, 180, 182–3, 184 n. 115
'Sapientia', 147
Sarracenus, John, 149; Peter, 111
'Satis ut accepimus', 120
Savelli, Cencio, *see* Honorius III; Giacomo, *see* Honorius IV; Haimericus, 1; Luca, brother of Honorius III, 5; Luca, senator, 4–5; Pandulf, 4; Perna, 4; Pietro, 4 n. 22
Savelli estates, 1, 4–5
Savelli family, 1, 4, 5 and n. 25
Sawston, Benedict of, bp of Rochester, 176
Say, William, 250
Scambio, Mag., of Como, *see* Como
Scarsus, Mag. Nicolaus (n. s.), papal scribe, can. of Cambrai, 44, 205
Scolari, Paolo *see* Clement III
Scot, Mag. William, archdcn of Worcester, bp elect of Durham, 73, 120, 260
Scots, 169, 170, 175
Scots, king of, 214; chanc. of, 170 n. 42; composition with English king, 64, *and see* Alexander II; William I
scribes, episcopal, 16
scribes, papal, 41–6, 197–207, 208–11; abbreviators appointed from, 33; calligraphy of, 118; in Chamber, 30, college, 16–18, 19, 49; copy for Tancred, 89, 91; and correction, 46; hands of, 208–9; number of, 51–2; output of, 50–2; punctuation by, 96; rewards for, 44–5; *sigla* of, 17, 44, (individual) 197–209, 211–61
scribes, royal, 16
scriniarii (archivists), 28, 76, *and see* Iohannes 'Leonis'; Ricardus
Se, B., papal scribe, 47 n. 158
Séez (Sagio), Simon of, 172
Segni, Lothario dei Conti di, *see* Innocent III

Selby (Yorks. WR), Ben. abbey, 178 n. 83
Selling (Kent), ch., 110
Senlis (France), d. of, 36–7
Set, P., papal scribe, 45
Sevenoaks (Kent), chapel of St Nicholas, 105, 154
Sexto, Guido de, 38
Shaftesbury (Dors.), St Edward's, Ben. abbey, 64, 110, 181
Shelford (Notts.), Aug. priory, 102
Shifnal (Salop), ch., 184
Shipley (Sussex), 110
Shrewsbury, St Alkmund's ch., 105, 122
Shrewsbury, Robert of, bp of Bangor, 114
Siegfried, abp of Mainz, 163
Siena, Bandinus of, 47
'Significantibus..priore ac', 260
Silano, G., 136
Simon, 127, 243
simony, ruling on, 145
Simplicius, pope (468–83), 65
'Sincere fidei et', 62
Sinebaldus, Reginaldo, preb. of Salisbury, 179
Sinibaldus, papal chamb., can. of S. Maria Maggiore, 2, 30, 174, 187
Sinibaldus (Fieschi) *see* Innocent IV
'Solet annuere sedes', 100, 109–10, 112, 121, 220, 223, 224, 249
souls, care of, 154. See also benefices
Southampton, Peter of, cl., 173
Southwell, prebend of, 111; can. of, *see* Malclerc
Southwick (Hants.), St Mary's, Aug. priory, 57, 95, 114, 256
'Staldeford' (Norf.), 103
'Stanford' (unidentified), 112
Stanhope (co. Durham), ch., 204
Stanley (Derbs.), 251
Staunford, I. de, ? proc., 249
Stavensby, Alexander, bp of Coventry (and Lichfield), 62, 159, 177
Stelzer, W., 20
Stephanus, Mag. (S?), papal scribe, 202, 206, 250, 258
Stephen V, pope (885–8), register of, 65
Stetchworth (Cambs.), ch., 111 n. 105
Stewkley (Bucks.), ch., 40
Stigand, bp of Chichester, 102
Stockton (Lincs.), ch., 172
Stratford Langthorne (Essex), Cist. abbey, abb. of, 215
Street (Som.), ch., 105